Global Servants: Cross-cultural Humanitarian Heroes Volume 3: The Art and Heart of Agency Care of Cross-cultural Humanitarian Heroes

A Three-Volume Series

Lois A. Dodds, Ph. D.
Laura Mae Gardner, D. Min.
Alice Chen, MD.

Heartstream Resources, Inc.
101 Herman Lee Circle
Liverpool, PA 17045
www.heartstreamresources.org
email: info@heartstreamresources.org

Second Edition, 2021

Online electronic version available
At Heartstream Resources, Inc.
www.heartstreamresources.org and

101 Herman Lee Circle, Liverpool, PA 17045
Printed copies also available from the above.

Cover design by Alan Furst

Library of Congress Cataloging-in-Publication Data
Lois A. Dodds, Laura Mae Gardner and Alice Chen.
Global Servants: Cross-cultural Humanitarian Heroes.
Volume3: The Art and Heart of Agency Care

ISBN: 978-0-9832307-3-1
1. Title   2. Humanitarian workers   3. Development of
humanitarian workers   4. Cross-cultural workers   5. Lois A.
Dodds   6. Laura Mae Gardner   7. Alice Chen
8. Developmental psychology   9. Missions

Dedication

To our beloved colleagues,
Lawrence E. Dodds, M.D., M.P.H.
and Mary Lazarides, M.Div.

Larry and Mary began this book project with us,
contributing to the structure and the content,
and bestowing their wisdom,
knowledge and myriad skills.

Their imprints are throughout the book.
We miss them intensely!

You may read their stories on the next pages.
They both exemplify the kind of hero
we write about in this book.

Acknowledgements

As authors, both of us have teams who help to make our visions become reality. Our own life commitments have included profound and intentional interdependence with others, as we advocate in this book. We are deeply grateful for those who have worked alongside of us and encouraged us with this project. Helpful readers have included Dr. Harry Boonstra, Joyce Parks, Dr. Alice Chen and Peggy Hill. Each of them gave us valuable suggestions. Dick Gardner patiently allowed Larrie to be away more than once so we could work together. Marion Matter, Elijah-Jason Love, Dr. Lee and Pat Maliska, and Dick and Sue Steward gave logistical support and encouragement. We are also grateful to Alan Furst for designing the book cover.

We also thank the hundreds of graduate students and thousands of cross-cultural humanitarian heroes whose lives have educated us about the topics we write about. Our lifelong learning, reflected in this book, is the gift of all of those who have allowed us into their lives and life work. We are deeply touched and humbled that so many have trusted us to invite us into the sacred spaces of their lives and hearts.

Table of Contents

Preface
By Lois Dodds

This planet we call home is an ever-changing place, now home to approximately seven billion persons. During our lifetimes, the number of inhabitants on our globe has more than doubled. Projections are that it will double again within the next couple of decades, with more than half of the world's population being in the vulnerable stages of childhood and adolescence. This population growth alone poses staggering problems! Since the events of 9/11 and the global financial meltdown of 2008 and 2009, a much greater percentage of the world's inhabitants have been plunged into poverty, danger, starvation, wars and other devastation. Even nature herself has created cataclysms greater than we have previously known in recorded history, such as the tsunami in Asia. Even that one event devastated millions of lives and multiple countries. Hundreds of caring agencies rushed in to attend to the overwhelming destruction, displacement and human losses. We have seen similar attempts to help after hurricane Katrina, the loss of millions of homes in Pakistan due to flooding, and the deaths of nearly one quarter of a million people due to the earthquake in Haiti.

Caring and altruistic people worldwide feel the staggering costs of these events for both the individual and society. How are we to help? What can we do to reach out to stem the flood of human sorrows and political turmoil? The tragedy we see is that our human "progress" can simply be wiped out in a few strokes of nature or human malfeasance. We have seen this firsthand, and it is most recently evident in the ways the fall of Wall Street, banks, and global financial markets have plunged humanity into deeper troubles that threaten to engulf both people and cultures. Yet, there is hope.

We write this book from the standpoint of hope. As Westerners, centered in the Judeo-Christian ethic, we believe people have choices which can change the future. We have hope that enough people will reach out to help others so that we can collectively make a difference. A review of history reminds us that most positive changes have happened because a few people cared enough to devote their lives to abolishing evil and promoting good. The abolition of slavery and of child labor, women's rights, worldwide promotion of literacy and health care, and most other good has come about not from governments, but from individuals with the will to care and to act.

As (four) authors, we have more than one hundred and forty years of combined experience working in many roles in multiple humanitarian organizations in dozens of countries. We know firsthand that individuals worldwide have huge impact in bringing about significant and lasting change—in safe water, sanitation, health care, literacy, and a host of other advances. Hundreds of these persons of impact have been our own graduate students or colleagues from and in many nations. We write from the perspective of being university professors, medical practitioners, public health officer, candidate selection and psychological assessment and training specialists, developmental psychologist, seminary graduates, linguists, translators and pastoral care givers, all serving in a variety of grass roots and top leadership roles in international organizations. (Yes, we have worked out of all of these disciplines and roles!)

Our purpose in this book is to promote meeting the human needs in the world by strengthening the hundreds of thousands of persons working through the thousands of organizations that provide humanitarian aid throughout the world. This book is about how to identify and choose the altruistic persons, of any culture or country, who will pursue careers in the care of others, specifically in humanitarian work. To address the vast needs of an ever-increasing world population, we must come together in multi-cultural teams. We must select persons with the vision, passion, personal strengths, hardiness and resiliency to endure the hardship conditions under which most humanitarian work is conducted. We must provide appropriate training for these roles, and practice the kind of ethical care which enables our servants of humanity to thrive over the long haul in spite of chronic high stress.

Tragically, during the writing of this book, we lost our two beloved co-authors, Lawrence Dodds, M.D., M.P.H., and Mary Lazarides, M.Div. Their contributions are undying, however, and we have retained their input and personal imprints.

Foreword
By Laura Mae Gardner

In September 2000, world leaders came together at United Nations Headquarters in New York to adopt the United Nations Millennium Declaration, committing their nations to a new global partnership to address eight Millennium Development Goals, which are:

1. Eradicate extreme poverty and hunger
2. Achieve universal primary education
3. Promote gender equality and empower women
4. Reduce child mortality
5. Improve maternal health
6. Combat HIV/AIDS, malaria and other diseases
7. Ensure environmental sustainability, and
8. Develop a global partnership for development

World needs are felt by individuals. These millennial goals are compassionately and pragmatically intended to provoke action towards meeting the needs of individuals, whether these needs are literacy, treatment of disease, justice, clean water, or health care for mothers and babies.

A more ancient mandate comes from the Old Testament prophet Isaiah:

> Is this not the fast that I have chosen?
> To lose the bonds of wickedness,
> To undo the heavy burdens,
> To let the oppressed go free,
> And that you break every yoke?
> Is it not to share your bread with the hungry?
> And that you bring to your house the poor who are cast out;
> When you see the naked, that you cover him?   (Isaiah 58:6-7)

The same concern expressed through the prophet in the Old Testament is expressed by Jesus in the New Testament book of Matthew. His words clearly underscore God's care for the needy:

> "I was hungry and you gave me something to eat, I was thirsty and you gave me something to drink. I was a stranger and you took me in. I needed clothes and you clothed me. I was sick and you looked after me. I was in prison and you came to visit me."

> "When did we see you a stranger and invite you in or needing clothes and clothe you? When did we see you sick or in prison and go to visit you?"

> "Whatever you did for one of the least of these brothers of mine, you did for me" (Matthew 25:34-46).

None of these altruistic efforts will be accomplished by accident. They must be deliberately addressed by nations, organizations, and individuals—our cross-cultural humanitarian heroes. This book is concerned with the care of those global servants. We want to share the perspectives, principles, and strategies which will allow humanity's special servants to go beyond merely surviving the rigors and challenges to thriving. Far too many idealistic, compassionate young people have burned out prematurely in their humanitarian endeavors due to lack of care.

The four of us who conceived of and began the writing of this book address the realities of what kind of persons are equipped to provide care in this troubled and tarnished world. We identify the factors which make persons effective. We speak of the ways in which agencies can enable their heroes to thrive throughout their terms of service. We want to facilitate the process of providing the world's peoples with the good news that people matter to God, and that they matter to us. We want to send this same message to both the people in need and to those ministering to the needy. We care.

Alice Chen

Alice Chen was born in Taiwan and grew up in Regina, Saskatchewan, Canada and trained in medicine and Family Practice at the U. of Saskatchewan, U. of Ottawa and U. of Western Ontario. She has served in Asia in medicine, training, community and preventive health, outreach projects and member care since 1990. She worked as a family doctor at the then-TEAM hospital, Logefeil Memorial Hospital in Taitung, Taiwan, from 1990 to 1993, and after pursuing theological studies at Canadian Theological Seminary in Regina, started working with the Shanxi Evergreen Service in China in 1995, where she continues to serve.

Her work has been diverse and includes clinical care, chronic disease management, village health worker training, well-baby and antenatal work, health education, Family Practice training, preceptoring Chinese and foreign medical students and residents, hosting visiting medical experts, coordinating staff development, coaching and mentoring Chinese staff and expatriate members, Christian education training, counseling, and supporting local church leaders. A significant portion of Dr. Chen's energies are directed towards providing member care, not only for the Evergreen team in advocating for healthy policies and lifestyles, but also through work done with Heartstream, in medical consultation, counseling and teaching, and within the international community in China.

Dr. Chen has spoken extensively on medical work in China, including community health development, rural health worker and Family Practice training in China, working with government agencies, preventative medicine, health education and member care issues and is co-author of a number of papers and book chapters on these topics. She was also a member of the Christian Medical Dental Association (CMDA) Working Committee of the PRISM study, "Patterns and Responses in Intercultural Service in Medicine" and is on the International Advisory Board of *Christian Journal for Global Health.*

Dr. Chen's passions include cross-cultural training, helping international workers to remain "healthy, effective and happy," and coaching or "leading from behind" as she supports emerging leaders as they grow into their leadership roles. In 2013, Dr. Chen was recognized as "Cross- Cultural Doctor of the Year" by the CMDA (USA). Dr. Chen continues to work full-time in Yuci, Shanxi, PR China with Shanxi Evergreen Service and makes Toronto her base when she is on home assignment in Canada.

One of Our Own Heroes
Essence of Humanity Award
Lawrence E. Dodds, M.D., M.P.H.
United Way of the Capitol Area, 2007

Dr. Lawrence Dodds, of Liverpool, PA, retains the amazing dedication to care for others which has typified his life of service as a physician. In his ninth year with ALS (Lou Gehrig's Disease) and confined to a wheel chair, he continues to work full-time as a volunteer for a non-profit organization devoted to the care of humanitarian, cross-cultural workers. He teaches, coaches, counsels, provides medical consultations, and carries on a worldwide network of communication. Everyone who knows him is inspired by his cheerfulness, upbeat attitude, and his "I can do" approaches to his many physical limits. Once able to fly jets and helicopters, do surgery, and build furniture, he now has lost the use of limbs and even fingers. After typing with a chop stick in his teeth for months, he now uses an "eye-gaze" computer and makes phone calls using a puff of air. He keeps in touch with his former graduate students, whom he has taught in about thirty countries, and with humanitarian workers around the globe. His ability to reframe situations and come up with a new solution has enabled him to adapt to continuous physical losses for over eight years with ALS.

Dr. Dodds' wife, Lois, a psychologist, licensed counselor, writer, and professor, estimates he has given away over $2,000,000 worth of medical care during his thirteen years in Peru and twelve years as a volunteer on the staff of Heartstream Resources, Inc. During most of his professional life he has received a minimal living allowance or no salary at all. His dedication, self-sacrifice, enthusiasm, and high energy continue to inspire many people. When he spoke to medical students at Hershey Medical School last spring, both faculty and students found him inspiring. One said, "You and your story are the most inspiring things I have encountered during medical school."

Dr. Dodds trained as a young man to fulfill the vision of his life purpose, discovered at age eight when he read the biography of David Livingstone, a Scottish physician who went to Africa in the early 1900s. After attending medical school at University of Southern California

(USC), Dr. Dodds served an internship at Huntington Hospital in Pasadena, CA, and was chief resident at Ventura County Hospital in California during his training in family practice. He wavered once during this time, typified by 120-hour work weeks (300 beds and 7 residents!) when he applied to return to the U.S. Army in the Space, Aviation and Astronaut programs in which he had trained earlier. After tough considerations, and down to the last signature for re-enrollment, he persevered by sticking with his childhood call of serving the poor.

After a tour of duty as the flight surgeon for the flight detachment of President Lyndon Johnson, Dr. Dodds was assigned to Viet Nam. There he took care of Vietnamese villagers during his spare hours serving as a flight surgeon with a flight battalion in Quin Yon. He found it very fulfilling to care for the people who had little or no care, finding courage to treat cholera, plague, and other contagious diseases.

Before going to Peru to serve the native peoples of the Amazon region, Dr. Dodds became the only full-time emergency room physician which Ventura County Hospital had ever hired. He also directed the County's Drug Rehabilitation Service. He loved the challenge of facing any problem which came through the door, and he found great fulfillment in caring for patients in crisis. Dr. Dodds, his wife Lois, and their three young children, then ages four, six and eight years old, spent six months training in jungle life in Southern Mexico. They learned to live a simple life, building their own shelter, mud stove, furniture, and household items. The goal was to be prepared for the worst that could happen and to be able to sustain themselves should they crash in the jungle or be lost. During this time Dr. Dodds trained other candidates for overseas jungle service in basic medical care, such as giving injections, pulling teeth, and stitching up wounds. The first night at camp their son David, aged 8, almost died of asthma due to DDT in their mud hut; it had been sprayed for mosquitoes and during the night the powder drifted down from the thatch roof into David's mosquito net. An hour's flight from any medical care other than himself, in the middle of the night, he felt helpless at the lack of a hospital in which to care for his son. He used what medication he had, and he prayed for God to bring his son through the crisis. Days later, David and several others were bitten by a rabid dog, presenting another huge challenge to a young physician full of enthusiasm, with excellent training and knowledge, but no access to modern medications or equipment.

Miraculously, an airline pilot heard Dr. Dodds' plea on short-wave radio and was able to deliver rabies vaccine to the jungle camp.

In Peru, Dr. Dodds devoted his time to caring for persons of about sixty indigenous people groups throughout the Amazon of Peru, an area about the size of the state of California. He frequently flew to far villages, landing on the rivers with a float plane. He encountered patients with illnesses and situations such as Jesus faced in New Testament times, and often wished he had the same power to do miracles. At the center of the Summer Institute of Linguistics (SIL), near Pucallpa, where the Dodds lived, Lawrence provided medical care to local indigenous groups, those from far-flung villages in the Amazon, and the adults of SIL and their children assigned to the linguistic study center. There they analyzed the indigenous language, developed alphabets and primers, taught literacy, and translated the New Testament and other important documents and books. He and his staff also trained community health workers selected by their villages.

Originally one of three medical doctors at the center, Dr. Dodds served as the only doctor for seven years, but continued providing medical care for the same groups throughout the jungle. He often traveled by canoe or float plane holding clinics for two or three weeks at a time, sharing in the hardships of the people of tiny villages. Once, after a flood of the huge Ucayali River, which destroyed all the fields and gardens, the people had nothing but boiled green bananas to eat for weeks; Dr. Dodds shared this meager food. He continued serving, even sharing their diseases such as whooping cough, hepatitis, and tuberculosis. His strength of character and dedication kept him working even during those times.

Without any screening methods, and living almost next door to the clinic, Dr. Dodds was on call 24/7 for seven years, with few breaks. He finally became so exhausted that he felt he would die. At that time he was transferred to Lima, to serve as the SIL-government liaison officer. He loved that job, changing from his khakis and sandals to a three-piece suit, meeting with generals, cabinet members, and other high officials to represent SIL's work with indigenous peoples.

Dr. Dodds returned to the U.S. for recovery, taking a position in the Public Health Department of Ventura County, back in the hospital where he had trained. Always loved and respected by the medical community there he was appointed to head the department. County personnel called his department "The Promised Land," or "The New Jerusalem" because so many persons wanted to join his staff of 240. Ten years there provided time for recovery, earning another graduate degree and specialty (preventive medicine).

One day while pondering why he had chosen a career in medicine and why he had ended up with such diverse phases of practice, it occurred to him that every venue had one thing in common: serving people who would not otherwise get care--the Vietnamese villagers, the addicts off the street, traumatized persons, indigenous peoples of the Amazon, and missionaries who had chosen a life of service in an extremely harsh environment.

During the twenty years of overseas travel and teaching in a Master's Degree program with Azusa Pacific University, the Dodds began to formulate the idea of creating a care center for international humanitarian workers. Everywhere they taught, in country after country, many expatriates from various countries were in burnout and crisis, needing a place of respite and various kinds of care. Together they began to dream of providing multi-disciplinary care for these dedicated and self-giving people, willing to work in impossible circumstances in difficult places. So, in 1992 Dr. Dodds resigned his job and began, with Lois, the process of incorporating a non-profit organization. They began with no salary, but with great expectation that if this was God's call to another phase of service He would provide. Doctor Dodds has worked twelve years already as a full-time volunteer, receiving no compensation for his medical services.

Three years after being diagnosed with ALS, Dr. Dodds also began treatment for cancer. Each treatment for that caused some step-down in his physical strength. Though the typical patient with ALS lives only two or three years, and only about ten percent live beyond five years, Dr. Dodds continues to have a very full life, continually engaged with others in need. He says he decided immediately that ALS is not his identity--it is just something he has to deal with. With his robust singing and hearty laughter, the ability to speak, and his mind still bright, he contributes inspiration, enthusiasm, love, compassion, and up-to-date knowledge within the organization and programs. Those who attend are amazed at his wisdom, gentleness, acceptance, and sense of humor.

Dr. Dodds is still active as a father, visiting and talking with his children and eight grandchildren regularly. They call him for advice (such as, "Grandpa, could you help me with my school science project?") and for fun. Dr. Dodds believes that this full-life engagement and the sustaining love and grace of God have enabled him to continue living such a full life.

Post script: Dr. Dodds died in June 2008 due to treatment for a third fatal disease. He worked until his death, and inspired us all in more ways than we can count.

Another of Our Heroes
A Tribute to Mary Lazarides

Most of us know our Mary as Mare. Her life was not easy or ordinary.
It was unique, a journey which included many valleys and mountains,
occasional meadows and deserts, and most recently a beautiful green
pasture with a quiet stream flowing from God's heart. Her life
demonstrates the resiliency that comes from a deep vision and passion
and to a commitment to things much bigger than her.

Mare gifts were multiple. From being a serious and shy little girl, she
grew into an unconventional and contemporary masterpiece of
humanity. Fresh out of graduate school she longed to serve those who
served in difficult and far-away places. She devoted her life to the care
of these global servants through her gifts in music, counseling,
psychological testing praying, helping in technical work, writing,
baking, and even in doing dishes and sharing herself in so many other
ways. She often said, "This is what I love to do! This is what God
created me for! "Shortly before her untimely death she said, "My vision
of twenty-three years ago is now fulfilled!"

One first noticed Mare as a humor therapist, with her fabulous sense of
humor, able to joke around even in Latin and a little French and Hebrew.
She was like the "Far Side" cartoons, seeing the absurd just around the
corner, finding deeper but funny implications and perspectives in life
than most of us do. The poet Gerhard Manley Hopkins wrote: "Glory be
to God for dappled things..." Mary's version would likely be "Glory be
to God for daffy things..." because she loved to spot the irregular and
funny things of life.

How did Mare get to be so funny? At a very early age she determined
to make people laugh; it was a good way to deal with her sadness. She
credits her father's sense of humor as her inspiration: a funny word, a
unique perspective, could change the emotional climate. She honed this
gift and used it to bring joy to many. Her gift of humor served people
literally around the world.   Unlike most comedians, Mare never used
her humor to hurt others.   One recent series she invented features me!
"Waiting for Lo" series is what she created at odd moments when we

were out shopping, traveling or something. She taught me to laugh at myself through the outrageous text messages she sent to friends. E.g.; "Waiting for Lo. We're in Dallas airport. Lo just stormed up to the counter and demanded an upgrade to first class. Poor Lo. She doesn't realize she's at the Dunkin' Donuts counter! Guess I'd better go rescue her."

Gifted as a musician, Mare credited her big brother David for helping her develop her gift. She learned hundreds of hymns and songs by heart and it seems she could play and sing any style, from the sublime to the hilarious, she even a wrote a song in tribute to the parasite medicine, Flagyl, after a trip abroad, when she boasted, "Now--I am a real overseas worker! I've got a parasite too!"

Some memorable times when Mare used her gift of music to encourage me and others included sitting at the piano in a home in North Africa with our hosts from another country. As Mare and I relaxed at the piano after teaching all day, we sang and sang. Sensing motion behind us, we turned around to see this lovely couple dancing, oblivious to us. A few months later at the end of an international meeting no one got up to leave. We just sat there--waiting for something. Then, Mare begins to play songs from memory. Miraculously it seemed she chose songs we all knew--people from several nations and languages. We sang for over an hour. It seemed a benediction to our week together. A week later as Mare lay dying so unexpectedly, on her forty-ninth birthday, I reflected on this treasure—it was a benediction on her life.

Mary had an academic gift too; she was blessed with a big brain! When she would tell her life story, she would end her PowerPoint with scans of her brain. She would say, "Since I don't have kids or grandkids to show you, I'll show you my brain. I'm the only one in this room who can prove I have a brain, because I've seen mine!" In high school Mare was chosen to represent her school at Girls' State; she was the valedictorian. When she felt called to go to seminary, she says she got confused, because she loved it over at the theology school "where the guys were" more than in her counseling classes. She became the grader for the Greek and Hebrew classes! This was amazing, as she was an MA student, not yet into a doctoral program. If you see her PowerPoint life story, you catch her humor even in the sacrosanct environment of seminary!

One fruit of Mare's academic love and skills is that she helped to create a CD-ROM called "The Translators' Workplace" which brings together a whole library of translation texts and commentaries. It reduces a huge library to one compact disc! She saw this project through three revisions over sixteen years. It is widely used by hundreds of translators around the globe.   Mare was also a great researcher, with immediate recall of where to find references or quotations; this gift has been a great help in launching this series.

Mary was a gifted, effective and delightful teacher, finding new ways to teach concepts and get learners to say "Ah ha!" She nearly danced as she taught, so full of enthusiasm was she. Her musical self and her most-light-hearted self got woven into the content in a way that made every class great fun and memorable learning.   Her skits, impersonations, and cartoons are unforgettable. Mare got to use these gifts in several countries.

Mare's growth in spirit and soul, emotion and expression allowed her to become a warm and loving counselor to others. She asked the right questions, and had great insight. She faithfully followed her students, especially with "skyping" and text messaging around the globe, giving practical guidance and encouragement.   These two activities illustrate "Mary the Techy." She has been a huge help in setting up our systems and finding and creating documents. She became an excellent writer and an editor with a quick eye in graphic design as well.

Mary has been a loving friend to many, many people. She especially enjoyed giving gifts of service. Even her affirmations were zany. We were walking the streets of Casablanca when she told me, "Being with you is almost as good as being alone"

Mare's humor emerged on another trip when our luggage did not arrive. After waiting four days, we tried to wash our clothes in what she dubbed the "French Beast"—a washing machine which refused to give up our only clothes, so that we had to borrow from our hosts. Her "25 ways to reframe the dismay of no luggage" included "free underwear from Air France." The pack of eight Air France paid for turned out to be a family pack, with two tiny (she would say "wee") undies, two small, two medium and two large. We still laugh at that.

Mare was not just a fun, funny and loving person. Her character and personality made her thorough, conscientious, honest, transparent, open, reliable, quick to give, generous, understanding, accepting, approachable, and able to create a climate of safety for others.

Mare was gifted with words too. She loved the Word of God.   Mare became a writer of poems, to her own astonishment! It seems this reflected the opening of her heart and emotions to receive more of God's love and the freedom to express more of it, as it is written in the Psalms.

There is so much more to Mare than our words can say--so much more that we can reflect on here. She was a contemporary woman, born into this culture. She was earthy and straightforward. She would not consider herself a "saint" (unless one looks at it theologically). But she loved God with all her heart, her mind, and her soul. She found healing in so many experiences of life through her reliance on the sacred Word. She learned to walk with God in the dark and to rely on Him.

Global Servants: Cross-cultural Humanitarian Heroes

Lois A. Dodds, Ph. D.
Laura Mae Gardner, D. Min

Volume 1. Factors in Formation: A Developmental View

Introduction to Volume 1. Why is formation relevant to effective functioning in international service? What are the most formative factors and dimensions and stages of human development which have bearing on these? How and why are these inter-related?

Chapter 1. Family of origin—Cradle of Eminence or Cradle of Emptiness. The most powerful influence in the development of a person is the family which rears him or her. The family may be either the cradle of eminence or the cradle of emptiness, or some place of influence in between the two. Parental backgrounds and styles, the degree of nurture or neglect, the coherence and function of the family system, communication habits, and attitudes arise within the family. The family is the microcosm of the culture. It is the center in which the self develops and the earliest and most lasting learning takes place. Later relationships usually repeat patterns learned within the family.

Chapter 2 The Self and Identity. The self is the core person, formed through the multitude of influences described here. One's self-esteem, self-concept, "multiple selves," and identity formation are all inter-related. These form the foundation for our life "stance" such as optimism or pessimism, our ego-strength and our competence. The process of adjustment to one or more other cultures requires adaptation in our understanding and perception of self. Examples illustrate the importance of a solid sense of self, of identity, and competence in cross-cultural functioning. Stress response and coping skills relate to the self.

Chapter 3. Stages of Psychosocial and Emotional Development. The major dimensions of human development discussed here are psychosocial and emotional. These are experienced and achieved in stages or levels. Developmental problems or blockages in any one of these have impact on all the others.   These major theories of development are described and related to one another, as well as to cognitive development and brain function.

Chapter 4. Stages of Moral and Spiritual Development. One's motivation and vision for serving the needs of humanity are usually rooted in spiritual life, very often in a sense of divine call. How well one carries out the vision, purpose and goals of the organization depends on how well developed one is in terms of moral conscience and behavior, as well as spiritual maturity. One's ability to endure, to find strength and grace in adversity, and to emerge from suffering with a renewed commitment comes from spiritual understanding and connection. Making sense of the presence of evil and injustice as well as mankind's capacity for good are enabled by spiritual and moral perspectives.

Chapter 5. Cultural and Historical Context and Religious Factors. The family is rooted in and embedded in both culture and history. The individual is shaped by myriad forces which are aspects of culture, such as type of schooling, political system, etc. Attitudes towards other persons, cultures and roles arise from these forces and have bearing upon the person's capacity and motivation to become a "person for others" devoted to serving the needs of the world. One's assumption and expectations about privacy, space, and material possessions affect one's formation and future effectiveness! One's spiritual development and religious background are also crucial factors in who one becomes—and in becoming "a person for others."

Chapter 6. Integration of Developmental Dimensions. The degree of development in the five major dimensions work together to create a person who is more or less capable of reaching full potential and fulfillment (Maslow's actualization). Personality type and one's stage of "personal power" (the ability to influence one's environment) play a large role in a life of service. The capacity for growth and change, including resilience and coping, shape one's effectiveness in cross-cultural or multi-cultural contexts. Motivation, appropriate or faulty, results from a combination of developmental factors.

Summary of Volume I.   The family of origin and the culture and history in which it is embedded give rise to a person's sense of self. The self grows in various dimensions of development, including emotional, psychosocial, cognitive, moral and spiritual. Each one of these informs our understanding of a person's formation and his or her potential for effectiveness in cross-cultural humanitarian work.

Global Servants Volume 2: 12 Factors in Effectiveness and Longevity of Cross-cultural Humanitarian Heroes

Introduction to Volume 2:   Twelve factors contribute to the effectiveness and longevity of a person serving in cross-cultural or multi-cultural humanitarian work. These are all shaping the person to some degree, and are also outcomes of the person's development. When these twelve are maturely developed, a person has the capacity for making a significant and lasting impact on the groups or people's he or she serves. Becoming a hero is a combination of all of these.

Chapter 1. Personal boundaries.   Boundaries may be healthy or shaky, leading us to express needs, limits, etc., appropriately or inappropriately and without discretion. Learning assertiveness skills is foundational to good adjustment. Bridging the culture gap is partly a function of knowing our boundaries and learning the aspects of self we can change and those we must retain in order to maintain integrity of the self.   Maintaining healthy boundaries is a major challenge of humanitarian work, particularly in cultural contexts vastly different from our home culture. How far can one go in adjusting to the new without losing one's self? Examples illustrate healthy and disturbed boundaries.   Communication habits and styles and relationship boundary outcomes of passivity, aggressiveness and appropriate assertiveness are compared and contrasted.

Chapter 2. Impact awareness. How does one learn to understand his or her impact on another person, a group, a culture, an environment? What do we do with what we learn? Lack of awareness can create obstacles in adjustment and in one's acceptance in the new culture, as well as harmful outcomes for the groups we seek to serve. Healthy awareness enhances our function and enlarges our influence.

Chapter 3. Resiliency. What enables a person to cope, to expand one's coping resources, to grow over time, even in the face of set-backs and obstacles? What are the personal factors and resources which enable one to bounce back after disappointments, hardships, dangers? What keeps one going for the long haul, even when it can take decades to bring about positive change in the groups we serve? Why is this an important personal quality? What impact does resiliency have in overcoming traumatic events, personal life-expectancy, and career longevity?

Chapter 4. Emotional, moral and spiritual maturity. What are the characteristics of these dimensions of maturity? How are they inter-related? What harm is done in relationships with colleagues and host culture when immaturity rather than maturity is prevalent? Examples illustrate outcomes.

Chapter 5. Effective communication. Relationships at all levels are built and improved, or devastated by, communication habits, attitudes and skills. Active listening, refraining from assumptions and projections, appropriate non-verbal and good verbal skills are crucial in managing relationships even in one's own culture. The importance of these is magnified as more cultures are represented within a given context. Much conflict arises through mismanagement of communication, especially through projection and making wrong assumptions. Learning how to communicate well and to handle conflict across cultures is a key to effective functioning.

Chapter 6. Being an agent of change. Roles related to serving mankind, whether in medicine, education, religion or the political arena, implicitly involve creating change. Persons go out to serve in order to bring about positive change in other persons, environments or contexts. Understanding the factors involved in introducing change, dealing with and overcoming resistance, providing or creating new models, etc., is a crucial aspect of effectiveness in a cross-cultural or multi-cultural humanitarian role. This is another capacity of a person related to the self, to self-concept, communication, and personal competence.

Chapter 7. Coping with and managing stress. Stress is defined as anything which requires our energy to adapt. Adaptation is the key word for going across cultures, therefore positive adjustment requires energy. Life in most cross-cultural and multi-cultural contexts involves high, chronic stress. Whether a person engages in healthy coping or maladaptive stress responses is another function beginning with self-concept and ego-strength. Persons can increase their knowledge, skills and resources in coping through training, and over time become better able to withstand high stress. Stress responses are idiosyncratic; each person has a different "threshold" for over-stress. A person can learn to recognize his or her own stress responses. Four major categories of stress symptoms are discussed, along with strategies for self-help and interventions for mal-adaptive coping. Examples illustrate both positive and negative outcomes of stress challenges.

Chapter 8. Preparation for service. The effective functioning of a person in a cross-cultural, multi-cultural context is influenced by preparation for service. Research points to personal preparation as most important--that is, self-study and interpersonal skills are a more important foundation than is "education" or job-training per se. Preparation varies immensely, dependent on role, area of the world in which service takes place, language acquisition required to fulfill one's role, and so on. Illustrations show the value of appropriate cultural orientation, knowledge of allocation, language acquisition, and help during key periods of culture "shock" or adjustment. Criteria for effective training are included.

Chapter 9. Good fit. Matching a person to an organization or agency, to the appropriate role, a workable allocation, and to a culture into which he or she can "fit" is crucial to effectiveness. Adaptability, values, ethics, and other factors influence "fit." Lack of "fit" explains why some people do not become effective; changing a key factor may result in a better fit which allows the person to function effectively.

Chapter 10. Organizational and systems issues. Some estimates by leaders highly experienced in cross-cultural contexts indicate that "problems" in field settings may be systems-induced in as high as 70 percent of cases. Individuals are embedded in systems whose functioning may either enhance or diminish their personal effectiveness. Some key systems issues are ethos or culture styles of leadership, management and administrative decisions, ethical frameworks, financial policies, team dynamics, and relationships of organizations to partner agencies. Discussion of ways to create healthier systems and foster the effectiveness of persons within the system is included.

Chapter 11. Situational factors: wars, evacuations, disasters, displacement, assaults, crime. Personal effectiveness and positive functioning are severely challenged and may plummet when situational crises occur. This chapter defines the importance of pro-active, strategic planning for risk assessment and contingency designs and preparation. Examples illustrate both positive and negative outcomes of real situations involving the unexpected.

Chapter 12. Theology of suffering. Another crucial factor in the effectiveness and longevity of a cross-cultural humanitarian worker is the person's understanding of suffering. One needs to have a framework or foundation out of which one can make sense of the things that go wrong in the world, particularly as one works to alleviate suffering and injustice. Understanding that evil is real and that one is in a spiritual battle against it helps to make sense of why there is so much suffering. Having inner, spiritual resources to battle evil and to enable one to overcome setbacks, hardships, adversities, and one's own suffering while doing good makes the difference in whether one gives up the fight or finds courage and strength to go forward.

Summary of Volume 2. "SPARE Yourself" tool for quick assessment of effective functioning.

Introduction to Volume 3

In this series, we have come now to consideration of how agencies need to care for their people, based on the many factors which shape their members and their many dimensions of need. In Volume One, we examined the ways in which our cross-cultural or multicultural humanitarian workers are formed, especially the role which family of origin has in shaping their attitudes and life stance. In Volume Two, we have considered the twelve factors which enable humanitarian workers to become effective and to last over the long haul, to achieve longevity in their roles and missions. In this volume, we focus on what the agency or organization needs to do to care for its members.

Care begins in the recruitment process and is especially needed in the screening, assessment and selection phase during which candidates are seeking the right fit with an organization, based on vision and mission and the candidate's qualities and qualifications. Thus, thorough psychological and medical screening is essential, both to promote the mission of the organization and to protect those who may lack the resilience or hardiness to endure the foreign life experience. Consistently, overseas life includes many risk factors inherent in living and working in an overseas or multicultural setting. Four of these needs particular attention, proactively (prevention) and in terms of response (treatment): burnout, depression, post-traumatic stress disorder, and adjustment disorder.

We advocate for a special person and role to oversee care giving: The Member Care Facilitator. Five domains or dimensions of human need and care form the basis for what care needs to be provided, and how it can best be carried out. In addition, grief and loss are among the common experiences of the humanitarian worker; they seem innate given the goal of caring for the world's poor and needy. Other risks inherent in field work are illness and extreme stress. When people do become ill or disabled, there is usually a visible pattern of "cascading downward" or "spiraling downward," beginning with one incident of illness or trauma, progressing to more frequent problems and ending at a crisis level. At times, it becomes necessary for members to leave their field assignment, either because of illness or some failure. Moral failure of various kinds especially result in thorny problems and difficult decisions. Some members may choose to leave voluntarily, also contributing to attrition.

Although all workers need basic care, the unique challenges faced by several groups within a team or agency membership require particular awareness, alertness, and care tailored to their needs. This includes families, children, mothers of young children, single parents, singles, those whose homes are their workplaces, and leaders. We consider these in looking at the scope of care. A personnel care audit is one way an agency can assess the morale of its people and health of itself as a system.

Attending to the qualities and character of leaders and the many factors which influence their effectiveness is also part of agency care. Leaders primarily create and influence organizational structure and ethos, and their influence is pervasive. Therefore caring for them, at all levels, is a wise and essential agency responsibility.

Lastly, this volume includes medical advice for international workers, with information about finding medical help abroad, medications, food handling, common medical ailments, trauma, immunizations, emergency planning, creating a safe haven, and other useful resources.

Chapter 1
Care Begins with Screening and Selection
With Alice Chen, M.D.

The art and heart of caring for our cross-cultural and multicultural humanitarian heroes begins with good screening and selection. The persons motivated to be engaged in any effort to improve the welfare of the peoples in need around the globe are typically excellent—competent and well motivated. Yet, the roles and locales this kind of service involves are challenging and most often exhausting. To identify candidates most likely to be effective and to thrive in the process of service requires careful screening and selection. We do not want those who are unqualified or unable to serve to be endangered by situations for which they lack resilience and coping ability. At the same time, we do not want to miss out on those who are able to meet the challenges and are hardy enough to serve over the long haul.

This chapter will cover the general rationale for screening, what qualities and factors we are screening for, who is best equipped to do screening and assessment, and how the agency can conduct or oversee both medical and psychological screening. We will look at ethical implications of screening.

Why Do We Care about Screening and Selection?

We present these recommendations based on many decades of experience in cross-cultural, multicultural and humanitarian agencies and missions, many of these years directly involved in selection and training of candidates and various other aspects of personnel work. We have served in many roles related to the care of these workers, including teaching, training, crisis care, psychological and medical care. Our experience has been repeated in dozens of countries and cultures. We care personally, as authors, because we have been devoted to caring for cross-cultural and multicultural workers, especially those in crisis. This has all been highly valuable experience; we have learned a great deal about **what** is important in the selection, training, and care of people. We have learned that **who** is chosen and **why** the person is chosen and for **what** qualities has direct impact on effectiveness and longevity in field settings. We have learned that **who does the assessment** and selection and **how it is done** are also crucial. As agencies, we care because the fulfillment of both the vision and the persons engaged in carrying it out are dependent on the factors we discuss in this chapter. We have a moral and social obligation to do the very best job of screening, assessment, and selection for each individual and each agency. **Screening and selection** for and by any humanitarian mission is from the very beginning an ethical pursuit. We cannot escape the fact that ethics are involved in the recruitment, assessment and selection of persons. Choosing the **right** people is crucial to the survival and development of the person as well as being crucial to the organization's effectiveness. We believe that inadequate assessment and casual selection is a violation of ethics, for we have an ethical, moral and spiritual responsibility to select people suited for the complex and heavily stressful cross-cultural experience. Choosing and sending out those who lack the personal resources of spiritual maturity, resiliency, hardiness, solid ego-strength, and relational skills is to set people up for failure and loss. If inappropriate selection is compounded by inadequate training, we increase the likelihood of failure or crisis on the field.

Four Purposes for Screening

The four most important reasons for screening include 1) risk assessment, 2) identification of baseline strengths and weaknesses of the individual which are important to a person's functioning in the organization, 3) implications for growth for the persons selected, and 4) relationship to team functioning.

1. Risk assessment:
Screening in essence is a risk assessment of the applicant or candidate, determining what risks are involved in sending out an individual, couple, or family into a stressful, often physically demanding and

challenging cross-cultural setting. The process looks for answers to questions such as, "Does this worker have the psychological maturity and resilience necessary to handle these additional stressors?" and "How effective will this worker be when living under such conditions, not only with regard to carrying out his or her work assignment, but also in functioning as a balanced, well-adjusted spouse, parent, friend, neighbor and colleague?" (Edlin, 2005). Screening helps to identify those who are most likely to enjoy health in all spheres—physical, emotional, relational, and spiritual, as they work and live in a cross-cultural setting. Intrinsically, pre-field screening also serves to identify those who are unsuitable for international service. In general, screening for those who have medical conditions which preclude international service is less problematic than screening for those with disqualifying psychological conditions. Some psychological conditions are not readily apparent. These include conditions such as personality disorders, which require specialized expertise for evaluation. It is estimated that somewhere between two and ten percent of the general population have personality disorders, so we can assume that a proportion of those who apply for international service will likely come from that segment of the population (Schubert, 2002). An individual with a condition such as obsessive-compulsive disorder (OCD) or bipolar disorder or borderline personality disorder may be able to function adequately in the highly-structured context of school or job in their home culture and country, but may deteriorate rapidly in the often chaotic adjustment to overseas living (Wickstrom, 2002). Such a scenario can cause severe interpersonal conflict, exhaustion of field resources and unnecessary personal failure for the individual himself or herself. Interview with persons who have known the applicant or candidate well over time are one important source for information in all these categories. While references are followed up, a second-tier of referees can be identified and consulted through the recommendation of the first referees.

2. Identification of baseline strengths and weaknesses:
Evaluation of the candidate's general medical and psychological condition through careful screening by trained professionals is invaluable in informing the agency about the suitability of the candidate. Interviewing of references is important in this.[1] The more reference

---

[1] In one study, by Kenneth Wiggers of SIL, negative feedback from referees turned out to be more predictive of problems than was positive feedback predictive of success on the field. It seems that people speak more readily about strengths, but when they

persons interviewed, the broader the picture of the candidate that can be gathered. If the applicant is accepted, the same results help the agency make wise decisions about deployment or placement of the individual and/or family.

In addition to the tests and assessments for physical and psychological soundness, a second category of assessment is very helpful. The tools in this category are not related to psycho-pathology, but are helpful in understanding the applicant's preferences or usual ways of interacting. Foremost in this second category are personality type assessments, which help to identify to the person and the agency the strengths and weaknesses of the individual. This is invaluable for teaching people how to best work together, for allocation to teams and host cultures, and for tracking changes which might later reflect distress. (For example, if a person who is typically very outgoing and talkative suddenly becomes silent and unable to communicate, it can be a signal of major over stress. Knowing about personality type can make people more sensitive to such a shift.)

The collected information from all sources helps to answer the following questions:

a. Where could this individual serve most effectively, in view of his or her unique personality and strengths, health conditions, and/or limitations and family situation?

b. Which traits or aspects of his or her psychological make-up would allow him or her to complete a cross-cultural assignment successfully and which ones may cause problems down the road? Which ones might be detrimental or counter-productive in a field setting?

c. What support does this individual or family require in dealing with areas requiring further growth and maturity? Where and how

---

tell about a candidate's weaknesses or past problems, those carry greater significance. (L. Dodds, personal communication, 2013). Two questions which correlated highly with field success or failures were asked by training staff personnel: "Would you be willing to work with this person?" and "Would you be willing to live with this person?" Negative answers to these questions, even though intuitive, were predictive of future problems.

can this support be accessed? What are resources available in the field settings where this person might be assigned? (Here, caution is required, since a person may be sent to one place based on available resources, and then be moved without consideration of resources in the new locale.)

3. Implications for Growth:

Pre-field screening also provides the opportunity for the individual to learn many helpful facts about himself or herself, including both psychological and physical factors. The person, under guidance, can learn to manage various matters related to his or own well-being. For instance, under some circumstances the person may be accepted with some degree of a medical condition such as hypertension and can learn to manage that aspect of health. A person who may be prone to depression, perhaps due to a previous bout, can learn to practice good self-care in order to manage his or her mood. For most candidates, learning about personality style, communication habits, and other vital aspects of themselves can provide challenge for growth in relationships and life stance. Whether candidates are ultimately chosen or not, the process of going through screening and assessment can provide "teachable moments" for the person to develop a growth plan, especially related to health maintenance, to minimize future risks.

Psychological evaluation may uncover areas of needed personal growth and development. With guidance the person may develop strategies for recognizing and managing stress, improving interpersonal skills and mastering cognitive behavioral techniques for self-help whenever anxiety and depression arise.

While screening and assessment are the responsibilities of an agency, it is crucial to acknowledge and emphasize that the individual is the one primarily responsible for maintenance of his or her own mental and physical health. Having identified issues and strengths and weaknesses does not mean the organization is responsible to "fix" or "heal" the person. The agency helps to equip and educate in the process but the person bears ultimate responsibility. We believe this means agencies should not take on people who do not measure up to the standards required by the role with the intent or plan to "fix them." (For instance, not to use "conditional acceptance" with the hope that people will change by the time of their allocation.) Medical follow-up studies have shown that when people are actively involved in their own care and management of their health, there is less chance of medical mistakes, as well as increased improvement in symptoms. There are also fewer hospitalizations and emergency room visits (Weingart & Wilson, 2000; Vincent and Coulter, 2002). Related to physical health, this process requires educating the candidate, providing resources, and articulating the importance of his or her key role as the only consistent member of his or her own health care team (Gamble, 2008).

4. Relationship to team functioning:
With the current and ongoing focus on team engagement in international projects, the formation and maintenance of strong and healthy teams is a top priority. One is likely to work in a cross-cultural team which *especially* requires healthy people because relationships are more complex. Pre-field evaluation can offer insights about individuals which, when shared appropriately, can help teammates to understand each other's personalities, communication styles, preferences, and priorities. They can also help to match gifts to teams and roles, and to enhance mutual accountability, clear communication, and respect (Wickstrom, 2002).

Results of Poor Screening and Selection

One study showed that premature return or overseas performance failure occurs in between thirty-seven and sixty-one percent of cases of international workers (Dodd, 2007). Losses include the initial expenses of moving, relocation, and orientation, as well as the long-term costs associated with the loss of productivity, morale, personal and organizational face. Frequently it may lead to resentment, conflict and

intense human cost to spouses and families. A study of 1,770 expatriates living in rural regions of several developing countries showed that thorough pre-travel health screening lowered both the number of in-country medical emergencies and the number of air medical evacuations (Callahan, 2008). Another study indicates that expatriates have a forty percent higher divorce rate than their peers who have not gone overseas and that their children have a fifty percent higher high school dropout rate than children who are not in an overseas situation (Harris, Moran & Moran, 2004, cited in Dodd, 2007). Statistics from Cendant

International Assignment Service and the American Training and Development Society indicate that two-thirds of workers fail their foreign assignments (Dodd, 2007). Yes, these are shocking statistics! We would imagine that in families in communities of faith and working with missions, these figures would not be as high as they might be in military or other settings.

Studies of religiously motivated international workers show similar attrition rates, though not necessarily for the same reasons; up to fifty percent of those embarking on their first term of service fail to return for a second term. In fact, the impact of such attrition is the driving force for the efforts devoted to the emerging field called "member care," of which these books are a part. In 1992, the World Evangelical Fellowship's Reducing Missionary Attrition (ReMAP) Project studied leaders from fourteen nations and found that seventy-four percent of problems reported as causes for premature return and attrition could have been addressed and corrected pre-field (Dipple, 1997). The most frequently cited reasons include the adjustment, education, health, and behaviour of children (accounting for 14.4 percent of stated reasons for early departure from the field) and issues related to mental or physical health (11.6 percent). Bloecher and Lewis (1997) further conclude that "a large investment in candidate selection and pre-field training is useful in reducing the Preventable Attrition Rate (called PAR)" (p. 117). Screening which included "sense of call," health factors, family status, and adequate financial support and other factors showed that these contribute to a lower PAR.

In view of these statistics, it is clear that thorough and careful screening is vital for selecting suitable candidates for international service. As pressing as it may be to fill an urgently needed position or to more quickly allocate a seemingly well-trained person in an international

assignment by short-changing the screening and selection process, this is never a good idea. The time, effort, and financial resources expended in assessing potential workers are very well spent if they result in the selection of workers who have the lowest risk of experiencing harm to their health and the highest possibility of success for their mission.

The case study in the box illustrates some of the ethical issues involved and the heavy toll exacted when an individual or a family is sent and then recalled in international service. This example relates to a complex medical situation which resulted in a profound blow to the physical health and had serious emotional and spiritual implications for the individual and his or her family. Sending a worker entails a tremendous outlay of resources by the sending organization and the community, in both the host and home countries. Overall, failure in an assignment represents serious social and economic losses. We could relate many examples such as this, resulting from social, emotional, spiritual, or marital issues which were not assessed appropriately.

Case Study
Example of Costs of Poor Screening and Selection

Bill and Linda, a young American couple, had a long-time desire to serve as cross-cultural development workers. Since meeting as college students as short-term workers in Taiwan, their common goal had been to be involved in long-term development work in South East Asia. Professionally, they prepared by taking graduate level development and linguistic studies as well as cross-cultural training, all with the view of entering international service. While working part-time to pay off their school loans, Bill also completed a pastoral internship. After repaying their loans, the couple applied to a small agency which was keen to receive such an eager and well-qualified couple. However, the agency had a limited screening protocol for new candidates.

It was a banner day when Bill and Linda were accepted and appointed to a host country in SE Asia to start language study in preparation for development work amongst the urban poor. Subsequently, they spent another two years preparing for the field, learning to live simply, working with an expatriate citizens of the host culture and raising a support team.

They enjoyed generally good health, but Linda had allergies to smoke and molds, and had suffered from asthma as a child. As an adult living in the American Midwest over the previous ten years, however, her condition had been stable; she had had only several episodes of wheezing which resolved readily with the use of a bronchodilator puffer. However, within days of their arrival in Asia, she developed a cough with wheezing and breathlessness. She attributed her symptoms to a cold but when her wheezing worsened, she sought help at a local hospital where doctors treated her with bronchodilators and intravenous antibiotics. These medications helped initially, but failed to provide lasting relief. By the end of her second month in country, she had developed a chest infection which did not respond to several types of antibiotics, and she was hospitalized. With the heavy humidity and air pollution of the area, she was never able to start full-time language studies because of fatigue, shortness of breath and what eventually became a chronic cough. Bill also withdrew from his language studies in order to care for her and to accompany her on medical visits.

After almost weekly visits to the emergency department and three hospitalizations in six months, Linda's general condition had deteriorated to the point that the home office advised that she leave the field. The couple returned to the US after having spent only eight months in their chosen country of service, deeply discouraged, demoralized and questioning their original call. Linda's physical condition stabilized gradually under specialist care, but she struggled with feelings of guilt, believing she had "failed" in letting down her husband as well as their family and church that had sent them off with such high hopes. Bill grappled with finding an adequate explanation as to why God would allow this to happen to them. He developed symptoms of depression and had trouble finding a job. Not surprisingly, the couple underwent significant stress in their marriage, for which they sought counseling. Bill abandoned plans for future ministry altogether within two years of returning home. (This kind of outcome is very typical when people must return but then do not get appropriate follow-up and restorative care.)

What are we Screening For?
Eleven Key Factors or Qualities
in Candidate Selection

We believe the following are key factors in the selection of cross-cultural and multi-cultural humanitarian workers, based in our experience and observations of over forty years—or over one hundred combined years of the three authors of this chapter! These criteria, when identified and chosen as relevant by an agency or a sending organization, should be described in writing during both recruitment and screening. The written materials should show why they are relevant and important. It is important to validate the importance of these selection factors. One can document why good mental health, emotional resiliency, and purity of life are essential requirements for anyone entering cross-cultural humanitarian work. One's beliefs and practices are relevant to ministry in cross-cultural settings! Significantly, in January of 2012, the U.S. Supreme Court ruled that religious organizations have the right to establish and require candidates to adhere to a set of beliefs and practices.

Ideally these factors should first be identified in candidates at the local level, through their volunteer service or formal roles in their synagogues, churches, or community agencies, since the selection process for humanitarian missions usually begins in one or more of those. These organizations have a key role in getting to know those whom they recommend for or refer for cross-cultural, humanitarian service. Both the sending and receiving agencies and organizations share the responsibility to assess the following factors in the person's life, because these qualities and skills exert great influence on survival, longevity and effectiveness in cross-cultural work. In reality, the home and community groups probably have the best opportunity for assessment, as they will have a history with the person over a longer time than the receiving agency.

In Chapter 9 of Volume 2 of this series, we describe at length the following factors in selection (See pages 185 to 193.)

1. **Spiritual maturity**—the ability to mobilize spiritual resources and to love and care for others, as well as to find meaning in the face of difficulty.

2. **A life history of altruism**—one begins caring and giving long before applying for a formal role in a humanitarian organization.

3. **A sense of call**—believing one has a destiny or calling to a vocation of service to humanity is profoundly important, especially in maximizing effectiveness and longevity. This kind of call gives persons the ability to endure through hardship.

4. **Emotional health and maturity**—knowing how to relate with ease to other people, being able to love and to put the needs of others first helps to maintain balance and increases effectiveness.

5. **Relational maturity**—being able to relate and connect with others, able to work through conflicts and difficulties, able to maintain relationships over time.

6. **Coping ability**—accepts, identifies and manages stress well; has the ability to adapt to unexpected and changing circumstances, uses healthy strategies for going through troubles; avoids mal-adaptive habits which compound problems.

7. **Record of service**—well established service record in reaching out to others in caring roles; has demonstrated ability to stick to a job and to be faithful and competent in carrying out responsibilities.

8. **Job skills and work experience**—demonstrated abilities to do a job and to transfer skills to new roles and environments, with sufficient experience that job skills are learned before the complexities of cross-cultural environments are added.

9. **Resourcefulness**—creative and innovative in the use of opportunities, challenges, material goods, finances; able to adjust to changing needs.

10. **Ability to generate support of all kinds**—having the ability to relate well emotionally, and to present ideas with good cognitive skills; attractive to others in soliciting care and cooperation.

11. **A theology or philosophy of suffering**—able to make sense of suffering and hardship without losing heart, losing faith, or giving up when obstacles are encountered in the process of doing good for others.

Of course, the twelve factors in effectiveness and longevity which form the contents of Volume 2 are in themselves attitudes, qualities, and skills we want to discover and assess. Assessment and screening are all about identifying persons who will be effective and will last over the long haul of humanitarian service. In the process we also identify persons who will not have sufficient internal resources, hardiness or resilience to work effectively. In spite of their initial disappointment, it is definitely not a service to accept those who lack hardiness and resilience.

Some Additional Factors for Screening and Assessment

In addition to the factors listed previously, an assessment should include a review of the following (R. Pruitt, personal communication, April 8, 2011):

- professional training[2]
- past experience in work and relationships
- areas of interest and gifting
- language-learning ability
- cross-cultural competency
- interpersonal communication style
- style of conflict resolution
- personality preference

Other information required by some agencies includes a criminal background check and a credit check. All this information should then be reviewed carefully by the candidate selection committee. It is helpful to have a master form to collect all the data from each area of screening. A summary of the screening and assessment should include a clear

---

[2] With the current emphasis on professional service as a platform in creative access countries, the candidate's technical qualifications are increasingly important. Finding a meaningful niche without marketable skills in a foreign setting can be very stressful, not only for the individual, but also for the agency.

statement about the suitability of the candidate—to recommend or not, and with what, if any, conditions (Edlin, 2005a).

Who Should Do Assessment and Screening?

Screening of candidates is two-pronged. At best, it is a cooperative partnership between the person desiring to become involved in humanitarian work and the agency seeking the right personnel to carry out its vision. Each party has important roles in determining whether a given person is right for the job, the organization, the mission, and the host country or culture. Ideally the two will arrive at a mutually helpful decision about suitability.

The Agency Process:

The first part of the assessment engages the resources of the organization, with it taking the lead in the means, methods, and content of screening. Those doing the screening and assessment should always keep in mind that the outcomes have impact on the agency, as well as the individual under scrutiny. The reputation of the agency and protection of its investment of personnel and financial resources are at stake, as well as the obvious fact of effective accomplishment of its goals. Financially, an agency investment for one family may be in excess of $500,000 (U.S.), beginning with recruitment and extending through allocation (Gamble and Lovell, 2008). (Depending on the location and assignment, costs may vary.) These costs include recruitment, assessment, selection, training in language and culture, allocation, moving costs, and orientation to the host culture and country. Another financial consideration for the agency is the expectation of the cost of health issues, particularly when an agency is self-insured. Will the candidate's medical needs place an undue burden on a self-insured program, especially if adequate national medical facilities are not available at the site of the assignment? (M. Pocock, personal communication, January 30, 2011). Errors early on in the process of personnel acquisition can become very costly indeed!

The medical and psychological assessments must be done by qualified medical professionals, usually a physician and a mental health psychologist or counselor. Generally, these are done separately, as clinicians qualified in both disciplines are rare. Candidates and spouses should be interviewed separately, though part of the assessment should be conducted together, in order to observe their interaction and to discuss their marriage relationship. (See later sections on these two specialized areas of screening and assessment.)

The Candidate's Personal Process of Self-Assessment:

Ideally, the agency and the individual are partners in the process of screening and selection. The second half of assessment is to be done by the individual himself or herself. It involves the individual in self-study which enables him or her to anticipate what lies ahead and to know how to minimize health and other risks that will be encountered in a cross-cultural humanitarian role and place of service. Volume 2 of this series has a section on self-study. The whole process of screening and selection should be one of mutual discovery, so that applicants are assessing the agency while it assesses them. Arriving at a mutual decision about "fit" between persons and organizations makes for the best outcome.

What are the Best Methods for Screening and Assessing?

Four methods of screening and assessment allow for the best selection of candidates.

1. **Attending a group residential program** such as a candidate orientation program which allows in-depth, face-to-face time for staff to get to know and observe candidates, and *vice versa.*

2. **A psychological assessment** with various methods and inventories.

3. **A life history evaluation**, with a questionnaire and written autobiography followed up with one or more face-to-face interviews.

4. **Other information**, including references and checking for any police or criminal record. Secondary references are also helpful. Those are derived by asking the persons providing the first references if they would suggest two or three others persons who know the candidate well

who might be willing to provide a reference. Let's consider each of these four in depth here.

1.　In-house Assessment in a Residential Program

The "whole life" approach takes place in a venue shared by staff and candidates. It provides the best environment in which various screening and assessment tools may be used. The goal in this kind of program is to get to know the candidate in all life dimensions. Ideally, an agency should have a residential training session of two or more weeks in which current staff of the organization and candidates live and learn together. The sharing of life together throughout the days of the program allow for multiple times of exposure to each other and sufficient time for self-study, orientation to the ethos of the organization, classroom time, a variety of formal and informal activities. People can get to know each other best in this kind of safe learning environment. Learning about each other as candidates and current organizational members is mutual. The candidates need to choose the organization, just as those entrusted with assessing and screening them also must choose them. In this context tests, inventories, questionnaires, interviews, and mutual dialogue can be easily accomplished. This is far superior to screening and assessments done by telephone, mail, email or skype.

The candidate program should be typified by open and intensive dialogue, when issues and concerns are brought out in the open. Candidates need freedom to inquire and to reflect; staff members need freedom to dialogue, discuss, and observe the relationships of the candidates with each other and with those who represent the organization. This amount of time and degree of interaction makes possible a far better assessment and screening process than any done by telephone interview and paperwork.

The program needs to include a variety of activities, such as classroom time, doing chores together, fun activities, interactive discussions, and others which allow for multiple kinds of interaction between staff members and candidates. These also allow for trained staff members to observe candidates interact with each other, including with family members.

Some agencies require potential recruits to attend **candidate school**, which varies in duration ranging from several days to six months.[3]

During this time, the agency can observe how the individual/family interacts with others in a close, community setting that simulates some aspects of international living. However, the transition to life, study and work in an altogether foreign culture is much more dramatic and potentially more traumatic than pre-field orientation at home can simulate. We recommend that two courses be offered, the first one being specifically for screening, assessment, and selection, and the second for training once the agency has accepted the candidate.

All kinds of assessments, including psychological (see next section) are best done within this organizational group context. For special areas such as medical and mental health, a competent physician or psychologist who is knowledgeable about the organization and the allocations and cultures it serves is best. Ideally this person is included in the residential program for in-depth time to get acquainted and to observe the person at work and in relationships. Testing and interviewing can best be done within this residential context. When that is not possible, outsourcing to organizations which provide skilled and trained mental health professionals may be used. It is imperative to include psychosocial and psychological testing! To overlook or exclude these will likely result in sending persons abroad who are not suited. For instance, in a group setting, with shared chores and activities, it might become clear that a "job qualified" person lacks the interpersonal skills to work well with others and to thus be a good team member.

"Outsourcing" the Candidate Program:
Outsourcing candidate screening and assessment and aspects of selection and training to *programs* conducted by agencies which exist for that purpose is the best approach for agencies and organizations too small to host and staff their own programs. We recommend Missionary Training International (MTI) in Colorado. A great advantage of the programs of these organizations is that the staff is trained to interact and

---

[3] One consortium of organizations which provides this resource can be found at http://www.missionsinterlink.org.au; a similar but abbreviated program for short-term workers is also offered by this Australian organization (S. Rowe, personal communication, January 12, 2011).

to observe, and to make knowledgeable judgments about behaviors observed in candidates.

Outsourcing is far superior to a haphazard process done in a small agency by persons not specifically trained in screening and assessment. A typical organizational personnel or human resources person is not very knowledgeable about human development and human behavior; he or she may not know what to look for in candidates or how to observe and evaluate what is being manifested. In addition to the agency named above, which does general assessment, some professional organizations provide services specifically for medical assessment. These include InterHealth (www.interhealth.org.uk), Edinburgh International Health Centre (www.eihc.org) and International Health Management (www.ihm.ca) in Canada (Beattie, 2007). As of 2021, interhealth.org.uk and eihc.org sites no longer exist.

Outsourcing resources are available for psychological services as well. One organization is Mandala Foundation based in Australia (www.mandalafoundation.org.au). We also highly recommend Dr. Charlie Schaefer, psychologist, Dr. Frauke Schaefer, psychiatrist, and Dr. Esther Schubert, psychiatrist. All of these are currently available in the U.S. and are experienced in overseas service. Each one has lived and worked abroad in humanitarian contexts. Many other fine professionals provide such services. We believe it is crucial to engage professionals who themselves have worked abroad and understand the unique stresses and challenges of cross-cultural work. They are best able to determine suitability of candidates with such a background.

2. Psychological Assessment

Our humanitarian heroes need good mental health screening as well as medical and general life evaluation. An international assignment requires, in addition to other skills and qualities, a high level of psychological health that can be maintained under stressful conditions over a period of time. The candidate's psychological and emotional health must be able to withstand the challenges of a rigorous environment while he or she maintains a growing personal and spiritual life, healthy interpersonal relationships, and intimacy, whether married or single. (Edlin, 2005a). Member care workers concur that many issues stem from emotional, mental, and spiritual sources, with relationship problems often being an integral part of the picture (Pettigrew, 2011). People who are well-adjusted, with a good sense of self-esteem, flexibility and openness to change and experience are best equipped to meet these challenges of international life and work. (J. Potz-Hartford, personal communication, January 12, 2011).

Some important issues regarding psychological assessments:

1. Consider all the information: Recommendations should take into account all information that has been gathered, including psychological inventories, interviews, references, life history questionnaires, etc. and not depend solely on one component.

2. Bounds of normal functioning: The goal of a psychological evaluation is to determine when a mental health issue would impair the individual's performance on the field. If the candidate requires medication to manage a mental health issue, this places him/her immediately into the classification of "conditional assignment" or "recommendation with reservations," in other words, acceptance on the condition that the psychological issue is satisfactorily controlled by psychotropic medication at the site of the assignment (R. Pruitt, personal communication, April 8, 2011).

3. Qualifications of evaluators: Organizations differ as to what degree of impairment falls within the acceptable bounds of functioning, as there are no concrete guidelines regarding these criteria. Therefore, the responsibility for determining the level of impairment often falls to the psychologist who is doing the assessment, highlighting the importance of the mental health professional's training and knowledge (R. Pruitt, personal communication, April 8, 2011).

Minimum qualifications for the psychological evaluator are as follows (Edlin, 2005):
- Minimal educational level of a master's degree in counseling or related field.
- Counseling experience, the equivalent of obtaining a license.
- Considerable life experience, especially in working in a cross-cultural context.
- Proficiency in the heart language of the individual being evaluated.

- Specialized training and certification required for the interpretation of psychological inventories.

4. Quality of information: Another important factor contributing to an accurate psychological evaluation is the quality of the information that is gathered (Edlin, 2005): All efforts must be made to maintain ethical standards of confidentiality, quality of reporting, etc. in order to ensure the quality of this data.

Use of assessment tools:

Much has been written about the pros and cons of using pencil and paper psychological tools in screening. This debate is beyond the scope of this chapter. However, many agencies recognize the value of using psychological screening tools in the pre-field evaluation of candidates. In general, the larger and older the agency, the more careful the screening and the more exhaustive the assessment, for they have learned over time the high value of this process. Younger, smaller, and newer organizations often lack the resources to do appropriate screening and assessment, and thus may end up with a higher ratio of individuals who are unsuited or will struggle excessively. The following inventories are used commonly for screening.

MMPI-2 (Minnesota Multiphasic Personality Inventory 2). This is the most commonly used tool for assessing mental health for many agencies, seminaries, embassies, NGO's and so on. Its purpose is to discover potential areas of mental health concern by providing a psychological profile. It identifies problems and potential problem areas in personality functioning (Wickstrom, 2002a); it is also useful for detecting personality disorders (Schubert, 1992). It must be administered by a trained mental health professional and the full written report must go only to another professional. A *summary* of the findings may be placed in the hands of the candidate and the agency. It is important to note that it identifies tendencies and possibilities and does not predict what may happen, that is, it cannot set the degree of risk which a person assessed may represent. Therefore, findings must be judged by a professional on the basis of possible or potential problems, in light of the person's history and current functioning. It should be administered face-to-face.

Some other instruments which shed light on an applicant's mental functioning:

- Personality Assessment Inventory (PAI) looks at psychopathology and diagnostic information (Leslie Morey).
- Millon™ Clinical Multiaxial Inventory (MCMI)—identifies psychopathology.
- Beck Depression Inventory. This is a self-administered questionnaire useful to a person which may provide a basis for seeking professional help (see Chapter 2).

Additional inventories such as the following may be used for specific issues:

- NEO Personality Inventory (NEO-PI). This instrument assesses normal functioning and qualities such as extraversion, agreeableness, conscientiousness, neuroticism, and openness to experience.
- Firo-B™ looks at styles of behavior especially in work and management based on Fundamental Interpersonal Relations Orientation™.
- 16 Personality Factor (PF) is used to assess normal personality traits, and functioning in various settings.
- Baron EQ-I is a self-inventory of emotional intelligence which is helpful in understanding one's emotional ability and relationship style (MHA Online Assessments)
- Marital Satisfaction Inventory—identifies differences in perceptions in couples and provides information for possible interventions when a marriage is troubled
- Prepare-Enrich couples' assessment (Life Innovations, Inc.)
- Burnout Inventory (Ken Williams, Strengthening Your Interpersonal Skills Workshops)
- Myers-Briggs Type Indicator® (MBTI). This personality type inventory is very helpful for self-insight and use in team-building.

It is essential that the result of *any instrument* is analyzed and interpreted by a trained professional who sees the person face-to-face and has interviewed him or her in person. This is especially true for instruments looking for psychopathology. Assessment from afar is not the best or most ethical choice. Neither tests nor self-help inventories provide a "black and white" picture of a person's health. None of them is meant to be used as the only measure of psychological health. Each one, and the combined results, always needs to be examined in the context of in-depth interviews with a trained and experienced professional. Even then evaluators must also take into account other information, such as references and life history. The best evaluation takes into account many facets of the person, like a three-dimensional figure. Rather than relying on a two-dimensional "pencil and paper" view, good screening and assessment requires multiple views of the candidate.

We recommend that personnel making assessments of candidates take at least one college level course in testing, to gain understanding of the limits and validity questions about every instrument. Given that results from any test or inventory on any one day or occasion represent a *sample* of behavior, no one score should be used alone.

When agencies lack trained and experienced professionals in-house to conduct assessment and screening, psychological assessments can be outsourced. One organization is called Mandala Foundation based in Australia: www.mandalafoundation.org.au. Many reliable mental health professionals might provide these services. We strongly recommend selecting one with cross-cultural experience so that findings may be better interpreted in light of demands of overseas work and living.

3. Life History Evaluation

This process is complex and comprehensive, including a questionnaire, written autobiography and an extensive interview. The questionnaire is usually given in written format. Guidelines for the written autobiography should be described to the candidate, including the length and depth desired. These two should be submitted and reviewed as preparation for the in-person interview. The form should include questions about family background, personal background, and marital background.

In conducting the interview, the interviewer should be watching for "red flags." These include personal or family history of alcohol or drug abuse, sexual abuse, sexual identity issues, history of child abuse or neglect, adoption or divorce, and unresolved feelings of guilt, grief, anger, fear or excessive anxiety.

Of course, skill in asking questions is crucial, so that the candidate is drawn out and does not feel like he or she is being interrogated. The skilled professional should ask appropriate, probing and definitive questions to try to validate the authenticity of the inventory results. Also, by correlating the results from the life history questionnaire, the evaluator will be able to obtain a clear picture of the candidate's past and current level of functioning. There is a tendency, when a candidate looks very promising, or has a great background, to shy away from asking the normal inventory of questions, as it may appear unseemly to ask the necessary questions (M. Pocock, personal communication, January 30, 2011). The interviewer should intentionally resist this tendency in order to obtain an accurate and thorough assessment.

The goal of the life history questionnaire is not so much to obtain very specific details but to identify issues for further discussion. It provides a way to gain valuable context in the interpretation of the psychological inventory profile, as well as to create questions for the interviews. Given that the best predictor of future behavior is past behavior, attending to what the candidate says about his or her habits of responding in trauma or distress is crucial, as this reveals the likelihood of future success or difficulty in adjusting to the demands of field life.

Below are listed the main points that should be covered in the life history process. Interpretation principles are noted. This section draws heavily upon the experience of a major sending agency in the screening of new candidates (Edlin, 2005a).

A written autobiography, including a detailed vocational and social history should be submitted ahead of time for the interviewer to study. Work or vocational history should be verified by outside sources. (Individuals with personality disorders and other psychological conditions often have checkered work histories indicative of sub-optimal function which is predictive of future performance, Schubert, 2002). The interview should cover these aspects of the candidate's life.

a. Family of origin:

An understanding of the family of origin such as the birth order, the parents' occupation, personality types, parenting styles, and their marriage relationship (including divorce or separation, etc.) can help identify the forces that shaped the candidate's psychological makeup. The state of the siblings' relationships with the parents and their view of the family also shed light on the values and styles of coping that were modeled in the family of origin. If there is indication of significant dysfunction in the family, it is helpful to find out how the candidate has dealt with this in the past and how he or she handles it now (e.g., by withdrawing, by acquiescing or submitting, by joining a healthier "alternate family" or such). (See Volume One of this series, which emphasizes the formation of persons, especially the role of the family of origin.)

1) **Unresolved issues** from the family of origin can cause significant stress after departure to the field. All efforts should be made to help the individual or couple deal with "old baggage" relating to relationships with parents or siblings before leaving for a cross-cultural assignment.

2) **Lack of parental support** for the candidate's decision to apply for international service can cause great stress. Grandparents may be very resistant to the prospect of having their grandchildren move so far away. Asian parents, especially, may have trouble releasing their grown children for service because of expectations related to filial piety. Exploring these issues and how the candidate has dealt or is dealing with them is vital.[4]

3) **Inadequate separation** from the family of origin. When emotional enmeshment is part of the family style it can continue after the individual leaves for his or her field assignment and may result in a difficult adjustment.

b. Current level of functioning:

The candidate's present level of psychological functioning should be assessed. How is he or she functioning in the current job? How has the

[4] See Vanessa Hung's article "Filial Piety and Missionary Calling" in *Worth Keeping* (pp. 78-79) for creative solutions to this problem.

candidate dealt with stress in the past and how has this affected his or her work? What is the person's level of self-esteem? It is useful to gain a sense of the candidate's flexibility and openness to change and experience, (Arthur, 2008), not only as it relates to adjusting to a new culture, but also with respect to the need to change personal habits that have an impact on health and well-being, such as stress management strategies, and adjusting to a different style of worship.

c. Personal life-style attitudes, values, and experience:

Does the candidate have any history of alcohol or substance abuse? Has the candidate ever been arrested or imprisoned? Is there a history of angry outbursts or lack of forgiveness? Does the candidate have any compulsions or obsessions? Any of these that are current in the person's life create complexity and "red flags" for acceptance. A past history of these issues has serious implications regarding the candidate's future functioning. It is important to recognize and validate that personal change can take place and that a person may make significant life-style changes so the past must always be interpreted in light of the present. Each "red flag" area of concern should be explored in depth in the interview. An example of this is the use of pornography or sexual addiction. A person who has overcome an addiction and is currently free of these behaviors can easily relapse under the weight of chronic high stress in another culture. Such matters are very important in risk assessment, for the candidate's future as well as for the agency's risk of accepting the person, who could damage the mission or the reputation of the organization with relapse into addiction. Privacy and confidentiality for the person are outweighed by the realistic need to know and predict based on the past.

d. Occupational history:

A spotty occupational history with unaccountable lapses of time may reveal evidence of problems such as a personality disorder or work time lost due to addictions. The behavioral description interview, which operates on the premise that the past is the best predictor of the future, has been used for screening new employees. This type of focused interview may have application in pre-field screening, in revealing how the individual has coped with various situations or challenges in the past (K. McClean, personal communication, January, 30, 2011).

A very positive occupational history demonstrates such qualities as responsibility, conscientiousness, competency, and ability to relate well to others in the work place. It can provide excellent guidance for role placement, assignment to a team, and allocation to a host culture and country. It is important to note that candidates who are "on their way up" in career development may change roles frequently once they master a given level of responsibility. This is especially true of intuitive-thinkers (as seem in the MBTI). These changes induced by upward mobility should not be confused with an unstable work history.

e. Past history of psychological problems:

Have there been any issues for which the candidate has sought or considered counseling? What was the outcome of the counseling? Willingness to go to counseling is generally viewed as a positive in that it shows recognition of a need for help and a desire to change something. A person's choice to engage in counseling should not be negatively sanctioned or viewed with suspicion as seeking help and guidance is a sign of awareness and desire to grow. It is important to ask if the candidate has had problems with depression or anxiety or has been diagnosed as having a personality disorder. The important factor is not the details of any past situation but rather how the person has dealt with difficulty. Even when a person has received help and recovered, depression or other mood disorders may resurface when the individual is placed in a stressful, cross-cultural setting. This is important for both the candidate and the agency to recognize and prepare for. Personality disorders, on the other hand, are usually trait stable and do not change, hence candidates suffering with such disorders are usually not acceptable candidates for the hazardous occupation of cross-cultural humanitarian work.

f. Sense of call:

Gaining understanding of a candidate's motives or "call" to overseas work and his or her expectations about that can also be useful. Some candidates may mistake a psychological agenda for a genuine call to service (e.g., a need to be needed) (Schubert, 2002). The role of family of origin expectations is important in this. A good interview will help to differentiate a healthy desire and motivation to serve from compulsive or unhealthy motivations. This is especially important if serving in a humanitarian organization will add prestige or status or significantly higher pay, or when a person may desire to marry an expatriate or enable the person to gain entry into the partner's homeland. Most often, motivations are actually a mix of a genuine desire to serve others and such things as an adventurous spirit and wanting to see a larger world. However, accepting candidates driven predominantly by unhealthy motives leads to a great deal of damage and may compromise the reputation of the agency and the outcome of the project.

g. Sexual history:

The interview should assess the candidate's degree of self-knowledge and attitudes about sexuality and sexual practices. Though most people will find it embarrassing and difficult to discuss such a personal topic, it is very important to do so. What sexual experience has the candidate had? Does the person have a history of sexual or physical abuse or assault, such as rape? Has the candidate been sexually active outside of a marriage relationship or been promiscuous? Has he or she ever had an affair while married? Has he or she had a problem with pornography? Does he or she have any history of pedophilia or sexual involvement with a student, minor or parishioner? These would not only be "red flags" but should rule out acceptance; the danger of relapse, as well as criminal violations and their consequence, are too great a risk!

Is the person sexually attracted to individuals of the same gender, and how has he/she dealt with that? In most cultures and countries same-sex relationships are not acceptable, and may even carry severe punishments, so any international organization must exercise great caution. Is there any evidence of compulsivity in the candidate's sexual behavior? If so, how has the candidate dealt with it? Sexual indiscretion usually indicates immaturity, emotional neediness, impulsivity, or unresolved past issues of sexual identity or abuse. Because sexuality is such a sensitive aspect of human life and is an area of vulnerability behaviors can easily shift from healthy to unhealthy. Unhealthy habits of the past over which the person gained control can easily emerge again in the stress of adjusting to a cross-cultural setting, especially early on. The person conducting the life history interview should review with the candidate what help has been sought and what steps he or she has taken to deal with any problems. Has he or she put an accountability structure in place? It is crucial to recognize that in many cultures, standards and values, and even definitions of sexuality, vary from western cultures. In some cultures that means standards are more permissive, but in other cultures violating those standards can lead to death! Violations of any country's laws about sexual conduct has serious impact on the whole organization!

h. Marriage relationship:

A couple should be assessed individually and together. An instrument such as the "Marital Satisfaction Inventory" is a helpful tool for a starting review. The interviewer should explore the marriage relationship, asking about the strengths of the marriage as well as areas of needed growth. What is the current status of the couple's marriage? What does the couple say about the strengths and resilience of their marriage, such as the ability to communicate, resolve conflict, and maintain physical and emotional intimacy? What are the motivations for and commitment to international service? For each one? Candidates who are newlywed should be strongly encouraged to take time, at least one year, to work on their marriage relationship before taking an overseas assignment.

i. Current family issues:

A primary reason for worker attrition is "family" issues which have impact on the family and colleagues.

1) **Careful evaluation of the children** is part of a good family assessment. The children's reactions to leaving friends and school need to be soberly considered. Teenagers, in particular, should undergo pre-field assessment along with the parents and should be seriously considered in the decision to move overseas, given the trauma of being uprooted. (An angry teenager acting out not only can create much heartache for the family, but also can do irreparable damage to the reputation of the team and agency, Wickstrom, 2002). Teens may not readily see the advantages of such a move. Thus, assessment of their openness to being transplanted is important. Friendly, adventurous children will find it easier to find peers within the host culture, which can be very helpful to their social well-being and adjustment (P. Fischer, personal communication, December 28, 2010). For younger children, parents need to be cautious to not be so "child-centered" that they allow

a young child to have undue influence in the decision-making process. We encountered this in one family, in which the parents and child thought the eight-year-old should have an equal vote with the parents. Learning disabilities, ADD/ADHD, and the adjustment of adopted children are other issues which should be addressed, despite potential sensitivity on the part of the parents. Further testing should be requested, if required, to assess the potential impact of these issues on the family's effectiveness and health on the field.

2) **Observe how family members relate** with one another. Interviewing the children individually and together without parents can reveal valuable information about family dynamics, parenting styles and behavioral issues which might not otherwise be apparent (Wickstrom, 2002). Problem areas that are identified should be brought up and recommendations offered.

3) **Address marriage and family issues** and create a plan to help resolve them before commencing overseas service. (If this is done, another review needs to happen before departure for the field.) If problems are not addressed while home country resources and energy are available, they are likely to grow out of proportion under the chronic high stress of field life. Someone has said, "Cross-cultural living is like pouring Miracle-Gro on all your weaknesses, dysfunctions and sins."

j. Social relationships:

Asking about the candidate's social relationships, including friendships with persons of both genders, is appropriate. For the single candidate, ask if he or she is able to manage issues such as loneliness and sexual desire in emotionally mature ways. Does he or she have the skills to build and maintain friendships and establish accountability, as well as enjoyable, healthy and intimate social relationships? What kind of social support network does he or she maintain? What history has he or she had regarding relationships with members of the opposite gender? Are there areas of vulnerability here? Is he or she engaged or considering marriage? What is his or her attitude about this relationship? (We recommend a fiancé go through the same screening process.)

For couple's a social relationship history is also helpful. Are they able to form friendships quickly? Do they have good friendship skills? Do they have any ideas about how their marriage will suffer pressure from the extreme stresses in life in a humanitarian setting and from some cultures which do not value marital fidelity? Do they understand the importance of developing a social support system quickly in the new context?

k. Spiritual and religious history:

Besides assessing the positive aspects of the candidate's religious history, it is important to explore whether the person has had any involvement in religious practices focused on or based in the occult, such as demonism, tarot cards, Ouija boards, idol worship, witchcraft, voodoo, and so on. These are all practices of concern because they can be pathways for evil spiritual forces. Both religious and non-religious workers often experience great darkness and even terrifying physical attacks in other lands. They may actually encounter demons directly, or in human form. Any past experiences which would leave an open door for such attacks should be remedied. In my experience in Peru (Dodds), several anthropologists and embassy personnel sought us out for advice because they were terrified of the evil forces they encountered. They knew they felt the presence of evil but they did not know how to cope. A very common experience was to feel that someone or something invisible was squeezing their chests so tightly that they could not breathe. Others have heard terrifying sounds or seen frightening apparitions. These experiences are doubly of concern in that some psychological illnesses come about because of such spiritual, behavioral, and cognitive aberrations.

Given that the humanitarian efforts worldwide primarily exist because of the needs of people and cultures created by the reality of evil in the world, it is not surprising that persons doing good and serving mankind in positive ways will at times be subjected to evil forces which attempt to stop them. A strong faith in God and in goodness and the belief that good can triumph over evil is crucial in the foundation of a person who will be effective and can endure over the long haul.

4. Other Salient Information Gathering

Additional background information about the candidate supplements the inventory results and life history questionnaire and interview, allowing the evaluator to increase the understanding of the candidate in order to make a thorough assessment. This information is usually obtained through references, police records and other tools. If candidates are likely to work in sensitive situations, such as caring for children or handling finances, background checks are warranted.

Personal references and letters of recommendation should be sought from colleagues, employers, friends and pastor, rabbi, or other spiritual or religious leader (as appropriate) and followed up by a personal telephone call. While referees may be reluctant to identify or elaborate on problems in writing, they may be frank in speaking of them when asked (Schubert, 1992). Seeking further references from the referees offered by the individual may also produce revealing information.

Caveats in Screening to Consider

1. False positives and difficulty in determining actual risk: As important as pre-field assessment is and as thorough as it may be, it is still limited in its ability to predict successful service. The risk of developing a physical or psychological problem hampering effectiveness and vitality will never be entirely eliminated (J. Potz-Hartford, personal communication, January 12, 2011). In the final analysis, the assignment itself is the definitive test of a worker's fitness for a particular assignment (Gamble, 2002). Even those candidates whose pre-field screening shows no indication of previous problems may struggle significantly when thrust into the crucible of international work. For example, a study carried out by Deborah Lovell (1997) (as cited in Gamble & Lovell-Hawker, 2008) showed that forty-six percent of aid workers reported experiencing depression either during or after service. The majority of these workers would be considered at low risk, having never experienced psychological problems prior to entering aid work. This underscores the fact that screening does not eliminate all risk for medical and psychological issues: pre-field assessment is not an end-point in itself, i.e. "passing" is not the ultimate goal of such an assessment. Rather, it is more helpful to regard screening as the first step in a commitment to providing ongoing care for international workers (Gamble & Lovell-Hawker, 2008).

2. Varying levels of risk tolerance between agency and candidate:
Another issue regarding risk involves differences in risk tolerance between the organization and the candidate. On the one hand, the question is how much this individual with this special challenge is willing to put up with, seeing that his or her decision to enter international work puts him or her at risk (C. Loong, personal communication, December 30, 2010). On the other hand, the organization must consider how much risk it is willing to absorb in approving the individual. This is important because the agency itself takes on responsibility for the health and well-being of the candidate and his or her family. It also must consider the needs of the team to which the person may be assigned. Making this call requires good communication, a careful review of all available materials, and wise judgment.

3. False negatives and the screening out of potentially effective workers: Conversely, pre-field assessment may result in screening out candidates who will not actually go on to develop problems on the field, thus ruling out potentially valuable workers. A notable example is Gladys Aylward who was rejected early in the twentieth century by the China Inland Mission (CIM) for poor health and insufficient education, but went on to serve in China for many years. Her work, especially in saving the lives of 100 children when the Japanese invaded China, was so impressive that a classic Hollywood movie was made about her; "The Inn of the Sixth Happiness" starred Ingrid Bergman as Gladys. Another example is a gifted and productive couple who did not pass the medical screening of one agency for their known, but stable, medical conditions. However, after being accepted by another agency, this couple went on to serve fruitfully and without medical incident for nearly twenty years. Another example is a blind man who was rejected by one agency but accepted by another and served for decades in very fruitful and effective roles.

4. Disqualification vs. inadequate development: In the process of screening and assessment, it is important to differentiate those factors which disqualify a person and those which are solely matters of development. How the information in a recommendation or rejection is presented is very delicate and important. It is unethical to imply to candidate who has been "screened out" through disqualification that he or she may qualify for service with further development. If the evaluation committee truly means, "You are not qualified and most likely never will be," that message should be stated concretely and clearly (Edlin, 2005). It is better to tell the truth kindly without giving false hope than to have a person try harder and become disillusioned later. In situations where a person is not yet acceptable developmentally, perhaps due to age or lack of training, appropriate hope and guidance may be offered.

5. Availability of resources to help workers grow: A related caveat is that for a newly accepted candidate to grow there must be commitment, time, accountability, mentoring, and other valuable resources from the organization. Agencies need to ensure that these resources are in place and available *before* accepting a candidate conditionally, with stated goals for growth and development in specified areas (Edlin, 2005). In this, too, it is better to tell candidates at the beginning what is or will not be available than for them to be disappointed or disillusioned later.

6. Legal constraints: Various agencies and organizations differ in the degree of screening they perform, in part, because of legislation which seeks to protect individuals from unfair discrimination. In today's increasingly inclusive political environment, any screening of candidates may open an organization to charges of discrimination, an obvious deterrent to the appropriate screening of appropriate workers (L. Gardner, personal communication, January 7, 2011). However, a recent encouraging decision by the U.S. Supreme Court has clarified that religious organizations are not discriminating as employers when they uphold standards consistent with their beliefs and practices (Jan 11, 2013).

7. Confidentiality: Confidentiality of reports generated from interviews and instruments needs to be clarified in accordance with best ethical practices (Griffin, 2007). Clearly, tension exists between maintaining appropriate confidentiality for the candidate and still providing leaders with sufficient information for good selection and to monitor the person in their field assignment when negative behaviors might   influence   his effectiveness or have the potential to harm others. Leaders have a legitimate need to know information which allows them to appropriately support the worker in the field or to turn down a potential assignee (P.

Davis, personal communication, April 2, 2011), as they, as well as personnel in the home office, need to make appropriate team and locale assignments. The following example illustrates the complexity of the matter of confidentiality:

> A new worker, with a history of sexual abuse as a child, is approved by the head office and sent on an assignment. Her previous history is withheld from the field leadership in order to protect her privacy. However, soon after arriving on the field she begins to struggle with feelings of low-esteem and depression and withdraws from her teammates. This seems to be related to her history and memories being triggered by current field events and factors. The field leaders are at a loss as to understanding her behavior and how to help her. When they contact the head office about her symptoms, they are informed of her previous psychological history. The worker is eventually sent home for counseling. After the incident, the field leaders are confused and angry that the head office would send such a candidate without informing them of her history; personnel in the head office feel constrained by legislation regarding disclosure of information and confidentiality, as well as the desire to prevent misinterpretation of such information by leaders who are not trained mental health or medical professionals. The field worker feels betrayed because she felt her privacy was violated by the field leaders being told, without her consent.

This tension should be addressed upfront by the agency and a policy formulated *ahead of need* which is adequately responsive to specific circumstances in order to meet disparate needs. One policy and possible solution would be to obtain consent from the candidate at the time of his or her pre-field assessment to disclose the history to the field member care personnel and the leadership *as needed* (R. Pruitt, personal communication, April 8, 2011). An explanation about the impact of her or his history during a period of especially high stress of adjustment in the field would be logical and helpful, so she or he would not think it is an arbitrary decision to share such significant information.

With appropriate information, the field member care personnel can provide necessary support and/or monitoring. As illustrated in the case above, this is potentially problem-laden, so every care must be exercised to ensure the information is not shared with anyone outside the "need to know" circle. The risk of not sharing the information must be weighed against the risk of it being known by those who have no need to know!

Another matter that should be considered in regards to the use of screening and assessment instruments is that appropriate feedback should be given to the candidate. Typically this means that they are told honestly what is revealed and how it has bearing on their selection. Only in situations where an MMPI reveals very significant information which the candidate would be emotionally or mentally unable to handle should information be withheld. We believe any person has the right to be informed about the implications of any information about him/herself which he or she has voluntarily shared. (See below.)

Despite the potential pitfalls and caveats, thorough assessment of candidates is essential. It has great bearing on the future well-being of the individual or family and many implications also for the organization. Much more harm is done by failing to do a thorough assessment and screening than is created by the complexities we have considered.

What Happens to the Results?

Preparing a summary of all the findings from various sources is a crucial part of the process for screening, assessment and candidate selection. It requires considerable time—probably at least several hours. Making use of the summary in formulating a recommendation for the agency and then providing feedback to the candidate all require wisdom, insight, and knowledge.

1. **Preparation and summary of results.** The final results of the whole life and psychological assessment should take into account all information that has been gathered, including psychological inventories, interviews, references, life history questionnaires, etc. The evaluator should summarize all the findings in writing and make a recommendation to the candidate selection committee regarding the potential of the candidate for effective international service. Recommendations should *never* depend solely on one component!

2. **Sharing with the candidate**. It is important to "get it right" and to "share it right." Results of all assessments, evaluations, testing instruments and interviews should also be reviewed with the applicant.

Each candidate needs to have the opportunity to talk with the professional who has done the evaluation to help him or her to interpret the results of the assessment (Wickstrom, 2002). He or she should be

allowed to read any written summary and recommendation. In the event of the discovery of a serious issue, such as a personality disorder, the candidate deserves to know the findings of the information that has originated with him or her, as well as what other people have provided. A face-to-face discussion is crucial to help the candidate understand why or why not he or she is going to be accepted for membership or as personnel of the organization.

Even the undesirable news of rejection as unsuitable for the cross-cultural endeavor is best understood by the candidate when it is carefully explained in the light of his or her own needs, limits, vulnerabilities, and future health. So, too, with the positive news of recommendation for acceptance. *To not provide face-to-face presentation of the pertinent information about the candidate is unethical, and can be very damaging to the person who hopes to be accepted for humanitarian work.* Even less-than-good news can help a person learn and grow about himself or herself and the stresses of cross-cultural life. This process is enlightened in "Stressed from Core to Cosmos" (Dodds, 1997). The first time we presented this paper at a conference, a pastor stood up and said, "Aaahhh! For the first time I understand why an organization does not accept everyone I refer to them!"

Assessments carried out professionally and ethically can also prove to be a powerful learning experience for the candidate and disclose areas of potential growth in self-knowledge and development. However, if not explained completely, psychological inventory results may lead to the candidate drawing erroneous conclusions, especially if the report is not positive. A negative evaluation may possibly lead to disillusionment and discouragement at best, and at worst to a fatalistic view which may perpetuate negative behavior. An overly positive evaluation, in contrast, may contribute to the candidate's developing an overblown self-image and may create resistance to future feedback and input. Thus it is important for the evaluator to review the results carefully with the candidate and then to assess what interpretation may have been made and its impact on the candidate. This process should be very transparent, without hidden agendas, and could lead to a deeper level of self-knowledge and desire for growth for the candidate.

3. **Making a recommendation to the agency or organization**. After completing all the assessments, the evaluators should prepare a thorough report of findings, using standard report formatting or standardized in-house forms. This would include a recommendation about the potential of the candidate for effective international service (Edlin, 2005a). These reports and recommendations then form part of the overall data that an assessment team will consider in making the final decision. We do recommend "selection committees," as a small group of professionals or trained assessors can arrive at a more realistic decision than can one person alone.

4. **Clarifying who owns the records**. This should be done initially. If the organization is paying for the assessment, they own the records. However, the outcomes of testing should always be shared orally with the candidate. In most cases this should also be done in written form. Depending on the instrument the whole written assessment may not be put in the hands of the candidate. (For example, an MMPI written report is not ever intended for any lay person. On the other hand, a written report of personality type information is helpful to the candidate.)

5. **Having clear expectations of evaluators.** Selection committees and agency personnel overseeing assessment and screening should be sure to clarify expectations of evaluators. It is crucial to provide a clear, concrete set of criteria to those asked to evaluate an applicant. They must be trained to know what they are looking for and know how to recognize it when they see it.

a. **Strive for accurate decisions:** Avoid making incorrect, unethical and illegal judgments, by ensuring that the results are reviewed carefully and that recommendations are made by qualified professionals or trained evaluators.

b. **Establish clear communication:** Once a candidate is selected, further open communication is important, with both the person and the field entity. The selection committee must strive to communicate very clearly with field leaders about the needs and any limitations of the person. Erroneous conclusions can result when an adequate, incomplete, or inaccurate written report is not provided, even if the assessment is made by a trained professional. Clarification is especially important if an agency leader on the field is not trained in mental health issues or is unfamiliar with the evaluation instruments used (Wickstrom, 2002). The report should clarify any matters about the candidate which indicate he or she may need special support.

c. **Work together with any outside professionals who are providing screening and assessment:** In-house selection committees should rely on the help of consultants in interpreting assessment results and handling specific circumstances and issues that require further investigation. This can strengthen the relationship between the professional and the agency. Later on, the professional may consult or give advice regarding specific problems or the placement of candidates he or she has screened. Intervention in the event of a crisis or problem or help in mediating interpersonal conflicts may be another way the professional can re-enter the client's life in the future (Wickstrom, 2002).

d. **Implement recommendations:** Obviously, the results of a careful assessment made by a trained consultant, should be taken seriously! The recommendations should be acted upon! To not do so is a waste of resources and leads to problems. One former candidate director commented, *"What I found is that we did not get into trouble because we did not know enough about the candidates, but because we did not do what we should have about what we knew!"* [5]

---

[5] M. Pocock, personal communication, January 30, 2011.

Summary

Pre-field screening is an essential first step in the effective career of any international humanitarian servant-hero. The more thorough and careful the screening, the more accurate the assessment, the more careful the selection, the better overall outcome can be expected. Every investment in this process is worthwhile and pays rich dividends for the agency.

This will be reflected in monetary savings and in better achievement of the mission of the agency. The individual too benefits. Those who are accepted will know that they have passed through rigorous screening and careful selection. Those who are not accepted, if the process of feedback is handled well, will understand that "rejection" is in their best interest because placement abroad under chronically difficult conditions is not the best choice for them.

Appendix:
Resources for psychological health

- People in Aid, www.peopleinaid.org is now hapinternational.org
- Antares Foundation, www.antaresfoundation.org
- Headington Institute, www.headington-institute.org
- InterHealth, www.interhealth.org.uk
- Global Member Care Network,
  http://gmcn.globalmembercare.com/
- Aidworkers Network, www.aidworkers.net
- Columbia International Graduate School, Dept. of Member Care. In the doctoral program for "Member Care," one class offered is "Church & Mission Health." The class focuses on five domains of health (Emotional, Relational, Spiritual, Financial and Physical), with the view of helping the candidate develop a personal health profile as well as a plan to address deficiencies. www.ciu.edu (R. Pruitt, personal communication, April 8, 2011).
- Heartstream Resources, Inc. www.heartstreamresources.org

Heartstream Resources, Inc., publisher of this book, is an invaluable resource for information regarding psychological health. Heartstream conducts two graduate level training courses per year in the care of cross-cultural workers, conducts recovery programs, and consults with agencies. www.heartstreamresources.org

References and Recommended Reading

Arthur, N. and Pederson, P. 2008. Case incidents in counseling for international transitions. Alexandria, VA: American Counseling Association.

Beattie, S. 2007. Candidate selection and medical matters. In R. Hay, V. Lim, D. Blocher, J. Ketelaar, S. Hay. Ed. Worth keeping. Pasadena, CA: William Carey Library. (pp. 85-88).

Bloecher, D. and Lewis, J. 1997. Further findings in the research data. In W. Taylor Ed. Too valuable to Lose: Exploring the causes and cures of missionary attrition (pp. 105-125). Pasadena, CA: William Carey Library.

Callahan, M.V. and Hamer, D.H. 2005. On the medical edge: preparation of expatriates, refugees, and disaster relief workers and peace corps volunteers. *Infectious Disease Clinics of North America*, Mar 19, pp. 85-101.

Chicoine, J-F and Tessier, D. 2008. International adoption. In J. S. Keystone, P. E. Kozarsky, D. O. Freedman, H. D. Nothdurft and B. A. Connor. Eds. Travel Medicine. Chapter 28. Available from www.expertconsultbook.com

Davies, J. M., Barnes, R. and Milligan, D. 2002. Update of guidelines for the prevention and treatment of infection in patients with an absent or dysfunctional spleen. Clinical Medicine (Journal of the Royal College of Physicians of London), 5, 440-443.

Davis, P. 2011. Personal communication.

Dipple, B. 1997. Formal and non-formal pre-field training. In W. Taylor. Ed. Too valuable to lose. Pasadena, CA: William Carey Library. pp. 217-228.

Dodd, C. H. 2007. Intercultural readiness assessment for pre-field candidates, Intercultural Communication Studies XVI: 2, 1-16.

Dodds, L. and Dodds, L. 2003. The stress of ministry hurts! How to thrive anyway! PPT presentation for Refresh! Thailand. Heartstream Resources, Inc. 101 Herman Lee Circle, Liverpool, PA, 17045, USA. www.heartstreamresources.org

_____. 1997. Stressed from core to cosmos. AACC World Congress.

Douglas, P. 2011. Personal communication.

Draper, P.L. 1980. Evaluating candidates for missionary service. Paper presented at Mental Health and Missions Conference, Angola. IN.

Edlin, S. G. 2005. Psychological assessment of overseas workers (unpublished paper).

_____ 2005. Instructions for Psychological Evaluations with Missionary Applicants (unpublished paper).

Fischer, M., Lindsey, N., Staples, J. E. and Hills, S. March 12, 2010. Japanese Encephalitis Vaccines. Recommendations of the ACIP. Recommendations and Reports, 59(RR01), 1-27. Retrieved from www.cdc.gov/mmwr/preview/mmwrhtml/rr5901a1.htm

Foyle. M. 1986. How to choose the right missionary. Evangelical Missions Quarterly Online.

Gamble, K. 2002. Intersections of physical and mental health. In J. Powell, J. Bowers. Ed. Enhancing missionary vitality. Colorado: Mission Training International. pp. 265-274.

Gamble, K. and Lovell, D. 2008. Expatriates. In J. S. Keystone, P. E. Kozarsky, D. O. Freedman, H. D. Nothdurft & B. A. Connor (Eds.). *Travel Medicine* (Chapter 30). Available from http://www.expertconsultbook.com/

Gardner, Laura Mae. 2013. *Healthy, resilient and effective in cross-cultural ministry: A comprehensive member care plan.* Published in Indonesia. Available from the author Larrie Gardner.

_____. 1999. The hardy personality. Dallas, TX: Wycliffe Bible Translators, International.

Harris, P. R., Moran, R. T. and Moran S. 2004. Managing Cultural Differences. 6th ed. New York: Elsevier.

Hay, S. 2002. Selection: health and psychological assessment. In R. Hay, V. Lim, D. Blocher, J. Ketelaar, S. Hay. Ed. Worth Keeping. Pasadena, CA: William Carey Library. pp. 81-84.

Hung, V. 2007. Filial piety and missionary calling. In R. Hay, V. Lim, D. Blocher, J. Ketelaar, S. Hay. Ed. Worth Keeping. Pasadena, CA: William Carey Library. pp. 78-79.

Jones, M. and Gamble K. 2002. Helping missionaries start healthy and stay healthy. In K. O'Donnell. Ed. Doing Member Care Well (pp. 349-364). Pasadena, CA: William Carey Library.

Lankester, Ted. February, 2011. Pre-travel preparation of aid workers and volunteers. Presentation at CMDA-CMDE Symposium, February 14-24, Chiang Mai, Thailand.

Lindquist, S. 1988 Psychological assessment. In K. O'Donnell, M. O'Donnell. Ed. (pp. 55-61). *Helping Missionaries Grow.* Pasadena: William Carey Library.

Loong, C. 2010. Personal communication.

Lovell, D. 1997. Psychological Adjustment Among Returned Overseas Workers. Bangor, Wales: D. Clinical Psychology Thesis, University of Wales.

McClean, K. 2011. Personal communication.

National Cancer Institute, National Institutes of Health. September 22, 2010. FactSheet on mammograms. Retrieved from www.cancer.gov/cancertoics/factsheet/detection/mammograms.

Northrup, C. 2001. The Wisdom of Menopause. New York: Bantam Books.

Pocock, M. 2011. Personal communication.

Potz- Hartford, J. 2011. Personal communication.

Richardson, J. 1992. Psychopathology in missionary personnel. In K. O'Donnell. Ed. (pp. 89-109). Missionary Care. Pasadena, CA: William Carey Library.

Rowe, 2011. Personal communication.

Schubert, E. 1992. Current issues in screening and selection. In K. O'Donnell Ed. (pp. 74-88). Missionary Care. Pasadena, CA: William Carey Library.

_____. 2002. Personality disorders and overseas missions: guidelines for the mental health professional. In J. Powell, J. Bowers. Ed. (pp. 333-342). Enhancing Missionary Vitality. Colorado: Mission Training International.

Weingart, S. N. and Wilson, R. M. 2000. Epidemiology of medical error. British Medical Journal, 320(7237), 774-777.

Vincent, C. A. and Coulter, A. 2002. Patient safety: what about the patient? Quality and Safety in Health Care. 11(1), 76-80.

Wickstrom, D. 2002. Choosing the right people: factors to consider in pre-field assessment. In J. Powell, J. Bowers. Ed. (pp. 219-225). Enhancing Missionary Vitality. Colorado: Mission Training International.

_____ 2002a. Tools used to assess missionaries. In J. Powell, J. Bowers. Ed. (pp. 227-230). Enhancing Missionary Vitality. Colorado: Mission Training International.

Chapter 2
Risk Factors in Humanitarian Service and Four Disorders Requiring Proactive and Reactive Care
Depression, Burnout, PTSD, and Adjustment Disorder

In your role as a member care giver or a personnel director, you may see people with serious needs who require intervention either on the field or in the home country. Four of the extreme responses to risk are described in this chapter, with the criteria listed to help you recognize serious symptoms and to distinguish between major problems which frequently occur with altruistic workers.

The most common conditions we encounter both in our residential programs and in field situations are depression, burnout, post-traumatic stress disorder and adjustment disorder. These all result from long-term stress and crises as well as sudden, traumatic crises. The circumstances of stress and the personality and background of the individual all are factors related to which of these conditions will develop. All of these conditions need some major intervention. Usually intervention means allowing the person to get away from the environment filled with stressors and providing counseling, medical, and other help for them.

People need care for many reasons, and a healthy organization must provide both proactive (preventive) and reactive (healing and restorative) care. Even the most hardy and resilient persons benefit from care, as they are subject to many forces which challenge their coping. In this chapter, we will examine factors which put people in humanitarian work at risk and some important interventions and responses of leaders.

Lack of resources, special circumstances, spiritual forces, isolation, chronic high stress, leader and team dysfunctions, and unclear expectations are some of the factors which increase risk of personal problems or group failure. Certain groups within organizations are at higher risk: leaders, mothers with young children, highly idealistic and young workers. Individuals, families, teams and organizations are all put at risk at times.

1. Risk Factors Inherent to Humanitarian Work

Humanitarian work is inherently dangerous, because we who are global servants are fighting the forces of poverty, human cruelty, natural disasters and cataclysmic events, and wars, all the while in opposition to forces of evil which would prefer to see us knocked out. Therefore, the risks are built-in to the humanitarian endeavor itself. Here we will examine some of the most common risks; this is by no means exhaustive.

a. Inadequate development or unresolved family of origin issues:
These *should* have been discovered during the selection process. When they were not and the person goes to the field, these issues predispose the worker to having more and more intense reactions to on-field events and stressors and likely create undue stress for the team and the agency. A few things in someone's history should preclude cross-cultural and humanitarian service or ministry—extreme self-centeredness, lack of love and concern for people, lack of integrity, poor interpersonal skills, and low levels of moral, spiritual, and psychosocial development. Other factors which should rule out someone being accepted for field service include unwillingness to change, entrenched family of origin issues or unresolved issues related to child sexual abuse.

b. The problem of evil:
This stress and risk factor plagues every humanitarian aid worker. Most often, he or she is in a locale and agency whose very existence has its origin in fighting injustice, scarcity of resources (often due to greed or mismanagement of charitable gifts or goods intended to meet that need), corrupt governments, and evil practices. Human trafficking, oppression of women, gender inequality, poverty and hunger, genocide, child and maternal mortality, scarcity of educational opportunities or facilities,

and environmental depletion are often evidences of greed and corrupt systems. To this must be added the unseen spiritual forces of pure evil.

The recent world news headlines about the government of an Asian country preventing an international organization from giving humanitarian assistance to their people is a shocking example of power corrupted. So too are political regimes in Africa which starve citizens of their own countries. They are dominated by self-seeking leaders whose goals and policies are destructive to millions. The massacres and genocides in the last decade are further evidence.

What could a sending agency do in situations like this? Even acknowledging the fact that evil is real can stimulate awareness and provide hope and help. Religious communities have many spiritual resources, such as asking for God's protection and seeking guidance through prayer. Persons in both humanitarian aid and religious and altruistic agencies can be encouraged to share spiritual resources found in prayer and in sacred writings. Sending organizations should equip and encourage spiritual preparation and the resources to resist evil forces. They must prepare their workers through awareness of this reality, and identification of resources. The organization must encourage their workers to establish a team of those who will pray for them in their cross-cultural ministry endeavors. Nonreligious global workers must also seek divine help and care because the problem of evil is real whether one is religious or not.

c. Hostile environments:
Humanitarian workers encounter hostility of many kinds, including political, cultural, and spiritual. This is true whether people are "Christians" or not. We know many who work and live in dark places of the world who have experienced overt evil against themselves, even when they are not religious persons. What we may refer to as "spiritual warfare or engagement with hostile ideologies" is a significant reality in some parts of the world—worship of man-made "gods," evil powers, corrupt systems, and evil people infused with destructive energy. When a person bringing hope enters the locale to serve, he or she can expect to be battered and bruised. Idealistic young workers and young families inexperienced in strange cultures are vulnerable and deserve to be equipped through preparation, and monitored once they engage in that

setting. Often the children are also at risk for attack by evil forces. We have witnessed and counseled many persons in such situations, anthropologists and embassy personnel specifically.

I (Gardner) remember vividly my first night in an Asian country where prostitution, pornography, and a vigorous drug trade are prevalent. Small spirit houses on poles stood outside every residence. The oppression I experienced on our first night was real, and I felt powerless to resist it. Thankfully, my husband was with me, loving and praying against this oppressive evil force.

Living with overt ideological hostility creates both internal and external stress. Internally, this stress may originate from:
- Knowing your mission and message, if received, could cost someone his or her life.
- Knowing that your local friends may reject the most important thing in the world to you—your faith.
- Having to be cautious about something you are not at all ashamed of—your faith or your values.
- Feeling unskilled in living and fighting against evil persons and evil practices, as well as evil intent.

External stress may come from:
- Living with blatant and overt evil.
- Living in a society where unchecked passions are given free rein.
- Living surrounded by temptation, evil, oppression, powerful evil forces, and perhaps corrupt power systems.
- Discovering that in some countries the police or other "helpers" are in fact culprits, participating in or multiplying the effects of crime.

These costs are almost unthinkable, taking a huge emotional and spiritual toll on sensitive people of integrity. Spiritual resources are most necessary to survive, even if a person has never been religious! Only God can protect one's mind and spirit from such powerful hostile forces. This is possible—we have seen people emerge from the most astounding situations!

A friend of ours literally lived under the nose of Saddam Hussein during his reign of terror. Our friend was there to assist the Kurds with humanitarian services while they were being terrorized and had become refugees. He had incredible resilience and endurance and managed his mission of good will under the most threatening circumstances.

One of our graduate students worked in the U.S. embassy in Kenya when it was bombed. Fortunately, her life was saved but she lost all her textbooks. Her resilience allowed her to take a new assignment, order new books, and continue her studies.

Another graduate student from the Congo walked for four days and then rode the bus for three days the first time he attended our university courses in Kenya. Later, he had to bury his books and all his course work during raids and destruction of his and other homes during an uprising. When he dug them up, they had rotted. He made the incredible trek outside his country to classes the following year and re-wrote all his papers from borrowed books. When he and his wife returned to their country, they were blocked at the border and held for six months, unable to return to their children. This amazing man got home and rebuilt his school and continued teaching the dispirited people of his community!

d. Lack of resources:
This is a reality so pervasive in the non-profit, humanitarian world that major donor campaigns and government endeavors are perpetually working to acquire what is needed. Both at an internal and personal level and at external and organizational levels, there is seldom sufficient time to fill the invisible gaps and the tangible needs. No individual or organization has sufficient finances, personnel, or assets to meet every contingency. These stresses ramp up the need for care. Especially in remote locations, staff who work day and night to attend to human needs have greater than usual challenges. Creative resilience and wise self-care must go hand in hand with caring oversight from encouraging leaders.

e. Traumatic circumstances:
Events which even in the home country are stressful or traumatic will be even more challenging in a foreign place. These may overwhelm one's coping ability. My first miscarriage in a foreign country resulted

in a hospital stay (Gardner). I was cared for by nurses whose language I could not understand and who seemed more interested in learning English than in attending to me. They sat on my bed and tried to persuade me to converse with them. I was frightened, alone and needy. Circumstances such as war, armed robbery, or kidnapping of a family member or a colleague are other experiences which call for extraordinary internal resources. Even how we define coping or surviving reflects the extremity of such situations.

Humanitarian workers must cope with stresses far beyond normal. Ted Ward tells us that "Coping is a matter of handling something effectively that might otherwise become a problem. The emphasis is more on the fact that you actually do handle it than on the judgment that you were highly successful. To cope is more a matter of surviving against odds than a matter of conquering" (1984).

Bob Klamser, of Crisis Consulting International,[6] describes a crisis trainer discussing with trainees situations of armed robbery and how to behave under threat. He said, "The fact that you're alive is testimony that you handled it successfully" (Bob Klamser, personal conversation).

A friend of ours exemplifies the role mental attitudes play in overcoming traumatic events. She was sound asleep when a group of armed, masked men broke into her home, which was in a war zone. They beat her on the head with iron rods; it should have killed her. Yet, she felt as though God put a protective helmet on her head and the blows brought no pain or damage. Instead of developing PTSD (the expected outcome), she emerged triumphant due to drawing upon her spiritual resources.

f. Isolation—aloneness.:
Alone when your child has scarlet fever. Alone when guerillas surround the village where you live and begin to loot, rob, torture, and kill. Alone when there is a medical emergency and you have neither medical training and supplies nor an advisor. All of these things happened to my family in our isolated village situation (Gardner). Feeling alone in the face of danger is one of the most debilitating of life experiences.

---

[6] Crisis Consulting International, founded by Bob Klamser, serves the humanitarian world through negotiating for hostages, helping agencies prepare contingency plans, and doing risk assessments for security.

An illustration from the air industry illustrates how *not being alone* in a crisis makes a huge difference. United Flight 232 had suffered what the airline industry calls a "catastrophic uncontained failure." At 37,000 feet, one hour and seven minutes out of Denver, the Number 2 engine literally broke apart. Over 70 pieces of shrapnel ripped through the skin of the aircraft at high velocity. The heavy plane was virtually unflyable. But amazingly, the captain rallied support from several sources, and together, they worked creatively to somehow land the jet.[7]

Having others available in a crisis makes a huge difference! Yet many cross-cultural workers are allocated alone and must face any and all crises virtually alone. Placing individuals or inexperienced couples in remote and difficult situations alone is unacceptable! A tragic, real-life situation bears this out. We were asked to provide help to a young family who lived for six years in a foreign culture, to establish a business for their company (Dodds). During those six years, no one visited in person to encourage them or help keep them accountable. Their training was inadequate, thus they did not know the risks of including a national man in their household for work in their business. Gradually, he seduced the husband, then the wife. He was in the process of seducing the children when the situation exploded. The husband attempted suicide and set the house on fire. The wife ran with the children.

The husband woke up from a coma in the hospital to overhear his supervisors (who had never visited his family) discussing how to dispose of his personal property. Had this couple been adequately

---

[7] Captain Al Haynes later described the scope of the damage: "With no hydraulics we had no ailerons to bank the airplane. We had no rudders to turn it. We had no elevators to control the pitch (that is, nose of the airplane up or down) of the aircraft. We had no spoilers that come up on top of the wing to help us descend or to slow down on the ground. And, once on the ground, we would have no way to steer the plane to keep it on the runway, and we had no brakes to stop."

The outcome? A team of people, including flight attendants, air traffic controllers, pilots from a humanitarian group, and several dozen different ground rescue and emergency agencies worked together to achieve unprecedented results. They found ways to handle this airplane and brought it in for a landing. Unfortunately as the plane was landing, some of the malfunctioning parts kicked in and threw the plane into a spin, resulting in the death of 112 passengers. But—184 miraculously survived. Captain Haynes gives tribute to the people and resources rallied to focus on his need. Imagine facing this crisis alone!

trained regarding cultural values and given a team for regular encouragement and accountability, the situation would likely have been avoided. They were placed "in the jaws of the lion," so to speak, through the failure of leadership to prioritize appropriate training and care.

In humanitarian organizations, the assumption seems to be that compassion and technical skill is enough to ensure success in the field. This assumption is flawed! Besides appropriate training, in crises we all need the comfort and strength of colleagues. Even in the business world, this principle is acknowledged.[8]

Another young couple who experienced extreme hardship due to isolation said, "We think our company put us here just so they could add another country to their letterhead!" Obviously, the agency had not provided appropriate care in their social isolation.

g. Chronic high stress:
Andrews lists 50 stressors faced by religious workers abroad (2004). According to Lois Dodds in "Love and Survival: Personality, Stress Symptoms and Stressors in Cross-cultural Life" the level of stress has to do not only with the stressors identified here but also with the stage of field experience. Typically, a worker in the firsts five years of field time experiences far more stress than at any other stage. Dodds also identifies stress scores by country of service. Some countries are more stressful places to live and work, due to geopolitical instability, climate, hostile factions, density of population, or remoteness (2000). Here are five types of stress which can typify humanitarian work.

1) Escalating sporadic stress without a return to normal between episodes. We know that stress is additive and cumulative when there is insufficient time to return to equilibrium between stressful events. Each significant event has "a tail" of time, usually about two years, with physical and psychological impact. These mount up. For example, a family we know was living in a country with simmering political unrest, competing armed forces, and abounding threats to safety. They heard gunfire nightly. For a while, nothing happened to them, but they had to

---

[8] According to business consultant Pat Macmillan, "Business in the 21st Century is a Team Sport" (2001, p. 17).

remain vigilant. Periodically, nearby buildings were destroyed, followed by a quiet period. Each episode became more dangerous and threatening than the last, causing their stress levels to escalate without relief. The periods of quietness were not returns to normal safety. They stayed on "high alert"—vigilance was exhausting!

The price of living in such a perpetually dangerous situation can include several responses arising from defense mechanisms:

- A distorted perspective, thinking things are at a baseline level of normal when they are not.
- Loss of care for others or possible disdain for those who manifest fear.
- For certain personality types, a sense of exhilaration and potential addiction to excitement of stress and danger (via heightened adrenaline levels).
- Impatient with peace and stability if one has become addicted to adrenalin.
- A sense of invulnerability. "Nothing has happened; therefore, nothing will happen. It can't or won't happen to me."
- An inflated sense of righteousness or pride from living and working in such dangerous circumstances.
- Physical illnesses brought on by high levels of cortisol, the stress hormone.

The norm in perpetual, extreme high stress is to develop stress-related illnesses, both mental and physical. But occasionally people emerge well. We were asked to consult regarding a couple who chose to remain with their children during the U.S. bombing of Belgrade. They were equipped with long experience, hardiness and resilience, and strong spiritual resources. They desired to go through the hardships with the people they served. They had birthday parties in the underground shelters and in other ways shared daily life with their friends. Their personality types were "perfect" matches for the situation; the husband (MBTI type SP) loved challenges and variety. The wife was a born nurturer (MBTI type NF), poised and caring in a way that lent stability to everyone. They emerged very healthy and triumphant. Colleagues who chose to leave would likely not have had the inner resources to thrive in the midst of the trouble. Of course, we followed the couple to watch for any delayed reactions to the extreme stresses.

2) Living under surveillance: Having one's phone lines tapped, mail opened and read, your movements monitored, and your meetings reported on are all highly stressful. When constant observation and suspicion are the norm, people experience very high stress. Some symptoms people may exhibit include:

- Hyper-caution—caution that is habitual and ingrained.
- Vigilance eats up energy and raises adrenalin and cortisol levels, which can cause physical damage.
- Distrust and alienation from local citizens.
- Reduced spontaneity.
- Less willingness to be vulnerable and to trust when in community.
- Increased anxiety and suspicion, even of friends.

My husband I (Gardner) had made friends of an attractive young couple during their training days. They were "beautiful people," extroverted, friendly, outgoing, pleasant, and interactive. After several years, we met them again at a conference in Europe. We looked forward to spending time with them, and hearing how their first period of service had progressed. Over a meal we asked the usual question, "How are things going with you two?" Their faces closed. After a few minutes of silence, they asked, "Why do you want to know?" We realized that their reluctance was a symptom of caution that comes from living in a setting pervaded by suspicion and surveillance. It cost them something to have to weigh every word, every question, every interchange.

3) Living with danger as a way of life: Just as with the above, living with a constant threat to life, property, or family is exhausting. Some humanitarian workers must constantly exercise security precautions including overprotecting their children. Either the worker or his or her family may live with death threats. Even death threats not specifically directed towards them indicate a high level of danger.

I (Dodds) have a very personal example of this. My daughter and her husband lived for twelve years in a country where the "Shining Path' Maoists created havoc in the country. Many foreigners were targeted for death, including my son-in-law. Time after time, their friends were killed or injured in bombings. They accompanied the bodies of two aid workers back to the U.S. on one occasion. My son-in-law took a different route to work each day. My daughter was robbed in daylight by a man claiming to be from the "Shining Path." Her greatest fear was that he would abduct their son in his stroller with her. "I have eight people watching you," the robber said. So she ran past groups of friends in her neighborhood, pushing the stroller, unwilling to acknowledge any of them lest they too be targeted. It was a terrifying experience! Only the immediate debriefing by trained people from her organization and her strong spiritual resources got her back to equilibrium. That and other dangers, however, took a lasting toll.

The cost of living with perpetual danger can include:
- Numbness
- Recklessness stemming from a sense of denial
- Hyper-vigilance
- Suspicion
- A sense of invincibility (the "frog in hot water syndrome") as a situation gradually worsens
- Post Traumatic Stress Disorder

4) Hostage situations: Having to manage a hostage situation is at the extreme of personal stress! Whether you are the victim or someone you know is, kidnapping is a disaster! If you are the leader with responsibility to negotiate and manage the crisis with the press and all your people, that too is inordinately stressful.

The level of stress and fear in a hostage situation varies with the age and gender of the hostage. A child's kidnapping causes agony to the parents and the whole community. When a female of any age is kidnapped, a concern for rape and other sexual assault adds to the terror. We have seen this in multiple cases, such as in Afghanistan in 2000 when two young women were held by the Taliban and in North Korea when a female journalist was taken.

A small research project that I (Gardner) did a few years ago studied what kind of person best endures being kidnapped as a hostage. I discovered that those hostages who seem to survive best were healthy, middle-aged men with ample life experience, a strong faith, and knowledge of his spiritual resources. Survivors also typically had a solid self-concept and were creative and diligent about self-care while in captivity. These men also had a secure sense that energetic efforts were being exerted to obtain their release. Of course, their capture dramatically increases stress for their spouses, children and extended family.[9]

Another amazing real-life example of survival is a family captured by the "Shining Path" in Peru. Expatriate language workers and a national colleague were captured while driving in the Andes. The terrorists explained their plan to kill the family. The husband, a very resourceful man, offered to teach them how to drive the captured van and how to use the movie projector they had along. During the day, the children played soccer with the village children, conversing easily in their language. The couple interacted kindly and personally with their captors. By morning, the village "tribunal" decided to let them live and to leave the area. The terrorists kept the van and projector and even showed the film to the local villagers! The captors reasoned that these were good people, because they knew their language and even their children valued the village kids as their peers (Dodds, personal knowledge).

Another example is that of a colleague personally known to both Dodds and Gardner, imprisoned for 810 days by terrorists in the South American country of Colombia. He treated his captors well, made friends of them, and won their confidence so that he was eventually freed (in addition to much effort by his organization).

Though many hostages situations have a "happy ending" with the release of the victim, we are concerned for the stress placed upon the negotiators. I (Gardner) have closely observed hostage negotiators. They bear a heavy responsibility for a process that can easily end in the death of a friend or colleague. The process of negotiating may last a long time, requiring constant vigilance. The negotiator's stress can seem almost equal to that of the hostage.

---

[9] In a teaching series by Bob Klamser of Crisis Consulting International, one man tells his story of how he survived hostage-taking and helped himself to be found and rescued. This is an inspirational story!

Given the fact that the final outcome and ongoing control is primarily in the hands of the kidnappers, the hostage negotiator may experience:

- Feeling 'jerked around' by the kidnappers.
- Alternating between hope and despair.
- Alternating between cynicism and optimism.
- Learning to live with being misunderstood by colleagues.
- Learning to live with a feeling of deceit, in not revealing everything to all parties.
- Learning to live with a sense of emotional flatness when there is no news.
- Learning to live with boredom.
- Being prepared, even on edge, waiting for the sudden communication or release of the hostage.

5) Evil on one's own team! Sometimes the evil or hostile person is a member of the field team itself—or he or she may have posed as a friend! His or her efforts to sabotage and destroy the work may be subtle and persistent. Other members on the team cannot bear to think that "one of us is the enemy," so tend to overlook destructive words and actions which could be tip-offs to a hidden agenda. A small team located in a remote place is very vulnerable to such internal betrayal. A friend of ours was bound up for death and dumped in a remote area by a group of his "friends" in the local culture. Fortunately, he escaped and was rushed out of the country by his agency.

6) Dysfunction of a leader or team member: A tragic and avoidable stress is having a person on your team, or even your leader, become dysfunctional, either due to his/her own difficulty in coping with prolonged stress or because the initial screening failed to catch someone with a personality disorder or other mental health problem. If the leader is arbitrary or uncommunicative, uncaring or impulsive, the whole team suffers and may have no outsiders for counsel or appeal.

2. Four Conditions Requiring Proactive and Reactive Care

All of the risk factors we have identified expose humanitarian workers a greater-than-average risk of suffering some serious consequences. Not

all do, of course, because over time such persons learn to cope and adapt at a faster pace and to sustain higher levels of stress. However, there are four conditions which require both proactive care and reactive intervention. We hope to prevent these from occurring by providing appropriate ongoing support and maintaining healthy organizations. We need to screen regularly for these and be prepared to provide intervention and resource for recovery when they do happen.

a. Depression

Depression is a common human malady. It is much more commonly recognized and diagnosed in recent decades than in the past, and some researchers wonder if it is, in fact, been "created" or "manufactured" by the influence of the fields of medicine and pharmacology in the last one hundred years.[10] Currently, many therapists and considerable research concur that most people will have some mild or severe depression, based on current criteria, sometime during their lifetime, Most of the time, depression "heals itself" and the darkness or sadness lifts without treatment (for reasons we don't understand) within about six months. By today's measurements, we do know that certain populations are at higher risk for depression, including some within the multicultural, humanitarian sector.

Serious symptoms of depression can often be seen in four types of mood disturbances and personal functioning:

1)   Impairment of body functioning, indicated by disturbances in sleep, appetite, sexual interest, unusual responses of the autonomic nervous system, and gastrointestinal activity.
2)   Reduced desire and ability to perform the usual expected social roles in family, at work, in marriage or in school.

---

[10] Greenberg, 2010.

3)   Suicidal thoughts or actions.

4)   In very extreme cases, disturbances in reality testing, manifested
        by delusions, hallucinations, or confusion. (These can also be
        caused by other mood disorders or by medications, so a careful
        assessment is essential.)

The major symptoms attributed to depression are listed in the box. These
are described in the Diagnostic and Statistical Manual of Mental
Disorders (DSM-1 to DSM-5). They are also identified and discussed in
much popular literature and many professional sources. In the section

on help and intervention in this chapter, we will include ways in which
depression may be attended to by individuals and leaders.

Symptoms of Depression

- Feeling sad, low, despondent, hopeless, gloomy, blue
- Inability to experience pleasure
- Loss of energy, fatigue, lethargy
- Retardation of speech, thought, and movement
- Change in appetite, usually weight loss, but sometimes weight gain
- Sleep disturbance, usually insomnia
- Bodily complaints
- Agitation (increased motor activity experienced as restlessness)
- Decrease in sexual interest and activity
- Loss of interest in work and other activities
- Feelings of worthlessness, self-reproach, guilt, and shame
- Diminished ability to think or concentrate with complaints of slowed thinking or mixed up thoughts
- Anxiety
- Lowered self-esteem and negative self-concept
- Feelings of helplessness
- Thoughts of death or suicide impulses, gestures, attempts

Proactive prevention of depression is best achieved by helping each person maintain healthy relationships within the family and the team. Regular breaks for renewal, talking about stresses and field situations, open discussion and communication with leaders about relevant issues are all helpful in keeping one's emotional balance. Periodic screening, through personnel interviews or with member care facilitators can be very helpful. Creating a climate of emotional safety in which workers are encouraged to talk about their needs, limits, and stresses leads to healthier attitudes and relationships. Pencil and paper questionnaires can also be helpful for screening. The sooner depression is identified, the more likely it can be readily treated. When it has developed to a serious or severe level, professional help is important.

We recognize that in many field locations, finding professional help is difficult. A leader, such as the Member Care Facilitator, should make every effort to identify the symptoms and relay the information by Skype or telephone to a professional, who can then make a recommendation for diagnosis and treatment. Many home-country based professionals are open to providing counsel and advice in such situations. At the time of this revision, most counselors are now willing to do distance counseling due to the pandemic (2021).

b. Burnout

Another one of the four most common outcomes of extreme stress is burnout. We especially see this condition among medical workers, crisis care personnel who work in refugee situations and persons engaged in ongoing disaster situations and relief. We will give this syndrome more attention here, proportionately, because it is seldom described or understood.

Many people jest about burnout. Some people say, "I would rather burn out than rust out." But—both are bad options! There is a better, third option. When we are engaged in professions addressing human predicaments, disasters, catastrophes, and the evils of systems, we are "running a marathon"—one with an elusive finish line. Such endeavors are not like "sprints"—none of the problems we address are solved quickly, so we want to run effectively for the long haul—we want to cross the finish line! This requires pacing ourselves for endurance. Yet, that is a huge challenge because human need is always with us, sometimes coming at us unceasingly and in overwhelming degrees. Burnout may result when we try to do too much too quickly in response to urgent need, rather than pacing ourselves so we can "finish the race."

Burnout is a commonly, and sometimes carelessly, used word but it represents a serious condition. The term comes from rocket science. Solid fuel rockets ascend to great heights with great speed; then after using all their fuel, the empty fuel capsules fall back to earth and crash. People may respond in a similar way after attending to extreme need. They may make a very good beginning, be productive, and contribute significantly through whatever their role may be. Those who burn out are often high-achievers—people of action and purpose. Often they are leaders who are well-liked. They may be enthusiastic, energetic and optimistic, but they can become overcommitted or overly dedicated. Their very strengths and positive character can become detrimental in terms of personal energy expenditure. They can get used up to the point of having nothing more to give.

Burnout occurs over time—often years—when the expectations of the person are dramatically out of sync with the realistic demands for energy and role requirements. This is exacerbated in the humanitarian world because most agencies cannot go out and hire more people due to their limited revenues. Conscientious persons persist in trying to reach fulfillment of their own or others' expectations, often in roles which the work is never "done." Because they are, in fact, often superior in motivation, intellect, skills, and training, they may believe they are not as limited as others. They likely have succeeded in the past through hard work and devotion and expect they can continue in that pattern. Over time they may, however, sacrifice sleep and other personal needs and simply run out of energy so that they have nothing more to give.

Burnout is a slow, corrosive process. As the person runs out of energy, he or she may anesthetize his or her feelings and go about the daily routine in a mechanical way—"going through the motions." The person may mask feelings of inadequacy and failure because of the sense of "losing one's edge" or previous competency.

Some of the causes of burnout are related to the individual's inability to perceive his or her limitations while they value self-giving. People who suffer burnout often have:

- Pushed themselves too hard for too long without adequate time for recuperation.
- Started out with great expectations and been unable to adjust along the way.
- Have been exposed to human suffering, failures and misery in the work they do (such as medicine, social work, relief work).
- Become overcommitted and over-dedicated.

- Embarked on their present course because it was expected of them.
- Followed standards they set early in life (often in childhood) which the individual accepted before he or she was equipped to make a more accurate assessment or balance.
- A combination of good intentions and some unwise choices regarding personal, legitimate needs.
- An excessive work load.
- Dependence on one's job for feelings of self-value.

Ten characteristics of those "most likely to burn out"
- Idealistic
- Young
- Submissive, passive and non-assertive
- Low sense of control over one's own life
    - Fails to set limits
    - Yields to the demands of others
- Lower involvement in decision-making
    - Feelings of being trapped
- Exceptionally eager to please and gain approval
- Impatient or intolerant of host country people or realities, making it harder to "go with the flow." This leads to frustration.
- Anxious or fearful
- Lower than usual self-esteem
- More conventional

The burnout syndrome begins slowly. Often it is not noticed in its early stages. Most people who end up with burnout are competent, self-sufficient men and women who hide their weaknesses well and work hard to compensate for the gradual loss of energy. Some early signs are:

- Loss of their appreciation for the people they serve; maybe a sense of boredom with them.
- Growing perception that once noble causes seem trivial.
- Physical distresses.
- Things that used to energize become fatiguing.
- Fatigue which is not remedied by sleep.
- Having little energy to do routine tasks.
- Having to "push" to accomplish one's usual work.

At the beginning of the exhaustion process, the "burning-out" person may work harder in an effort to deny what he or she feels; yet the feeling persists and creates worry. The individual goes on to feel abused, then detached and cynical. Burnout is now been included in the psychological DSM guides to diagnoses, and it is described in the medical and popular literature. It is generally considered to have four stages:

Stage 1. Fuel Shortage:

a. Exhaustion: One of the primary signs is loss of energy and feelings of weariness not relieved by normal rest. People feel they are "running on empty" with insufficient energy and personal resources to meet the demands of work. They tend to push harder to make up for being less effective, and thus become more depleted. As an example, a pastor does not recover from the stress of caring for people and preaching on Sunday when he takes Monday off. He becomes more and more exhausted over time, so that he needs days to recover from what once took only hours or one day.

b. Denial: "I am really okay. All I need is more rest." The symptoms that usually warn someone that something is wrong become enemies to resist or ignore.

c. Detachment: Emotionally stepping back from involvement in the work begins as a self-protective device to help ward off pain caused by extreme demands for energy. By separating oneself from people and events, these lose their power to hurt. Unfortunately, this tactic also diminishes their power to uplift or inspire or bring a sense of fulfillment. Detachment is the first step in a process of disengagement, distancing, dulling, and deadness.

d. Boredom and cynicism: Boredom may become a problem, particularly if work is unchallenging and routine. The most deadly combination is overwork and under-challenge. A person may overwork due to long hours or heavy demands (such as too much interaction with people) and yet be under-stimulated or under-challenged intellectually. For example, a highly trained physician may treat a hundred cases of diarrhea in a day, which is exhausting but not intellectually stimulating. At this stage, a person may question the value of activities and friendships, or even of life itself. He or she may become skeptical of people's motives and blasé about causes they once held dear. In extreme cases, he or she may laugh at newcomers "caring," waiting for them "to see reality." Escape activities become appealing: reading too much, drinking, drugs, self- medicating, compulsive eating or sex, shopping sprees.

e. Psychosomatic complaints: Physical or emotional symptoms are often an early sign of distress. Real illnesses develop as a result of the impact of the emotions on the body.

Stage 2 Chronic Symptoms: At this stage the person's symptoms worsen because the energy loss continues. Most likely the person continues to work hard and to try to compensate for loss of energy or competence, but in the process continues to expend inordinate energy, without ample opportunity to re-energize.

a. Impatience and heightened irritability: As burnout increases, ability to accomplish things diminishes and impatience grows and spills over into irritability with everyone around. The person may experience anger flare-ups that seem totally out of character.

b. Tunnel vision from loss of perspective narrows one's sense of options. A person may come to think he or she can or should "do it all" and thus not delegate. Part of the distortion is believing that he or she alone can handle the problems and jobs.

c. Anger and a sense of being unappreciated: With a decrease in energy comes an increase in effort, but not necessarily an improvement in results. Blind to that, a person may feel irritated by a lack of appreciation. This leads to feelings of bitterness and resentment.

d. Paranoia: One can progress from feeling unappreciated to feeling mistreated and "used" by the organization or co-workers. Unwittingly, as burnout worsens, the person tries to find a reason for perceived mistreatment. This may lead to increasing suspicion of the work or ministry environment and people.

e. Disorientation: Disorientation and lack of concentration may develop due to low energy. The self goes into "survival mode" because

of the threat of excessive demands. (That is, the demands exceed the energy available for meeting them.) The demands or expectations are not necessarily unrealistic; rather, they exceed the resources of the person. As burnout advances, the individual may feel a growing separation from his or her environment. Things seem a little out of kilter, which can heighten agitation and paranoia. A person who is burning out often has trouble with thinking clearly. Speech patterns may falter; one may forget what one started to say. Names and dates may seem elusive. Concentration may become more difficult. This in turn affects perceptions, judgment and the ability to make decisions.

f. Depression: In contrast to general depression, the depression associated with burnout is usually specific and localized, pertaining more or less to one area of life—usually work. Yet there can be a "spill-over" into other areas of life, particularly in vocations such as the ministry, where life and work meld together. A vicious cycle may ensue, as sleep disturbances (waking at 2 or 3 am) result in even less energy and cause other symptoms to intensify. Loss of libido, loss of appetite or excessive eating, loss of the meaning of life, and guilt for not "producing" are other outcomes. Combined, these distresses may lead to suicidal thoughts, with a loss of hope. Negative feelings, such as "Who cares?", "I could care less!', "It doesn't matter!" may predominate. One may feel churned up and not know what to do about it.

Stage 3. Crisis is here:

At this stage a person may feel deep pessimism that the situation will ever change. He or she feels stuck, trapped, wondering how to escape. And there is no energy left to try to change. Self-doubt kicks in, especially as one works harder and harder but accomplishes less and less. A person feels like a victim and may look for escape by daydreaming or fantasizing. Functioning is seriously affected at this point.

Stage 4. "Hitting the wall:"

The loss of hope is pervasive and hope seems irrecoverable. Tunnel vision has gradually occluded all the light so that one sees no possibilities or options. One's career and life are in danger. Because of hopelessness, suicide may be considered as a way out of one's painful life situation. If intervention is not sought and provided, the person may sink into a perpetual state of disillusionment and fatigue—we liken this prolonged state to what happens to a burned out chunk of charcoal. It can be consumed and yet retain the shape of a briquette, but it is grey rather than black and easily crumbles to ashes when any pressure is applied.

Intervention for Burnout!

Burnout is reversible. We can stop what is happening, and a person can recover. This takes a commitment to the restoration of the whole person—spiritually, physically, emotionally, and intellectually. Restoration usually occurs *after* getting out of the situation. People do not get over burnout while staying in the situation. We need to help a person through the process of recovery. The individual must learn to attend to what is vital to his or her own personal survival to return to healthy functioning as persons. The ideal is to re-learn how to live at an optimal level of health and maturity, so that one can best serve the needs of others while of others while retaining joy and energy in the process. We have to pay attention to what is vital to life. The leader in member care or personnel must take this syndrome very seriously, and get the person out of the context in which burnout has occurred, plus providing resources for recovery.

Self check-up for possible burnout:
Self-awareness is an essential first step in identifying burnout. It is important to "get in touch with" your inner self, and to understand the image you project to the world (the one that others expect so much from) and the hidden and perhaps denied suffering self.

Critical questions to ask yourself if you are feeling burned out.
a. What were my expectations when I started this task?
b. Where did these expectations come from? Myself? Others?
c. Are these expectations realistic and appropriate?
d. How have I taken care of myself— how have I done with self-nurture and development? How have I not taken care of myself?
e. What is it I really want to do in order to best use the gifts and history God has given me?

Burnout Requires More than Stress Management!
Burnout is a life-threatening situation! It carries the potential for actual death, either by physical illness, psychological and spiritual death, or suicide. Burnout requires intervention by someone who can identify the process trapping the person. It will not go away by itself. Intervention must be made with the utmost care and delicacy, to preserve the fragile self-esteem and self-concept of the suffering person. Intervention must never be punitive or judgmental! The goal is saving life, promoting health, restoration to wholeness and return to service.

Immediate time-out from responsibilities is essential when burnout occurs. Postponing help means a greater threat to the person, the family and the organization.

A major goal for the treatment of burnout is to help the person learn appropriate self-care. For example, the person needs to sort out distorted "spiritual" values which conflict with appropriate self-care, such as, "I am always supposed to be self-giving even if I have nothing left to give."

Professional resources should be maximized to help the individual. These helps include:

a. Counseling can enhance understanding of underlying causes of burnout, such as one's motivation to serve, and self-concept related to over-commitment.

b. Medical assessment to learn what is needed for physical restoration. Many physiological results of long-term stress can develop during burnout. Restoration can be enhanced through improved nutrition and physical activity as well as treating any medical conditions. A condition such as hypothyroidism may be hard to spot but can contribute to the continual fatigue a person in burnout experiences.

c. Spiritual, pastoral care is essential to work through spiritual questions (such as, "Has God let me down?" "Have I let God down? "Where is God in all this?")
d. A supportive caring community in which the recovering person will be accepted, loved, and understood as being exhausted from giving and serving rather than being judged as inadequate or as a failure.

Intervention and arrangements for care should always be made in cooperation with the person suffering burnout. The importance of time-out and time off must be stressed. Allowing and encouraging the person to get away from the physical place and the assignment in which he or she has experienced burnout is also crucial, as "staying put" means that all the same stressful influences which led to burnout will still be there.

People in depression, burnout, PTSD or with adjustment disorders are fragile. They need love, support, wise intervention, help--not criticism, judgment or insensitive treatment. Statements such as, "We want you to take time off because we love you and want you to get better..." are essential. Leaders must be careful to not imply, "You have to go home because you can't do your job anymore." Such a statement when making interventions can be experienced as punitive.

Resources for Coping with Stress and Burnout

1. Spiritual: True spirituality nourishes, nurtures, sustains, and energizes. True spirituality is deeply personal and is not simply a set of cognitive exercises or religious forms.

a. Sacred writings, such as the Old Testament and the New Testament offer us instruction, encouragement, comfort, hope, and examples for change. Meditation and other devotional methods literally feed our spirits and emotions, and affect our physical health. (Studies show that meditation and contemplative prayer reduces the heart rate, blood pressure and adrenalin levels.) In recovery, it is helpful to not just "study" per se but rather to enjoy the sustaining and renewing of our emotions and spirit.

b. Prayer, dialogue with God, heart-to-heart conversation with him, has many spiritual, emotional, and physical benefits. It unleashes our burdens, sorts our thoughts, and gives an outlet to our "groanings which cannot be uttered" [11] Prayer invites God to help us in the seeming impossibilities of our lives and work challenges. Many empirical studies are confirming that prayer changes many things, including our physiology, our body chemistry (such as through expression of our tears) and our attitudes.

c. Our community of faith is a rich resource to us, as we are part of the whole and are designed to need each other. Praying together, meeting in small support groups, worshipping together, receiving instruction, and singing all renew us. Also within our communities of faith, we find wise and gifted persons who can help us.

2. **Professional resources** such as counseling and books are very helpful and will speed up the recovery process. We believe it is helpful to counsel with someone who has experience in cross-cultural life and knows the right questions to ask of the person in recovery.

3. **Renewing activities** with time scheduled for activities which a person loves to do or enjoys doing. We recommend that blocks of

time, such as a whole afternoon or a whole evening, at least once a week, be set aside for activities which are undertaken solely because they bring enjoyment and pleasure. Activities and responsibilities that bring on an "Oh, no!" feeling should be avoided.

4. **Emotional nurture** is also essential to regain energy and belief in oneself. Often in burnout, a person has become somewhat distant from

---

[11] The New Testament, Romans 8:26.

the relationships which can sustain and renew. The gradual increase in negative emotions and numbness may have led to emotional starvation.

16 Ways to Help You Prevent Burnout

- Exercise during breaks and lunch time for releasing stress, even short walks or something simple like "jarming" (jog with your arms). Exercising gives you a greater sense of power and mastery, feelings of relief, improved outlook on life. Find the way that works for you.

- Change attitudes! Pessimist sees the light at the end of the tunnel and says "Oh, oh, here comes a train!" An optimist sees a welcome space and opportunities.

- Note your attitudes about work and the people you work with. Wrong attitudes can poison your mind, body and spirit.

- Build a support group, people not related to work.

- Practice meditation and relaxation. Be calm to quiet inner chatter. This is a learned skill that comes with practice. Deep breathing is a useful way to relax. In a recent book James Nestor (2020) gives a wonderful explanation of "Breath" and an array of techniques.

- Take more vacations; build them in to your schedule. Make mini-vacations on weekends; take a break in the day. Change your pace— conduct an orchestra with a CD!

- Keep a healthy sense of humor. Have fun, play, and laugh. Develop hobbies, activities, and interests away from work.

- Pamper yourself! Massage, soak in a Jacuzzi, read a book, go on a hike.

- Make a list of priorities designed to keep you balanced (daily, weekly, and monthly). Set achievable goals for these priorities. All you have is NOW so let go of guilt about the past, obligations unfulfilled, and worry about the future.

- Re-negotiate or re-structure your job. Break the routine by re-arranging your schedule. Delegate responsibility.

- Cut down on overtime and leave the job at the office. Guard and control what you think about.

- Don't try to be superhuman. Get rid of perfectionistic attitudes.

- Learn to be detached from problems outside your areas of responsibility or when you cannot help.

- If you are in a dead-end job, find a new one. Do what you love and that will help you to stay energized.

- Avoid blaming others for the problems you are having. Avoid becoming judgmental, critical and negative, and placing blame.

- Love yourself! Have appropriate self-esteem based on being God's creation. He made you as wonderful, capable, talented, unique, and loveable. Remember how precious and special you are to God.

c. Post-Traumatic Stress Disorder (PTSD)
Diagnosis[12] and Intervention

A huge amount has been learned in the last two decades about what happens to normal people who go through abnormal, traumatic events. Brain studies show that actual changes take place in various anatomical regions of the brains of those who develop PTSD. We find it occurring fairly frequent in humanitarian workers, particularly those in war zones or regions with much political upheaval. Going through a calamity, even when one survives, can be exceedingly distressing because of what one

---

[12] Diagnostic Criteria for Posttraumatic Stress Disorder, from DSM-IV, Code 309.81. American Psychiatric Association, 1994, pp.427-429.

sees and hears, the sudden nature of many disasters, and the great sense of helplessness one feels in the face of overwhelming forces.

Persons working in refugee situations, war zones, and host countries which experience earthquakes, tsunamis, and other violence of nature are at risk for developing PTSD. (About one in ten develop PTSD.) Later, we will discuss the importance of debriefing and Critical Incident Stress Debriefing (CISD) as a means of reducing the likelihood of PTSD.

The key features and symptoms of PTSD include the following:

A. The person has been exposed to a traumatic event including both of the following:
    1) The person experienced, witnessed, or was confronted with an event or events that involved actual or threatened death or serious

    injury, or a threat to the physical integrity of self or others.
    2) The person's response involved intense fear, helplessness, or horror. Note: in children, this may be expressed instead by disorganized or agitated behavior.

B. The traumatic event is persistently re-experienced in one (or more) of the following ways:
    1) Recurrent and intrusive distressing recollections of the event, including images, thoughts or perceptions. Note: In young children, repetitive play may occur in which themes or aspects of the trauma are expressed.
    2) Recurrent distressing dreams of the event. Note: In children, there may be frightening dreams without recognizable content.
    3) Acting or feeling as if the traumatic event were recurring (includes a sense of reliving the experience, illusions, hallucinations, and dissociative flashback episodes, including those that occur on awakening or when intoxicated). Note: In young children, trauma-specific reenactment may occur.
    4) Intense psychological distress at exposure to internal or external cues that symbolize or resemble an aspect of the traumatic event.
    5) Physiological reactivity or exposure to internal or external cues that symbolize or resemble an aspect of the traumatic event.

C. Persistent avoidance of stimuli associated with the trauma and numbing of general responsiveness (not present before the trauma), as indicated by three or more of the following:

1) Efforts to avoid thoughts, feelings or conversations associated with the trauma.
2) Efforts to avoid activities, places, or people that arouse recollections of the trauma.
3) Inability to recall an important aspect of the trauma.
4) Markedly diminished interest or participation in significant activities.
5) Feeling of detachment or estrangement from others.
6) Restricted range of affect (e.g. unable to have loving feelings).
7) Sense of a foreshortened future (e.g. does not expect to have a career, marriage, children, or a normal life span).

D. Persistent symptoms of increased arousal (not present before the trauma) as indicated by two (or more) of the following:

1) Difficulty falling or staying asleep
2) Irritability or outbursts of anger
3) Difficulty concentrating
4) Hyper-vigilance
5) Exaggerated startle response

E. Duration of the disturbance (symptoms in Criteria B, C, and D) is more than one month.

F. The disturbance causes clinically significant distress or impairment in social, occupational, or other important areas of functioning. When the duration is three months or less, it is considered *acute.* When it is three months or more, it is considered to be *chronic*, and when symptoms do not occur until six months or more after the event, is diagnosed as *delayed onset.*

We have seen in debriefing persons after crises how the debriefing process is enormously helpful. We have met with various families who went through the earthquake in Haiti, the tsunami in Asia, and various other traumatic events, particularly in Africa. Amazing things come to light from such experiences through the debriefing process, and even when debriefing is delayed beyond the recommended time, it brought about very positive outcomes. One family with children was stopped at gunpoint by uniformed men impersonating police. They demanded that the family all lie in the ditch. While there, the family witnessed other people being shot and was terrified for their own safety. Three months later at the debriefing, a tiny toddler was able to quote, *verbatim*, every word the men had spoken, including using the regional dialect the men spoke. An older child confessed tearfully that he was "a very bad boy" because he had "not been brave" and had not been able to defend his siblings in the encounter. Without the debriefing, the parents would not have known of the huge guilt the child felt for something that was not at all a failure of his.

Another family had to evacuate due to a crisis in their host country. In this debriefing too, the parents discovered misinterpretations the children had made about why they had to leave—believing it was because they as children had "not been good enough." Debriefings are enormously helpful in uncovering a child's "magical thinking" that they are somehow responsible for events totally outside of their control. Adults too gain perspective about themselves and what occurred in the traumatic event through debriefing. One father was able to tell his children how it felt for him to cry and to be unable to change the events that had occurred.

d. Adjustment Disorder

Adjustment Disorder is the fourth common outcome of extreme, chronic stress. Some individuals are unable to make adjustments fast enough when confronted with many simultaneous and ongoing stresses. This should not be regarded as a failure of the person, but as a reflection of the excessive demands that the person has experienced—too many changes in too short a time.

I was once asked to consult with a mission leader who was concerned about a worker who was "not doing well." Her story was a sad one, and her responses illustrate what happens in adjustment disorder. She had been accepted to go to work in a rural, agrarian village in a poor country. Her ticket was purchased and her plans were all in place when her mother died of suicide. She attended her funeral, and not wanting to waste her precious financial resources, continued on with her plans. She went straight from the funeral to orientation classes held by the agency in a major U.S. city. That venue and environment were nothing at all like her allocation, so that program was not in any way adequate to prepare her for the life that was ahead—life in a rural village. After a few days, she flew overseas and took up her assignment in the village. The culture and language were totally different, and she had not been given any language training or cultural orientation. Food resources were scarce and even ordinary amenities were lacking. She worked with a team totally new to her. Overall, the degree and number of stresses were more than she could handle in the aftermath of her mother's suicide. The suicide of a loved one, along with murder, evokes a highly complex grief that requires more time and deeper inner resources than do most deaths. All the cumulative field adjustments were overwhelming—it was simply too much for her to handle all at once. We recommended time for her to grieve and for her to regain her equilibrium.

Typically, a person confronted with an overwhelming amount of stress begins to adapt through attempts to regain balance in fruitful ways. However, when the stresses are unremitting and the person can no longer stretch to meet the demands, the attempts to change may include choices which create even more stress. We can use the analogy of a rubber band. When it is fresh and new, it has a great deal of elasticity but when it is overstretched for too long a time, it becomes brittle and may break. In the process of cultural adjustment, we have to change our own selves and our habits of dealing with everything, so we must be stretchable or flexible or "plastic" in order to fit the new situation. We aim in the long run to bring change to the situations in which we find ourselves and serve in, but in the process, each of us also must undergo a great deal of change. (See "Am I Still Me," Dodds, 2003.)

Adjustment Disorder is one of the conditions which may lead to a *maladaptive response* to stress. When ones effort to adjust actually creates more stress because rather than continuing to use positive coping strategies, the person begins at some point to use unwholesome or unhealthy attempts to cope. *Mal* or *bad* attempts to cope actually impair functioning rather than helping the person to regain equilibrium. These attempts lead to problems in one or more areas: 1) social (relationships), 2) cognitive, 3) behavioral, and 4) physical. A typical example of maladaptive coping is choosing to use alcohol to escape the pain of adjustment, which then leads to addiction and relational problems. Or, a person may begin to use drugs to dull his or her pain, and that leads to additional problems. We may see maladaptive coping in something as simple as reading too many romance novels (at the expense of getting one's work done) or in severe situations, physical illness, child abuse, spouse abuse, or suicide.

In Adjustment Disorder a person manifests "worse than usual" symptoms of distress. (The full set of symptoms must be distinguished from other conditions which manifest some of the same symptoms.) Symptoms severe enough to compromise the functioning of the person usually begin within three months of the onset of severe stresses. If help is not available or the load of stress is not reduced, symptoms may persist for many months.

The DSM-4 identifies nine ways in which adjustment order may be manifest:
1. with depression
2. with anxious mood
3. with disturbance of conduct
4. with disturbance of emotions and conduct
5. with mixed emotional features
6. with physical complaints
7. with withdrawal
8. with work or academic inhibition
9. not otherwise specified

Diagnostic Criteria for Adjustment Disorder:

1. We could call this a "too much too soon" reaction to a major stressor or many unremitting stressors. One cannot adjust quickly enough for the intensity or number of stressors. An attempt to cope may lead a person to use alcohol or drugs inappropriately, may engage in sexual acting-out, over-eating, or escaping in other unhealthy ways. These symptoms usually begin within three months.

2. The maladaptation is evident as either:
   a. Impairment in function, such as at work or school, or disturbed relationships.

   b. Exaggeration of stress-related symptoms so that they are

experienced in greater degrees or frequency than what would be usual or expected in a given   situation (of course, this judgment is highly subjective, especially since stress responses in general are idiosyncratic—that is, everyone is unique in reacting).

3. Frequent manifestations of the maladaptive reaction. (This is an important factor, as a one-time occurrence of some reaction may be indicative of other issues. For example, an adverse reaction to some medications, especially those that pass through the central nervous system (CNS) barrier can lead to episodes of paranoia or psychosis. These require immediate medical intervention and should not be misjudged as simply symptoms of stress.)

4. Duration not usually exceeding more than six months, according to usual statistics. However, we see people in the humanitarian world whose symptoms may last longer when the unremitting stress is not identified as the cause of distress. Often persons do not get help until their condition is entrenched, due to lack of resources, lack of awareness, and reluctance to give up on the humanitarian vision or goal. It is quite typical for stress to be internalized and to lead to physical illness, especially in highly motivated persons who find it hard to withdraw from their field location or project.

How to Survive and Thrive

What is it that helps workers to survive and thrive when they have been experiencing the kinds of risk and stresses described here? What must they do for themselves? What should an organization do before the fact, during the workers' in-country time, and after their members leave these stressful environments? Specific suggestions are described in Chapter 6 on Interventions.

At the personal level, *resilience* is the quality most needed to cope with escalating stress, surveillance, and unexpected or hostile forces. Resilience is that elasticity of the total person that enables one, when knocked down by life or circumstances, to recover and utilize the experience for increased growth. Gardner has recently written about this vital quality in field workers (2013). (Also see Volume II, Chapter 3, page 49 and forward for a thorough look at resilience.)

Summary

Myriad risks and dangers are inherent in the life and work of humanitarian heroes. In this chapter we describe many of them. We identify and discuss four of the most common negative outcomes of severe, chronic stress: depression, burnout, Post-traumatic Stress Disorder and Adjustment Disorder. We provide diagnostic criteria to help leaders understand and assess what a worker may be experiencing. The agency has a responsibility to provide "primary intervention" in the form of proactive resources to promote health and to prevent crises, as well as to intervene at each level of problems. Prevention is least costly and most effective; the longer any condition goes on untreated, the more costly it becomes to provide treatment and to restore health. In Chapter 6, four levels of interventions are described, applicable to the four conditions described here and many others.

Appendix:
The Beck Depression Inventory[13]

Give yourself a score for each question by circling a number from 0 to 3.
See the significance of the scores at the bottom.

1. 0 I do not feel sad.
   1 I feel sad.
   2 I am sad all the time and can't snap out of it.
   3 I am so sad or unhappy that I can't stand it.

2. 0 I am not particularly discouraged about the future.
   1 I feel discouraged about the future.
   2 I feel I have nothing to look forward to.
   3 I feel that the future is hopeless and that things cannot improve.

3. 0 I do not feel like a failure.
   1 I feel I have failed more than the average person.
   2 As I look back on my life, all I can see is a lot of failures.
   3 I feel I am a complete failure as a person.

4. 0 I get as much satisfaction out of things as I used to.
   1 I don't enjoy things the way I used to.
   2 I don't get real satisfaction out of anything anymore.
   3 I am dissatisfied or bored with everything.

5. 0 I don't feel particularly guilty.
   1 I feel guilty a good part of the time.
   2 I feel quite guilty most of the time.
   3 I feel guilty all of the time.

6. 0 I don't feel I am being punished.
   1 I feel I may be punished.
   2 I expect to be punished.
   3 I feel I am being punished.

---

[13] Beck, A.T., Steer, R.A., & Brown, G.K. (1996). Manual for the Beck Depression Inventory-II. San Antonio, TX: Psychological Corporation.

7. 0 I don't feel disappointed in myself.
   1 I am disappointed in myself.
   2 I am disgusted with myself.
   3 I hate myself.

8. 0 I don't feel I am worse than anybody else.
   1 I am critical of myself for my weaknesses or mistakes.
   2 I blame myself all the time for my faults.
   3 I blame myself for everything bad that happens.

9. 0 I don't have any thoughts of killing myself.
   1 I have thoughts of killing myself, but I would not carry them out.
   2 I would like to kill myself.
   3 I would kill myself if I had the chance.

10. 0 I don't cry any more than usual.
    1 I cry more now than I used to.
    2 I cry all the time now.
    3 I used to be able to cry, now I can't cry even though I want to.

11. 0 I am no more irritated by things than I ever am.
    1 I am slightly more irritated now than usual.
    2 I am quite annoyed or irritated a good deal of the time.
    3 I feel irritated all the time now.

12. 0 I have not lost interest in other people.
    1 I am less interested in other people than I used to be.
    2 I have lost most of my interest in other people.
    3 I have lost all of my interest in other people.

13. 0 I make decisions about as well as I ever could.
    1 I put off making decisions more than I used to.
    2 I have greater difficulty in making decisions than before.
    3 I can't make decisions at all anymore.

14. 0 I don't feel that I look any worse than I used to.
    1 I am worried that I am looking old or unattractive.
    2 I feel that there are permanent changes in my appearance that
      make me look unattractive.
    3 I believe that I look ugly

15. 0 I can work about as well as before.
     1 It takes an extra effort to get started at doing something.
     2 I have to push myself very hard to do anything.
     3 I can't do any work at all.

16. 0 I can sleep as well as usual.
     1 I don't sleep as well as I used to.
     2 I wake up 1-2 hours earlier than usual and find it hard to get back
       to sleep.
     3 I wake up several hours earlier than I used to and cannot get back
       to sleep.

17. 0 I don't get tired more than usual.
     1 I get tired more easily than I used to.
     2 I get tired from doing almost anything.
     3 I am too tired to do anything.

18. 0 My appetite is no worse than usual.
     1 My appetite is not as good as it used to be.
     2 My appetite is much worse now.
     3 I have no appetite at all anymore.

19. 0 I haven't lost much weight, if any, lately.
     1 I have lost more than five pounds.
     2 I have lost more than ten pounds.
     3 I have lost more than fifteen pounds.

20 0 I am no more worried about my health than usual.
     1 I am worried about physical problems such as aches or pains, or
       upset stomach, or constipation.
     2 I am very worried about physical problems and it's hard to think
       of much else.

     3 I am so worried about my physical problems that I cannot think
       about anything else.

21. 0 I have not noticed any recent change in my interest in sex.
     1 I am less interested in sex than I used to be.
        2 I am much less interested in sex now.
         3 I have lost interest in sex completely

Scoring points usually are interpreted as follows:

1 to 10 points normal
11 to 16 mild mood disorder
17 to 20 borderline depression
21 to 30 moderate depression
31 to 40 severe depression
Over 40 extreme depression

References and Recommended Reading

Andrews, Leslie A. Ed. 2004. The Family in Mission: Understanding and Caring for Those Who Serve. Colorado Springs: CO: Mission Training International.

Cloud, Henry. 2010. Necessary endings. New York: Harber Business.

Diagnostic and statistical manual of mental disorders. 2013. APA.

Dodds, Lois, and Dodds, Lawrence. 1997. "Stressed from Core to Cosmos." AACC World Congress, Dallas, Texas, Nov. 6 – 8. Booklet available at www.heartstreamresources.org.

_____. 2000. "Love and Survival: Personality, Stress Symptoms and Stressors in Cross-cultural Life." AACC Conference, Dallas, Texas, Oct. 19 to 21. Booklet available at www.heartstreamresources.org.

_____. 2003. Am I still me? AACC World Congress, Nashville, TN, Sept. 23 to 27. Booklet available at www.heartstreamresources.org.

Gardner, Laura Mae. 1999. (Book Review of *Ten Mistakes Leaders Make*, by Hans Finzel. 1994. Wheaton: Victor Books.)

_____. 2013. *Healthy, resilient, and effective in cross-cultural ministry. A comprehensive member care plan*. Bandung: Indonesia. Percetakan Surya.

Greenberg, Gary. 2010. *Manufacturing depression: the secret history of a modern diseases*. New York: Simon and Schuster.

Hagberg, Janet. O. 2003. Real Power: Stages of Personal Power in Organizations. Salem, WI: Sheffield Publishing Company.

Klamser, Robert. Crisis Consulting International.
https://cricon.org/about/consultant-profiles

MacMillan, Pat. 2001. The Performance Factor: Unlocking the Secrets of Teamwork. Nashville, TN: Broadman & Holman Publishers.

Nestor, James. 2020. *Breath: The new science of a lost art*. Riverhead Books, New York.

Schaefer, Frauke, and Schaefer, Charles, eds. 2012. *Trauma and resilience: a handbook*. Condeo Press. www.condeopress.com.

Taylor, William. Ed. 1998. Too Valuable To Lose. Pasadena, CA: William Carey Library.

Taylor, William. Ed. 2007. Worth Keeping. Pasadena, CA: William Carey Library.

Ward, Ted. 1984. *Living Overseas: A Book of Preparation*. New York. Free Press.

Chapter 3
How People Get Sick and Wounded:
Preventions and Interventions

Practicing the art and heart of care for the heroes we call global servants requires a solid understanding of how people get sick or become wounded. Getting sick and becoming physically and emotionally depleted is usually a complex, multifactorial process. It is not one simple thing which turns a person from health to sickness. In this chapter, we will look at what we call the "spectrum of health" and the typical process by which people become depleted physically and emotionally, and end up with chronic exhaustion, disease, or wounded spirits.

We take our model from public health, which tracks the cascade downward once a process of illness or disease sets in. Because cross-cultural, multicultural workers are exposed to multiple hazards which affect the immune system, there is typically a spiral downward with one thing after another affecting healing or health. For example, one may lose sleep due to international travel, which induces a cold or other viral illness. (Even a three-hour loss of sleep interferes with the function of T-cells, which fight infection). In this weakened state, the person may develop a chronic sinus infection, especially if there is a prior history of severe allergies. A predisposing factor for all of this may be multiple vaccinations for diseases expected in the host country. These too will have taken a toll. The person may arrive at the allocation to experience chronic air pollution and unfamiliar microbes or pathogens in the water, bringing on asthma and perhaps gastrointestinal problems. Treatment for these infections or parasites is often harsh, creating some harm to the system as well as killing the culprits. This leads to further decline. Treatment of one problem may trigger a new problem, and so the downward spiral may continue. When I (Lois) was first treated for amoeba many years ago, the recommended dosage was triple the dose currently recommended, and I developed "hind leg paralysis"—so called because beagle dogs used for testing developed this side effect. So, in addition to feeling sick with amoeba, I was immobilized a few days and lost time from my assignment.

The physical health issues are compounded by emotional, social, and sometimes spiritual issues, such as loss of work time and stress on relationships, and may lead to a questioning of one's vision and call. Thus, a psychosocial, philosophical, or spiritual corollary develops and compounds the physical health issues. The key to preventing or halting this cascade downward lies in understanding the process, preventing or avoiding as many negative factors as possible, providing good screening for health changes at the right point, and making timely interventions at each stage. These can enable the process to move upward, back towards optimal health.

We examine in this chapter the levels of prevention and intervention (what to look for, how to help, and how to empower). We will see the interactive dimensions of health in a foreign country context, and the interaction of these dimensions during various life stages and critical intersections of life and career stages.

Glossary of Terms
Public Health Model of Disease Development

Healthy Organism: We are born about as healthy as we will ever be, biologically. Immediately, at birth, some preventive measures are made, such as vitamin K for the prevention of bleeding in the newborn.

Need for Primary Prevention: After birth, we want to nourish for growth and to prevent damage from occurring. Common examples of interventions are immunizations, water treatment, proper nutrition (such as eating a low fat/high fiber diet), and exercise.

Healthy Organism at Risk: Because of learned behaviors, habits, environment, etc., we accumulate injuries/insults. For example, eating a high fat/high cholesterol diet will result in elevated blood cholesterol levels. Physical inactivity and smoking also increase cholesterol. Genetics plays a part in the kind of elevated blood lipids we may have.

Need for Secondary Prevention: At level two, we seek to detect abnormalities or deviations from normal in order to intervene to restore "normalcy." For example, screening tests can detect elevated levels of cholesterol and triglycerides which indicate the individual has a higher risk of coronary heart disease. Interventions may consist of education about making dietary changes, physical exercise and stress management.

Asymptomatic Organism with Signs of Disease: At this stage, biochemical and/or tissue changes have accumulated, but no symptoms have appeared as yet. For example, an individual may have elevated serum cholesterol and perhaps also have elevated blood pressure, which is another risk indicator.

Need for Tertiary prevention: At this level, we seek to prevent further damage and attempt to restore function as much as possible. This usually occurs in a hospital or consulting room.

Symptomatic Organism: Tissue damage has occurred, but it is not irreparable. For example, the person may have elevated blood pressure leading to angina pectoris. Because of pain or decreased function, the individual seeks treatment. Treatment is directed at alleviating symptoms and trying to reverse as much as possible contributing conditions in order to return the person to full function.

Need for Crisis Care: Intervention to save life. (The hospital is a monument to failure.)

Return to Asymptomatic State or Death: Function is seriously compromised and death may overtake the person. For example, heart attack or stroke with paralysis puts the individual at great risk of dying. Often vigorous therapeutic interventions can save the person's life and he or she is restored to life, although with serious "scars" which reduce function. If the damage is too great, the individual dies. The goal of each of the interventions made at the different stages of disease is restoration in order to allow the person to function at a level as close to optimal as possible.

Dodds, Dodds
Heartstream Resources

Spectrum of Health

Healthy Organism

**Primary
Prevention**

**Healthy organism
at risk**

**Asymptomatic
with signs of disease**

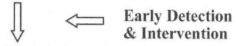

**Early Detection
& Intervention**

**Symptomatic
(no irreparable damage)**

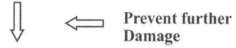

**Prevent further
Damage**

**Clinical disease
(damage but recoverable
function)**

Crisis care

**Permanent loss of function
or Death**

Spectrum of Health continued:

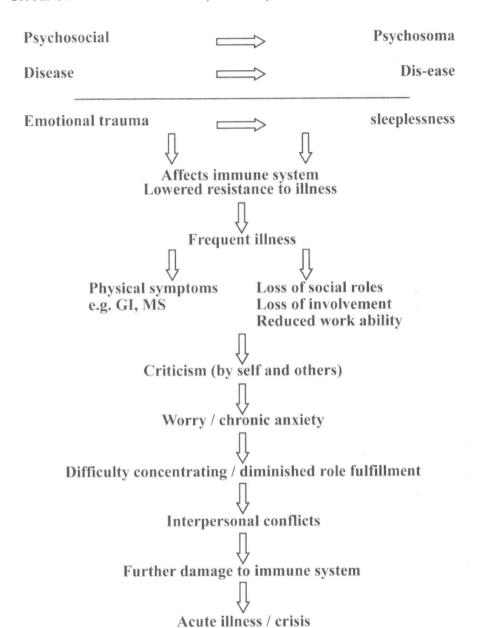

Psychological Corollaries
to the Physical Disease Process

"Dis-ease" in the emotional, spiritual and social dimensions of the person follows the same kind of progressive development as does disease in the physical dimension. Researchers are continually discovering more and more about the immediate and complex interactions between the *psyche* and the *soma*. Our minds, emotions, and spirits clearly create conditions in our bodies, and vice versa. (See illustration next page.) We can trace such dis-ease progression by looking at a case study illustrating the perpetual interactions of emotional/social/spiritual dis-ease and physical disease. Here is one hypothetical example.

Gina has spent many years preparing for and anticipating a career overseas in a semi-professional role. She has grown up in a family with very high expectations; they expect her to do everything well and to never question authority. She has earned excellent grades and is affirmed by her peers as being inspiring, dedicated, and with "a lot to offer."

When Gina arrives at her first field assignment, she is dismayed to discover that they don't know about her professional training and experience. She is assigned to a job which she believes is beneath her abilities, and appears to waste the years of training she worked so hard for. However, she does not question the assignment, assuming that the directors have the right to tell her what to do. Organizational values favor unquestioning obedience, self-sacrifice, and serving without expectation of rewards. Gina doesn't express her disappointment to anyone except her husband. She finds it hard to sleep, wondering why she has been assigned to a job which doesn't make use of her abilities.

No one communicates to Gina what she is expected to accomplish in the job handed her. It is assumed she will know how to do it and will produce "the right thing." Gina asks for no feedback, and gets no direction until she is criticized. "That's not what we wanted!" she is told. Gina feels unappreciated and disappointed. She has worked hard and done her best to get the job done. She wonders, "Why is God allowing me to suffer like this? Doesn't He see how hard I am working for Him?"

Gina cries often at night and begins to feel ill many mornings and doesn't want to go to work. Her supervisor criticizes her further for not being motivated; being late or absent, he says, means she doesn't care. Older workers comment, "These new recruits just aren't committed!" Gina internalizes the criticisms and tries harder. Finally she gets the job done, but receives no thanks. "Yeah – that'll do," is the only feedback she gets. Gina is handed the next assignment without guidelines, but fears to begin work on it. She is afraid of further criticism and feels paralyzed to accomplish anything.

At home, Gina's husband tells her to "snap out of it." He's feeling great! Why can't she? She should try harder, be more spiritual, and not let things slip at home as she has been doing. Gina speaks harshly to her household helper, who has grown lax in getting the household tasks done. Later she feels very guilty and finds it hard to speak to the young woman at all. When their time in the house does overlap, she stays in her room to avoid having to interact with her.

Gina becomes ill with hepatitis. During this time, she develops severe food allergies so that even after she recovers, she finds it very hard to eat and to find foods that don't cause intestinal problems or other allergic symptoms. She consults the nurse, who tells her it's "just stress" and that the symptoms will go away when she feels better.

A supporter back home writes that it is morally wrong to feel frustrated; it shows Gina isn't trusting God, she writes. Gina's level of energy drops even lower. She finds it harder and harder to interact with others, and even on Sundays sometimes avoids going to church so that she doesn't have to expend the energy to look cheerful and be friendly. She's afraid someone will see her looking gloomy and exhausted; they'll judge her to be unspiritual and not able to cope. She drags herself to work a few hours a day, but finds work unfulfilling. She prefers to close the door and work alone rather than to interact with anyone else, especially the supervisor.

Gina becomes increasingly depressed. She loses twenty pounds in the next four months due to her food allergies and the limited food choices available. She knows some people are criticizing her for not "doing her share" and for letting something that "is all in her head" rule her life. She stops going to work, pleading exhaustion and illness. She doesn't want visitors; it hurts too much to have anyone see her in this depleted and defeated state. She hasn't got the energy to get out of bed. Her hepatitis flares up; she goes into shock and is hospitalized.

Comment: In Gina's case, we can trace the pathway and process of how unattended emotional and social wounds contribute to a person's developing a style of behavior which contributes further to disease, so that symptoms of illness finally occur. Treatment is usually not sought or offered until the acute or crisis level, after much damage has already occurred. Some of the damage may be irreversible, locked forever into the tissues or organs of the body in the form of scar tissue, non-functional cells, etc. Attempts to treat the symptoms may bring relief to the sufferer, and move the process of decline backwards to a lesser level of damage. However, without help in the psychosocial dimension, for example in Gina's case, to help her learn healthier ways of responding and relating, it is likely that full recovery will not take place. It is important to impart to Gina at this point, as part of the treatment, that her disease is real, that even though it may have begun through damaged emotions and social conflicts, the daily stress has produced very real physical changes which must now be reckoned with. Though these changes were psychogenic, they became physical, starting at the cellular-chemical level and continuing until tissue and organ damage occurred.

Additional examples might be useful: 1) Early life abuse causes a child to formulate certain mental constructs (such as, people in authority always betray you). These constructs lead to certain attitudes, which spawn certain behaviors. These in turn create a relational style, such as aggression or passivity, to protect one's self from perceived threat. This creates conflict which causes many kinds of harm. 2) A cold parenting style will influence negatively a child's self-concept and self-esteem, which foster certain attitudes, such as feeling unacceptable. This leads to isolation, diminished communication and ultimately to a failure to thrive.

Levels of Prevention and Interventions
See full chart of levels on page 119.

The underlying assumption at all levels is that the person seeks homeostasis, to regain balance and to self-heal in order to return to optimal functioning. The more frequent and the smaller the "adjustments" back to the optimum, the better the level of functioning.

Level 1

Focus	What we see	Goal of P/I[14]	What we do: methods
Primary level: "Isn't she/he beautiful!"	Health; normalcy[15] Optimal development Life satisfaction	Protect, prevent, strengthen, enhance normalcy & **optimal** growth	Teach, model, nurture, communicate, inoculate, give skills, make healthy groups and organizations, pastoral care

Note: Prevention is not dramatic or glamorous: e.g., preventing twenty children from being hit and run over by cars gains less attention than saving the life of one who is run over. Saving 100,000 lives through proper sanitation is less captivating than curing dozens with typhoid. Thus, the importance of prevention is often overlooked and prevention is neglected. **Most health and care providers (and humanitarian agencies) overlook and neglect the crucial importance of this level.** Care extended at Level 1 is the least expensive; the most cost-effective, i.e., securing the most gain for the least investment. (Some insurance companies recognize this and provide for preventive measures in their coverage.)

---

[14] "P/I" denotes "Prevention/Intervention."

[15] Normalcy here does not mean "average," as that is generally below or less than that which is optimal. For example, Winter and Winter express their ambivalence about recommending psychological care for overseas workers because of the emphasis on "self" in today's society and the fact that today so many people seek such care in order to be "normal" (1982).

Level 2

Focus	What we see	Goal of P/I[1]	What we do: methods
Secondary level: "Catch it quick!"	Microscopic changes & minute disturbances indicating the beginning of disease	Detect incipient changes/problems, reverse the process, restore to normal	Screening, tests, inventories, questionnaires, train, teach, repeat Level 1 interventions. urge lifestyle changes

Note: There are no overtly noticeable symptoms of disease or distress at level 2, but the damaging process has begun. As in level 1, interventions at this stage are not dramatic; correcting and instructing twenty children who have dashed into the street do not gain the attention that stitching up one who is wounded does. Discovering and treating *Giardia* in the water supply doesn't make the news unless it happens too late and someone becomes ill. **At this level, trained observers and appropriate testing can detect the signs of disease or dis-ease not noticeable to the untrained.** (Example: detecting abnormal levels of cholesterol in blood which indicate the incipient disease process which puts the person at risk.)

Level 3

Focus	What we see	Goal of P/I[1]	What we do: methods
Tertiary level: "Please help!"	Symptoms appear, trouble comes to awareness, pain or distress	Diagnose problem, discover root, alleviate symptoms, remove cause, reverse process, restore function	Testing, assessment, interview, examine, counsel, treat, prescribe & proscribe, urge lifestyle changes

Note: Intervention with treatment may become dramatic at this point if symptoms are acute. Efforts are directed towards reversing the disease process and restoring normalcy. Chances are, however, that the optimum cannot be fully restored. Lasting damage has likely already occurred at the tissue/organ level; scars may remain even after treatment.

Level 4

Focus	What we see	Goal of P/I[1]	What we do: methods
Crisis level: "Call 911!"	Life threatening: physical illness or psychosocial crisis	Save life, seek to heal in order to reverse process of disease, restore function	Life-saving measures, ongoing treatment and therapies, change lifestyle radically

Note: Crisis level intervention is the most dramatic because the threat to life is manifest. It is also the most costly. Most health care dollars are spent at this point, both in managing physical disease and emotional dis-ease.

Levels of Intervention

Level	What we see	Goal of P/I[1]	What we do
1. Primary: "Isn't she/he beautiful?!!"	Health: normalcy, strength, development, life satisfaction	Protect; prevent, strengthen, develop, enhance normalcy & **optimal** growth	Teach, model, nurture nourish, communicate, inoculate, teach group skills, promote healthy groups and organizations, pastoral care

2. Secondary: "Catch it quick!"	Microscopic changes: minute disturbances which are the beginning of the disease	Detect incipient changes/problems, reverse the process, restore to normal	Screening tests, inventories, questionnaires, train, teach proactive, good health habits, urge lifestyle change
3. Tertiary: "I hurt!"	Symptoms appear, trouble comes to consciousness: pain or distress	Diagnose problem, discover root, treat symptoms to reverse process, restore to normal function	Testing, questions, interview, examine, counsel, treat, prescribe & proscribe, urge lifestyle changes
4. Crisis: "Call 911!"	Life-threatening physical illness or psychosocial crisis	Reverse process of disease: seek to restore function, save life	Manage crisis, life-saving measures, long-term treatments and therapies, change lifestyle, radically

Examples of Prevention and Intervention at Various Levels

These levels apply to various dimensions of development: physical, spiritual, relational, emotional, and mental— as well as the organizational dimension. We include interventions of the organization because individuals function within the organizational system and setting. Ill health or disturbances in the organization leads to ill health in the individual, and vice versa (Smith and Berg, 1987).

1. **Primary level (prevention)**: The importance of this cannot be overstated. All areas of life warrant preventive measures to promote

optimal functioning. (Example: What would you do to prepare a soldier whom you will send into battle six months from now?)

a. Personal--psychosocial, spiritual, relational
- Teach/train in personal growth areas, such as communication and interpersonal skills.
- Teach how to create personal support networks, such as care groups. Increase personal awareness, of self, others, impact of culture, etc.
- Practice values clarification; resolve conflicting values resolutions (e.g., how does the need for "Sabbath rest" conflict with value of giving hospitality, feeding the hungry, etc.?).
- Teach and practice coping skills and mechanisms.
- Teach about burnout, depletion, over-adaptation, stress management, etc.
- Teach and practice good spiritual habits and use of resources for coping.
- Encourage accessing pastoral and other supportive care **continually** to enable return to optimal as soon as possible after each "insult" or experience which disturbs equilibrium.
- Promote regular spiritual retreats.

b. Physical
- Teach and practice physical fitness via appropriate nutrition, regular exercise, avoidance of addictive substances, etc.
- Have regular physical examinations for early detection of problems, especially being alert to signs and symptoms of over-stress, such as psychosomatic manifestations.
- Encourage regular vacations of a week or more, plus mini-vacations as needed.
- Ensure sufficient sleep. Many cultures promote sleep-deprivation!

c. Organizational
- Create climate of trust and openness.
- Provide optimal environments as models and for intentional analysis and direct experience (e.g., in training/candidacy process).
- Practice conflict resolution; consensus making.

- Affirm, encourage, build-up to foster maximum growth.
- Match jobs and persons appropriately; examine and clarify roles and expectations. .

- Examine and correct organizational structures, ethos, culture, attitudes, values, expectations, etc., especially identifying organizational factors which are contradictory to good health. (E.g., not communicating clearly role expectations, confused lines of leadership, hurtful policies.)
- Teach group dynamics and process and needs of individuals in groups.

Gardner (1987) provides an excellent list of various proactive means of preventing illness by attending to needs before overt problems arise.

Some organizational practices or behaviors constitute "malpractice." These may be due to ignorance, lack of awareness, poor policies, and inadequate leadership. Even though there may be no bad intent, decisions made can be very harmful to the personnel involved.

I (Dodds) was teaching a group of expatriate leaders overseas a number of years ago. One of them was the director of a non-profit humanitarian agency. He asked to speak with me at break time, and invited my advice about what to do regarding one of his staff.

"What seems to be the problem?" I asked.

"Well," he said, "she is just not doing well."

"Can you describe how she seems?" I asked. After listening to the symptoms he related, I said, "What you are describing seems to be grief and depression. Has anything happened to her since she came here?"

"I don't think so. But her mother died just before she came—a suicide. She insisted on coming here soon after the funeral since she had bought her ticket in advance and didn't want to lose the money."

I learned more of the woman's story. She literally had flown within hours after her mother's funeral to New York City, where she went through three days of orientation for life in rural Africa. So, she had triple the stress one might normally face in taking an assignment abroad—coping with her mother's death, dealing with the grief of her suicide, and trying to adapt to a vastly different lifestyle, climate, and work environment with "training" that was mostly irrelevant. Any suicide leads to the most complicated grief and is much more difficult to resolve than death by some other means.

"Her reactions all make sense," I told him. "She needed time to grieve, all the more so since her mother's death was by suicide, as that

is very complex. Even with a more expected death, one needs time to grieve. She took no time. And, having three days of orientation in New York City for life in rural Africa makes no sense at all. It would not have given her any realistic experience or preparation for the adjustments that she has had to face. It's a wonder she has been functional at all."

All these events exposed the woman to far more stress than is healthy and to more than she could cope with in the new environment, with a whole new set of people. A more experienced and wiser personnel leader and process would have kept her in the U.S. to grieve, even if it meant losing her investment in her ticket. It would also have been wiser to provide training and orientation that was relevant to what lay ahead for her, for example, a longer, residential program in a similar environment, such as a rural village where she could make some of the adaptations with support and guidance.

Another example illustrates the complexity involved when someone begins a downward cascade of distress. I was teaching overseas, and being housed in a children's home for expatriate workers, when the young couple who were house parents asked to talk with me. They were in their mid-twenties. The wife was nursing a six-week-old infant and had a toddler of about two cuddled up beside her.

"We aren't doing very well," the couple told me. "We are failing and feeling worse and worse." This led to tears.

"Tell me what you do," I asked. What I learned was astounding.

This young couple was house parents to twenty-three children and teens, ranging from first grade to high school. They had six national workers to supervise in cooking, laundry and other household chores.

"Wow!" I said, "Even for a much older couple this would be an overwhelming load. No wonder you feel overwhelmed! Is there anything else you do in addition?"

"Yes," said the wife, "when the airplanes are flying in the interior of the country, I follow them on the radio to track their progress by writing down their check points, in case they have any trouble."

"Yes," said the husband, "I am also responsible for purchasing, packing, and shipping supplies out to the folks in the interior. They really rely on me to get their mail to them, as well as other necessary things such as medicines."

"No wonder you feel like you are failing," I said. "I don't know anyone who could do all this, let alone two very young persons such as you! You deserve a medal for trying, but what you have been asked to do is just not realistic!" More tears followed – of relief this time. I helped them see that they were having a very normal response to a very abnormal work load.

What was wrong in this picture, leading this young couple to feel like failures? First, placing such a young couple at the stage of early marriage and early childrearing in charge of twenty-three children to parent was totally unrealistic. Because they were very eager to prove themselves as good workers, they did not want to complain. They reasoned that if the leaders asked them to do this, it must be possible. They did not see that the issues were based in the system, not in themselves. Because they did well enough in the beginning in the house parenting role, and did not give any feedback to their leaders about their limits, the leaders added more and more responsibilities on them. Their experience illustrates how life stage issues (young, idealistic, new marriage, new parents) were superimposed upon their first years of field experience and their need role fulfillment. Combined, these were too much for them to retain optimal health and to feel they were doing a good job.

I helped the couple to formulate some statements about their needs and limits and then to approach their leaders about cutting back on the responsibilities they were carrying. Had they gone on trying to juggle such hugely unrealistic challenges, the agency would have lost a fine young couple. My intervention allowed them to regain balance and to remain on the field with a reasonable chance of ongoing success.

2. Secondary level intervention:
a. Personal
- Repeat screening tools at critical times: entry into candidacy, early training, various stages of training, departure for field, arrival on field, pre-furlough, re-entry time; special attention to be paid on relationship assessment, self-esteem and self-concept

levels, communication skills and job satisfaction.

- Dialogues or interviews to pick up early signs of dis-ease and disequilibrium.

b. Physical
- Regular physical examinations and screening, looking for early signs of incipient disease, such as psychosomatic disturbances.

c. Organizational
- Assess the role of the organization in addressing budding problems, such as unclear job expectations, confusion about roles and responsibility.
- Make appropriate changes in order to support individual in roles, etc.

3. **Tertiary level interventions:**
a. Personal
- Provide supportive care to diagnose and attend to problem(s).
- Mobilize support network and look for alternative behaviors and solutions. Change   lifestyle, work habits, schedules, etc., as needed.

b. Physical
- Assess physical state and stage of disease.
- Provide appropriate care.
- Take time off for recovery.
- Adjust nutrition and exercise according to need.

c. Organizational
- Proactive climate of trust, open communication.
- Communicate care: "You are more important than your work."
- Consult; trouble shoot organizational role in problem.
- Teach ongoing skills in conflict resolution, etc.
- Re-structure job roles, lines of authority, etc.
- Place positive value on seeking help **before** crisis occurs;
- Remove the stigma of shame or guilt or blame from help-seeking.
- Allow time out or time off to remedy problems.

- Provide resources (e.g., insurance, counselors, and physicians).

4. **Crisis level interventions**
a. Personal
- Cry for help! Heed the cry for help made by others!
- Act and respond immediately! You are worth saving! Each person is worth saving!
- Communicate care: "You are more important than your work or the organization. We want you to be well!"

b. Physical help
- Time off and time out to restructure life, work, role expectations, etc.
- Hospitalize or get emergency care.

c. Organizational
- Don't "punish" person for having or expressing a need.
- Mobilize resources immediately! Support group, physician, and counselor.
- Always take the cry for help seriously – even if it doesn't "look" so bad. Mobilize or send crisis team after disaster, such as terrorist attack.
- Reassess organizational issues which helped to create the crisis (e.g., years of failure to confront obesity which has put the individual at risk; authoritarian practices which allow no dialogue or discussion, appeals, etc.).

Three Interactive Dimensions of Development of Humanitarian Workers

Various dimensions of life interact continually to influence a person's current state and status. O'Donnell (1988) examines the interplay of an individual's personal development and the family life cycle the mission career stage. Here we focus on the interaction of life stages and mission career stages with the individual's basic health status (involving physical, psychosocial, etc.).

a. **Basic health status:**

This is the sum of all dimensions of health. Basic health status is the foundation, or underlying matrix, on which life development and mission career development takes place. SPARE is a helpful acronym by which to remember these.

> **Spiritual**—concepts of God, of self? Grounded in the Scriptures?
- Able to feed self and others through Word?
- Accustomed to prayer? Power of Holy Spirit?
- Aware of Christian standards?
- Able to resolve guilt and shame?
- Feel unconditionally accepted?

> **Physical**—any limitations?
- Chronic diseases?
- At risk behaviors or hereditary predispositions?
- General level of fitness and energy

> **Actualization/Mental**—able to seek stimulation?
- Handle boredom?
- Seeks challenge?
- Content to be under-stimulated?
- Able to apply new learning? (Even Mensa geniuses lose intelligence when under-stimulated and/or not using their mental capacities regularly.)

> **Relationships**: having skills necessary for establishing intimacy
>   - Able to confide in others.
>   - Able to verbalize stresses, etc.
>   - Healthy ways of handling conflict.
>   - Appropriate attitudes to authority.
>   - Able to create a caring, supportive network for self and others.
>   - Family of origin issues are overcome or laid to rest.
>   - Mental constructs affecting behavior.

> **Emotional health and maturity:**
>   - Appropriate self-esteem.

- Good self concept.
- Any "unfinished business."
- Healthy mental constructs governing behavior.
- Flexibility.
- Degree of self-awareness.
- Ability to cope.
- Any "unfinished business"?
- Degree of flexibility.

b. **Life Cycle Stages:**
Predominant or primary issues emerge from **life cycle stages** and are particularly heightened by involvement in humanitarian missions and cross-cultural life. We have made a special column for financial concerns because these are a continuing part of the matrix of life and a major source of stress.

Life Stages and Critical Issues

Age, By Decade	Chief financial concern (heightened concern due to "living by faith", etc.)	Primary issues of life stage (heightened concern due to overseas setting, restricted social networks, etc.)
20 – 30 years	$ to get started in life and ministry/field	sexuality – who will love me?[2] where & how to get affection my "place" -- what are my gifts, what job is right?

According to Erikson and other personality theorists, some persons may experience a prolonged adolescence, so that at this age they are still grappling with questions of identity, attempting to define the self. For men, particularly, identity is formed primarily through job or career. If identity is still confused, the person's ability to be self-giving (through intimacy) and to become fruitful or productive (generative) is hindered. For women, especially those who marry and bear children early, identity is more influenced through and concurrent with generativity.

30 – 40 years	Can I provide for my family?	What about my children? Does my job match my gifts? If single: biological clock pressure
40 – 50 years	$ College for kids?	Is this all there is? (Life's over half gone!) Is my career move upwards? downwards? Flat? Are there any more rewards coming to me? Can my kids make it back home without me? Can I still grow and learn?
50 – 60 years	$ Will there be $ for retirement? Support of aging parents?	My body is betraying me! I still think young! Can aging parents get along without me? Must I return to care for them? Have I maximized my potential? I want to be with my grandchildren.
60 - 70+ years	$ How can I live now? If I "retire" will I get $ support?	With whom can I grow old? Who will take care of me in old age? How much time do I have left? Energy? Is there still a place for me? (Where? field? Home culture? With children?) Does anyone want me? What am I leaving behind?

c. **Stages of humanitarian career** also interact with the basic health status and life cycle stages.

Stages of Humanitarian Career

Stages of mission career	Time duration	Issue
1. Pre-candidacy, seeking	1 to 10 years	What is my mission? Where?
2. Candidacy, orientation	1 to 3 months	Am I acceptable?
3. Intermediate training	0 to 5 years	Let's get going!
4. First field term & furlough	2 to 5 years	They never told me... Can I survive? Where *is* home now?
5. Middle career (usually on the field) Time varies according to age at commencement of career; may be subdivided	5 to 30 years	Now I'm getting comfortable and useful. This is old hat... been there, done that. Is there a new challenge?
6. Late career (often home)	5 to 10 years	Our job is about done... Where will I go? Will there be a job for me?
7. Retirement (usually home)	1 to 15 years	Am I still useful? Can I fit at home after 40 years abroad?

Cumulative Stress during Certain Stages of Career

One factor in the interactive dimensions of cross-cultural, humanitarian life which needs to be researched and addressed further is the effect of cumulative stress. Particularly during the first four phases or stages of the mission career, stress may mount up to very significant levels because of the progression of the orientation and training process. In one large organization devoted to language analysis and literacy, for example, individuals and families must move through a series of programs, each of which takes them away from home into a new environment, a new group, a new set of expectations and a new learning challenge. (See graph on stress and cross-cultural worker career stages.)

This initial process may take as long as five or six years. The candidate first attends an entry level one-month program, returns home, goes on to an intercultural communication course, returns home, then takes special training according to job destination, attends one or more semesters of linguistics and translation training, returns home to continue gaining financial support, and eventually goes to the field – only to be faced with more moves as she or he is assigned to learn the national language for a year or two. By the time the linguist/translator has reached the field assignment, several years have passed. He or she has had to make literally hundreds of new acquaintances, learn one or more languages, move every month or two or four, and then arrive on the field -- and try to give the impression of starting the field assignment "fresh from home." At least, that is the expectation of the tired field personnel awaiting his or her coming. We ourselves (Dodds) moved 19 times in two and a half years, with three small children, beginning with the first candidacy program and ending with moving to our own house in the jungle after completing our national language study program.

Other organizations also have a very long-term initial screening and training process. For example, Helimission, based in Switzerland, is devoted to providing crisis care, including food, medical and other relief to remote areas, as well as transporting medical passengers who have no local access to care. Those who join as helicopter pilots are sometimes engaged in the whole process for a decade, as they move through progressive stages of training. Such a long and complex process of preparation for service is in itself highly stressful, as one competency after another must be established and the cost of training is inordinately high, as compared to other academic routes.

In some agencies, the cumulative stresses are compounded by the "staged acceptance" process, in which candidates are not fully accepted until they have successfully completed all phases of training. We believe this unnecessarily adds to already-high levels of stress; to not feel that one is fully accepted and that the organization is not yet fully committed to one's success adds an extra burden, keeping the trainee on edge and under scrutiny for as long as five or six years.

A number of studies have considered the levels of stress which cross-cultural, overseas workers or missionaries experience (Mueller, 1977; Foyle, Lindquist, 1982; Chester, 1988). Our own experience (Dodds), through living in and teaching overseas in about 30 countries is that people often live perpetually with levels of stress which are astonishing. We have used a "stress event scale" (Holmes-Rahe), altered to accommodate cross-cultural realities, with many groups in many locations worldwide. Most expatriate individuals in the groups we have studied average 600 points on the scale, three times the 200 points considered to put a person "at risk" in the U.S. In one location with young people recruited to work in a refugee program, we found that these workers regularly average 900 points (in three separate inventories over a two-year period). These young people were specifically recruited because they had grown up outside of their home countries, and thus had better coping skills and higher levels of adaptability than their home culture peers, yet it was exceedingly stressful. We have encountered some individuals coming into a training program or new phase of career with points as high as 1,500.

What keeps most cross-cultural workers healthy enough to live with such stress levels? It appears that for most of them, coping ability gradually increases to meet the demand of the stressors. They learn to use more resources for growth and coping, especially spiritual resources. In general, cross-cultural workers succeed amazingly well in adapting to the challenges they face. However, understanding the levels of stress they habitually carry certainly helps us to see why they do somatacise over-stress and occasionally are overcome by it. Most global servant candidates are disciplined and persevering, and very motivated, factors which contribute significantly to their success (Britt, 1983).
We must always keep in mind that responses to stress are idiosyncratic; what causes stress and how it is somaticized varies greatly from person to person, based on personality type, genotype, and many other factors. The threshold from bearable stress into over-stress is highly variable.

In the graph attached, we trace what seems to be a fairly typical pattern of increasing or cumulative stress during various career stages. The shaded area represents the rather usual, daily levels of stress experienced by ordinary people. The graph illustrates how persons who go across cultures often encounter stress upon stress as each new stage (involving multiple changes) demands adaptation.

Our observation is that the stress level most often peaks mid-way into the first field term, unless one is a short termer who stays in the "honeymoon" or tourist phase. Mueller, et. al, 1977, found that culture shock and culture fatigue are major causes of dropout. Citing several studies, they found that 38.1 percent of those who dropped out did so during or at the end of the first field term. Both from our experience and other studies, it appears that half-way into the first field term is a critical period, worthy of extra support of individuals by the organization. The fact that most cross-cultural workers "make it" is remarkable, considering what Daniel (1981) writes: "The cost of burnout is high.... The average length of stay in many people-helping professions such as social workers, poverty lawyers, child care workers, pastors, etc., is two years or less." (Chester, 1983).

For many workers, stress peaks again at furlough time, with the uncertainties of re-entry. Once back on the field there tends to be a decline and leveling out of the stress pattern. However, another researcher found that more personnel left the field halfway into the second term than at any other time. This study did not include measures of stress, but we could infer that a long build-up of stresses would contribute to premature departure.

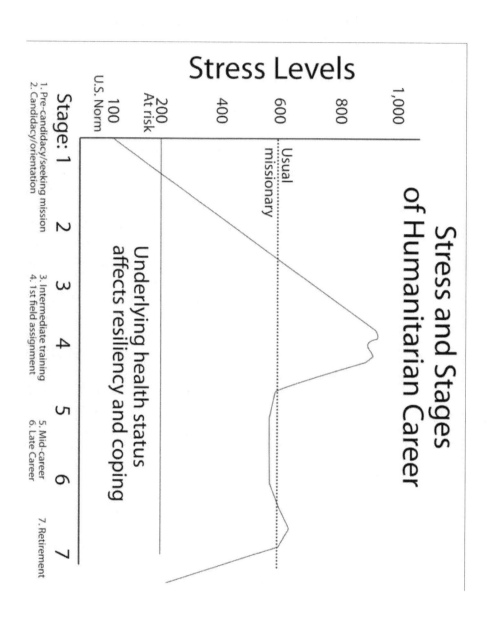

Stress Levels

Stress and Stages
of Humanitarian Career

Underlying health status
affects resiliency and coping

Usual
missionary

1,000
800
600
400
200
At risk
100
U.S. Norm

Stage: 1   2   3   4   5   6   7

1. Pre-candidacy/seeking mission
2. Candidacy/orientation

3. Intermediate training
4. 1st field assignment

5. Mid-career
6. Late Career

7. Retirement

For the very long-term worker abroad who has successfully made the cultural adjustment, a new threat to well-being arises: that of under-challenge or over-adaptation to an unchallenging situation. If persons are not provided with continued opportunities for personal and professional growth, or are deprived of their primary, significant job role (such as a pilot losing flight status) they may experience a decline in their overall functioning that is akin to chronic burnout. We see persons manifesting the ashen, grey, prolonged state, which we could call "ongoing burnout," characterized by low levels of energy, loss of hope, loss of self-esteem, negative self-concept, loss of job satisfaction, little sense of meaning, despair, and other negative states. Perhaps such a state is the ongoing outcome of burnout not previously attended to, indicating that an earlier total depletion experience may not have been rectified. We need to investigate to what extent organizational values, such as an emphasis on faithfulness and submissiveness to authority rather than on personal growth and continued challenge, influence the person's depleted state.

5. Interactions of Three Progressive Dimensions and "Unfinished Business":
These three processes, life cycle stage, mission career stage and basic health status, interact continually. The degree of health or the particular stage of a process that one is in directly impacts the other processes. Assessing and understanding the basic level of health at entry level into the mission career is **essential, as it is foundational to all further development**.

a. **Critical intersections**: Certain critical periods or events, when intersecting, increase vulnerability and put the person at greater risk. For example:

1) Bearing first child in early field years.

2) Empty nest with recovery of memories of early childhood trauma.

3) Empty nest with loss of significant ministry role or change of field assignment.

4) Going to field for first time with unstable or late teen or early adult children remaining at home, or at the onset of one's parents' decline.

b. **"Unfinished business:"** The heavier the load of disease or dis-ease, whether undiagnosed or known, and the greater the extent of unresolved earlier life issues, the sooner the individual will move to the next level of symptomization on encountering the next round of stresses. (For example, entering mission service just after the suicide of a parent, without taking time for grieving or resolution of issues aroused will hasten the development and outbreak of disease in both the physical and the emotional dimensions. These pre-existing burdens will lower the threshold for sustaining additional stress, use up the person's energy and thus lower adaptability and coping abilities.) The recent book on trauma and resilience by Schaefer and Schaefer is an excellent resource which examines this issue (2012, Schaefer and Schaefer).

Caution is needed: In assessing a candidate's basic health it is very important to ask: "What is his/her present level of functioning given his or her background? Where is she/he now compared to where she/he came from."? It would be highly unfair and unrealistic to eliminate a person based on background if he or she has been able to achieve a healthy level of functioning.

Some persons are "self-correcting," self-renewing, self-healing and otherwise resilient so that they change and grow and function well in spite of serious background issues (See Dodds' research, 1992). We need to research what makes the difference between such persons and those who either fail to recover or continue to decline (See Volume 2, Chapter 3, pages 49 to 78).

Summary

The public health model of disease progression is helpful for demonstrating and understanding the developmental nature of both physical disease and psychosocial-spiritual dis-ease. Easily visualized and understood, the model provides a useful and easily applied framework for assessing the needs of a person and for making interventions appropriate to the level of illness. The model also illustrates the need for ongoing prevention (or maintenance) **to enable the person to return as quickly as possible to the optimal state**.

The basic health status of an individual is the sum total of her or his health in all dimensions of human development, such as the physical, emotional, relational, spiritual, mental and organizational spheres of life. Though the organization exists external to the person, each individual lives and works within the organizational system and setting, which exert direct influence in myriad ways on the well-being of that individual. Thus, we consider that both prevention and interventions must include assessment of the organizational factors related to the person, and the making of appropriate changes by the organization.

Both the life development stages and the stages of the cross-cultural career are taking place upon the foundation or matrix of health of the individual. Thus, understanding and attending to all dimensions of health is essential. These three dimensions, each in itself a progression, interact continually to create the person's immediate state. Certain intersections of life cycle stages, mission career stages, and health status create particular vulnerabilities in persons, putting them at high risk for crisis.

References and Recommended Reading

Allen, Frank. 1986. Why do they leave? Reflections on attrition. *Evangelical Missions Quarterly*, 22, 118-129. Reprinted in O'Donnell and O'Donnell, 1988, p. 421-431.

Britt, William G., III. 1983. Pre-training variables in the prediction of missionary success overseas. *Journal of Psychology and Theology*. 11, 203-212.

Chester, Raymond M. 1983. Stress on missionary families living in "Other Culture" situations. *Journal of Psychology and Theology*. 2, 30-37. Reprinted in O'Donnell and O'Donnell, 1988, p. 164-185.

Daniel, A., and Rogers, M. L. 1981. Burn-out and the pastorate: A critical review with implications for pastors. *Journal of Psychology and Theology*. 9, 232-249. Quoted in Chester, 1983.

Donovan, Kath. 1992. *The pastoral care of missionaries: The responsibilities of church and mission*. Melbourne, New Zealand: Bible College of Victoria, Sept.

Gardner, Laura Mae. 1987. Proactive care of missionary personnel. *Journal of Psychology and Theology*. 15. p. 308-314. Reprinted in O'Donnell and O'Donnell, 1988, p. 432-443.

Hart, Archibald. 1991. *Adrenalin and stress*. Waco: Word, Inc.

Hawkins, Don; Minirth, Frank; Meier, Paul; Thurman, Chris. 1990. *Before burnout: Balanced living for busy people*. Chicago: Moody Press.

Horowitz, Mardi Jon. 1992. *Stress response syndromes*. Northvale, NJ and London: Jason Aronson, Inc.

Kobasa, S. C. 1979. Stressful life events, personality, and health: An inquiry into hardiness. *Journal of Personality and Social Psychology*. 37, 1-11.

Lindquist, Stanley E. 1982. Prediction of success in overseas adjustment. *Journal of Psychology and Christianity.* 1, 22-25.

Maslach, Christine. 1982. *Burnout: The cost of caring.* NY: Prentiss Hall.

Mueller, D., Edwards, D. W., and Yarvia, R. M. 1977. Stressful life events and psychiatric symptomatology: Change or undesirability. *Journal of Health and Sociology.* 18, 307-316.

O'Donnell, Kelly S. and Michele L., eds. 1988. *Helping missionaries grow: readings in mental health and missions.* Pasadena: William Carey Library.

O'Donnell, Kelly S., ed. *Missionary Care.* 1992. Pasadena: William Carey Library.

_____: Developmental tasks in the life cycle of mission families. *Missionary Care.* p. 148-163.

Schaefer, Frauke C., and Schaefer, Charles A., Eds. 2012. Trauma and resilience; A handbook. Condeo Press.

Schein, Edgar. 1992. *Organizational culture and leadership.* San Francisco: Jossey-Bass.

Smith, Kenwyn K. and Berg, David, N.: 1987. *Paradoxes of group life.* San Francisco: Jossey-Bass.

Thoits, P. A. 1981. Undesirable life events and psycho-physiological stress. A problem of operational confounding. *American Sociological Review.* 46, 97-109.

Vinokur, A. and Selzer, M. L. 1975. Desirable versus undesirable life events: their relationship to stems and mental distress. *Journal of Personality and Social Psychology.* 33, 329-337.

Winter, Ralph, and Winter, Roberta. 1992. Foreword to *Missionary Care.* O'Donnell, ed. p. ix.

Chapter 4
Grief and Loss

Grief and loss are unavoidable aspects of life for a humanitarian worker, especially in another culture and country. Because we are engaged in efforts to confront and correct evil, and we live in a fallen world, none of us escapes the sorrows of losing people close to us whom we love and others whom we serve. Especially when our investments of life, time, energy, and passion have been intense and longstanding, the shocks of loss can shake us to the core. At such times we need the love and care of friends, colleagues, those whom we serve, and our leaders. Even in our home cultures and countries, we face the loss of family members and friends, and other tragedies. In our cross-cultural humanitarian work, certain losses can seem especially overwhelming and tragic. This is even truer when losses come about because, though we are "there" to do good, we have enemies who would destroy us and our work and because the corruption of systems and persons betrays us.

The role of our leaders and agencies is crucial at times of grief and loss. Members of organizations look to their leaders for practical help, guidance, and comfort. Helping to "make sense of" tragedies of all kinds is an important function of leaders at all levels. The seeming senselessness of so many acts of violence and cruelty which bring about losses and plunge us into grief is part of the grief itself. Global servants need help in identifying reasons why it has occurred and to help in somehow making sense out of the senseless. A leader must recognize and care for grief and loss at a personal level, among her or his own people who are affected, and for large populations at the cultural or societal level when catastrophe occurs.

One suffering person has summed up beautifully what we need in times of grief and loss.

Wanted: A Grief Helper

A strong, deep person wise enough
To allow me to grieve in the depth of who I am;
Strong enough to hear my pain without turning away.
Not too close, because then you couldn't help me to see.
Not too objective, because then you might not care.
Not too aloof, because then you couldn't hug me.
Not too caring, because then I'd be tempted
To let you live my life for me.

I need someone to believe that the sun will rise again, but who does not fear my darkness, someone who can point out the rocks in my way without making me a child by carrying me, someone who can stand in thunder and watch the lightning and believe in a rainbow.

J. Mahoney[16]

Grief is often chaotic, and can seem unremitting and unending. If we have lived very long, we know that truth from experience. Grief will not be scheduled or postponed. The events that send it crashing down upon us are not predictable. Crisis never happens by appointment or at our convenience.

To be human is to suffer. Suffering affects everyone, and that is why thousands of humanitarian organizations have sprung up around the globe. Yet, for those who choose to be part of the humanitarian solutions, the rewards come at a high cost. Engaging in a life of service to others may carry with it a disproportionate amount of grief and sadness. This is yet one more reason why we want to select resilient and hardy persons for roles involving the needs of humanity. To be effective and to endure over the long haul requires us to be able to grieve, and to recover, and to somehow surpass and triumph over the unimaginable. Unless we learn to face the pain that comes into our lives and deal with

[16] Source is not known

it in appropriate and healthful ways, we run the risk of losing our ability to serve. We will tend to close off emotionally and socially and encase important aspects of ourselves in tight defenses, leading to emotional numbness which limits our ability to respond. We have only to see the daily news to know that many, many wonderful people and their causes are snuffed out by violence, hatred, and corrupt regimes. We know this first hand from tending to the griefs of humanitarian workers who have seen colleagues killed in the aggressions of war and assault, and who have suffered the loss of dozens and even hundreds through the calamities of nature. The losses and griefs cannot be minimized.

In *Half the Sky*, WuDunn and Nicolas present astounding stories of women and girls who have endured unimaginable horrors and yet have rebounded with amazing strength and enough courage to go on to save and strengthen others. They tell also of innumerable global servant/heroes who have dedicated their lives to helping the suffering overcome their losses and tragedies and to then mobilize others to do the same.

We have another beautiful picture of someone who was acquainted with the bitterest grief, and who died on behalf of those whom he loved. Jesus, our prime example and model of purposeful and willing suffering, was called "A Man of Sorrows." When we too love those whom God has created and loved, we will experience as Jesus did the pain of disappointment in man's cruelty and hard-heartedness that breeds corruption and other evil practices. We will end up mourning, as he did, for social injustices. Those of us who choose to serve mankind in the hardest places and circumstances, and to confront the evils in the world, are by nature sensitive persons. Thus we are more easily bruised and damaged, and wounded by the sufferings of others which we encounter. We suffer more due to our values and empathy and compassion. (See David Martin Lloyd-Jones, 1965.)

In every culture, people experience grief at some point from inexplicable events—profound, indescribable grief. However, there is often a dimension of grief inherent in the vocation of global servants that goes beyond that experienced by those who choose other career paths. In this chapter, we will acknowledge griefs that are common to us all and, in addition, we will explore kinds of grief more likely in the humanitarian community. We will recognize three common temptations we experience in grief and look at four ways to protect ourselves and facilitate coping and growth. We will provide basic guidelines of how leaders can help during times of grief.

Universal Human Griefs

Some of the griefs we all face sooner or later are:
1. The "large" losses inevitable to life
    - Death of spouse, child, any significant other.
    - Chronic, debilitating, and terminal illnesses.
    - Sudden disaster—earthquake, tornado, flood.
    - Attack—robbery, kidnapping, bombing.
2. Life-stage losses
    - Family of origin deficits—loss of a happy childhood without loving parents; a safe childhood; things we didn't have, lack of or loss of status.
    - Shift from singleness to marriage—loss of independence and of some relationships.
    - Marriage without children—mourning the absence of children (infertility, miscarriage, or the death of living children).
    - Married with children—growth/independence adjustments, rebellion, grown children leaving the nest, release of control.
    - Midlife—life is passing by, and the loss of opportunities, some forever.
    - Retirement and aging—career changes; health (general slowing down; aches and changes in the body).
    - Divorce.
    - Death of spouse.
3. Loss of hope and things we never had but we hoped for
    - Unmet expectations.
    - Lost opportunities.
    - Consequences which seem to trap us—our own or other people's.
    - Certain kinds of relationships.

4. The "little," common losses familiar to us all

- Cherished objects, such as a hat, a chair, a book, a car, a knife, a diary.
- Comfort objects, such a bathrobe, a teddy bear, a pillow.
- Creatures we love—our pets.

Particular Griefs for Global Servants

Some losses more likely experienced by persons in cross-cultural or multicultural humanitarian vocations:

1. Image and related losses—to ourselves, a spouse, our children, extended family

- The relative lack of status and financial security experienced by the cross-cultural worker in the non-profit sector, compared to the benefits of persons in for-profit companies (what some misguided people call "real" jobs) he or she might have taken.
- Changes in self-concept, self-perception, self-esteem, sense of worth and value (See "Am I Still Me?" Dodds, 2003, and *How Do I Look from Up there?* 1985.)
- Moving from pre-field idealistic "expectations" to the "reality" of field life.
- Loss of freedom for women in cultures, countries, and situations in which women are repressed, having low status.
- Role changes—e.g., from being in a "front-line," active position on the field to an administrative role back home or other job change, title change or benefit change.
- Loss of dreams associated with uncontrollable events or forces in the field setting. For example, "We won't be able to go where we envisioned," "I had hoped to finish my language or literacy project, and now I know I won't be able to." "I thought my daughter would go to college but she wants to stay in this host country and marry a national citizen."

2. Relocation—this is a very frequent occurrence for the sojourner, bringing with it a constant movement of people in and out of our lives. In my own life (Dodds), my husband's and my engagement, along with our three young children, in our life-long dream of providing medical service and spiritual care for those who lacked it led to an enormous amount of change. During the two and a half years of our training and preparation, we moved twenty-three times (counting as "home" anywhere we stayed for a month or more), learned two new languages, and lived in two new countries and several new cultures. With each phase of training and change of location, we had to get to know dozens or hundreds of new people and adjust in myriad ways. Once we arrived in our jungle allocation, we were already quite exhausted from all the stresses of change. Yet we had to "move house" again several times while our home was built. Once settled in our home we still had to change locations periodically for home leaves and educational updates.

a. Some stresses of "normal" or usual moves in the cross-cultural world
- Family, friends and possessions left behind.
- Reluctance to relate to new people because of the loss of loved ones.
- Exhaustion at the thought of the need to find new friends, new church, doctor, dentist, mechanic, bank, food store, and a host of other contacts and services.
- Limited amount of time to pack and move.
- Stress of insufficient money to finance move.
- Guilt for the things left undone in the last allocation.
- Loss of automatic "right" responses, such as, "I knew how to get things done when I lived there. I didn't have to hunt or ask or worry; I was used to driving on the other side of the road."
- Misunderstanding by others about our motives for choosing a difficult life without the usual benefits available in the for-profit world.

b. Closing of an entity or termination of a project brings losses
- Frustrations of why it happened.
- Losses from premature closure; unfinished projects.

- Possible anger and ambivalent feelings.
- Doubts about administration or agency or government.

c. Emergency such as evacuation or crisis
- Possible negative feelings toward host country which has control.
- Heightened sense of danger due to war or hostilities.
- Lack of closure.

3. Disillusionment— This can cause a severe grief because it strikes at the core of our being. Loss of illusion, loss of ideals, the fear that what we have believed in was not or will not be possible, and the sense that we may have "labored in vain" are very difficult to cope with.

- Loss of ideals, hopes and dreams.
- Unable to change the world in ways we had planned.
- Loss of faith in self due to high stress which brings out the "shadow side."
- Burnout which leads to being callous in the face of great need.
- Loss of faith in God—we may feel he acts too slowly, that he seldom answers our prayers, that he does not come through or does not keep his promises as we expect.
- With our calling to serve—we may have assumed that our commitment would be followed by "success" and we would be blessed.
- With my organization—when we discover leader have "feet of clay," when leaders seem inflexible, uncaring, penurious, or we see political jostling that seems so antithetical to our values.
- With my colleagues—we may see people striving for positions of power and for titles to satisfy their egos. We may see pettiness, gossip, selfishness and laziness (And— I may find some these same attitudes and behaviors in myself!).

These kinds of losses can be anticipated and, to some degree, prepared for. What we are generally unprepared for, however, is the sense of internal chaos when we undergo significant loss. Such turmoil seems to be an intrinsic characteristic of many service-related griefs. When we try to understand the incomprehensible, to find meaning in a jumble of inexplicable or unforgivable actions, we can easily experience inner chaos. It is easy to get lost there and forget our call and our purpose.

We are also generally unprepared for the continual barrage of griefs that come into our lives, both globally and locally. We all felt the shock of the 1995 Oklahoma bombing, followed by other crises. Then came the attacks of 9/11, followed by more horrors and the sense of chaos in our world. The 2004 tsunami in Asia seemed to occur on the heels of 9/11. The earthquakes in Haiti and Chile soon followed. It is hard to regain balance with a stream of disasters. Our grief is not simple and our losses are compounded when they are ongoing. All these acts of violence and the upheavals in nature brought compounded grief to hundreds of thousands of people. We feel each new shock, both personally and as a population.

The sense of chaos may continue for a long time as we try to sort out the effects of the losses on our own lives and those more directly affected. This sense of chaos has been captured in the recently dedicated memorial museum to those who died in the Oklahoma bombing. When asked why chaos was so graphically depicted, the key developer of the museum replied, "There was so much of it!"

In our own work, we see the multiple outcomes of disasters and often debrief and care for those who have endured them personally as well as rushed to the rescue of the suffering. We have cared for people whose homes collapsed on them in the Haitian earthquake, those whose homes were swept away in the tsunami, assisted those injured in bombings and terrorist attacks, cared for those working in extreme refugee situations and other crises most of us will never experience. Seeing the resilience of these cross-cultural workers truly restores hope that all our efforts in reaching out to a world in need does indeed pay off!

How Can I Keep on Giving in the Face of so Much Chaos?

When we find ourselves in situations of unremitting grief and chaos, most of us encounter three temptations in coping with our grief. We must face these squarely and work our way through them to regain equilibrium. We can do this if we remember to draw upon our four most crucial resources.

Face our three temptations:

1. Getting stuck in the grief and sadness—being unable to hope for the future.
2. Getting angry and becoming bitter—refusing to consider the possibility that good can still happen in the future; this may be expressed as cynicism.
3. Becoming callous towards heartache, suffering, and sadness—both our own and others' as a means to protect ourselves from future disappointment.

All tragedies leave scars. Pamela Reeve, in The Parable of the Forest, likens major losses to lightning bolts and avalanches.

"They leave things charred. Strewn with debris. Seemingly ruined. Sometimes these strikes occupy our whole vision. ...We stumble along through the rubble. But God says, ... 'In these very places, as you look closely, you will see My hand at work, planting seeds to bring forth beauty.' Those seeds can, if you let them, produce flowers of fragrance for you, for all whose lives you touch. Because of the avalanche, you can have a broader view. See out far beyond yourself. Where the lightning bolt of death comes, I purpose, in my time, to renew that area. Life shall reign – not death." (pg. 25, 26).

In God's economy, as one thing dies – if we will but allow it – new life springs forth. Death is the secret of fruitfulness. God says, "Even as you rightfully grieve, I plant the seeds of new life."

Draw upon four valuable, key resources:

We are reminded of these precious resources by some heroic writers of the past.

1. **Remember our source**: Thomas Merton quotes some words of comfort and instruction from Abbe Monchanin; he reminds us that God is there in all our suffering.

    For us let it be enough to know ourselves to be in the place where God wants us, and carry on our work…. Now is the hour of the garden and the night, the hour of the silent offering: therefore the hour of hope…

2. **Remember our purpose and calling**: Fyodor Dostoyevsky has said,

> Love in action is a harsh and dreadful thing compared with love in dreams. Love in dreams is greedy for immediate action, rapidly performed and in sight of all. Men will give their lives if only the ordeal does not last long but is soon over, with all looking on and applauding as if on the stage. But active love is labor and fortitude.

3. **Remember our divine resources:** We find great encouragement and counsel for ourselves as individuals and for our teams or group life in the sacred writings of our Judeo-Christian heritage, specifically the Old Testament and the New Testament of the Bible. Some of the counsel is directed to organizations, or systems, or groups, particularly in the Old Testament when the prophets spoke primarily to groups. In the New Testament, Jesus often spoke to the Pharisees, the leaders of the religious system of the times, but most often the messages of the gospels and epistles are directed to individuals.

The Scriptures do not promise us that in this world we can avoid pain. Rather they promise God's presence and comfort in our pain. For example, the psalmist wrote about God's response to the suffering of his people, "In all their distress he too was distressed, and the angel of his presence saved them. In his love and mercy he redeemed them; he lifted them up and carried them all the days of old."[17] The Psalms and other Old Testament books include myriad statements about God's concerns for and responses to our distresses.

We have many promises about the future, when God will redeem his creation and make all things right. He tells us that even when his own people have lost their way, he will turn them around. So, too, will he turn around evil systems. "I will give you a new heart and put a new spirit in you; I will remove from you your heart of stone and give you a heart of flesh."[18]The meaning of the word "heart" is "...soft, living, malleable, sensitive, throbbing," "the very ground of one's being, the root and source of all one's own inner truth."[19]

---

[17] Isaiah 63:8,9 NIV
[18] Ezekiel 36:26, 27 NIV.
[19] Saint Macarius, one of the Desert Fathers.

Many other devotional and inspirational writers can help us sort out and cope with our griefs. The Psalms and poetry are especially helpful in restoring a sense of peace and calm. So too is reading aloud to one another. The rhythm of speech actually calms the heart and lowers blood pressure.

Our "divine" resources also include each other, especially those with whom we work and fellowship. While we are puzzling our way through the aftermath of grief, we can find a wealth of encouragement in our friends who know how to listen. Telling what we have experienced and how we are feeling about our loss is proven to be a crucial help in recovery, as well as in the prevention of Post-Traumatic Stress Disorder (PTSD). Jeffrey Mitchell pioneered an approach to debriefing which has proven to be very effective in prevention of PTSD. See his work on Critical Incident Stress Debriefing (CISD).

4. **Remember our heart responsibilities:** These have to do with the condition of our hearts.
a. **Assess our hearts.** Identify anything that can cause our hearts to harden. These include being self-centered, emotional fatigue, pain, previous wounds, unresolved hurts, ingratitude, depression, unforgiveness, resentment, bitterness, and remaining perpetually needy.
b. **Tend our hearts.** We must guard our hearts against the temptations and conditions listed above. We want to live out of pure hearts, being undivided in our commitments and having understanding.
c. **Offer our hearts.** We must allow our hearts to be broken in order to serve. The prophet Isaiah wrote centuries ago, "My eyes are drawn to the man who is humble, whose heart is contrite and crushed, who trembles at my word. This is the one I esteem."[20] A more contemporary author, C.S. Lewis, wrote, "The pastor who is most Christ-like is not the one who is most gloriously fulfilled in his ministry but the one whose ministry has in it unbelievable elements of crucifixion." Amy Carmichael, a beloved cross-cultural worker whose poetry touches many wrote, "No wound? No scar? Yet as the Master shall the servant be; And pierced are the feet that follow me; But thine are whole; can he have followed far who has no wound or scar?" (1957.)

---

[20] Isaiah 66:2b NIV.

d. **Seek healing for our heart's wounds**—a life-long process. As Henry Nouwen explains in his book, *The Wounded Healer*, we are called to receive healing of our own wounds and then to become healers for others. We will likely bear the scars, but will use the past pain to help the grieving. Our own personal experience and understanding of woundedness allows us to come alongside the hurting, to encourage them in their journey. As our hearts are healed, and we become ever more whole and healthy, we are increasingly able to help carry the griefs of others. We are able to offer hope because we have experienced the outcome of it.

e. **Know what a healthy heart looks like.** A healed and healthy heart is truly free to love, to rejoice, to weep, to mourn. It is free from defensiveness. It does not need to be protected. A healthy heart is resilient. It differentiates right from wrong. It can stand firmly on the side of the right and resist society's trivialization and commercialization of wickedness. It refuses to "get used to it!" A healed and healthy heart is a servant heart.

Nothing in this process of keeping a right heart in the face of overwhelming grief and disaster is easy. To keep a "heart of flesh" rather than developing a "heart of stone," we must examine ourselves and move past our brokenness to restoration. Then, we must continue to grow. We are never "done" with grieving or loss or being wounded and scarred, but we can go forward and serve with even greater love and compassion having gone through with it.

What Can Leaders Do for the Grieving?

The most significant way in which a leader can provide comfort and support to his people when they are grieving is to show up! Presence speaks more loudly than any words! This principle is powerful! Even presidents and other national leaders are judged by how soon they visit after a disaster or other crisis.

Listening too is powerful. Often words are completely inadequate in the face of grief and loss. Listening, both to the articulated words of the aggrieved and their "under the surface" meaning, is healing for those being heard.

In these ways, a leader first shows himself or herself to be a friend, sharing in the sorrow and the loss, expressing empathy and concern.

A second important function of a leader is to help people "make sense of" what has occurred. To know and understand is an urgent human cognitive need, and our minds and heart search incessantly to come to grips with tragedies and disasters. Mitchell's CISD process is very helpful, especially in the immediate aftermath of crises and disasters. "Making sense of" may at times be a group process.

The third phase of caring, which may be immediate and concurrent with the above, is, of course, for a leader to assess what is needed, and to begin the process for drawing into place resources to address the plight of those who are suffering and grieving. This effort may require purely local provisions, or it may mean a massive international effort. The leader will be remembered, and judged by, his heart and the art of caring as well as by the organizational and other resources he brings to the aid of his people.

Summary

Grief is a common and inescapable experience of being human. It has a profound impact upon us throughout our lives. In humanitarian work, it is compounded by myriad factors, more frequent encounters and more intense engagement. Much humanitarian work exists specifically to alleviate grief and suffering and to provide for people in their losses. Those doing the work of caring are themselves subjected to more griefs and losses because of their helping roles. Leaders of agencies, teams, or groups devoted to the care of others need to be attuned to the needs of their own people, and be alert to care for them as they care for others on a larger scale.

Appendix One: Our Dreams

Our Dreams
Sometimes the pages won't turn in our book of dreams
and we are left clinging to a life
we never lived…
just wanted to.

Stuck in the stark reality
of unlived dreams,
we sniffle and tread water,
or we go in search
of the Holy One
who will wipe the tears
from our eyes
and offer to us
the only dream
that lives.

Ann Weems, *Kneeling in Jerusalem*

Appendix Two:
Some Biblical Passages Dealing
with Grief and Loss

We are called to join in Christ's suffering: "Now if we are children, then we are heirs – heirs of God and co-heirs with Christ, if indeed we share in his sufferings in order that we may also share in his glory" (Rom. 8:17).

We are called to not waste the pain we have experienced: "…(Christ) comforts us in all our troubles, so that we can comfort those in any trouble with the comfort we ourselves have received from God. For just as the sufferings of Christ flow over into our lives, so also through Christ our comfort overflows" (2 Cor. 1:5).

"I am glad when I suffer for you in my body, for I am completing what remains of Christ's sufferings for his body, the church" (Col 1:24, NLT).

When we bear and share in others griefs and pains, we join Christ in acting out his love. "We always carry around in our body the death of Jesus, so that the life of Jesus may also be revealed in our body" (2 Cor. 4:10).

"I want to know Christ and the power of his resurrection and the fellowship of sharing in his sufferings, becoming like him in his death, and so, somehow, to attain to the resurrection from the dead" (Phil. 3:10).

References and Recommended Reading on Grief

Albon, Mitch. 2000. *Tuesdays with Morrie*. New York: Doubleday.

Carmichael, Amy. 1957. The Poem, "No Scar." It has appeared in several of her books, including *Toward Jerusalem*. London: Holy Trinity Church, Marylebone Road, N.W.

Didlon, Joan. 2011. *Blue nights*. (On her daughter's death.) New York: AA Knopf/Random House.

Dodds, Lois. 2003. "Am I still me: Changing the core self to fit a new cultural context." AACC World Congress, Nashville, TN, Sept. 23 to 27.

_____. 1985. *How do I look from up there?* Wheaton: Scripture Press.

Dostoyevsky, Fyodor. Cited in Kisley, Lorraine, 2000, in *Ordinary Graces*. New York: Bell Tower.

Haught, Molly, and Langermann, Cindy. 1996. "Resilience in Missionaries: Effects of a Theology of Pain and Suffering on Missionaries." Dallas, TX: Dallas Baptist University project.

Kisley, Lorraine, ed. 2000. *Ordinary Graces: Christian Teachings on the Interior Life*. New York: Bell Tower.

Konigsberg, Ruth Davis. 2011. *The truth about grief (on the new science of mourning)*. New York: Simon and Schuster.

Kushner, Harold S. 1981. *When bad things happen to good people*. New York: Shocken Books.

Martin Lloyd-Jones, David. 1966. *Spiritual depression, its causes and cure*. Grand Rapids: Eerdmans.

Merton, Thomas. 1971. *Contemplative Prayer*. New York: Doubleday.

Nouwen, Henri. 1972. *The wounded healer*. New York: Garden City.

Reeve, Pamela. 1989. *Parables of the Forest*. Multnomah Press.

Rosenblatt, Roger. 2012. *Kayak Morning—on love, grief and small boats* (on losing his child). New York: Ecco.

Sittser, Jerry. 1996. 2005. *A grace disguised: how the soul grows through loss*. Grand Rapids: Zondervan.

Weems, Ann. 1993. *Kneeling in Jerusalem*. Westminster: John Knox Press.

WuDunn, Sheryl, and Nicolas, Christopher. 2009. *Half the sky*. New York: Knopf.

Yancey, Phillip (1988). *Disappointment With God*. Grand Rapids: Zondervan Publishing House.

Chapter 5
What is Member Care?
The Member Care Facilitator and
Five Domains of Need and Care

Member care is the ongoing preparation, equipping and empowering of humanitarian aid workers for effective and sustainable life, ministry and work. A personnel care audit is useful to reveal how successfully an organization is implementing principles and practices of member care. (See Chapter 9.)

Member care enhances recruitment, increases morale, stimulates effectiveness and productivity, decreases attrition, and promotes health and resilience. It is also cost-effective because in caring well for its members throughout their life cycle, it decreases loss of many kinds. It is also the right thing to do!

Member care is primarily a preventative function, promoting personal and interpersonal health, and enhancing relationships between members and administration. The commitment to member care is evidenced by an adequately trained staff, a budget, and an agreed-upon job description for the MCF, with clear boundaries and reporting relationships. This should be done both on the field and in the home office.

Even though there is a huge range of variability in humanitarian organizations, they share many common characteristics which provide a basis for creating approaches to care for the needs of their members and workers. Those whom any mission serves have the same human needs, but our focus here is on how to best care for the needs of the cross-cultural, multicultural workers themselves.

Agencies vary greatly in their available resources, their awareness of the needs of their members, and their ability to enact care across the dimensions of human need.

Increasingly we are seeing small struggling organizations merging with larger, more stable ones to enhance their caring resources. We also see many cause-driven organizations springing up quickly in response to a specific need. These are very attractive to idealistic young people, but do have some drawbacks. Such an organization may grow quickly but it may outpace its infrastructure for care. It is also quite likely that the leader of a new organization is young and inexperienced in people-needs.

For example, I (Dodds) was asked to consult with a rapidly growing agency about ten years old. The leader was in his 30's and the staff members were also very young. Some of their policies, born of idealism untempered by realism, were actually counterproductive. One policy dictated that a member stay in the "cheapest place available" without regard for other factors. The "cheapest place available" for my stay as a consultant led to instant asthma; fortunately, the young leader was willing to waive the requirement for my health's sake. In another new, young, highly idealistic mission, workers were experiencing burnout after an average of only six years of service because the demands of their service were so rigorous and idealistic. Their steep drop out rate was tragic, a result of the mission's inexperience and lack of a solid program of care. My own son (Dodds) and his peers and other young people who grew up speaking Spanish were recruited (while still wearing their college graduation robes!) for a crisis refugee program, in which they were entrusted with inordinate levels of responsibility, extreme stress, and little opportunity for daily balance or refreshment. Lack of appropriate care led many of them into burnout and disillusionment.

Expectations of a person who joins a religious or humanitarian organization must take into account the age of the worker, infrastructure, availability of resources, and leadership style. Thus, it is very important for someone choosing an agency to gain a full understanding of it before joining.

The Member Care Facilitator

The discipline called "Member Care" is less than three decades old. It has come about through the efforts of a core of mental health specialists who began small meetings during the 1980s. From that core grew a conference which recently celebrated its thirtieth anniversary. Out of that conference has sprung a host of agencies and professionals devoted to the care of humanitarian heroes/servants worldwide. It has become a global movement, with continent-wide conferences. It spawned the first World Congress in 2012 and a second World Congress scheduled for 2015. Participants in these conferences have created most of the literature in this discipline devoted to caring for cross-cultural and multicultural humanitarian workers. This volume, third in a series of three, is one outcome. This series, *Global Servants*, is one of several books dedicated to member care. Most of them are anthologies, with as many as fifty authors. Each one has contributed significantly to many aspects of this field. This series is the first in the field to take a developmental approach to the preparation and care of humanitarian workers.

Heartstream Resources was the first agency in the world to begin to offer formal training for persons who wished to learn more about member care and to increase their level of professionalism, building on what had been learned in the MH&M Conferences.[21] In our first graduate courses in 1997, with about thirty participants each time, we wrestled, like others before us, with a definition for what has come to be called member care.[22] We also worked together to create a name for the role of a person dedicated to caring for the members within an agency. We decided on the term Member Care Facilitator, modeled after the term Health Promoter, which is used in much of the world to

---

[21] This Mental Health and Missions Conference meets annually in Angola, Indiana, and is currently organized by MTI International. It is open to mental health practitioners, physicians, mission personnel, and students. See www.MTI.org.

[22] These graduate courses have been accredited by Azusa Pacific University as part of the M.A. Operation Impact program, which is offered worldwide each summer in about 25 countries. We have conducted the courses in Pennsylvania, Australia, New Zealand, the Philippines, Morocco, and other places. It is a portable program, easily "taken on the road" and fit to the context. Heartstream offers courses regularly in Pennsylvania.

designate someone who introduces and oversees the care of people at the grassroots level.

As this discipline has come of age, more and more organizations have come to realize its value and to send people for training. Increasingly, workshops and conferences are offered in various parts of the globe. We recently helped to sponsor the third Asia Care Network conference.[23] Various care centers have been developed throughout the world. [24] Columbia International University graduated its first doctoral students in this field in the spring of 2012.

We advocate that every agency appoint a Member Care Facilitator (MCF).[25] This is a key role for every organization. We encourage agencies of all types and sizes in the humanitarian world to train persons specifically for this vital role. Besides appointing a "head" or "lead" MCF, having someone in every field or allocation is also important, to bring the care "closer to home" where people are serving. Though some of the tasks involved have in the past been part of personnel care, the role of the MCF may include them as well, but it reaches out much more broadly. It is helpful to differentiate it from personnel roles (usually more technical and records focused) and the roles of pastoral care and counseling. All of these are necessary to promote life-long health for members; the MCF is the role with the broadest overview of human needs, in light of high stress and life-long needs.

We suggest that the role of Member Care Facilitator be an administrative position, reporting to the director. Ideally it is filled by a person who is trained in member care who has longevity and credibility within the organization with both members and leaders. However, the member care person does not have administrative authority for people.

The goal of an MCF is to develop and oversee a program of structured, comprehensive care for the members of a given mission. This is to be

---

[23] For information, contact Heartstream Resources, www.heartstreamresources.org
[24] Heartstream, for instance, now has partners in Korea, New Zealand, and the Philippines. Various centers exist in Africa, Asia, and Europe.
[25] In the Member Care Training course offered by Heartstream Resources in various locations, we include a major emphasis on who should be selected for the MCF role, including history, qualifications, personal character and personality traits, and a complete description of the role.

based on personal knowledge of the organization, its vision, mission, and ethos. It should encompass the span of ages, status, cultures, roles, and other factors of the members. This should be seen as an "over-arching" role, not limited to any one task.

The MCF role involves raising consciousness of the need of care for both members and leaders. The person becomes a *facilitator*, that is, *a promoter*, of health in many dimensions. He or she is not a sole provider; rather he or she draws many people into the actual attitudes and tasks of caring and helps to shift the organizational ethos towards continuous caring. He or she creates and provides for many ways that both self-care and community care can be exercised. (For qualifications and suggestions about this role, contact Heartstream Resources.)

The member care role is the nerve system of the organization. The MCF's role includes having his or her finger on the pulse of the membership, especially attending to the quiet people, the remotely assigned people, and the strong introverts.

The Member Care Facilitator becomes a specialist in brokering care for persons in the agency, based on the values, resources, and needs of its people. Ideally, the MCF has a history and some longevity in the organization, knowing its ethos, policies, personality, vision, etc. He or she should receive training to develop knowledge about a wide assortment of resources which can be made available to persons, families or teams for ongoing development or at times of need. Resource brokering is a helpful concept, implying that this person does not *provide* all the care; rather he or she *facilitates the provision of care* by bringing together needs and resources. Just as a real estate broker connects buyer and seller, a resource broker connects members in need with available resources.

Ten Ways the MCF Can Serve the Agency:

1. By giving input into administrative decisions that affect members before these decisions are made, and by monitoring the implementation of painful decisions in change and transition, helping members through these stressful times.

2. By helping administration understand differing needs within the service cycle; for example, what do new arrivals on the field need? What do folks need at mid-career? What do those ending their field service need in order to finish well?

3. By providing corporate memory having to do with changing historical procedures, sites, or life events and the emotional importance of these matters.

4. By serving as a sounding board and consultant to leaders and managers, helping to mitigate the impact of decisions and understand the uniqueness of the membership, and the individual tolerance for change and stress. and or/stress.

5. By helping Human Resources personnel to ensure that Best Practices are followed in decisions that have to do with members (i.e., assignments, change of roles, discipline, leaving the country or the organization).

6. By attending to crises, both in preparing people for pending crisis, supporting them during the crisis event(s), and arranging or doing debriefings   following   crisis.

7. By linking people to necessary resources for family needs, or by referring them to counselors for therapeutic help.

8. By arranging for periodic seminars and workshops on such topics as marriage enrichment, parenting, children leaving home, Sharpening Your Interpersonal Skills, managing transitions, encouraging spiritual vitality, spiritual formation and spiritual growth, etc.

9. By prompting celebrations, recognizing awards and milestones, honoring productivity, longevity, and so on.

10. By identifying and honoring the "story-tellers" of the group and to encourage their gifts.

Member care works best in an organization which desires to develop and maintain an ethos of care. Ethos begins with leaders and flows downward. An ethos of care is especially compatible with the "servant leadership" model. In this philosophy of leadership, leaders see themselves as "the first among equals" and present themselves as approachable and responsive leaders.[26] They value being caring and operating within an ethical framework. Regardless of the size and longevity of an organization, an agency can grow intentionally in developing its ethos of care. (See Chapter 9 for more on ethos.)

We recommend that member care be extended to paid employees (who may be on a different pay system than those who are categorized as volunteers on donor support) and local workers. Ideally, the person appointed to provide member care for local workers would be of the same nationality, speaks the local language and knows the local culture.

How the MCF Can Get Started: Identify Needs of Members

Identifying the needs of workers engaged in altruistic activities is a first step. We suggest an acronym which provides a simple model or framework around which to create a structure and plan for care. Though "felt needs" are usually the starting place for providing care, it is important to gain a comprehensive overview of all needs so that nothing is missed in the long run. This provides for care with longevity, as well as effectiveness, in mind.

The MCF may begin by gathering some demographic information, being aware of the spectrum of members in his or her organization— adults and children, couples and families, single persons – as well as noting the country of origin of team members. The Member Care Assessment Tool can help to gather detailed information about the group (Appendix 1). The Continuum of Care is designed to gather similar information by collaborating with the group's local leader (Appendix 2). Working together to obtain information is a beneficial way to build a relationship between the MCF and the leader.

---

[26] See Volume 2, Chapter 11 for more on servant leadership, as well as Chapter 10 of this Volume 3. Also, this philosophy of leadership is included in the Member Care Training Course offered by Heartstream Resources in Pennsylvania and other locations.

Dr. Laurel McAllister, working with a number of Canadian organizations, formulated the Code of Best Practice in Member Care for the Evangelical Fellowship of Canada (2001). This document suggests a set of principles and guidelines for incorporating member care in an agency. Some religious organizations have found it to be very helpful. We recommend perusal of this document.

"SPARE" —Five Domains of Need and Care

Since humans are multi-dimensional in their development, we have needs for sustenance and growth in several dimensions: spiritual, physical, actualizing, relational, and emotional. To these five basic domains, we can add needs related to organization and culture.

1. Spiritual Needs and Care

When an agency can encourage and provide for the spiritual care of its member, this strengthens each one individually and the community of faith. This may require creativity, and certainly commitment, especially when there are few speakers of the "home language." It is helpful, when possible, to affiliate with local groups who share the faith. Even without knowing the language at first, there is strength in the common bond of belief. Leaders can also encourage each person to be responsible for his or her individual spiritual care and nurture through personal study, singing, and prayer. Keeping up our spiritual health even in remote places is life-giving. It becomes an essential means of countering burnout and the loss of hope that human suffering can bring about.

Opportunity for worship: Most cross-cultural humanitarian workers come from some sort of religious background. A community of faith and relationships and practices based on our faith is an important part of our lives. Each of us needs some kind of spiritual leader, pastor, priest or rabbi. We benefit from regular worship, especially in the style to which we are accustomed—liturgical, charismatic, baptistic or other. Even though we may be located far from our preferred religious setting, receiving spiritual care is crucial to maintaining health and well-being.

It is possible we may have to alter our times or style of worship or fellowship, or even the language. In Afghanistan, we worshipped on Fridays. I was surprised at my own slight unease with this different time, even though I have long experienced worship across many cultures (Gardner). Learning to enter into worship in an unfamiliar setting is an important skill and attitude.

When my husband and I were assigned to a remote location in the mountains of a Latin American country, we were not near a church, so we carried on worship within our little family of four (Gardner). I really missed taking communion, so we decided that it would be appropriate for us to follow this spiritual ritual as a family. My husband went on one of his supply trips (200 miles by motorcycle on mountain trails, gravel road, and main highway, the journey taking two full days). In the major city 100 miles away, he purchased tiny glasses and a little tray to hold the elements of communion. It was a boost and encouragement to my faith, and gave me spiritual strength. Sometimes in caring for ourselves, we must do some unusual things.

Vision, motivation and our moral guide all come from our spiritual belief system. Thus, if we do not retain our spiritual vitality, it weakens us. Attrition studies reveal that loss of vision saps energy and perseverance.

Encourage small groups: This can be the most vital aspect of maintaining one's spiritual life! A small group provides opportunity to share about life regularly, to support one another (and practice the "one another" injunctions of Scripture), to pray and study together, and in other ways become spiritually stronger. Such a growth group may be from persons across agencies and culture, or within a larger team. We had a most wonderful group when we lived in the jungle of Peru—we called each other life support! Later, in the city, our group of ten was made up by persons from six cultures and five languages. We all agreed we were much closer to each other, and found far greater understanding, than with our families and friends "back home"—home being in six countries. See Appendix 3 for how to create small groups.

Teach devotional and study methods: Even persons who have grown up in churches or synagogues can benefit from learning a variety of devotional methods and ways to study the sacred writings. Methods such as *lectio divina* are enriching to persons of any religious background. Meditation, contemplations, practicing stillness and listening to the divine, time enjoying the beauty of nature—all are ways to nourish the spirit.

Encourage music and art: Learning more about, and listening regularly to, sacred music can be a daily way to enjoy connecting with God and others. Other kinds of music can also meet the needs of the spirit. The world of art is rich in devotional images. For example, Marc Chagall's magnificent images in stained glass and paintings are inspirational and provide continuing opportunities for reflection. For instance, his "White Crucifixion" is a stimulating and profound painting. He said it reflected the "suffering of Jewry" more than any image he could imagine. It helps us now to reflect on suffering and the dominance of the human spirit in moving forward against all odds. His painting "Jacob Wrestling with the Angel" can inspire us to keep wrestling as well. So too the work of Peter Paul Rubens whose larger-than-life scenes of Jesus and other biblical characters provide on-going beauty and reflection. Michelangelo's "Pieta" and his astounding work in the Sistine Chapel and other places lift the spirit. Many other artists have given us a legacy of incredible images and sounds to keep us spiritually attuned. Salvador Dali's image of God holding man and woman in his hands, in the "Divine Comedy" gives opportunity to ponder the divine in human matters. Who can gaze on "The Gates of Hell" or the "Burghers of Calais" by Auguste Rodin without realizing that our war with evil is an age-old one which is still worth fighting, and that the battle will someday be won?

For me and my family, taking an extra day away to search out good art is renewing. Whenever we travel, we look for museums and art galleries (Dodds). Most great cities of the world are full of them, and even small towns can have wonderful art which inspires the spirit. Even a half day with art can be a mini-vacation. Thus, giving members leeway in planning their travel schedules to explore art can contribute to their spiritual nurture.

2. Physical Needs and Care

The second dimension of need and care relates to physical health. By and large, those who enter humanitarian service in most forms are healthy physically, at least in the beginning. When we are young and vigorous, we give little thought to the needs of our bodies. Yet, over time, it is easy to neglect good nutrition, staying fit, and keeping up with annual exams. We often live in environments with many health benefits, but may also suffer consequences related to traveling or more frequent exposure to disease. Over a lifetime, most global servants suffer many assaults to the immune system due to travel, new water and climates, different foods, parasites, medical treatments and perpetually high stress. Other benefits offset these to some degree. In many locales, we get sufficient movement as part of our work, so that "exercising" is a result of daily life rather than a separate activity.

Staying fit: I grew up on a farm (Gardner). My mother was not a very good cook, but our food was simple and nourishing. I didn't worry about exercise because riding horses and doing barn chores, walking a mile each way to and from school and wrestling with my brothers provided all the exercise I needed.

As an adult, my life was quite different. My husband and I lived in a remote village in the mountains of a Latin American country. Getting to this location was a matter of riding a mule twelve miles, or walking, and the trail went up and down over two ranges of mountains. We were pretty healthy! Additionally, my husband gave me a gift to promote my health—he would get our little sons ready for the day and prepare breakfast while I exercised each day by jumping rope.

Exercising: As time went by, my duties became less vigorous and more sedentary. Graduate school, leading a counseling office with a world-wide outreach, and serving as International Vice President for Personnel didn't allow much time for exercise. One day, a good friend said to me, "You're getting a little chunky, aren't you?" I didn't think so, but I began to pay more attention to my health, diet, and weight. I still jump rope for twenty-five minutes a day, do floor exercises, and run-walk a half marathon each December. While in Thailand recently for a conference, I ran a Ten K. Of course the Kenyan runners outstripped me quickly! Healthy practices are not onerous for me because one of my lifelong values is to 'be as well as possible.' The proverb that states, "When the body is fit, the soul dances" has been true in my case.

Though the individual has responsibility to practice good health habits, an organization can do much to promote health. I am currently writing this book in a beautiful home in central Pennsylvania at a member care facility. To my great delight, the hosts and founders have included an exercise room. As care is extended and health is promoted at this facility, a healthy diet and regular exercise are integral aspects of care in promoting health.

Nutrition and diet: These are important no matter where we live. Sound nutrition has a huge influence on health and longevity! An agency can promote health in this by educating its members about nutrition and the local availability of foods. They can advise on ways to compensate for what is lacking. A crucial part of this is training in food handling to avoid parasites in food and water. A doctor can recommend supplements according to the need.

Inoculations: Before departure for the field getting required vaccinations is important. Once there, an agency physician or consultant should keep members apprised of updates and changes.

Vacations are another essential way to maintain both physical and mental health, so we encourage every agency, through personnel departments or MCFs, to assess the policies relating to time off. The more intense and dangerous the environment, the more frequently workers need respite by time away in a safe environment. Though this may seem costly compared to the "usual" vacation time taken in the home country, it will help to ensure health and longevity; healthy people will be less likely to drop out or need more specialized resources. Extra days off for mini-vacations, especially when traveling for the agency, can be a boost to help offset jet lag and fatigue.

Annual check-ups: See the recommendations in Chapter 12.

Health insurance: See Appendix 3 about this in Chapter 12.

3. Actualization Needs and Care

Actualization is a term developed by Maslow in the mid-1900s. It refers to one's fulfillment when using all the gifts and talents God has given. An actualized person believes he or she is making a difference in the world. He or she has energy for life's work and challenges, and maintains a positive outlook as well as being oriented to growth and learning.

We are devoting more space in this chapter to actualization needs than to the other needs identified in SPARE. This is because this area of human need is seldom considered by agencies and organizations, whose focus is on fulfilling its vision and mission rather than on the development of each of its members. Workers' needs usually come last in most humanitarian work, because of the urgent nature of the task and the unending human need with which teams are faced. Yet, actualization can be fostered in the built-in challenges inherent in fulfilling humanitarian visions.

Actualization is enhanced when we are encouraged by others to develop our gifts of intellect and talents and when we risk reaching out beyond our normal comfort zone. Encouragement and success are part of the "fuel" which motivates us and enables us to grow. What a gift it is when we have a supportive spouse, a caring supervisor, and a leader who values learning.

The agency can help to foster actualization in many ways.

Become a "learning organization:" One crucial way in which the agency or organization can foster development so that people can experience fulfillment and become "actualized" is by itself become a "learning organization." Jeffrey Kotter, a Harvard expert on change, advocates this.

Help members identify their gifts: A worker may not know the full extent of his or her giftedness at the beginning. He or she will benefit by devoting time to discovery periodically as experience and interests grow.[27] Doing jobs we did not go to do may help us discover we have a gift or gifts to develop. Feedback about our effectiveness in unaccustomed roles can build confidence and validate gifts we are discovering. Personality type inventories, such as the Myers-Briggs Type Indicator, are enormously helpful in identifying the strengths of

---

[27] *Now, Discover Your Strengths* by Buckingham and Clifton, 2001 and *StrengthsFinder 2.0* by Tom Rath, 2007 are excellent guides for a strengths discovery journey.

various personality types and encouraging persons to "own" both strengths and needs for growth in rounding out the "least preferred" sides of themselves. We recommend MCFs become qualified in the use of this instrument as it has application to every area of life and work.[28]

Provide career testing periodically: This benefits both the agency and the member and we recommend it be provided for members at various stages of their career. Typically in their forties people are at a different career juncture than when they joined at an earlier age. Due to maturing and having gained a great deal of experience, plus perhaps identifying with a different or more focused vision, this is a ripe time for change. It is better to help workers in the search for their most fulfilling role than to ignore their need. Many new ventures and visions are launched at midlife. Of course, from an organizational perspective, supervisors want to keep productive and congenial team members, so they may be reluctant to release the worker who wishes to move on. Another reason for periodic assessments of one's skills and desires is to prevent the person from being stereotyped in a role. For example, if a person has been a secretary for many years, it may be difficult for a supervisor to imagine her or him in any other role. Ideally, a supervisor will notice a worker's giftedness and arrange growth opportunities for him or her— and rejoice in the person's growth, even if it eventually means the loss of a good worker.

Sometimes by midlife a person is eager to move forward in career development but may be limited by incomplete degrees or formal studies. An individual can compensate by finding courses to pass for credit through exams or validating life experiential learning. Many colleges now offer this option. Keeping a list of one's accomplishments and on-the-job learning and training is helpful to demonstrating one has greater potential.

Attend to job fit: This is a shared responsibility between worker and supervisor. A worker is responsible to give input about "fit" in the role he or she has been asked to fill. Is this role a good fit? Can any adjustments be made to make it a better fit? Talking together is important, so a person does not feel trapped or stuck. Staying in a job

---

[28] MBTI® is owned by Consulting Psychologists Press. CPP provides training courses and materials. The instrument is available in various languages.

that does not fit may lead to burnout. An agreement to stay in the role temporarily may be needed, while searching for a better fit.

Make expectation clear: Providing clear expectations should begin in the recruitment and training phase and continue into the process of deciding about allocations and job roles. Expectations need to go beyond "work" to the whole of life in a new setting, so that each family member will have a sense of the culture, schooling available, how much help the agency can provide, what housing will be like, and so on. The more people know ahead of time and choose in light of what lies ahead, the more resilient they will be in the new setting. We might call this "stress inoculation" as it prepares and helps to equip everyone for the myriad adjustments that lie ahead. Unclear expectations, on the other hand, can cause one to flounder in uncertainty, sapping energy. Knowing more ahead of time increases confidence.

Offer annual job performance reviews: An annual review helps us as a member of any agency to know how we are doing, since we innately ask ourselves, "How am I doing?" This is especially true in situations foreign to us which require many adaptations. A review provides opportunity for valuable encouragement and any feedback needed for improving skills or attitudes. Additionally, members need accountability. This includes knowing to whom one reports and is accountable. In some humanitarian mission situations, this can be complex, particularly when national partners or cooperative projects are involved.

Promote life-long learning: When we analyze the lives and habits of outstanding persons, especially in cross-cultural or multicultural roles, we discover that they are committed to life-long learning. Long after they complete formal degree programs, they continue to read, discuss, seek interaction with knowledgeable people, and keep their eyes open to new discoveries. This stance towards life can be appreciated and promoted by an agency through provision of training times and courses, access to books, bringing in consultants who are stimulating, creation of work groups for project development and chances to travel (as opposed to keeping people "stuck" in some remote place without regular breaks to the outside). One agency we know of gives each member a financial stipend each home leave to spend on some kind of new training or education. That pays off!

At age twenty-one, I set myself a goal of reading a book a day (Gardner). As time went by, I discovered that was unrealistic so I revised my goal to read an hour a day and a day a week. Keeping this commitment has paid huge dividends. When I moved "up" to roles of teaching and leading, I devoted Thursdays to reading and study. Now my role as an international personnel consultant means that I travel at least half the time. Though it is not laid out as an hour or a day, this travel time is a great gift! I can read four or five books on each trip. (Having a Kindle reduces the weight of luggage!)

Provide or encourage continuing education opportunities: In many professions and roles, continuing education is a requirement for licensure or certification. Even when it is not, however, wise leaders make provision for people to have periodic home leaves or other breaks to pursue upgrading their knowledge and skills. Some work tasks can be arranged for actual educational credit. For instance, when the linguists we worked with in Mexico and Peru were working collaboratively with master linguists in advanced projects, they could sometimes receive graduate credit for their work. In my role as professor in a masters degree by extension program, I required my students to do projects that were "real life work"—part of their regular job which could be done for credit and in the process, produce a better outcome because it was integrated with their study program (Dodds). This is a valuable way to assist members to upgrade knowledge, skills, and academic level.[29] People earning degrees later in life, after years of service, can often validate their learning for credit by colleges in various ways so that their training activities on the job contribute to their degree programs.

Provide on-going leadership development: In many ways, any person who has the courage and resilience to leave home, enter another culture, and undertake risky endeavors to improve the lives of others is a leader. This is especially true when "getting there" requires raising funds,

---

[29] This takes place in the Masters Degree program of Azusa Pacific University, Operation Impact. Many other institutions currently offer programs overseas by extension and encourage their already-working students to use their real life work as the laboratory for their research and projects.

relating to donors, reporting to groups, public speaking on behalf of one's agency, relating to national governments, and other tasks or roles outside a typical home-culture job. Therefore, it is worthwhile for an organization to look at all its people as potential leaders for its own mission fulfillment, and to provide opportunities and resources for their development.

Healthy leaders are more likely to create a healthy work place. Thus, providing for existing leaders at all levels to grow in leadership knowledge and skills is beneficial to everyone. Identifying up-coming leaders through this process will enrich the organization over time.

4. Relational Needs and Care

Many studies have shown that interpersonal relationships are the most frequent factor determining either success or failure in overseas, multicultural work. This seems obvious in that in order to adjust to a whole new social and emotional environment, filled with myriad challenges, we have to relate to many new people and to build supportive relationships.

Prepare candidates for relationship building: Attrition analysis shows that a lack of ability and skill in interpersonal relationships may be the most frequent reason for workers to leave a field of service and return to their passport country. Here is why this matter of ease in relating can be so challenging!

When my husband, Dr. Larry Dodds, and I set out to fulfill our great life calling, we left home and all our familiar relationships. He was thirty-two and I was twenty-nine. We had three small children. During the process of preparation for our work and allocation to Peru, we were faced with living, studying, and working with several groups, all of whom were strangers to us. First came a summer of living in a university dorm with other families and singles and all the teaching staff of a graduate program. Then came six months of life in the jungle, in three settings, again with dozens of new colleagues being trained along with us and our teachers for the program. Then came months of living in a huge city for the study of Spanish, getting acquainted with dozens of other students, teachers, and colleagues in our mission, as well as new Peruvian friends. Then came life in our jungle village, with about 250 adult co-workers, dozens of children, and numerous members of indigenous groups whom we served. In all, we had to make hundreds of new relationships, all within two and a half years and twenty-three moves (counting only what was home for a month or more!). Even the hardiest persons are challenged by such rapidly changing environments and the need to establish so many relationships in such a short time. Teaching members friendships skills is invaluable!

Another example is our experiences in the early stages of service (Gardner). My husband and I served as staff on a jungle living training camp in southern Mexico near the Guatemala border. Later we served for a number of years as summer staff of a linguistic training course offered at a number of U.S. universities (The Dodds were our students the summer of 1969!). We made numerous moves with our two small sons, going back and forth to our village project. The effectiveness of our service in the village and the universities depended on our relationship skills. These are "real life" skills—not esoteric ones. Good relationships boil down to being good listeners, attending to what others say, giving caring feedback, and having positive interactions.

Make relationship skills and character explicit: Establishing and keeping good relationships involves character qualities, attitudes, and communication skills. I recently asked a retired military friend who has a long history of service in the military, civil service, and many service organizations what she looks for in a good friend (Gardner). She listed loyalty, dedication, integrity, humility, trustworthiness, keeping confidences, kindness, a loving, forgiving, and generous spirit, gentleness, compassion, understanding, a degree of cleanliness, organization, quietness and ability to remain calm. "I like to be around people who know who they are, and whose they are, and who they are with others." She said, "I love people for who they are, not what they do, though I appreciate what they do."

Becoming persons able to sustain friendships is not easy; it requires openness and continuing growth. (We use the term *person-able*, *personable*, to mean that a *person* has the (*able*) *abilities* to relate well.) This same friend identified characteristics or behaviors that she finds irritating—as almost any of us would. Arrogance, the need to be right all the time, making no allowance for others' opinions, being forceful and overbearing, refusing to make eye contact (when that is culturally appropriate), being evasive or deceitful, and not showing interest all contribute to the failure of creating relationships or to their death.

Harshness in speech, lying, gossip, malice, meanness, manipulation, slander, laziness, feeding on trivia, disrespect, and intentionally hurting others by words or behaviors all wreak havoc.

For further discussion of the need for self-awareness in relating to others, see Chapter 2, "Impact Awareness," in Volume Two of this series.

As we illustrate in our personal stories above, cross-cultural and multicultural service often involves periods of time in community living as well as quantitative intensity in interpersonal relating. (We recommend life in community as an important part of the screening and assessment process!) In these settings space is limited; people are crowded; high stress and pressure are the rule. For many people, these conditions can lead to harsh words, short tempers, angry flare-ups, avoidance, or withdrawal. For others, tolerance and generosity soothes relationships. For these very reasons, group living is a helpful way to discover a person's habitual reactions.

Provide workshops on relationship skills: We highly recommend that cross-cultural, multicultural agencies provide training called Strengthening Your Interpersonal Skills (SYIS). This workshop was developed by Dr. Kenneth Williams,[30] built on another long-running workshop, Counseling Skills for Administrators. This transcultural training is meeting needs around the world.

Spiritual life values and relationships: Both the Old and New Testaments of the Bible teach many ways we can interact within the family and with friends, colleagues, peers, supervisors, and outsiders.

---

[30] Dr. Williams began his career as a linguist and Bible translator. After earning his doctorate in counseling he became head of the counseling department for a large international organization, as well as participating in various screening, selection, and training programs. He developed SYIS workshop in these contexts. It is available in multiple languages and locales through International Training Partners (www.relationshipskills.org). As of 2021, this website no longer exists.

The Proverbs are rich in instruction about our mouths and character habits! Promoting the teaching and practice of healthy habits is another way an organization can promote relationship health! Promoting social times, such as celebrating different cultures and their customs and foods, birthdays, anniversaries, special accomplishments—all these build community. When our children graduated from their school in the jungle of Peru, people would stand in line for two hours to congratulate each graduate—even when there were only sixteen or twenty graduates! This kind of community support contributes to health (Dodds)! Given that most humanitarian efforts are devoted directly to the care of people, training members in relationship building is one of the best investments an agency can make.

5. Emotional Needs and Care

Agencies can do much to enhance the emotional health of their members. It includes all the matters we have discussed up to this point. To those, we add specific ways to foster emotional health and provide care.

Teaching verbal expression of emotions. Many people, especially men in certain cultures, lack a vocabulary for the emotional side of life. This is especially true when persons have grown up in non-expressive families in which emotions were not articulated or encouraged, those whose training centers on technical or professional training, and those serving in roles which require major cognitive skills. For example, a person reared in a non-emotional family who then trains to be a physician or military officer will be at a disadvantage when identifying and expressing emotion. This happens because emotion is deliberately set aside as "unfitting" when one has to stay very focused cognitively. The habit of closing off emotion or not exhibiting or expressing it is, in certain situations, helpful, but in life, in general, this is a hindrance. Though this allows for greater concentration on the cognitive challenges of a role, such as tending the sick, it is contrary to developing intimacy and building sustaining relationships. Allowing for and encouraging openness in emotional expression is positive.

Providing workshops on communication skills: This emphasizes that good health includes the ability to express emotions. Practice sessions, such as in role play or counseling, can lead to greater freedom in the expression of emotions. In this context, persons can also work on anger management or other emotional issues which create conflict and trouble in relationships.

Marriage and child rearing workshops. In these contexts, persons can be encouraged and trained to express emotion. To create close bonds as well as to remain healthy, a person needs to develop ease with their own and others' feelings. Families in which members are free to express emotion in positive ways, rather than acting out negatively, are the healthiest.

Allow for the role of emotions in group life and work settings. This can enable workers to address issues in the work place and their community life early on, before they become magnified by "stuffing" them down, ignoring them, or forcing them "underground" so that later they erupt into conflict. Healthy group life allows for this kind of interaction. Of course, it also implies self-control, so that emotions are expressed in positive ways that do not harm others. MCFs can teach skills through workshops for all ages.

Healthy and positive emotions, such as love, gentleness, tenderness, caring, empathy, and patience become the life-line, nurturing force in relationships. These emotions feed our spirits, our souls, our hearts. To endure the challenges and hardships of humanitarian work, we must have the ability to share our hurts, our pains, our sorrows and disappointments, and to draw on the positive emotions of others. Becoming hardened or closed off emotionally leads to stagnation and disillusionment.

Jamie Lawrence describes "twenty emotions and feelings that drive human motivation." Allowing for these, encouraging them, will benefit every agency and each member.[31]

---

[31] People in Aid, and HRZone.co.uk. May 23, 2013

Ten Additional Facets of Promoting Health

As we have just described, the agency plays a vital role in promoting and maintaining the international worker's health.   Additional recommendations for the agency involve creating an environment which fosters health and addresses the full spectrum of the worker's health concerns, from pre-departure to return from the assignment. This section draws heavily from the "Code of Good Practice" for international agencies developed by "People in Aid."[32] These additional key support functions of the agency add to the previous information.

1. Promotion of work/personal balance: The agency, starting with top leaders, should model and maintain an organizational ethos, structures and policies which support a healthy balance of work and rest. International workers often work long hours under challenging conditions so obtaining enough rest can be difficult. The U.S. Foreign Service estimates that sixty percent of problems encountered by their foreign staff are related to stress (Gamble and Lovell-Hawker, 2008). This is likely true of other humanitarian workers. To counteract this trend, policies need to provide for regular rest and adequate vacation. Funding for breaks and vacations should be built into the system of support raising, donor support, financial quotas or salaries. If finances are limited, MCFs or other leaders may help with other arrangements that can help members take holidays away from the work-site. One idea is to trade homes with other members for brief periods. Other policies should support lifestyle habits conducive to good health.

Of course, there is never any guarantee of daily life balance, especially in crisis response situations or conditions of war or refugee aid. What may be impossible on a day-to-day basis therefore needs even more attention at the meta-life level, with every attempt made to provide for regular, periodic relief from work pressures. In most situations, emotional engagement extends 24/7 even though physical work may remain within set boundaries. This is one reason why it is essential to PLAN and facilitate time-outs.

---

[32] People in Aid.org

2. Training for life as well as work: The agency should provide training in areas of stress management, effective teamwork, cross-cultural and multicultural training, transition, re-entry, and health maintenance. Other training can include lifestyle habits such as diet and exercise to cultivate self-care in sustaining long-term effectiveness and vigor. Other areas of training could include emergency response and care (what to do in the event of a tsunami, earthquake, theft, war, etc.). See Appendix 4 of Chapter 12 for contingency plans which cover disaster scenarios. All of this training should happen periodically, with some in the initial stages of orientation and allocation, and frequent workshops or other training in field sites. After re-entry, additional training can help in the worker's adjustment to the homeland.

3. Encouraging help-seeking behavior: Maintaining good self-care is essential for effectiveness and longevity. Seeking the help of health care professionals is also important. Facilitating access to medical care by providing resources and support is a vital function of the agency (Gamble and Lovell-Hawker, 2008). This includes the provision of a health insurance program which rewards effective self-care and has inclusive/reasonable policies regarding in-country medical care, hospitalization provisions, and medical evacuation (Riesland, 2008). Agencies can help at the local level by having a referral system for professionals, and in the homeland by having advisors who can communicate regularly with the MCF or on-field health care professionals.

4. Fostering communication within the agency: Observers have noted that effective communication with the international worker may be the single most important form of support in helping to lower preventable attrition (Bloecher and Lewis in Ritschart, 2008). Upon joining a sending agency, workers often find themselves struggling not only to adjust to their new host culture, but also to the written and unwritten rules of the agency itself. To facilitate this process, the agency should clarify how to give feedback to leaders or departments and how to make requests or ask for help (practical, psychosocial or spiritual). Clarifying avenues of communication is especially important in, but is not limited to, emergency situations. In addition, an environment where there is tacit freedom to acknowledge difficulties and to request help at an early stage helps to head off problems that lead to chronic stress (Gamble and Lovell-Hawker, 2008).

5. Providing effective personnel functions:

a. **Policy establishment and review**: Policies regarding health, security and safety should be regularly reviewed, and cover issues such as availability of and financial provision for educational options for children, reasonable housing, language study, compassionate leave, etc.

b. **Supervision and mentoring**: Just as lack of clarity about the task, vision and structure lead to problems, so too, lack of supervision can cause significant stress and premature return from the field. Involving the worker in planning and developing strategies and providing mentoring and coaching, especially in the early years, are also vital to the continued motivation and health of the worker. Efforts should be made to provide adequate staffing, finances and other resources to provide ongoing contact and support.

c. **Complete records** of injuries, illnesses and accidents, etc. should be kept in order to minimize the recurrence of such events.

d. **Regular reassessment of the job description** and appropriateness of placement should include a review of the security, travel and health risks of the region where the worker is posted.

e. **Openness to suggestions** from the worker for changes and improvements can improve job satisfaction (Gamble and Lovell, 2008). Lack of responsiveness of the leadership to the feedback from members leads to a sense of being devalued and an erosion of morale.

f. **Proactive assessment and monitoring of the worker's health** includes initial thorough and careful pre-departure health and psychological assessment as well as assessment of health risks on the field. Monitoring the worker's health and proactively addressing issues help to ensure the worker's continued health, well-being and effectiveness.

g. **Keep abreast of stresses**: Follow-up of the worker should be attentive to stressors such as changes in the worker's international environment (political changes, fallout of natural disasters, etc.), job description (change of location, promotion, etc.), and personal issues (changes in health status, children's education, the need to care for aging parents, etc.).

h. **Mobilize help when needed:**   If and when the worker develops medical or psychological issues which pose a higher risk of health problems, the agency should be ready to initiate and mobilize help. Note that this requires the building of trust in the relationship between the agency and the worker, a process which is ideally initiated at pre-departure.

6. Support for families' and children's needs:

Families who have children with special physical or psychological needs require focused attention both before departure and while on the field. The agency needs to ensure that adequate support is provided for such families. Ritschard draws from the experience of the U.S. military in identifying high-risk families and provides specific questions for carrying out an annual family "check-up" which helps to identify and address medical, spiritual and support concerns as well as educational issues (2002). In a study of 1,036 U.S. Army soldiers and spouses, McCubbin and Lavee (1986) found that families with preschool and school-age children required the most support in adapting to frequent moves (as cited in Ritschard, 2002, p. 414).

See Chapter 7 of this volume for additional information about family support.

7. Provide periodic updates in cross-cultural understanding: This can include a look at how values and practices may differ in the cultures represented in the work team. An excellent tool for this is presented in Lingenfelter and Mayers, who provide us with a very practical method for promoting understanding across cultures (1987, 1988, 2003).

8. Provide opportunity to members to discuss the health of the organization itself and what changes might benefit the agency and the members. Doing this regularly can address issues early on before they become sources of conflict, division, or disheartenment. When a major sending agency underwent significant changes related to financial difficulties, the leadership instituted some rather severe measures to address these issues. However, the leadership failed to keep its membership abreast of the financial difficulties and the subsequent changes so when the news was finally broken to the membership, it provoked a strong reaction, ranging from alarm, fear and a sense of being disrespected, to indignation and anger because they were not notified earlier. Clear and timely communication to the members and keeping them attuned to the status of the organization would have averted to these reactions, which added an additional layer of complexity to an already difficult transition.

9. Post-return, re-entry follow-up: A thorough review should be carried out upon the worker's return to the homeland. This should include an exit debriefing, a health check to follow up on known problems and the management of newly-diagnosed medical and psychological conditions, a review of issues that might affect further placement, counseling as needed, timely teaching about re-entry, culture shock, TCK issues for children (Gamble and Lovell, 2008) and provision for pension and career counseling as needed ("People in Aid," 2003). The degree of post-assignment support offered varies from agency to agency, but should provide follow-up of issues which developed as a result of the assignment.

10. Emergency support: This seems even more needed than in past decades, as both natural and man-made disasters are occurring at an intensifying pace. Just into this new millennium devastating earthquakes, volcanic eruptions, tsunamis, hurricanes, tornadoes, oil spills, nuclear reactor explosions, outbreaks and pandemics of infectious diseases, wars and terrorism all keep the world in turmoil. An agency's workers can be affected anywhere, any time! My teenage daughter narrowly escaped the bombing in Kampala and teens from my local area were wounded. Danger strikes when least expected! Therefore, maintaining regular communication and contingency planning and preparation is essential. When disaster strikes, bringing resources together to give immediate practical resources is vitally important. This area of preparedness includes:

a. **Crisis management team (CMT):** Appointing a trained crisis management team jumpstarts the management of crises, allowing the emergency response to be launched immediately and effectively. One important role of the CMT is to manage communication with headquarters, family and constituency as well as local authorities.

b. **Contingency plans**: The formulation and regular review of contingency plans with the aid of expert consults (medical, crisis management, etc.) allows for better preparedness. Briefing all personnel on these plans, clarifying roles and conducting drills all help to minimize the chaos and anxiety of crisis. See Appendix 4 in Chapter 12 for sample contingency plans for war, flu, kidnapping, etc.

c. **Support** in the event of detainment or quarantine: Public health hazards posed by natural and man-made disasters not only expose cross-cultural workers to the specific health risk, but may also result in their being quarantined or detained by local governments. The agency should be prepared to take on the role of negotiator, mediator and advocate in such cases.

Summary

Agencies do well to appoint and train personnel specifically for the role of Member Care Facilitator. This person becomes the meta-level overseer of care in the major dimensions of need. He or she practices "resource brokering," bringing together and matching various resources and the needs of members. In addition to the five basic dimensions of need and care, the agency's provision of additional facets of care is vital to the health of individual members, and the organization as a whole. Proactive care is essential for greatest effectiveness. The agency that neglects these vital functions does so at its own peril.

Poorly handled crises can have harmful fallout. A crisis may be worsened by lack of timely and appropriate intervention and care. The perception of members and outsiders of leaders' competence and caring at such times will persist long after the crisis itself recedes. Trust will be enhanced or diminished by responses.

Case Study[33]

In May 2003, at the height of the SARS crisis in China, a German nurse posted in one of the SARS hotspots developed a low-grade fever. It was just days before she was to return to her home country for home leave, and adhering to national regulations, she presented for a checkup to the local hospital mandated with assessing foreign SARS cases. She had been assured by a Chinese medical friend that this was merely a formality. The hospital, however, kicked into high gear, and much to her surprise and consternation, the nurse found herself admitted to the SARS ward, sharing an isolation ward with 23 confirmed SARS cases. Though her temperature remained low-grade and she did not develop any symptoms of SARS, and in fact, her lab tests suggested that she had a *Mycoplasma* infection which would explain her fever, the hospital quarantined her for monitoring for 5 days, fearful of being responsible for allowing the first SARS case to enter Germany. The nurse's hospitalization created great concern within her agency, prompting phone calls with the home office, discussing the need for medical evacuation. The agency also was the liaison with her family and constituency as the patient herself had no way of contacting them from hospital.

Anxiety escalated when a local TV station broadcasted a short video clip of the patient in the hospital SARS ward, as part of a "What were you doing on May 1, Labour Day?" public relations stint. Within minutes of this showing, the executive director of her agency received the first of dozens of phone calls from colleagues and neighbors who'd all had contact with this outgoing foreigner in the preceding days. In an already charged atmosphere of near-hysteria about this deadly and poorly-understood epidemic, this development only heightened the general level of suspicion and fear. The agency monitored the patient's progress closely, negotiating with the hospital for early discharge to avoid her being infected by the confirmed cases of SARS with whom she was hospitalized. In addition, the agency played a public health role, consulting and advising quarantine for known contacts, in keeping with national regulations. This was complicated by the fact that this occurred in the late spring when many of the known foreign contacts already had

---

[33] As in all our case studies and examples, the names, places, and details are changed to protect privacy.

made plans to return to their home countries after their university teaching assignments had finished.

The patient was discharged from hospital after five days, when her fever had subsided and she had not developed full-blown symptoms of SARS. She voluntarily underwent another week of quarantine in her home before returning to Germany. By June, 2003, the WHO proclaimed the SARS outbreak contained; China, in total, reported 235 deaths as a result of the SARS outbreak.

1. What are the main groups of people involved in this scenario who need attention? What issues are to be considered by the agency?
2. If you were the head of the agency to which this worker belonged, what concrete steps would you take in managing this situation?
3. What lessons were learned? How could this case affect future emergency and contingency planning?

Appendix One:
Member Care Needs Assessment Tool[34]

What is true for my agency now?
What direction are we going as an agency?
What is likely to take place in the next five to ten years? What structures, personnel, and funds do we need now? How soon?

1. Administrative and resource personnel: What is the proportion of administration to field teams? What is the pool for potential leadership in our agency? What mentoring is going on?
2. Services: What services are members asking for? What do we offer now? What would make a difference in effectiveness? Morale?
3. Children: Current education options? Age of children in the agency? Future needs of families?

---

[34] By Laura Mae Gardner, 1997 and 2009, SIL.

4. National involvement: Hospitality to national members? Vision for future involvement of nationals?

5. Proportion of membership—What is the membership makeup: Number and kinds (singles, widows, divorced, males/females), ages, and mission experience of membership? Number and proportion of cultures represented in agency language facility of other cultures? Issues of minorities--how handled? Number of childless couples; couples with children; attitudes in the agency related to women in leadership? Unique challenges and needs of personnel in cross-cultural marriages, such as "Which sending country will be 'our' country?" "Which culture will be our preferred culture in which to raise and educate our children?"

6. Attrition: How much is it? Why do people leave? Where do they go when they leave? Who leaves? (Are they potential leaders, families with teenagers, people who are discontented?) How do they leave? (Quietly; sadly; surreptitiously?)

7. Change: What change has happened to this agency? What is the attitude of this agency toward change? What change is likely in the future? How is the agency preparing for change? What mentoring and coaching programs are needed? What training programs for teams/administrators? What are the attitudes toward completion?

8. Hospitality attitudes of agency: Does it welcome visitors? Is it willing to ask for resources from international or regional offices?

9. Pastoral care: What is the felt need? Who meets it? To whom does the agency look for help? Are they open to help?

10. Management ethos of agency: What are the historic attitudes of the agency? How open is the agency to good management practices (planning, staff matters and personnel care, clear communication, performance reviews, encouragement, and providing for times of renewal)?

Appendix Two:
A Continuum of Care[35]

A Mechanism to Facilitate Awareness by
Directors, Administrators, and Member Care Facilitators

1. Analyze the context:
*   How many cultures are represented in your agency?
*   What is the proportion of administrative staff to membership?
*   What are the environmental challenges (climate; difficulty in travel; degree of linguistic difficulties; predictability of continuance or tenuousness of visas, etc.)?
*   What are the relationships with government (open; respectful; helpful; difficult)?
*   What is the degree of difference from sending countries?
*   What is the age of group (variety; aging; youthful); what are the ramifications of that?
*   What is the atmosphere of the country (hostile; suspicious; welcoming)?
*   What are the educational factors (presence of national or private schools; children's education resources, cost of education, degree of difference of national or agency system from sending countries)?
*   What is the reality of spiritual oppression and evil power?
*   What is the ethos of the country for good or evil (temptation; presence of national worship options)?
*   What is safety and security like (presence and prevalence of AIDS; kinds of crisis issues; health care)?
*   What is the amount of infrastructure (places and people of renewal, consultant help; help with visas, other technical services)?

2. Provision of standard care:
*   Orientation of new members (when, where, by whom?).
*   Language school or language learning expectations and facilities.
*   Method of assignment.
*   What happens when crisis comes? Does a new member know what constitutes a crisis, how he/she can call for help, what help will be forthcoming.

---

[35] By Laura Mae Gardner, 1997 and 2009, SIL.

- Children's education and enculturation (who will advise or assist a new family with these issues?)

3. Maintenance oversight:
- Participation of members (They will expect to have a voice; how can this be encouraged?)
- Accountability of members (How to establish and carry out?)
- Reporting of problems (New members wonder who cares and what do they care about? How will I ask for help for myself? For another member?)
- Measuring and maintaining morale (How can an administrator know what the morale is, when it needs attention and what kind?)
- Communication (internally and externally with constituency and extended family) in an atmosphere of suspicion and surveillance.
- Burnishing the vision; knowing when it's waning; keeping one's own vision fresh and alive.
- How to remain positive and confident as a leader in the midst of uncertainty, conflict, little progress?
- Promoting spiritual fellowship among the membership (How does a leader find time to be a shepherd to his people?)
- Accounting for spiritual oppression and evil power and standing against it (How does a leader do that?)
- Promoting bonding of lone rangers, introverts, computer people, isolated members.
- Sensing or perceiving when members of a family are having trouble and reluctant to ask for help (How will I know? What kind of help can I offer? What and where are the resources?)
- Helping members with personal dilemmas (expectations of extended family, home church, sending country).

4. Handling trouble when it comes:
- Problem-finding (How do I do that from a distance? How do I use a grapevine when our agency is so small?)
- Problem-solving (I'm so far away; I'm the authority; I may have to take action that a member won't like—how will I rebuild trust with him or her?)
- Maintaining confidentiality (Can I? When is it not wise?)

- Discipline (When, for what and how should it be implemented?)
- Getting help (When, where, and how?)
- Restoration and risk (What can stay on the field; what can't? For example: threatened or attempted suicide, possible multiple personality disorder, immobilizing depression, compulsive slanderer, non-functioning member, moral lapse offender, child molester. What is the degree of risk?)
- Confronting across cultures (How can I find out how people want to be confronted, how do other cultures manage conflict?)
- The price of living cautiously or distrustfully in countries with high security issues.
- Addressing interpersonal problems and conflicts between members (When? How? How do I discern right and wrong? Do I have the courage to take an unpopular stand and live with criticism?)

5. Helping in transitions:
- Changes in the family (new baby; health of a family member; child leaving home for boarding school or college)
- Furlough time for the family (How can I help them with furlough schooling? Fund-raising? Integrating with home church, extended family problems, expectations?)
- Expectations of extended family back home while worker is on the field?
- Change in assignment (new role; elected to administration; unsuccessful field assignment, lack of job fit).
- Transition to retirement, or other reasons to leave the field permanently; helping with good good-byes.

6. Crisis care:
- Things are no longer safe or predictable—threats, insecurity, uncertainties.
- Program disrupted by violence—can't continue.
- Evacuation due to war—great loss of goods, task, future.
- Spiritual issues—question God's leading, organizational care, insufficient resources; crises of faith—"God didn't protect us."
- Death, accident, loss, disaster, tragedy.
- Need for debriefing (Who, where, how, when?)
- Understanding impact of various kinds of crisis.

Some final questions:
- How can an administrator do all of this?
- What infrastructure is needed (funds, personnel, facilities, plan)?
- What can the sending country do?
- What can the sending church or religious community do?
- What must a member do for himself?
- What must members be prepared to do for one another?

Conclusion of Continuum of Care

Member Care Facilitators, as well as administrators and leaders at all levels of an agency must consider member care as one of his or her important roles; he or she must do more than see that the work gets done. Attending closely to members, making it safe for them to express needs, and doing whatever is reasonable and possible to meet those needs is crucial. So, too, is promoting inter-group, and perhaps inter-mission, care and sharing of resources. Promoting appropriate self-care, fostering hardiness, and encouraging members to rely on God and family is ongoing, before and after crisis.

Appendix Three:
How to Create a Growth and Care Group

Part 1: Guidelines for Group Members
Lois Dodds, Ph. D., and Lawrence Dodds, M. D.

Process for getting started:

1. Ask for guidance to identify six to ten other persons who are conscious of their need to grow, in spiritual, relational and overall development. Share your idea for a group with these persons to find out their interest. Ask each one to think about joining you.

2. Schedule a preliminary get-together to discuss the purpose and guidelines for a group.

3. Agree on a time frame, such as 6, 8, or 10 weeks as a trial time. This allows for an easy out or dissolution of the group if it doesn't go well. We find that two and a half to three hours per week is the best, allowing sufficient time for in-depth sharing and caring prayer.

4. Agree on a purpose statement and the guidelines to follow.

5. Agree on a leader for this initial period, or to share or rotate leadership in the group.

At the end of the trial period:

1. Discuss openly how the group has developed, sharing what you like, wish to do differently, what barriers might have arisen, etc. It is important to be honest in a loving way.

2. If the consensus is that the group is working well and moving towards its goals, agree to continue for a stated time, usually 3 to 6 months. Some may wish to drop out at this point for various reasons. If the barriers appear too great, you may wish to dissolve the group and make a new beginning with a different mix of people.

Sample purpose statement (you can write your own):

Our purpose is to help each other to grow through sharing our lives and hearts with each other. We understand that we are all wounded and sinful and that we can best grow as we open our hearts to one another by being honest, open, transparent and vulnerable with each other. Our purpose is nurture and growth in the community of faith, both directly and through the members in relationship to each other. We purpose to provide for each other the love, support, understanding and challenge which nurtures growth toward maturity in life, especially in our key relationships. (James 3:3 says "we all stumble in many ways," hence we need each other for support.) We agree to use the Scriptures as a foundation, source, and guide for our personal growth and our group process. We agree to "speak the truth in love" (Eph.4:15). We will devote an agreed upon portion of our group time to reading and sharing insights from the scriptures. (We suggest a simple process of 10 minutes for silent reading of a portion of 10 to 20 verses and jotting down insights, questions, etc. and then discussing these in another 10-15 minutes. Avoid usual "Bible Study" rules and a "head knowledge" approach, as well as homework, as these may create barriers to the devotional (heart level) and personal sharing.)

Facilitating Small Groups Part 2
Part 2: Guidelines for Facilitating Small Groups

These guidelines can help you lead a small group, such as a care group, in which you are committed to help each other grow.

Purposes of small groups:
1. To help you develop relationships and strengthen the bonds of love in the community of faith through sharing your ideas, feelings and experience with each other.

2. To provide an opportunity to interact with or process the ideas and content of the teaching sessions so that each person makes it personal.

Tips or guidelines for facilitating these purposes:
1. Clearly state the reason for meeting in the small group, the question(s) to be discussed, and the time allowed. Ask for confidentiality—for the group to agree not to take what they learn and share it outside the group.

2. Model the behavior you want others to engage in. For example, be personal in your sharing, but keep your comments brief and succinct. Always show respect in the way you facilitate staying on track, through comments which affirm the importance of the participants and their questions or concerns and yet allow you to lead the group in the desired direction.

3. Be sensitive to the needs of individuals, and at the same time keep the group "on task" in discussion. If a person has an overwhelming need to share his or her personal struggle which is outside the content area to be discussed, gently lead the person to defer until the end. For example, "Mary, I see that you are feeling very hurt (overwhelmed, angry, whatever) right now. This concern deserves more time than we can give you here. Could you and I talk about this when our discussion time is over (or before supper, etc.)?" If the specific concern can fit into the question or area of discussion, include it but be astute to the time any one person may take. Be sensitive to the moment, seeking to facilitate the group bonding and engage individuals with the content for discussion.

4. Try to draw everyone into the discussion, without going around in a circle. Extroverts naturally jump in and easily dominate the group time, so as a facilitator you need to moderate those too quick to speak, by saying something like, "Bob, I appreciate your willingness to share. Since we've heard from you three times, could you just hold your comment for now to give Carol time to share?" Ask persons who are reticent to share to participate (they wait to be "invited") by asking a question that requires more than a "yes" or "no" and is not threatening, such as "What is this (need, issue, etc.) like for you, Steve? Can you share something of your experience?" This gives the person the choice of how deep to go with the answer.

5. In facilitating discussion about the topic area or question posed, ask open-ended questions which invite more than "yes/no" answers and which allow the person to choose his or her level of sharing. Avoid questions so specific a person will be boxed in or feel cornered. For example, instead of asking, "Mary, do you agree with Judy?" ask "What do you think (feel, etc.) about this approach, John?"

6. Constantly monitor, keeping an eye on the time and task to invite participation by many rather than letting one person have it all. If a person gets "off task" gently remind him or her of your purpose in meeting and at the same time, affirm the importance of his or her concerns. For example, "Julie, what you're saying here is very important, but it's taking us away from our question. Perhaps we can talk about your experience (or concern, or whatever) after our discussion is over."

7. Be sensitive to the spirit of the group. If you sense people are very nervous, reluctant to share, or some other feeling which is hindering the group process, it is helpful to reflect that, gently. You can say something like: "I know it's sometimes hard to open our hearts to each other if we are new or haven't had time to build trust. What do you think we might be feeling now that makes it hard to get started?" "Is there anything we can do (agree to, etc.) to make it easier for each other?"

8. Summarize the discussion very briefly at the end, to give closure to the group experience. Say something like, "This has been a special hour together. I appreciate so much each one of you who has been willing to share. I think we can take away with us a greater sense of how God meets each of us in our needs" (or whatever the discussion as a whole has yielded). Head levels of communication include facts, ideas, judgments, generalizations. Heart level includes feelings, needs, personal responses, intimate disclosures, secrets. "Out of the heart flow the issues of life." (Prov. 4:3)

Facilitating Small Groups—Part 3

Part 3: Guidelines and Commitment for Group Members

As a group, we pledge to conduct our times together according to the following:

1. Confidentiality: Everything shared in this group will remain in the group. Nothing is to be told or repeated outside the group. We will respect and hold in trust the disclosures and secrets of each other. If a spouse is not part of the group, he or she will not be included in the disclosures shared. Such confidentiality is essential to creating safety and trust in the group. Trust is fragile and is easily broken, so it must be nurtured and guarded.

2. Use only "I" statements when talking about life experience, struggles, wishes, prayer needs, etc. This encourages "owning" one's own feelings, thoughts, experiences, etc. This eliminates the problem of talking about others, labeling or blaming others, and veering off course from the purpose of the group. Exercise the discipline of talking only about your thoughts, wishes, etc. and not those of other persons.

3. Invite sharing, but do not force it. Participants may ask for more sharing, to draw out someone who is hurting or reticent, but should never push for disclosures. Sharing must be voluntary, not demanded. You may ask, but I may say "no," or otherwise decline. We find an excellent approach given by King Solomon, "...the heart is like deep waters, but a man of wisdom draws them out..."[36]

4. Avoid giving advice or making judgments. The purpose of sharing is not to "fix" each other or judge each other (or those not present to represent themselves). It is to listen, to learn from each other, to give feedback which allows the one sharing to gain insight, understanding and strength.

5. Offer suggestions, encouragement, queries which allow for learning and exploration rather than those which cut off exploration. Some excellent guidelines come from the writings of the Apostle Paul,[37] such as, "stimulate one another to love and good works" (Heb. 10:24). Offer instruction or correction with humility (Gal. 6:1), knowing everyone may be tempted. Speak "truth in love," in the spirit of Ephesians 4. We should ask ourselves if our feedback or exhortation meets the three rules of Eph. 4:29: 1) Is it helpful for the hearer, 2) useful for building up, and 3) according to the need of the hearer (not[38] spoken according to one's own need to talk)?

6. Avoid discussion of general topics and generalizations of people. These often lead to differences of opinions, which generally don't promote growth or group cohesion. Sticking to heart level sharing of one's own life and experience, struggles, needs, etc., will promote growth in one's self and in others.

7. Practice being "HOT"—honest, open, and transparent. Only through speaking truth in love.

---

[36] The Bible, Old Testament, Proverbs 20:5
[37] The New Testament Epistles
[38] We are to "speak truth in love."

References and Recommended Reading

Bloecher, D., and Lewis, J. 1997. Further findings in the research data. In W. Taylor. Ed. Too valuable to lose: exploring the causes and cures of missionary attrition. Pasadena, CA: William Carey Library. Pp. 105-125.

Gamble, K. and Lovell-Hawker, D. 2008. Expatriates. In J. S. Keystone, P. E.

Kozarsky, D. O. Freedman, H. D. Nothdurft and B. A. Connor, eds. *Travel   Medicine*   Chapter   30.   Available   from http://www.expertconsultbook.com

Kohlberg, Lawrence. 1981. *The philosophy of moral development: moral stages and the idea of justice.* San Francisco: Harper and Row.

Lambert, Howard. 1972. *A comparison of Jane Loevinger's theory of ego development and Lawrence Kohlbergs theory of moral development.* Chicago: University of Chicago Library Microfilm Duplication.

Lingenfelter, Judith, and Sherwood. 2003. *Teaching cross-culturally— an incarnational model for living and teaching.* Grand Rapids: Baker Academic.

Lingenfelter, Sherwood, and Mayers, M. K. 1986. 2003. *Ministering cross-culturally.* Grand Rapids: Baker Books.

_____. 1988. *Questionnaire for ministering cross-culturally.* Grand Rapids: Baker Books.

McCubbbin, H. I., and Lavee, Y. 1986. Strengthening army families: a family life cycle stage perspective. *Evaluation Program and Planning.* Vol. 9, No. 3, pp. 221-231.

McAllister, Laurel. 2001. *Code of Best Practice in Member Care.* Evangelical Fellowship of Canada. Vancouver, BC, Canada.

People in Aid. 2003. Code of Good Practice. Retrieved from http://peopleinaid.org/pool/files/code/code-en.pdf

Powel, John, and Bowers, J.M. 2003. *Enhancing Missionary Vitality*. Palmer Lake, CO: Missionary Training International Publ.

Riesland, N. 2008. Healthcare abroad. In J. S. Keystone, P. E. Kozarsky, D. O. Freedman, H. D. Nothdurft and B. A. Connor , eds. *Travel Medicine* (Chapter 50). Available from http://www.expertconsultbook.com

Ritschard, Hans. 2002. *In Doing Member Care Well*, by O'Donnell, Kelly. Pasadena CA: William Carey Library. P. 414.

Chapter 6
When Should People Leave the Field?
At-Risk Situations, Interventions, and
Voluntary Departure

Sometimes in spite of good screening, workers on the field experience extreme situations which require more resources than can be provided in a field setting. This can also happen when inadequate screening allows persons or families to go to the field when they lack the personal resilience and coping skills to meet all the challenges. Discerning when a need has risen to this level requires good observational skills and open communication with the person or family who has encountered trouble.

Problems that generally cannot be handled on the field include physical illnesses or burnout. Serious psychological conditions may also need to be cared for off the field, such as severe depression, self-destructive behaviors, behaviors harmful to others (such as child abuse or family violence), and psychotic behaviors (unless it is a temporary reaction to a medication). Some severe mental disorders may "surface" due to extreme stress and plunge the person and family into crisis, including bipolar disorder and dissociative identity disorder. Recovery from being victimized through rape or assault may require care off the field. Maladaptive coping responses at their worst may require leaving the field, including addictions of all kinds, and moral failures (sexual, financial, and ethical). Any criminal actions require immediate and careful assessment, perhaps including consultation with the home country embassy and local law. Any illness so serious that death is pending will likely require evacuation to a safer environment with more medical help available.

Other situations which are not so serious may also call for the worker or family to return to the home or sending country for further assistance. These would include families in which discipline is too punitive or abusive. Chronic illnesses that do not improve with available resources or are due to the allocation (such as inescapable, severe air pollution) also necessitate the worker's return to the home country. If chronic illness also places heavy demands on the local support system (i.e., the team), the situation needs to be evaluated in light of the needs of all involved. If a person is persistently unproductive, for whatever cause, something is amiss and needs evaluation.

When entrenched anger is causing damage to relationships within the family or team or with national colleagues, this requires serious intervention. This kind of relational issue hinders the overall functioning of any group. If the angry person is responsive to help, is willing to own the problem and to work on it, he or she may grow while on the field. But, if all strategies for help are resisted, the field leadership team may have to require the person to return to the home country. When a worker is sent home, the stress of returning to the home country must be weighed against the detrimental effects of allowing the person to stay on the field. Once back home, the worker should be under accountability to the home office to ensure that help is given and progress is made.

Administrative Questions for
Sticky Personnel Issues:

1. What is the observed problem? What is wrong?
2. How serious is it?
3. Who is being hurt?
4. Are things getting better or likely to get better?
5. What administrative help does the person and the team need?
6. What has been tried? How was it received?
7. If we do nothing, what is likely to happen?
8. How much demand is the person making on support systems?
9. What responsibility do we as leaders have: spiritual, ethical, organizational, and legal?
10. What role should the sending country's home office play?
11. Have we consulted appropriately on this issue?

Include the troubled person: In every situation, the person or family involved must have input into the decision—to go or to stay. Often, people will not want to go home, as leaving entails a great deal of work and adjustment. The final decision should be made by the administrator in charge and knowledgeable resource people. The decision should take into account the needs of the local group of colleagues, such as the drain on group resources. Security and safety measures should be considered. The goal is to arrive at a decision which gives the best possibility of recovery for the person or family. It also involves assessing the impact of the detrimental behavior on the team and mission.

Follow protocol: Once a decision is made to return the person or family to their sending country for help, the supervisor and personnel worker or Member Care Facilitator (MCF) must follow existing procedures and policies. Policy should require a face-to-face meeting on the field to arrive at a decision about departure but also for discussion about issues and changes that must take place before a return to the field will be permitted. There must be a written record of this having been done while the member is still on site. This record should be reviewed by both parties, and copies kept for their reference.

A good personnel procedure is to document the problem—how it developed and how it has been addressed. Troublesome behaviors should be identified, specifically, and notes made about when they were called to the person's attention. The person should be given the opportunity to correct the written record. How the member is treated by administrators, leaders, and colleagues during this tense and embarrassing time will have an impact on the recovery process, and on the possibility of the member returning later. There is also the inevitable impact on the local group of colleagues. They must be informed. How this is done and how the troubled worker is treated will enhance or damage trust between the local group of workers and their leaders.

The organization is best served if the member can be restored and returned to a higher level of health and wholeness than he or she experienced before the failure. The member is best served if he or she receives compassionate attention and professional care so that return to service is recommended.

We could easily identify people who are prone to failure. However, any one of us is vulnerable. Anyone can become discouraged and seek comfort in the wrong ways and soon find that comfort has led to an addiction. It is important to understand that the "stress of the unexpected" often has unexpected consequences. It acts, as someone put it, like putting Miracle-Gro on our faults and flaws and weaknesses. A crucial factor is that in many places, the presence and strength of oppressive evil can debilitate us and frighten us.

Voluntary departure from the field also happens, for many reasons. We will discuss the most common reasons why people who have committed to humanitarian work sometimes make the choice to return to the home land.

Interventions and Leaders' Responses

Any intervention for any cause or need should always be made in cooperation with the person, stressing the goal of restoration. People in depression, burnout, PTSD, or adjustment disorders are in a fragile state. They need support and wise intervention, not criticism or judgment for their loss of energy and diminished effectiveness. This applies also to persons who have suffered some kind of failure or are stuck in a chronic state of sickness or need.

Four Levels of Intervention

These levels and kinds of intervention apply to the whole life process and life span. They are not only for situations of crisis such as depression, burnout, PTSD, or adjustment disorder. They also apply to other serious kinds of depletion. They are useful for sizing up and addressing almost any health-related issue.

Level 1. Primary intervention includes awareness and knowledge of the person's state of being when healthy and untroubled. At this level, leaders or other persons of influence declare, as with a newborn baby, "Isn't she/he beautiful!" It is a time of noticing and affirming health, and normalcy. It is a time for strengthening development, enhancing life satisfaction, protecting health and preventing illness, and promoting **optimal** growth. At this level, interventions are not dramatic. They include many "every day" activities to teach, model, nurture, nourish, communicate, inoculate against stress, encourage group skills, facilitate healthy groups and organizations and promote pastoral care.

Agencies can provide many resources at this primary level, such as culture classes, interpersonal skills workshops, marriage retreats, parenting courses, training of other kinds, counseling, performance reviews, and other job-related care. Access to spiritual and pastoral exercises and care is also very important, to build faith and to strengthen the community of faith. Opportunities for continuing education and periodic updates in one's career field or knowledge base can help to maintain and increase intellectual and job competency. Studies of personality type are enormously helpful in promoting both self-understanding and relationship insights to help teams. When people are cared for on a regular basis and there is ample opportunity to share with each other and leaders about daily life and work, ongoing positive adjustment and fruitfulness is likely to occur. Ensuring that workers take regular vacations is another important form of level 1 care.

Level 2. The secondary level of intervention needs to be activated periodically, not just when health or well-being seem to be deteriorating. This is the "Catch it quick!" level. With good observation and the right tools, one can observe microscopic changes and minute disturbances which reveal the beginning of the physical disease or social dis-ease. A trained person can detect incipient changes or potential problems in time to stop and reverse the process and facilitate restoration to normal.

In an agency the Member Care Facilitator or other person can suggest screening tests, provide inventories, and offer questionnaires to discover problems. The focus at this stage is on training and teaching recovery techniques to restore equilibrium which may be faltering. Each person can work proactively at good health habits. As leaders, we need to urge life-style change as both restorative and proactive steps for improvement.   At   this   stage   or level at which we can detect incipient damage, the agency can provide training to certain personnel to look for *signs* of trouble at the cellular level physically and in emotional responses and social relationships. Individuals can also be taught what signs of distress to look for in one's own life and in one's spouse and family.

Level 3. The tertiary level of interventions become necessary when the person feels or says, "I hurt!" The hurting person has become aware of *symptoms;* trouble or distress comes to consciousness. Others too may note that the person is in distress. (A *sign* is usually not detected until it becomes a *symptom*. For example, a person has *signs* of illness going on before a heart attack, but these may not be felt or be visible to the eye. Only when a *symptom* such as pain or shortness of breath appears, and perhaps a heart attack occurs, does the patient realize the damage that has already been going on.)

At this level, the Member Care Facilitator, the physician, or a mental health professional or another relevant leader needs to become involved in the process. This includes diagnosing the problem, discovering the root causes, and treating the symptoms to reverse the process and restore to normal functioning. Tests, questions, interviews, examinations, counsel, treatment, prescriptions and proscription are typical interventions for this level. Life-style changes become imperative at this point to prevent further and more severe states from developing. This may be possible in the field situation, but may need resources beyond those available in many allocations.

Level 4. Crisis, the fourth level of intervention might be termed "Call 911!" At this stage, a situation is life-threatening; there is a physical illness or a psychosocial crisis. The aim here is first to save life, then to reverse the process of the disease and to restore function. Typically once life-saving measures have been taken, long-term treatment and therapies are called for. To survive and recover, the person must be willing to radically change his or her life-style.
In humanitarian agencies, people may experience crises in their personal lives, their spiritual lives, or in job-related areas. Long-term discontent with one's organization, often resulting from a poor "fit," or from feeling that leaders are not responsive can erode relationships and health and lead to this dismal or disastrous level. Of course, traumatic events and dangerous environments also may lead to the crisis. Almost always, persons reaching this crisis level need to be allowed to give up their responsibilities and to return to their home

country in order to receive appropriate help and have time for recovery. This level of intervention requires the greatest investment of resources for the agency and necessitates the most change in the life of the person who is suffering.

Special Interventions

Debriefing—An Important Means of Assessment and Intervention
For decades the military and other institutions in society have practiced debriefing, which is to review a process or situation which members have gone through. The purpose has been to examine what took place and what the outcomes were, including whether things went "right," as planned, or whether they went "wrong," and to attempt to examine ways in which a similar, future situation might be averted. This has been adapted by the humanitarian, cross-cultural service world in recent decades, with the same purposes and goals—to try to understand what members have experienced and to improve the system and its approach.

What is debriefing?
- It is an intentional, specific and scheduled listening time during which a person tells his or her story, from his or her own point of view, to a caring and trained friend or small group.
- It usually follows an intense and unusual experience but may be routine.
- It is for the purpose of supporting the person, caring about and understanding the story as much as possible, accepting both the story and the person telling it without judgment.
- It provides an opportunity for feedback, perspective and help.
- It is for the benefit of the person being debriefed as well as for the group or agency.
- It includes both fact and feeling.
- Eventually, it will include reframing and integrating the story into the person's life experience.

Note: The debriefer facilitates remembering, sorting and consideration of the experience, but the information is "owned" by the person being debriefed. It is usually for the well-being of the individual that debriefing is being done.

What debriefing is not
- It is not counseling, therapy, social interchange or simply catharsis.
- It is not for the sake of the debriefer, to satisfy his or her curiosity or as an opportunity to share his own experience.
- It is not solely for the benefit of the organization (in the sense that an interview would be).
- Note: In an interview, the organization, not the member, is the client. This affects method, content, control and confrontation.

How Debriefing Helps:
- It helps us to process feelings, such as frustration, helplessness, vulnerability, irritability, nervousness, regret, grief, fear, hope, inadequacy, guilt, and denial.
- It is a scheduled and structured event which helps a person to sort out an experience and to discover that someone else can share the burden. It provides support, shares the burden and removes a sense of isolation.
- It can help to bring about change through reframing, in the person and in the organization.

Who Needs Debriefing?
- We all need it.
- Some people need more debriefing than others.
- Some events need more debriefing than others.
- Note: Positive experiences should also be debriefed, e.g., a major accomplishment, completion of a significant project, personal or family victories or achievements. Sharing the delight with people who know how to listen doubles the goodness and bonds people together.

Necessary Debriefing Skills:
- Listening, drawing out, and giving feedback in a nonthreatening way.
- Seeing and accurately interpreting verbal and non-verbal cues.
- Providing assessment and direction.
- Keeping confidences!

- Staying focused, with no tangents, emphasizing the most important things.
- Calmness under pressure and having faith in God.
- Managing intense feelings—your own and the person's.
- Maintaining perspective and helping the person to "reframe" the event or situation.
- Providing resources as needed.

What Happens When We Do Not Debrief?
- We brush the experience aside as unimportant.
- We suspect that we also, and not just the experience, are unimportant.
- We lose an opportunity to process.
- We do not receive validation or correction.
- We may not make necessary changes or grow as a result of the event.
- We may lose the opportunity to bring God into the event.
- We may not ask His wisdom to process the event, or to give Him praise.
- We lose the opportunity to pass our learning along to someone else.

Debriefer Integrity: What does the debriefer do or not do with the information he or she has heard? What does he/she do with the facts? What does he/she do with his or her feelings? The most important matter is to act with integrity, keeping confidences and being discreet, sharing only as it is appropriate to help the person or to inform leadership of necessary information. Sharing the information is to benefit the person and to help the organization improve. For the believer, the debriefer can also be a bridge to God and spiritual resources. He or she must never gossip or share the information inappropriately! He or she can follow up appropriately and periodically.

Conducting the Debriefing

For routine debriefings, such as leaving the field or re-entry to the home land, the following is a helpful set of guidelines. The next section will describe the process for post-trauma or crisis debriefings.

I. **Planning for the debriefing**

A. Choose the interviewer. Who should conduct the debriefing? The best person is one who genuinely knows and cares for the person, couple, or family, and not necessarily the "personnel person." Important personal qualities include warmth, caring, loving communication, a welcoming spirit, and positive attitudes. Important communication skills include careful and attentive listening, the ability to ask artful questions to clarify, give feedback and summarize.

B. Choose the place: Set up the interview in a comfortable room with living room type furniture, if possible. Avoid an office with distracting furniture and papers. Provide for privacy, not a place where people pass through or can observe. (Remember, you don't know what you might hear!) Turn off the telephone or have calls held. Create a calm and beautiful setting, if possible. How is the temperature of the room, taking into consideration the climate from which the person has just come?

C. Create the emotional climate or environment of safety: Creating the right climate is crucial! This is done through the physical setting, the personal qualities and communication skills of the interviewer and the emotions projected by the interviewer (both verbal and non-verbal). If a person feels judged, labeled, misunderstood, not believed, etc., these feelings will PREVENT an open and honest conversation. They promote fear and block you (the interviewer) from hearing the real needs (at the surface and deeper) of the person. You may never hear the whole story or all the truth. People will give you "safe" information which obscures the reality they have experienced. (Or it obscures other important information, such as the "real" reason they decide to leave the organization or the field.)

Create a climate of care. You might offer tea or coffee to put the person at ease. Communicate a genuine desire to know what the person or couple has experienced. Demonstrate caring. Be unhurried. Avoid defensiveness, especially if you hear something that might reflect on you, the leadership, or on the organization. Avoid being an examiner or inquisitor. Without interfering with the flow of the story, give frequent acknowledgment and appreciation.

D. Time frame: Be open-ended. Take as long as is needed. This might be two hours for some, and as much as four or five for others. Remember, you are reviewing YEARS of significant life! Each person needs to be heard, so take the time to let each one feel he or she has been heard. You are asking the person to share about life, health and ministry for the last several years. That deserves at least a few hours of your time! Choose a time which won't be fogged by jet-lag!

II. **Have your goals for the debriefing clearly in mind.**
A. Enable the member(s) to feel heard and cared for by the organization. (Loved, cared for, valued, appreciated, supported, welcomed back; that you are interested in the whole family and whole person, etc.)

B. Hear and understand the person's experience. This involves careful and attentive listening.

C. Empathize with the impact of the whole field experience; sorrow with them for the difficulties and rejoice with them for the good things.

D. Help the person to start gaining perspective on his or her time of service. This perspective may change as the person gets further away from the experience, but talking about it is the first step to gaining perspective.

E. Help the person summarize his or her experience in a way that will enable him or her to recount it to supporters and family.

F. From an organizational viewpoint, glean information and insight on what the organization and leadership are doing well and what could be done better.

G. Identify needs and mobilize resources to meet the member's needs.

III. **Conducting the debriefing interview**

A. Ask the person or couple to tell their story. "Tell me about your term? What was it like?" (With a couple, ask both husband and wife to tell their story. Give as much time to each one as needed.)

B. After you have heard the whole narrative, ask these questions, one by one:
- What were some of the high points?
- What were some of the low points?
- What do you feel you have accomplished? Ministry, relationships, language learning, cultural adaptation, impact upon the family, etc.
- What was the most difficult thing for you?
- Did you have people to support and encourage you emotionally? Did you feel   emotionally supported?
- How do you feel right now, overall, about your time in _____?
- Is there anything you wish you had done differently? Or that you would do next time?
- Is there something you wish you had known before you went?
- Did you feel you had enough support from the organization?
- In what way could your leaders or the organization have supported you better? (Part of this question is: what kind of things would let you know that you were cared for?)

C. Inquire about immediate and furlough needs:
- Right now, what are you feeling the need for? (e.g. rest, getting away for a while, not interacting with others, celebration, etc.)
- Would you like us to contact your pastor or supporting churches to let them know of your needs?
- What material needs do you have? (Car, housing, money, dental/medical, clothing, etc.)
- Who is going to help you with obtaining or arranging for these? How are your children doing with this transition?
- Can we help directly or by contacting or encouraging your churches or supporters?
- What's ahead for you right away? Is this plan what you really need? Do you feel "locked in" to some plan that isn't what you need right now? (For example, the furlough plan submitted six

months ago may not take into account the current exhaustion or changed   needs   of   the   person.)

- What's ahead of you in the next three to six months? (Help the person evaluate the plan for its reasonableness and attainability (For example, a plan such as visiting seventy churches in ninety days is neither reasonable nor healthy.)
- What's ahead of you in the next six to twelve months or longer? Help the person evaluate whether this is a realistic goal.

D.   Bringing   a   loving   closure   to   the   interview Summarize what you have heard. Tell the story back to the person in a nutshell, mentioning the good and the difficult. Recap the needs of the person. This is to demonstrate that you have heard, and to allow for correction of any errors of perception.

Validate the person's experience, especially the difficult ones. This means letting the person know that it was hard (or great, or whatever), that you do understand, that missionaries often feel that way, that normal people in hard situations often react as they have, etc.

Ask, "What could we as an organization have done differently?" Summarize and repeat back what you have heard.

Express appreciation for what the person has gone through and what he or she has accomplished. Give thanks from you, the organization, on behalf of the Kingdom of God! (If you don't express gratitude, who will?)

You might want to close with a prayer of thanksgiving to God for his protection, his enablement, and his leading for their time of home assignment.

IV. **Interviewer tasks after the interview**
Reflect on what you have heard. Assess whether any special needs exist which require special resources or help. For example, is this person depressed? Exhausted, depleted, burned out? Are they physically ill?

Does he or she LOOK and SOUND healthy? Should you or the person consult a specialist for some kind of care?

A. Write a summary of the person's experience—2 or 3 pages at least.

B. Write your assessment of how they are doing: well, exhausted, depressed, depleted, need for specialized care, degree of need, kind of support needed from organization, etc. Make it clear that this is YOUR assessment, YOUR impressions, not a diagnosis. Don't use labels!

C. Organizational resources to mobilize.

D. Issues for the organization to work on.

E. Review a copy of your report with the person before passing it on to anyone else. This will allow you to correct any errors of fact or perceptions, and allow you to clarify expectations. It will take you a step further in helping the person feel cared for and understood! You will also avoid any errors which might cause embarrassment for you or the person by making certain the story is accurate before it goes to anyone else. (That's worth a lot!)

V. **Follow up after the interview**
A. One to three days later:
- "I'm so glad we had the time together. How are you feeling today about what you shared? Is there anything else you would like to add or clarify?"
- "Is there anything I can clarify for you?"
- "Are you getting the resources that you need?"

B. One week later:
- "How are you feeling now as you have had more time to think? Anything more you would like to add?"
- "How are things coming together? Car? Clothing?"
- "Are your immediate plans working out?"
- Reinforce what you or the organization expects, such as that the person must arrange for counseling, medical care, skill development, education, etc.

C. One month or so later: Variable, depending upon the degree of need.
- "How are you doing?"
- "Do you have what you need?"
- "How are your plans working out?"
- "How has it been to come back to your family and your churches?"
- "Is there anything else we can do to help? Have any other needs arisen which you didn't foresee?"

D. End of six months of home assignment or at end of home assignment.
- "How has your time been?"
- "Are you feeling refreshed, ready to return?"
- "Are you needing anything before you return?"

If an agency provides regular debriefings members will feel more cared for. The agency itself will benefit, first by having personnel who believe the organization cares, and secondly because many valuable insights can be gained about system issues, policies, and practices. When a crisis or trauma has taken place, a different type and level of debriefing is needed. This might be a personal trauma such as a robbery or a home invasion, a group level crisis such as kidnapping of one of the members, or a natural disaster which affects the agency members and the surrounding population. This same process can prevent the development of post-traumatic stress disorder (PTSD) and enable everyone who participates to benefit from the knowledge and support of each other.

Critical Incident Stress Debriefing (CISD)[39]
An Important Means of Trauma Intervention

The origin of this process is Dr. Jeffrey Mitchell and his colleague George Everly. This is a crucial way to provide support after crisis or trauma and is well worth the time and the energy involved. It provides a way to connect, to listen, to support, and to give instructions on self-care following a crisis. This level of debriefing can be done by "laypeople" who have received training. It is considered a peer-to-peer kind of help rather than a professional mental health process. Dr. Mitchell developed it in the beginning for use by firemen, emergency medical responders, policemen and other responders. It has since been used with many groups and in many diverse situations. For crisis matters and critical incidents, this seven-step process used with groups or individuals helps to structure the chaos of the experience. The approach has been well-tested and has been adapted by the Gardners for use in cross-cultural ministry situations.

Stage 1	Introduction	To introduce intervention team members, explain process, set expectations.
Stage 2	Facts	To describe traumatic event from each participant's perspective, on a cognitive level.
Stage 3	Thoughts	To allow participants to describe cognitive reactions and to transition to emotional reactions.
Stage 4	Reactions	To identify the most traumatic aspect of the event for the participants.
Stage 5	Symptoms	To identify personal symptoms of distress and transition back to the cognitive level.

---

[39] See www.icisdf.org.

| Stage 6 | Teaching | To educate as to normal reactions and adaptive coping mechanisms (i.e., stress management). Provides a cognitive anchor. |
| Stage 7 | Re-Entry | To clarify ambiguities and prepare for termination of the debriefing. |

Voluntary Leaving

Though we have considered who should not remain on the field and reasons why, it is helpful to also remember that others may make the choice to leave based on none of the factors described. Sometimes a person or family prepares thoroughly for a specific work in a specific location, and once arriving there, finds conditions intolerable. Or, after an extended period of engagement with the task, the person or family may decide it is not a good fit. Leaving a field assignment is very difficult, especially because the decision to depart may look to other people like failure. Likely, this decision to depart will have impact at the personal and family level, on the team, on the agency, and on the constituency back home. Such voluntary departure from a field assignment and withdrawal from an organization is one cause of attrition. People involved at all levels will find it wrenching.

We discuss this with sensitivity, as we want to be careful to avoid causing shame or placing unnecessary blame on those who make this tough call. In general, attrition is defined as the act of individuals leaving their humanitarian assignment and returning to civilian life. Sadly, too often attrition has been defined as failure. To understand attrition, we must look at current trends in cross-cultural worker populations, the different kinds of leavings and the issues that often prompt the decisions to leave.

Contributing factors may include:

- Sense of entitlement—expectations were not clarified. Something was assumed to be the norm but was not met.
- Generational differences which make foreign work more difficult for some people—For example, some persons go into humanitarian aid work as a second career. Thus they are older,

often less flexible, and may be less prepared for hardship and deprivation because they have become used to a more comfortable lifestyle.

- False hopes—For example, younger persons may feel they do not understand, and are not understood by, older colleagues. Perhaps they have been told that they have leadership gifts and expect or demand a leadership role without first earning the credibility necessary to function well as a leader in a given place or entity.
- Dysfunctional family backgrounds may have left the person with acute personal needs or issues which worsen with the stress of field work.
- More involvement is expected or desired by the sending organizations than the person expected. Or, in a given society, the emphasis on charitable, humanitarian work may have diminished.

Some of the reasons why people leave voluntarily include discouragement, loss of vision, disillusionment, and health problems. A transfer within the organization to another location or another type of work, or secondment to another organization may prompt discontent and lack of fulfillment. Death of a spouse often causes the surviving spouse to want to return to the sending country to be nearer the extended family. Empty nest parents may feel responsible for their extended

family, and are often concerned for their children's education. They may also feel obliged to return to the homeland to care for aging parents. Sometimes these issues can be handled with a leave of absence, a study leave, or home assignment. We all recognize too that graceful, timely retirement is a natural cause for attrition. At times, someone leaves for the opportunity for marriage back in the home land.

Issues prompting reassessment or re-evaluation of assignment:
- Adoption—by singles or of racially mixed, special needs children.
- Aging—health care, retirement, financial matters.
- Crisis management and crisis care—aftermath, time out for recovery.
- Interpersonal relationships—conflict; multinational, inter-generational, gender issues.

- Cross-cultural marriages—partners from two cultures end up in a third.
- Administrative overload, leadership succession, lack of qualifications for leadership.
- Workload, over work, mismatch with gifts and interests.
- Complex and troubling personal and relational issues.
- Oppression and evil takes a huge toll on workers in the field setting.

All of these matters are the concern of the individual worker, the sending institution, and the field agency. Good assessment, training and placement <u>must</u> be coupled with lavish communication and a commitment to ongoing member care and support. Implicit in organizational health must be an ethos of care for individuals, families, and attention given to all phases of their life and work.

Fortunately, generosity prevails and characterizes the humanitarian world so that cross-agency help is frequent and vital. We know of many heart-warming examples of workers reaching across national, cultural, and organization boundaries to lay down their lives for one another. For example, during the evacuation of humanitarian workers in one war zone, some workers refused to leave in the airlift because their government only wanted to take their own citizens. They stayed until their colleagues could be rescued together with them.

We recognize that not all agencies are large and well-resourced, and not all humanitarian workers work in contexts where they can expect help from their agency. We know that some workers go out to serve independently. Some people work in very isolated settings, far from oversight and care. In situations such as these, the responsibility for attending to their needs will rest strongly on the individuals themselves. They must take initiative for their own emotional, spiritual, and physical preparation and well-being. We strongly recommend, always, that people go abroad with established organizations so that they have every advantage of good selection, good training, and on-the-field care. Most of the "worst case scenarios" of need and trauma we have seen have been in independent workers who have no backup system to help them when trouble strikes.

Summary

Every agency must make periodic assessments of their personnel, to establish whether their workers are still healthy and effective. Due to the extreme stresses and dangers of humanitarian service in many parts of the world, workers meet hazardous conditions, events, and troubles. Agencies must be alert to attend to their members, to determine how they are doing and whether help can be provided in the field setting or the organization. Some situations are too complex or critical to allow persons to stay in their allocations, so bringing them back to the home land is required. In other situations, especially those with a "poor fit" factor, voluntary departure may take place. At any level, agency leaders such as the Member Care Facilitator and human resources personnel must be prepared to intervene at the appropriate level and to provide resources to address the difficulties or crises.

References and Recommended Reading

Hay, Rob, et al. 2007. *Worth keeping: global perspective on best practice in missionary retention*. Pasadena, CA: William Carey Library.

Kinchin, David. 2007. *A guide to psychological debriefing: managing emotional decompression and post-traumatic stress debriefing*. London and Philadelphia: Jessica Kingley Pub.

Mitchell, Jeffrey, and Eberly, George. 1996. *Critical incident stress debriefing: an operations manual for the prevention of traumatic stress among emergency service and disaster workers*. Ellicott City, MD: Chevron Pub.

_____, and Resnik, H.L.P. 1981. *Emergency response to crisis: a crisis intervention guidebook for emergency service personnel*. Bowie, MD: R.J. Brady Co.

Taylor, William. 1997. *Too valuable to lose: exploring the causes and cures of missionary attrition*. Pasadena, CA: William Carey Library.

Chapter 7
The Scope of Care
Diversity—Who Needs Tailored Care?

Our goal in the field of member care is to provide what is appropriate for all the persons within an agency. This is a tall order, and requires foresight, insight, and awareness of the diversity within the membership. All that we have written is appropriate, and yet care can be tailored with the needs of certain groups in mind. Some of these groups are more "at risk" and thus deserve special consideration. Others are sometimes overlooked and thus it is worth making overt what is sometimes hidden or taken for granted.

The greater our awareness of who is among us and who we consist of as a group, the greater the likelihood that we will take the needs of everyone into account. Single parents face particular challenges. They and their children have needs that are somewhat different from two-parent families serving in humanitarian agencies, roles, and allocations. Young moms with pre-school aged children are at greater risk for depression. Couples need time to keep their marriages healthy. Single persons make enormous contributions to the humanitarian world, but may sometimes feel overlooked when family needs seem to predominate. Leaders may also be under-appreciated and their needs overlooked, as they are taken for granted because they are in positions of authority. Members who work with home as their "office" or workplace need special consideration and guidance. We want to address some of the concerns of these groups within the membership.

The Family in Cross-Cultural Service

When families go abroad to engage in humanitarian work, they go together. This is both a blessing and a challenge. They always have each other to rely upon and can learn together. They can support and encourage each other in the process of adjustment. They can take pleasure together in learning language and culture and seeing the fruit of their labors. They can speak their mother tongue even in a foreign culture because they have each other. Along with these wonderful advantages come complexities, for there are more adjustments to make with several persons in a household.

Finding proper schooling, a safe neighborhood, and special activities for their children adds to the adjustment load of the parents. The mother has to learn to cook differently, with different food, different shopping, and perhaps coping with household help to which she is not accustomed. Her adjustment will be more complex because as the "heart of the family," her responses have so much to do with the adjustment and happiness of the children. She will likely have to reduce her own contributions to the mission's goals because of the competing needs of the family. When children become ill or have special needs, this role conflict can increase. An understanding supervisor and organization are a great help!

A father's life as a husband and worker requires adjustment in fewer areas than does the life of the wife and mother. Chances are he will still go to work each day, and though his role may be new or he may have to enact an accustomed role in new ways, it will include fewer changes or adjustments than what his wife faces. It seems that mothers bear the brunt of adaptation, given that housing, food, homemaking, medical care, education of children, social life, and most other arenas of life fall to them. All of this is in addition to a mother's own career needs or contributions to the life of the organization.

One study emphasizes four elements of overseas effectiveness. Not surprisingly, they put family adjustment first. The authors cite 1) personal and family unit adjustment, 2) satisfaction with living overseas, 3) engagement in enjoyable activities, and 4) successful coping with day-to-day life as vital aspects of adaptation (Hawes and Kealey, 1984).[40]

Children on the Go

When parents take their children abroad, they become a vital part of the humanitarian effort itself. They become ambassadors, and often enable the parents to make friends faster and to be trusted more quickly. Those who are in need and being served are more likely to trust a family who comes to live among them. Children tend to learn the language faster and better, and thus help to build friendships with the local community. This actually may be a dramatic advantage. One ten-year-old we knew learned Russian so quickly, she began to conduct the family business and translate for her parents! We see this same phenomenon in our home countries when foreigners come to live among us. Parents take joy in their children, especially when they see them adjusting in positive ways.

Of course, having children can also bring about special problems and greater anxieties. If the environment is unsafe, parents may worry about their security. This may be related to people, or to other dangers. Friends of ours were shocked to learn their boys had been playing daily in an empty lot next door, where land mines were later discovered! Fear of kidnapping might be realistic in some countries. Having to restrict the public appearance of daughters is another realistic stress in some cultures.

Ted Ward reminds us of how positive outcomes outweigh the challenges:[41]

> In every family, the overseas sojourn will be good news and bad news, but as far as the welfare of children is concerned, the good news is likely to outweigh the bad news. For a start, consider the stress on the family unit as a whole. The move itself is likely to be quite stressful. Packing things up, giving away things that have meaning for the children far in excess of their value in the adult world, leaving friends and family far behind, facing the unknown of neighborhood, housing,

---

[40] In Ward, *Living Overseas: a Book of Preparations,* p. 176.
[41] Ward, p. 249.

schooling, and new friends of a different sort—all
these are understandable sources of anxiety or
unhappiness, and they aren't easy to face. But
children are likely to be less perturbed and more
resilient than their parents. Parents often worry on
behalf of their children about things that the
children themselves take in stride. So look at the
bright side: children who grow up in intercultural
environments can gain a global perspective that
will have a lasting influence on their appreciation
and acceptance of other human beings.

The literature about the great people of the world, especially those who
have become ambassadors and statesmen, is replete with the biographies
of men and women who grew up as children in cross-cultural or
multicultural settings. Outstanding writers, like Pearl Buck, have often
come from such a background.[42]

Having raised two sons overseas, I believe that the benefits greatly
outweighed the struggles (Gardner). Rearing my three children in the
Amazon jungle of Peru gave my children amazing advantages in life for
which they remain grateful (Dodds). They say they would not change
that experience. It has shaped their lives in innumerable positive ways.
It is impossible to place a monetary value on the ability to be bilingual
and bicultural, appreciating and living with diversity.

What an agency can do to enrich the children of the members is
important. Providing guidance about schooling, whether home-
schooling or formal schooling, is a huge help.[43] Making sure that any
special needs are addressed is very important. "Special needs" not only
includes remedial help for those who struggle but also opportunity-
related help for those who are gifted. We were privileged that in our
setting, one of our sons could play in the National Symphony because
our organization gave us flexibility which allowed him to travel
(Dodds). When another son needed emergency surgery, that same

---

[42] Novels by Pearl Buck include *Dragon Seed, The Good Earth, The Three
Daughters of Madam Liang, and Pavilion of Women.* Reading such works is a great
part of preparation for moving to another culture.
[43] SHARE is an organization for resourcing home school parents who work in cross-
cultural settings. Their book, *Fitted Pieces,* lists a marvelous array of resources.
www.shareeducation.org.

flexibility allowed my husband to travel for his care. Either set of needs, for help and care or for opportunity, may mean parents need more flexibility in work or vacation schedules in order to attend to the children's needs. Agencies can provide in other ways for children, such as by creating communities which are educative and supportive, so that all children are a vital part of the group. In return, adults gain friends and fun activities through the young among them. They can also connect parents to inter-agency resources. This is especially important in remote allocations and when parents home-school.

An extensive study was conducted during the 1990s called MK Cart CORE. A highly respected, well-qualified, and well-equipped committee studied families in foreign service, and the impact of foreign living on children. The term *Third Culture Kids* (TCKs) came into vogue as a result. (Later the term *global nomads* became popular through the work of Pollock and Van Reken.) We highly recommend taking a look at those findings.[44]

The study found that if field workers experience multifaceted support by their organization, they benefit in all aspects of family life. If the organization fails to support families, these families will experience higher levels of stress, expressed in resentment, discord, conflict, and lowered satisfaction.

Moms with Young Children

Various studies in recent years indicate that in North America, stay-at-home moms with pre-school children experience depression at a rate, higher than that of the rest of the population. A major factor in this is social isolation. The mother, likely young herself, has few social outlets and less life experience for coping with adversity. In the home land, members of the extended family are seldom available to help, as grandmothers and aunts are likely in the work force. Overseas, there is

---

[44] *The Family in Mission: Understanding and Caring for Those Who Serve*, edited by Leslie A. Andrews (2004).

almost never any family help. Children are often ill during the first few years of life, so a mom can feel trapped. Getting out is a problem, as either taking young children out is fatiguing or finding a trustworthy person to care for them is difficult. When children are ill, it may be impossible to leave home. Husbands or partners may work long hours or find it disagreeable to help.

We were asked to consult with one young family living abroad, to help them deal with their excessive stresses. They were allocated in a country where women are not allowed to leave the home without a male relative. Their little home was in a poor neighborhood. The children often played out of doors, where a huge drainage ditch funneled sewage and other waste water down the street. The father was gone long hours with his teaching job and riding public transportation. The children were ill more than usual, perhaps due to the polluted environment. We were not surprised to find both parents very depressed and disheartened. When we met them, they were very disillusioned with their organization, who they said had not even bothered to put them in touch with any other expats with whom they might have built friendships. They bitterly said, "We think they sent us here just so they could add another country to their letterhead!"

Even in the best of settings, MCFs (Member Care Facilitators) and other leaders need to be especially sensitive to the needs of mothers with young children. They need help, encouragement, periodic outings, and relief from some of the hard work of caring for a home and children. We believe that having an active role in the work of the organization is very helpful to mothers, even if it is for just a few hours a week. This provides some adult companionship, a way to know other members of the team, and a sense of significance and accomplishment. A study by Buehler and O'Brien (2011) showed that "Part time employment appears to have some benefit for mothers and families throughout the child rearing years." We have observed this first hand.

Couples and Marriage Care

Marriage care is needed for couples engaged in humanitarian work. Couples sometimes need help from their agencies to keep their marriages healthy. The pressures of life and work can be intense. Often housing allows less privacy or the culture does not permit wives and husbands to show affection when others are present. Due to cultural expectations or financial constraints families and couples may also need to share their homes or living space with others. Single co-workers or the children of colleagues may need temporary housing. If some parents must travel, they may want to ask friends to care for their children so their schooling is not disrupted. Most caring friends and colleagues help in such situations, but this of course puts more demands on their time and energy.

Helping couples keep their relationships vital and fresh is a long-term benefit! It helps to strengthen them and reduce the possibility of affairs or other moral failure.

Agencies can help by encouraging time away periodically. They may have a "housing exchange" program so couples can exchange homes and get a fresh experience periodically without high expense. We did this for a time in our jungle locale (Dodds). Since travel was very expensive and my husband needed breaks from being on call 24/7, we worked out a plan to trade homes for a few weekends a year with a couple in an isolated setting who needed more social life. We got solitude and they got social life in this way. The agency may invite special speakers to conduct workshops or retreats or marriage enrichment weekends, and also help members find resources for marriage when they go on home leave.

Single Parents

The incidence of single parents in overseas, humanitarian work is fairly low. Yet, there are many brave and resilient parents who make this choice. When our friend Beth lost her husband to an airplane crash, she bravely kept her commitment as a nurse and reared her four children in Indonesia. The outcomes in the children's lives have been profound— all four have chosen to devote themselves as adults to humanitarian

work in difficult places of the world. When our friend Pat lost her husband in commercial jet crash, she too continued in her linguistic and literacy work, bringing up two children in our jungle locale and helping a whole ethnic group achieve literacy and schooling. She has become an expert in her field of work, and continues as an international consultant in high demand.

As co-workers and agency leaders, we need to keep in mind that single parents, whether fathers or mothers, have a double load to bear. In addition to their contributions to the humanitarian effort, they must be both father and mother, with all the physical and emotional responsibilities that requires. Our support as friends, co-workers, neighbors, and leaders can help them to carry the extra load. We can provide time off and time away periodically, and see to their needs for stimulating learning and growth. A caring community can become like extended family, with "aunts" and "uncles" who truly care about the children. We also need to remember that as their children age, grow, marry, and have children of their own, our single parent friends are not "just singles who can work longer hours." They are also grandparents who need time off for being grandparents!

Members with "Home" as Office

One of the thorny problems encountered by many non-profit workers is that home becomes the work place and work space. Usually this is due to finances, being unable to afford the cost of renting an office. It may save much time in transportation and include less risk to public dangers. Sometimes it is because hospitality is an intrinsic part of the work, such as when caring for needy children, the distressed and homeless, or persons who need family and parenting. Sometimes becoming part of the neighborhood through continual hospitality furthers the connections to persons or communities being served. For whatever reason it comes about, working "at home" creates certain tensions.

One tension is space itself. Workers wrestle with, "Shall we use the dining room? Or is the bedroom a better space?" The first option means transferring papers, books, computers, and other work items each time a meal is served. The clutter can take over! Home does not feel exactly like home! If the bedroom is the office, it too can get cluttered. Working late may mean interfering with sleep patterns of one's partner.

Working at home usually also means it is hard to separate work time from family or personal time. This is especially true for the spouse and children, who may find it difficult to differentiate what is work and what is not. They may find it stressful to have to be quieter than usual or to refrain from interrupting the person at work in the family space. For some strategies to deal with these stresses, we recommend listening to radio programs devoted to this matter.[45]

Leaders

Though many people would say leaders get more privileges and more attention, this is usually not the case when it comes to humanitarian work. After all, the reward for success is usually more work! When that is in the context of minimally funded projects or missions, it seldom means one actually earns more or gets other "benefits" or rewards. What it does mean is giving more of oneself, more often, for longer hours, and bearing a greater load! I recall that in our linguistic work in Peru, as it is in many countries, the leaders had been on the field longer. This meant that they had probably lost some of their financial donors due to aging and death during a period of time in their personal lives when expenses gradually crept up due to growing children and inflation in the field economy. Thus, serving as leaders meant they had the privilege of spending *more* of their *lower income* to carry out their duties, such as through hospitality.

Any possible benefits of being a leader are at least matched by the risks involved, which mean we need to attend to the needs of our leaders. When we consider what puts leaders at risk in situations of cross-cultural service and ministry, we must conclude that leadership choice and development are of critical importance. To underscore this importance, here are twenty-four factors that put leaders at risk, or make their task difficult.

1. Imputed power, the belief that the leader can do more than he or she is able to do within the limits of the system, and the local context.

---

[45] MemCare Radio programs are produced by TransWorld Radio. Several sessions by Dr. Lawrence and Dr. Lois Dodds are devoted to the stresses of working at home. They can be listened to or downloaded as scripts (articles) from www.heartstreamresources.org or www.memcareradio.org. (As of 2021, site is no longer available.

2. Projection of qualities not there, i.e., assuming that because he is an excellent pilot or translator, he should also be an excellent administrator.
3. Expectations of being known by the leader so my needs will be met because he is my social friend.
4. Overwork is true of most leaders. There is more to do and less time to do everything, so some things are not done well.
5. Criticism when expectations or standards are not met. These may or may not be stated. "How could my leader be reading Tom Clancy or Danielle Steel?" Or "my leader doesn't control his family very well!"
6. Disappointment by the leader of him/herself, and by others if performance falls below expectations.
7. Style differences. Competence may not be respected because his/her style is different from that of previous leaders, or judgments such as "in my country, a leader behaves like this!"
8. Social or peer isolation. Status changes relationships. When someone is chosen to be the leader, others may draw back, fail to give feedback, or no longer relate personally to the leader.
9. Loss of family time. The leader's role and high pressure of the task can lead to marital or children's problems, and little or no support and affirmation from the spouse and family.
10. Loss of personal time. Leadership pressures limit time for self-renewal, time for hobbies, and other opportunities for refreshment.
11. "Middleman" crunch. Higher authorities in the organization have expectations; they may want things done differently than the local leader is doing them. And these expectations may also be different from the expectations of those served by the leader. He's in the middle, pleasing neither side.
12. Possible loss of self-esteem because of criticism, lack of affirmation, and not being able to "stay on top" of everything.
13. Information overload. The leader needs to know a great deal to do the job well. It is hard to read everything, collect it, process it, and synthesize or extrapolate from it. In many countries, there is the additional pressure of tracking political situations.
14. Lack of a confidant to process what is happening and the impact on him or her of the leadership role, no "safe" person for him or her.

15. "People pleasing"—that is, trying to do what people want rather than doing the best thing. A leader may also try to do things that make people like him in order to be affirmed, thus avoiding doing the hard thing.

16. Expectations that the leader knows everything that is going on. Leaders usually do not know "everything" going on unless they are told. They need to be told if there is a problem so they can address it.

17. Few compensations for leader's hard work, or overwork, his commitment, etc. The "privileges" of leadership usually mean spending more of one's personal funds, time, and resources to serve the group.

18. Lack of affirmation. His authorities above him or her do not always know how excellently he or she is performing, and those observing him every day are well aware that he is not getting everything done. So affirmation may be sparse or absent.

19. Making decisions. Leaders face the need to make sudden and important decisions especially when unexpected complications or outcomes arise. Often these decisions must be made with insufficient information, and sometimes without consultation. People usually like to have a voice in decisions that affect them, but this is not always possible, especially during a crisis.

20. Communication limits. Leaders may fail to get sufficient feedback and input from others due to their own style or because they are perceived as being unapproachable. This leads to more isolation and loss of confidence because of not being "in touch" with the group's needs and thinking.

21. Need to support others without sufficient resources for one's self, the emotional "outflow" exceeds the "inflow."

22. Delegation deficits. A leader may find it hard to delegate due to lack of trust or lack of competent people, so he does too much and controls too much.

23. Young leaders may not have personal resources or life experiences to handle the pressures of leadership successfully.

24. Confrontation. Fear of this most stressful interpersonal action or lack of knowledge of how to confront properly and well adds its own stress.

These are only some of a leader's stresses. Is it any surprise, then, that when a crisis comes, the leader may be overwhelmed and unable to think and act wisely, and at the same time care well for his staff?

Leaders above the individual at any level, plus those who work "below" him or her, or as a team with him or her do well to take these factors into account and to find ways to honor and encourage the leaders. We personally did this often in our life in Peru, such as by hosting special dinners when someone went "out of office" as director or other role. Though these were personal efforts rather than organizational, they were very much appreciated and enjoyed.

Single Workers

In the organization of which I am a member, about twenty-two percent of our members are single women (Gardner). Only about five percent are single men. These single workers deserve special attention because many of their needs are unique.

Many of us presuppose that "married" is the normal condition for adults. The implication is that singleness is a temporary, abnormal and possibly pitiable state. In formulating this chapter, we sought input from many singles. We trust it accurately reflects their concerns. We realize this cannot fully address all the issues included in the diversity of single members, especially knowing that singles on the multicultural team come from a variety of cultures and countries. A helpful new book about thriving as a single in cross-cultural work is coming out soon, by Hawker and Herbert (2014 projected).

Contributions of Singles

In our own experience, we have found our single colleagues to be effective and productive in every area—administration, leadership, academia, translation, linguistics, literacy, non-print media, communications, medical work, member care, staff training —literally, in all of the service functions of our organizations. Most have worked comfortably and compatibly with married teams to complete language projects, or completed these on their own. Their productivity and effectiveness has been awesome at times, surpassing the typical output of couples with family responsibilities. One single female team completed three translations of the New Testament in two Latin America countries. Another single woman completed the translation of two Bibles for a West African country. Written materials in linguistics, literacy, and translation have been produced by single workers. Some of our best consultants are single men and women. The contributions of single persons to the translation and language development task must be acknowledged and celebrated. This is true in the whole humanitarian sector.

One hazard for singles in an organization in which they are the minority is the unfortunate attitude by some people that singles can "do without" more easily than married people, especially those with children. Yet, whether married or single, we all have similar needs and wants. Single persons deserve the same kind of individual consideration and care that married workers do. We have seen this harmful attitude at play, particularly relating to housing, when singles might be displaced because the need of a family is considered to be greater. Or, the idea that because someone is single he or she does not need a home or opportunity to put their energy or funds into creating their own "nest." Member Care Facilitators and other leaders must be alert to damaging attitudes which hurt single members.

In some cases, a single person may need or warrant even *more* care than a couple or a family. Examples would be someone who is newly widowed or a single woman living in dangerous surroundings. At such times, the agency needs to be extra-alert to their needs. Travelling alone as a woman in many parts of the world is especially hazardous, and helping a single to find a travel or work partner is a great way to show care. We highly recommend personal GPS systems[46] for anyone traveling in dangerous areas, but especially for singles. While it is best to NOT travel alone, when it is necessary, it is a relief to know one can call for help! Part of the safety issue is that leaders, at both the local and the higher level, need to know accurately what the risks are for their workers. Local "partners" who are expected to oversee a foreigner may

---

[46] Personal GPS systems are available for an incredibly low price, compared to the value and safety of a worker. They can be set to alert various persons in the local or international offices so that the worker is immediately recognized as being in need and help can be dispatched.

not themselves recognize the dangers. One young woman was sent to a country, under the oversight of a local group, and encountered continual sexual harassment, to a truly dangerous level. Her local national leader's response was, "Oh, it's nothing. My wife has to put up with that too."[47]

Challenges for Singles

Opportunities for leadership, administration, advanced study—these exist for all members. Though the tendency of some leaders may be to look first at gender rather than ability, we advocate for equal rights and responsibilities for people of both genders, married or single. The glass ceiling has no place in the humanitarian world! We know that any single person can have the hardiness and resilience as any married person. They can just as readily serve as leaders, board members or as heads of academic institutions. Member Care Facilitators must be alert to any negative attitudes which limit a woman's or a single person's opportunities. Opportunities to advance professionally and to serve in visible positions of authority may have to be more energetically sought and earned, and they may come at higher cost than that accrued to the married person. When any members of the multicultural work team are prejudiced against women in leadership, the challenges of the single woman are very complex! So too if national partners do not regard women or singles as equal. "Headquarters" level leaders must be alert to these negative forces.

Another generally recognized hazard for single persons is the stronger possibility of loneliness due to the lack of an emotionally supportive confidante. Good self-care as well as agency care advocates the fostering of friendships to offset loneliness. Isolation must be avoided at all costs! If a person is "embedded" in the local culture, it is crucial that he or she be given regular breaks and opportunities to speak the mother tongue and to retain same-culture friendships.

---

[47] Lois Dodds, *Dealing Redemptively with Sexual Harassment and Other Forms of Violation,* 2004, 2017.

Advice from One Single Person
To Other Singles

Singles to Singles	Advantages of being Single and Childless:
✺ Get on with your life. If God wants you to marry, he'll provide—in and outside of your home country.	✺ We can devote more time to ministry.
✺ Develop ways of avoiding and dealing with temptation.	✺ We have more solitude, allowing us to more easily focus on our relationship with God..
✺ Remember that because of Christ's redemption, you are deeply loved, fully pleasing, and absolutely complete in him.	✺ We have more control of our time—to study, to travel, to visit.
✺ In acceptance, there is grace.	✺ Our schedules are more flexible. We can move, delay, stay late, and not affect another's plans.
✺ Worse things could happen to us than remaining single!	
✺ Life here is so short, why waste it wondering why God had you single. Enjoy it!	✺ Often we form a stronger bond with friends, both national colleagues and others.
✺ Adopt a family.	
✺ Make a home for yourself and your friends.	✺ We are stretched as we do many things for ourselves.
✺ Work at avoiding selfishness.	✺ We can switch roommates if we don't get along!!!

Reciprocal Community Care

One major difference in being single seems to be that a single person may not have a consistent relationship in which daily responsibilities are shared. In extreme allocations, this can be a huge need. This is where community comes into play. "Burden bearing" is part of our responsibility to each other. In a healthy faith community, we value each other, whether single or married, and show it through respect, appreciation, affection, understanding, time, opportunity, and loyalty. We all need a friend, someone who is loyal, who will listen, who will give corrective feedback, who will share freely. Singles and marrieds can meet these needs for each other. At times, more tangible, practical help is needed—car repairs, technological assistance, advocacy, financial guidance, or help in caring for elderly parents. Any one of us needs someone to pray with about major life decisions. Married friends can offer such to single friends. A single co-worker recently wrote, "I think the hardest thing for me as a single person is making decisions alone so much of the time. …especially about significant, life-changing decisions…"

Community care extends both directions, hopefully without harmful assumptions. Single persons need opportunities to give as well as receive. If a married person is unsatisfied with his or her spouse, it is frustrating to that person to have a single friend assume that marriage solves all problems. So too if a married person assumes that a single friend cannot understand his or her world. Acknowledging any gaps in understanding and continuing to be a loyal, loving friend will go a long way toward resolving potential tension in these areas.

Another drawback for single persons is the assumption others might hold about how much "free time" they have. In many situations, discretionary, personal time must be guarded carefully so the single worker does not do more than is healthy. This is because "free time" can be easily seen as time to give away. Personal free time is a legitimate need for both married and single workers. Giving it away must be a conscious, generous choice. When choosing to say "no" to a request for help, saying one would like to help, but cannot, eases the relationship.

Recreational activities for singles to engage in with married friends can include hospitality, sharing meals, birthday parties, and other celebrations. Hikes and treks are forms of exercise that provide social contact. My husband and I have climbed mountains in Vanuatu, New Caledonia, Malaysia, Nepal, South Africa, Gibraltar, Israel, Switzerland, Utah, Arizona (Grand Canyon) and various other places. Hiking, backpacking, camping have been family events for us (Gardner).

For those who prefer less strenuous recreation, scrapbooking and stamp clubs, snorkeling, scuba-diving, and various kinds of travel can be wonderful. This allows one to become more familiar with the geography and culture of one's host country and surrounding ones as well. These are activities that singles can also engage in to meet social needs, as well as to obtain exercise.

Whether married or single, survival in a remote locale or one with few amenities may require the worker to learn new skills. Successful cross-cultural living often requires technical skills as well as relational skills. The more a single person can learn and do for himself or herself, the more independent and secure he or she will feel. He or she will also have more to contribute to the community and may feel less needy. Married friends, including those with children, can visit and help singles in their allocations. I did this with my daughter in Peru; we visited our mountain teams and decorated, sewed, and cooked for them, and in general had wonderful times of sharing in their lives for a few days at a time (Dodds).

When a married member loses a partner late in life, adjusting to singleness can be a huge challenge. He or she is likely used to a regular division of responsibilities and may feel ill-equipped to do the things the other partner used to do. This can lead one to feel like a burden to the community. Friends, both married and single, can help widows and widowers with understanding and practical help as they adjust to this new and painful stage of life.

Some Additional Issues for Singles

These issues must be acknowledged and handled by some, if not all, single persons in humanitarian service:

• Finding and establishing a partnership or peer group for social and relational needs	• Feeling out of step with contemporaries who are now married with children
• Commitment to another single (How extensive should that commitment be? How long should it last?)	• Dealing with the desire to be married
	• Security—who will take care of me if I get sick, when I grow old?
• Getting and maintaining support; limited finances may mean sharing living quarters	• Adequacy
	• Traveling alone
	• Limited options for partnership
• Feeling rootless, not belonging anywhere	• Housing is unpredictable

• Contribution (satisfaction with work load)	• Being misunderstood by host culture, always having to explain self
• Trying to find a niche or role for self	• Issues of justice—is God really fair? Does he really supply my need? Why would he create me with these needs if they cannot be fulfilled?
• Loneliness, no confidante	
• Unmet sexual needs (and need for physical contact)	
• Attraction to national colleagues	
• A good partnership ending because of illness, marriage or death or change of assignment or location	• Finding identity in work and being tempted to overwork, overachieve
• Family of origin may not understand and care for her or him	• Hungry for affection, tempted to seek inappropriate intimacy
• Awareness that one's biological clock is ticking; opportunities for marriage and children are passing	• Insecure about appropriate boundaries with opposite sex
• Unmet expectations and hopes of meeting someone to marry	• Partnership may break up for many reasons, may bring guilt
	• Re-entry to home country alone, at furlough time or retirement
	• Many demands on furlough, only one person to meet them all
	• Single women expected to care for aging parents

Two papers on singleness may be helpful. 1) "Issues Facing Women on the Field: From A Single Woman's Perspective," by Cindy Langermann, a single field linguist who writes first-hand about loneliness, uncertain housing, and other issues. 2) "Responsibility for One Another," by Laura Mae Gardner, 1994.

Retiring or Retired Persons

Leaving one's field of service permanently in order to retire is another very stressful period for most people, bringing up all the life stage issues typical in one's later decades, as well as the loss of work and relationships established during earlier stages of life. Wise leaders look to these needs, appointing persons to help retiring and retired persons to connect with housing and other resources. It can be daunting to re-enter one's homeland after decades abroad and then have to figure out the current medical system, housing and utilities, and new social relationships. Even if one's former friends have survived they may be very different after so many years have passed, making it difficult to find common ground once more. Some agencies provide special housing units to allow retired persons from the same organization to live in proximity, providing each other with support, friendship, and a background of common, shared experiences. This also allows for more ease in living on small retirement incomes as well. Many retirees choose this option, as even living near their adult children may not provide the kind of understanding friendships and support they need.

Members with Mental Health Crisis

Humanitarian and religious workers are not exempt from depression, suicidal ideation, emotional illness, and despair. The complexities of life and work outside one's own culture can exacerbate these conditions. When seeking help, it is usually more effective to find a counselor experienced in overseas living. One such remarkable couple, who provided care for decades for people in our organization, was appointed to further counseling study, which added to their legal, pastoral, and psychiatric experience. Because of their character, communication skills, and commitments to the membership they were beloved and served well for many years. Good leaders encourage their members to seek appropriate care.

Sometimes, people in an agency may feel safer to go outside their organization for counseling or other mental health care. Today there are many places in the United States and across the world, staffed by people who are both qualified in providing therapy and experienced in cross-cultural ministry.

Summary

Within every agency or organization, various sub-groups have particular needs. A good agency attends to the needs of these diverse needs of their members. A wise Member Care Facilitator, as well as other leaders, needs to become attuned to the unique needs and issues of single persons. Mothers with young children, especially stay-at-home moms in restrictive cultures, also need a great deal of attention and care. Older personnel about to retire, or those who have retired, warrant care in the re-entry process and re-learning about their own home cultures. Those who work at home, away from the team, need help in bridging the gap and connecting as well as finding strategies for use of space and delineating work time from personal time. Leaders also need care, though they rarely manifest that need. The needs of each person, and every sub-group in the agency, should be given thought and be included in the member care plan for the agency.

References and Recommended Reading
On Singleness

Baker, Y. G. 1985. *Successfully single*. Denver, CO: Accent Books.

Buehler, Cheryl, and O'Brien, Marion. 2011. "Mothers' part-time employment associated with mother and family well-being." *Journal of Family Psychology*. Vol. 25 (6). Dec. Pp. 895 to 906.

Clarkson, M. 1978. *You're single!* Wheaton, IL: Harold Shaw Publishers.

Collins, G. R., ed. 1979. *It's O.K. to be single*. Waco, TX: Word Books.

Dodds, Lois., 2004, 2017. *Dealing Redemptively with Sexual Harassment and Other Forms of Violation*. Liverpool, PA.

Evening, M. 1974. *Who walk alone: A consideration of the single life*. Downers Grove, IL: InterVarsity Press.

Fix, J. and Levitt, Z. 1978. *For singles only*. Old Tappan, NJ: Fleming H. Revell Co.

Gardner, Laura Mae. 1994. "Responsibility for one another." Available from the author.

Hawker, Deborah, and Herbert T. Eds. 2013. *Single mission: thriving as a single Christian in cross-cultural ministry*. USA: Condeo Press.

Hsu, A. Y. 1997. *Singles at the cross-roads: A fresh perspective on Christian singleness*. Downers Grove, IL: InterVarsity Press.

Langermann, Cindy. "Issues facing women on the field: From a single woman's perspective." (Written by, a single field linguist who writes of first-hand experience with loneliness, uncertain housing, and other issues.) SIL Counseling Department, Dallas, Texas.

McAllaster, E. 1979. *Free to be single*. Chappaqua, NY: Christian Herald Books.

McGinnis, M. 1974. *Single*. Old Tappan, NJ: Fleming H. Revell Co.

Petersen, R. and Palmer, A. 1988. *When it hurts to be single*. Elgin, IL: David C. Cook Publishing Co.

Rinehart, P. and Rinehart, S. 1996. *Choices: Finding God's way in dating, sex, marriage, and singleness*. Colorado Springs, CO: Navpress.

Sroka, B. 1982. *One is a whole number*. Wheaton, IL: Victor

Weising, E. and Weising, G. 1998. *Singleness, an opportunity for growth and fulfillment*. Gospel Publishing House.

On Families and TCKs

Andrews, Leslie A., Ed. 2004. *The family in mission: Understanding and caring for those who serve*. Palmer Lake, CO: Mission Training International.

Curran, Dolores. 1990. *Traits of a healthy family: Fifteen traits commonly found in healthy families by those who work with them*. New York: Ballantine Books.

Hawes and Kealey. 1984. In Ted Ward, *Living Overseas: A Book of Preparation*, p. 176. New York. Free Press.

Loong, Cindy. 2006. *Growing up global: what a TCKs life is like*. Hong Kong: Shepherd International Church Limited.

Pollock, David, and Van Reken, Ruth. 1999. *The third culture kid experience: growing up among worlds*. Yarmouth, Maine: Intercultural Press.

_____ and _____. 2001 and 2009. *Third culture kids: the experience of growing up among worlds*. London: Nicolas Brealey Publ.

Pollock, David. 2000. *Global nomads: meeting the needs of third culture kids in schools*. Joimont, Victoria: 1ARTV.

Ward, Ted. 1984. *Living Overseas: A Book of Preparations*. New York: The Free Press.

Chapter 8
Dealing with Moral Failure

One of the most perplexing personnel issues in the world of humanitarian care is moral failure. In whatever way it occurs, it is usually scandalous and does serious damage to the individual, his or her family, the organization, the national partners in the host country, and the constituency "back home." It has far-reaching implications, much more so than other kinds of failure or maladaptation. It may be manifest in sexual behaviors, such as having affairs, inappropriate relationships, or abuse of a fellow member, a child, or a national. It may be financial malfeasance, including participating in corruption, embezzlement, and other misuse of funds. Moral failure may also be lack of ethical behaviors, such as misrepresenting the agency or cause, mistreatment of personnel, and lying. It is costly in any form. When laws have been violated, the consequences are enormous!

Moral failure of the humanitarian cross-cultural worker calls for specific kinds of awareness and interventions. From a compassionate human perspective, it can be viewed as a maladaptive attempt at coping with an overwhelming situation. In this light, leaders are to provide for and hope for restoration. But, from a practical standpoint, it must be viewed as a betrayal of the integrity and ethics of the organization. It must be viewed spiritually as failure to behave as God desires for one's own purity, and to act with integrity for the good of others, in a way that demonstrates unconditional love and care for all of those in one's circle. The person has chosen selfishly rather than for the good of others. From a psychosocial standpoint, any type of moral failure is an indication of deeper emotional and relational issues.

Though this is not a pleasant topic for any of us devoted to bringing about good in the world, it is essential that we understand what happens and how any kind of moral failure is disruptive and harmful. We will address the following questions:

- What kinds of moral failure happen in multicultural contexts by humanitarian workers?
- Who's being hurt anyway? What business is it of the organization if the individual engages in immoral behavior in his or her own home and free time?
- If an individual believes it is not hurting anyone, why is it wrong?
- Why do these things happen?
- What are the evidences or symptoms of such failure?
- Who should intervene and when?
- What intervention best serves the organization as well as the individual?

My husband and I were very new workers living in a small Latin American town when our first exposure to moral failure happened. A much more experienced couple living in the same small town returned to their passport country on home leave. Then word drifted back to the field leadership that this couple had separated and were divorcing.[48] We were stunned and devastated. It raised many questions for us, and created fear and self-doubt. Could we have helped in some way? Why had we not seen that something was wrong? If it could happen to them, it seems it could certainly happen to us. How could we prevent such a disaster in our own lives?

Since that time we have seen many kinds of moral failure. Our involvement in addressing failures has sometimes been as consultants, sometimes as therapists, and occasionally as decision-makers who had to figure out a course of action. We have heard stories that break our hearts, because the tragedies that result from any moral failure are wide-

---

[48] Though divorce *per se* may not be regarded as moral failure in many countries and cultures, it clearly has profound implications in the Judeo-Christian context, where fidelity to a life partner is considered a vow to God as well as to one's partner. It has much greater impact in this context than in the secular world. Though it has been de-stigmatized in some cultures, in other contexts and cultures, it carries serious expectations about its impact on ethical behavior and the penalties can be extreme.

ranging—and they are preventable! They need not happen! We come to this topic with compassion and courage. We do not want to excuse infidelity and all its related behaviors but we do want to look at moral failure through the lens of prevention, care, and restoration.

What Kinds of Behavior Constitute Moral Failure?

Marriage breakdown, including spousal abuse, child sexual abuse, incest and other kinds of molestation are moral failures in sexual behavior. So too fathering children out of wedlock, rape, the sexual abuse of women in any culture and the cultural values which encourage and permit it. Pornography is also a breakdown in moral values, and though its use may be in "private," it has many damaging outcomes. On the financial side, theft, embezzlement, manipulation of funds, false representation, taking kickbacks or selling goods meant to be donated are all forms of moral failure—dishonesty takes many forms! Other moral failures may be less visible, such as neglect, misuse of the internet, soliciting children into evil, lying, slander, gossip, uncontrolled anger, verbal abuse, persistent failure to forgive, holding onto bitterness and resentment, and false accusations. All of these do immense damage to the person and all those whose life is touched.[49]

What Does It Matter?

Why should matters of morality concern an organization? Some people would argue that if their members engage in these activities in their free time, it should be of no concern to the agency. Though this argument might be acceptable in the secular world and in one's home country, it is a naïve perspective in the multicultural and humanitarian world.

---

[49] Though in some Western countries homosexuality is no longer considered abnormal, it has profound implications in many contexts and countries, including the penalty of death in some. For religious organizations that base rules of conduct on the Bible, a candidate may not be accepted or may be dismissed for practicing a homosexual lifestyle, just as he or she might be dismissed for other behaviors considered to constitute moral failure.

Richard Gardner, international coordinator of a counseling office that serves a large multicultural agency, describes the cost and the ripples of impact to be widespread.

Immoral behavior carries with it an extremely high cost which extends to many areas and people far beyond one's expectations. The cost to the perpetrator includes shame, possible loss of role, perhaps loss of marriage and family, collegial respect, probably loss of financial support.

Let's look at some of the implications, as identified by R. Gardner:

- The spouse and children experience disillusionment, pain, anger, grief, loss, embarrassment.
- The victim will be wounded and may have scars that last a lifetime. Sexual abuse or molestation can result in diminished self-esteem, anger, susceptibility to depression, suicidal ideation, disillusionment, possible multiple personality disorder and a loss of trust. Later on, it may lead to an inhibited marriage relationship. Loss of trust may later extend beyond the perpetrator to the organization and other adults who may be perceived as having done nothing when they might have been able to rescue the victim. The organization pays too, in damage to its reputation, interrupted work, and decreased morale of the membership.
- The impact on field colleagues is heavy—pain, hurt, loss, disillusionment, guilt, anger, suspicion (such as parents wondering, "Did he molest MY daughter too?"). There is a heavy burden on colleagues to deal with information about immorality. They wonder what the limits of confidentiality are. If they learn about the failure by means of a peer before others do, they must grapple with the matter of whether they should report it, and when and to whom. The administrator or leader who has to investigate and make decisions about the offender experiences a surprising range of emotions--anguish, bewilderment, and other emotions related to the enormous output of energy involved with dealing with the situation, being the target of anger and blame, overload, dealing with the ramifications; the leader may feel like the police as he or she tries to determine the truth and may not know what questions to

ask or what to do with the answers when they are disclosed.

- The spouse of the leader to whom it falls to bring about intervention may also experience devastation as he or she receives the residue and reactions from the people involved, from uninformed members, from the spouse of the perpetrator.

- The local national community— those whom the agency serves—will experience☐ disillusionment that a foreign aid worker "could act this way." There may be cultural misunderstandings of the administrative response. People may believe he or she acted either too harshly or too mildly. Knowing how much to disclose to the local community, and how it should be done are taxing for the administrator. Such a loss of trust can destroy the credibility of the organization and result in failure of the vision and mission.

- The administrative staff who takes action may be recipients of misplaced anger and share in the ostracism which may be experienced by the administrator. They may know the "real story" but due to rules of confidentiality be unable to tell what they know. They may feel their hands are tied in defending their leader.

- The constituency of both the perpetrator and the organization pay a steep price in disillusionment, sorrow, regret, anger, and a sense of betrayal. Evil, deviant behavior has deep impact on those who trusted and supported the member in trouble. And, if the constituency can never be told "the full story" due to legal or political issues, there is sure to be misunderstanding and perhaps criticism of everyone involved in decision-making.

NOTE: The cost is particularly high when a violation of trust is not handled promptly, compassionately, and as openly as possible.

Who's Being Hurt, Anyway?

Moral matters are murky matters when it comes to multicultural life. Standards of conduct, values, and legal statutes vary enormously from culture to culture, country to country. What is acceptable, okay, and "normal" in one group may be abhorrent to another. For instance, in some cultures, caressing a child's genitals is considered to be a soothing gesture and nothing more. In other cultures, it is a criminal violation. Taking a child bride, as young as six or seven, is permissible in some countries, and criminal in others. A foreign worker can suffer incredible distress when exposed to practices which as outsiders we believe are reprehensible, and yet there is no legal recourse. How do you endure the crying in the night of your village neighbor's new bride, age six? In cultures where women are demeaned and viewed to be "fair game" for men, stepping in can be treacherous. Fortunately, over years of humanitarian work, especially in the last century, more and more "foreigners" have intervened, saving the lives of countless women and girls. Sparing the lives of widows in India is one example. Current efforts to outlaw and stamp out sexual slavery, human trafficking and female genital cutting are encouraging indications that "stepping in" does pay off. In their excellent work *Half the Sky*, Kristof and WuDunn give practical ways to join the battle against trafficking. (2009).

The use of pornography is another maladaptive response to stress which some people consider to be private and acceptable. They may be blasé and say, "What does it matter?" yet we know it has very damaging consequences for the individual and family, as well as for the agency. Even in the U.S., according to national news media, Wall Street investment banks lose untold millions because so many of their personnel wasted work time on viewing pornography.

Why and How Does It Happen?

Choosing to engage in humanitarian work often exposes people to risks they would not have encountered "back home." For instance, due to parents' strong commitment to altruistic service, they may take their daughters to an area of the world where women are viewed as bait. The girls may undergo pinching, touching, fondling, and caressing by nationals who consider it legitimate. The girls may hesitate to tell their parents. They may have no idea how to protect themselves so the violation continues. Sadly, we have discovered that some children (both genders) of humanitarian workers in other lands have been abused sexually and yet have never told their parents until adulthood, either out of fear, having been threatened, or thinking that telling on someone the parents have trusted as a valuable helper would create too much tension. Others may fear it will lead to their parents giving up the work they love.

Here are a few of the situations we have encountered which are outside the normal behaviors people would practice in their home culture:

- Two single women are assigned together to work in a lonely isolated place. Without close friends or colleagues, they turn to each other and begin to sleep together, not because they are lesbians but because they are lonely and crave attention and affection. News of this creates a scandal.
- Family members find themselves without funds for vacation or diversion, and in their weariness and boredom, someone in the family turns to pornography.
- Long hours of work and weariness lead someone to seek a massage, only to find it leads to sexual activity.
- An indigenous woman wants to bear a child and makes herself available to the foreign male. She may tempt him until the man gives in. If she is the maid or house-helper, her availability may compound the infidelity.
- A young couple is assigned to another culture which has widely different sexual values and practices. Out of loneliness and without sufficient orientation, they fall prey to seduction.

The path to moral failure seldom is clear. Yet, we can trace it in retrospect. People who serve in humanitarian organizations are deeply committed, caring, generous people. They do not plan to ruin their life and service or their marriage and family, but it happens gradually.

What becomes a serious problem usually begins with a felt need, followed by discouragement and the belief that that need will never be met, following by proximity to temptation. Temptation leads to fantasizing which leads to the desire to try it "just once." Then the person engages in the immoral action itself. This, in turn, is followed by a reactive process which may take any of four pathways:

- Downward spiral: Hiding, repetition, rationalization, dulled conscience, deception, and an increasing appetite for the activity.

- Repentance and confession: Conviction that this is wrong, confessing to appropriate people, facing the consequences, engaging in restitution, getting help through counseling and insight that is needed, and being restored to a greater level of wholeness.

- Getting caught through exposure: This leads to embarrassment, shame, anger, and possibly remorse, often projection and blame, and may result in bitterness and estrangement from close friends or family and authorities. (This is least hopeful, as there is less chance of resolution or restoration, and the person's service is usually over. The wound in both the perpetrator and the family may go unhealed, and continues to fester. Results are tragic and long-lasting.)

- Desiring to get caught: Reckless acting-out in an unconscious desire to be caught may be a cry for help due to feelings of guilt, remorse, and shame. A sense of trusting despair gives the person courage to own the wrong and ask for help. The person sees no other response than to face the consequences and pay the price for failure. Seeking help is the pathway to regaining wholeness for the self and the family.

What Evidence? How to Recognize Trouble

How is a Member Care Facilitator or an organizational supervisor to know that something is amiss? What are the symptoms that someone's behavior has spiraled down to a problematic level? Some of the observable indicators include:

- Loss of competence
- Not attending to work
- Ignoring the needs of one's family
- Frequent unexplained absences
- Missing group activities, especially spiritual
- Decline in motivation; may be unexplained exhaustion
- Vague explanations about why things are not done or why one is absent
- Seeming loss of spiritual vitality or desire to relate to God or

over-zealousness as a cover-up
- Funds that are missing or unaccounted for
- Falsification of records, especially financial or time logs
- Gaining material possessions beyond one's salary resources
- Lies and secretive behaviors

There may be other signs that someone is faltering, such as depression, hopelessness, and feeling trapped. A sense of entitlement to what has been "missed" in past experience and wanting to make up for lost rewards can also become a source of temptation.

Who Should Intervene and When?

When an agency or field entity has a Member Care Facilitator available, this is the appropriate person to intervene. Without someone in this role, the first intervention may be by a supervisor, department head, or local director. The sooner intervention happens after the moral failure is discovered or confessed, the better. The MCF likely knows each field member and has built rapport with that person and his or her family. It is likely that the MCF has good relationship skills, which are definitely needed in exploring or confronting the problem and then in intervention. By virtue of the MCF's training, he or she may be able to detect that something is amiss sooner than others might. Discernment is a valuable quality at such a time. By virtue of the role (resource brokering, fostering health and wholeness), the MCF will likely be able to intervene in a caring, rather than a punitive way, and to assist in bringing resources and aid to the troubled member. As a resource broker, the MCF will likely know the counselors and chaplains who can offer aid. If the behavior has reached an overt level so that it violates the moral standard of the organization, the MCF may accompany the offender to make confession to leaders. The MCF can advocate for the member by helping to formulate a plan for leaving the field and for getting into a program of restoration.

When should intervention take place? The sooner, the better. If the MCF monitors the field individuals or teams and knows the reality of the allocations where members serve, he or she will likely be aware of the potential for succumbing to temptation and discouragement. The MCF has hopefully established a bond of trust that allows for truthful communication. Obviously the MCF must be skilled in observation, discernment, intervention, and in confrontation.

A professional counselor can be helpful in situations of moral failure by helping field leaders understand the implications of behavior, especially of addictions. He or she may help the hurting member directly at this stage of assessment and intervention. However, if the counselor acts as a consultant or evaluator, he or she probably will not be able to serve the person later as a therapist. We will assume that in almost all cases of moral failure, the person will be removed from the field setting in order to get help.

It is important to keep distinctives of the roles in mind when making interventions. A consultant does not make management decisions, administer or enforce decisions, or function outside of the areas of his or her professional competence. A consultant does offer informed, comprehensive input, facilitate exploration of action alternatives and potential outcomes, and provide follow-up and input to current developments. Making final decisions and arrangements to leave the field, re-enter the home land, provide for restoration resources, and decide whether the member is to remain in the organization is usually a combined responsibility of field and home office leaders.

What Interventions?

A management decision should be made with collective input from relevant professional resources—if such resources are available. In this instance, "relevant" refers to individuals with a valid relationship to the case. "Professional" resources refer to those individuals who by virtue of their training, job title, or area of responsibility are able to and responsible to assess the situation. Resources may be local, on site, or more distant, such as at the level of the organization's international services. They may be in-house or sourced outside of the organization.

If a counselor is available, he or she could be a significant resource to both the community and the organization. For example, a counselor could identify the significant issues. A well-trained Member Care Facilitator or other leader may also make an assessment. Once the problem is identified, and treatment is sought, the following issues should be evaluated. It is best not to label with diagnoses at this point, but to identify the behavioral problem. These ten questions are helpful:

- Is there a clear antecedent or precipitating event/condition to this person's behavior?
- What is the duration of the behaviors?
- How pervasive is the impact of the behaviors?
- How intrusive are the behaviors on the person's functioning?
- What is the potential for the person to harm self or others?
- How do the counselor's training, experience, and/or available supervision match the person's treatment needs?
- Does the counselor's present schedule allow adequate time for treating this person?
- Are there more appropriate treatment opportunities available in the person's home land?
- What will treating this person cost the counselor in terms of other ministry opportunities or responsibilities?
- Will attempting to treat this person on the field prolong his/her recovery in the long run?

Twelve Questions for the Administrator to Ask:

The perspective of the local administrator or leader is important because he or she most likely has a broader perspective and greater responsibility than the counselor and most likely will better understand the implications of the moral failure in the context of the field, the team, and the cultural setting.

1. What are the potential benefits or liabilities to the entity of retaining this person or family on the field?
2. Does this person's behavior represent a threat to the organization's reputation or placement in the country?
3. What is the preference of the individual and/or family regarding getting help? How do they view the significant issues?
4. Are existing services able to meet the needs of this person or family? Will serving this person or family stretch services beyond their intended, typical function? Will other potential consumers of services be excluded because of this person/family's unusual needs?
5. What is the probable impact of this person's presence on community morale? On community security and/or safety?

6.   What is the potential impact of this person's presence?
7.   Is harm being caused or experienced by anyone right now?
8.   Is there a change in sight?
9.   Is the member willing to work toward change?
10. How much support service is needed?
11. On how many others persons does the presence of the "problem" person have an impact?
12. What does it cost (financial, emotional, etc.) to keep the person on the field?

Leaders at all organizational levels must also determine what legal ramifications, if any, result from the moral failure. If this is not attended to, there can be long-term consequences which harm the mission and may lead to expulsion of the group as well as individuals. In some situations, the laws of various countries may come into play, and even into conflict. The host country's laws most likely predominate, but laws of the home country or countries of the parties involved must also be considered.

Summary

Moral failure is one of the most difficult and thorny issues to deal with when it occurs in the humanitarian cross-cultural or multicultural context. Whether sexual, financial or ethical, the malfeasance exacts a great cost to the individuals who do wrong and to the team and agency. When such a problem is suspected or identified, leaders must exercise clear and appropriate methods for confronting, intervening, and rectifying the wrongs. Dealing with the failures immediately is very important to minimize the fallout among the members, the local persons who are on-lookers, the home constituency of the wrong-doer and of the mission itself.

References and Recommended Reading

Allender, Dan. 1999. *The healing path*. Colorado Springs, CO: Waterbrook Press.

Carder, Dave, *et al.* 1991. *Secrets of your family tree: healing for adult children of dysfunctional families*. Chicago: Moody Press. Also available in Chinese language.

Coles, Robert. 1990. *The spiritual life of children*. Two volumes. Boston: Houghton Mifflin Co.

_____. 1995. *The story of Ruby Bridges*. Picture Book. New York: Scholastic.

_____. 1997. *The moral intelligence of children*. NY: Random House.

_____. 1982. What about moral sensibility? *Education 81/82. Annual Editions*. Guilford, CN: Dushkin Publ. Reprinted from *Today's Education. J. of the National Assoc. of Education*.

_____. 1990. *The spiritual life of children*. Boston: Houghton Mifflin Co.

Dodds, Lois A. 2011. Twenty traits of emotional maturity. In Chapter 3, Volume 1, *Global Servants* Series. Liverpool, PA: Heartstream Resources. 101 Herman Lee Circle, Liverpool, PA. 17045. www.heartstreamresources.org.

_____. 1997 and 2003. Am I still me? Changing the core self to fit a new cultural context. AACC World Congress, Nov. 6-8, 1997, Dallas, Texas, and AACC World Congress, Sept 23-27, 2003, Nashville, TN. Available as a booklet at www.heartstreamresources.org.

_____. 1979. Ten gifts to give your children. *Eternity Magazine*. Dec.

_____. 1980. *How do I look from up there?* Wheaton: Scripture Press.

_____. 1992. *The perception and experience of supernatural spiritual power for personality growth and change: an analysis of twelve life histories*. U.C.S.B. Available through U.M.I., 300 N. Zeeb Rd., Ann Arbor, MI 48106, Order Number 9237798. File 3266.

_____. 1992. The role of the Holy Spirit in personality growth and change. 1st International Congress on Christian Counseling. Atlanta., Georgia. Nov. 11-15. Available at www.heartstreamresources.org. and in paper form in *Collected Papers*, Heartstream Resources, 101 Herman Lee Circle, Liverpool, PA, 17045

_____. 1995. "Stressed from core to cosmos: Needs and issues arising from cross-cultural ministry." American Association of Christian Counselors, March 22, 23, Philadelphia, and Pittsburgh AACC

September 22, 23, 1995. Later published in *Christian Counseling newsletter*. Fall, 1995. Presented again by invitation to ACMC in various regional meetings. Available at www.heartstreamresources.org.

_____. 1997. Selection, training, member care and professional ethics: choosing the right people and caring for them with integrity. In *Collected Papers*. Liverpool, PA: Heartstream Resources, Inc. Available at www.heartstreamresources.org

_____. 1998. "Stressed from core to cosmos" published in three parts in *Women of the Harvest*. Jan/Feb/March issue, 1998; April/May/June issue, 1998; July/August/Sept issue.

_____. 1999. The role of the Holy Spirit in personality growth and development. *Journal of Psychology and Christianity*. Summer. Pp. 129-139. (centerpiece article, by invitation).

Erikson, Erik. 1950. *Childhood and society*. NY: Norton

_____, *et. al.* 1959. *Psychological issues*. NY: International U. Press.
_____. 1959, 1968, and 1980. *Identity and the life cycle: selected papers*. New York: Norton.

_____. 1963. *Childhood and society*. Revised edition. NY: Norton.

_____. 1964. *Insight and responsibility.*   NY: Norton

_____. 1982. *Identity and religion.* NY: Seabury Press.

Fleagle, Arnold R., and Lichi, Donald A. 2011. *Broken Windows of the Soul.* GrandRapids, MI: Zondervan.

Gardner, Laura Mae. 1999. Making sense of and maintaining stability in a world of malignant uncertainty, corruption, and increasing evil." Waxhaw, NC. Pastors to Missionaries conference presentation. Available from the author.

_____. 2000. Moral and spiritual health. Counseling Department Bulletin, SIL, 7500 Camp Wisdom Road, Dallas, Texas.

Gardner, Richard. 2000. The high cost of immorality. Counseling Department Bulletin. SIL, 7500 Camp Wisdom Road, Dallas, Texas.

Gilligan, Carol. 1982. *In a different voice: psychological theory and women's development.* Cambridge: Harvard U. Press.

Guinness, Os. 2000. *When No One Sees: The importance of character in an age of Image.* Colorado Springs, CO: NavPress.

_____. 2005. *Unspeakable: Facing up to evil in an age of genocide and Terror.* San Francisco, CA: Harper.

Hall, Calvin S., and Linzey, Gardner. 1978. *Theories of personality.* New York; John Wiley and Sons, third ed., p. 26

Israel, Seun. 2013. *Sexual Battles: experiencing lasting victory over sexual sin.* Forerunner Publishing House. eBook format.

Kohlberg, Lawrence. 1981. *The philosophy of moral development: moral states and the idea of justice—essays in moral development.* NY: Harper and Row.

Kreeft, Peter. 1990. *Making Choices: finding black and white in a world of grays.* Ann Arbor, MI: Servant Books.

Kristof, Nicolas D., and WuDunn, Sheryl, 2009, *Half the Sky: Turning Oppression into Opportunity* NY: Random House, Alfred A. Kropf

MacDonald, Gail. 1991. *A Step farther and higher.* Portland, OR: Multnomah Books.

MacDonald, Gordon. 1988. *Rebuilding your broken world.* Nashville, TN: Thomas Nelson.

Morley, Patrick. 1997. *The man in your mirror.* Grand Rapids, MI: Zondervan.

Pittman, Frank. 1989. *Private Lies: Infidelity and the betrayal of intimacy.* New York:W.W. Norton & Company.

_____. 1998. *Grow Up! How taking responsibility can make you a happy Adult.* New York: St. Martin's Griffin.

Plantinga, Cornelius, Jr. *Not the way it's supposed to be: A breviary of sin.* GrandRapids, MI: Wm. B. Eerdmans Publishing Co.

Olthius, James. 1985. Faith Development in the Adult Life Span. Presentation to the Annual Meeting of the Canadian Theological Society.

_____. 1985. Faith development in the adult life span. *Studies in Religion.* Vol. 14, No. 4, Fall, pp. 497-509

_____. 1985. Straddling the boundaries between theology and psychology: the faith feeling interface." *J. of Psychology and Christianity.* Vol. 4, No. 1, Spring, pp. 6-15,

Rizzuto, Ana-Maria. 1979. *The birth of the living God—a psycho-analytic study.* Chicago: The U. Of Chicago Press.

Virkler, Henry A. *Broken Promises: understanding healing and preventing affairs in Christian marriages.* Grand Rapids, MI: Baker Books

Chapter 9
Personnel Care Audit with
Principles and Practices

A very important reflection of the "art and heart" of agency care is how the organization acts with integrity in caring for its personnel. Persons devoting their lives to bring about good for humanity deserve to be cared for in a variety of ways that enable them to be effective and to endure over the long haul of service. The commitment to care begins with screening, assessment and selection as we have seen in Chapter One, and continues on through periods of training and allocation. In field settings, it takes many shapes, addressing care for the individual and families in at least the five basic domains of human need.

While it is always tempting for leaders to focus first on the vision and mission of the agency or project, the most productive long-term outcomes are brought about by caring first for the persons who do the serving and caring. As Jesus said, "The poor you will always have with you."[50] It seems he meant that we can never finish the job of caring for all the poor and needy of the world, so we must attend first to other matters, such as our own health, our souls, and keeping our balance in life.

In assessing the health of an organization and its personnel, we can identify that morale rests on and relates heavily to two aspects of the agency. We see these two avenues as enhancing or diminishing many "markers of care." The first of these aspects is objective and measurable;

---

[50] Matthew 26:11, New Testament.

the second is more subjective and also more challenging. Though both are important, the second is more important.

Practical Organizational Structure

By organizational structure, or infrastructure, we do not mean organizational hierarchy. It is something more practical, more day-to-day. Though structure forms the "bones" of the system, it is more subtle than what we see at the surface. It does not necessarily end up on the "chain of command" chart. We see it in action more than on paper. It is expressed in philosophy, principles, policies, practices, and procedures. It is reflected in the allocation of resources. It is manifest in the nimbleness of the organization and its ability to cope with change and surprise. We see it in the relationships of leaders and in their availability and attitudes toward their fellow member-workers.

Infrastructure regarding personnel has a particular impact on the members. Besides the procedures for selection, orientation, assignment, and deployment we considered in earlier chapters, it includes oversight and care extended into field terms and re-entry. Based on it we can answer, "How are members treated? How are they selected, deployed, supervised, and cared for throughout the life of their service? Do they feel valued and respected?"

Perhaps the most visible aspect of infrastructure relates to principles, policies, and practices including guidelines for various matters. It is helpful to assess whether policies and practices are known to members and to look at how they are applied. We are familiar with the need for annual financial audits in any agency. We can benefit from a parallel process as it relates to serving our people. If a "personnel care audit" were being done, what would the auditor look for?

Ideally an auditor would first see the philosophy, principles, policies, and practices as beneficial, as granting opportunity and permission for growth. (The opposite is having policies and practices which are "prohibitive" or restrictive—that is, they say more about what cannot be done than about what is encouraged.) The policies and practices would be specific, clear, objective, published, and communicated to each candidate or member. The auditor would want to see a set of principles from which specific policies and practices emerge with regard to the treatment of personnel. He or she would want to see "below" them to the process by which the principles were derived. He or she would want to establish whether there was good communication in the process. Were members given opportunity for input?

To perform a good personnel audit, one must begin with describing what kind of organization is involved. We might call this an organizational profile, identifying the vision and mission and the most important values and characteristics. Having a clear understanding of the category of work and identity of the agency is crucial, as that has great bearing on day-to-day matters, such as where funding comes from, what members are paid, and to whom the agency itself is accountable. In most cases, humanitarian work reaches across boundaries of countries and cultures, may be religious or non-religious, and involved in disaster aid and more routine efforts to address the needs of humanity. Understanding the national and international structure, as well as their relationship to each other, is crucial. Does the agency act alone or in partnership with others?

A good example of this profile comes from "People in Aid," which describes their organization as follows:

> People in Aid is an international network of development and humanitarian assistance agencies. People in Aid helps organizations whose goal is the relief of poverty and suffering to enhance the impact they make through better people management and support. People are at the heart of humanitarian endeavor. They are the beneficiaries, the donors and, critically, the providers of assistance. Our sector is driven by the experience and knowledge of people rather than the functionality of goods or efficiency of services.

> People in Aid is a registered not-for-profit organization which provides support in NGOs wishing to improve their human resources management. We provide support for NGOs wishing to implement the Code of Best Practice in the Support and Management of Aid. As an organization founded as a central resource for the sector, we also undertake research, produce publications, offer training and other services tailored specifically to the human resources needs of NGOs" (from the Executive Director, Jonathan Potter, for People in Aid).

Principles: Since infrastructure for the care of personnel begins with a set of principles, it is helpful to have an example of them. Here are the nine principles of one North American NGO, based on those established by People in Aid. They have been adapted to serve an American-based organization with members serving internationally.

Principle 1: Our workers (members, employees, volunteers) are essential to the achievement of our goals. Their contribution is integral to our effectiveness. They are valued and treated with dignity and respect.

Principle 2: Personnel policies and practices aim for the highest ethical standards. Our policies and practices are congruent—we do what we say we will do.

Principle 3: Personnel policies are intended to promote both high integrity and high quality performance in all our workers.

Principle 4: Plans and resources are reflected in our responsibilities toward our staff.

Principle 5: Staff development is expected, resourced, and monitored for all staff.

Principle 6: Staff security is essential for the well-being of our staff, and to the degree possible, planned and resourced.

Principle 7: Our organization is committed to harmony and the maintenance of an environment where differences of opinion may be voiced and conflicts addressed and resolved.

Principle 8: Violations of internal standards and external legal expectations will be dealt with in such a way that the violation is addressed in thorough, culturally appropriate ways, the violator is treated with respect, and internal morale is not damaged.

Principle 9: Ethical treatment of staff includes appropriate attention to the families of our staff, including the well-being and education of dependent children.

These principles are communicated to all members of the organization. From these principles, specific policies and procedures are developed and implemented. The practices, or implementation of the principles, should be dynamic. That is, they should be changeable rather than static. They are responsive to new insights and information as these come to light and as situations change. They are dynamic without being capricious.

Practices flow from these principles in a way that reflects the uniqueness of a given organization. For example, Principle 2 says, "Personnel policies and practices aim for the highest ethical standards. Our policies and practices are congruent—we do what we say we will do." This principle might be enacted by some specific practices, such as:

- Personnel are recruited for their people management skills and are adequately trained.
- Each staff member has clear work objectives and knows to whom he/she reports.
- Benefits, such as health care, are provided and reviewed regularly.
- The organization monitors how well personnel policies achieve their objectives.

Principles of a faith-based organization may differ somewhat from these. A faith-based organization should abide both by legal and ethical standards in its treatment of personnel, and should even act at a higher level of care because of the Biblical standards held by Christian organizations. Law does not necessarily acknowledge the highest moral and ethical standard, so holding ourselves to an even higher standard is best. In Lawrence Kohlberg's stages of moral development, he places law at level four out of six, indicating that other levels, based on universal truths, are higher than law.[51] Democracy, he points out, is at level four, and the majority rule of law is not the highest standard.

A faith-based organization must never fail to adhere to sound principles

---

[51] Lawrence Kohlberg, a researcher, devoted his life to the study of moral development. Along with Robert Coles and Carol Gilligan, he provides us with very valuable insights into the development of morality and ethics. (1981)

just because its workers are highly motivated. For instance, overwork may be sanctioned on "spiritual" grounds, but it should not be demanded or expected because that violates the principles of appropriate care. Spiritually motivated workers need oversight and care just as any others and leaders should not assume their members can always make the right choices. Following a "higher spiritual authority" never exempts a faith-based organization from practicing ethical and caring oversight of its workers. The opposite should be true and accountability is always important as part of care.

An example of failure to care adequately for its workers due to a misguided "spiritual" reason might be neglecting to monitor civil unrest or to develop contingency plans and resources for evacuations because of their members' faith that God will protect them. The organizational leader must conduct "due diligence" in looking out for their people.

Organizational Ethos

This brings us to the second, more subjective aspect of an agency or organization—its *ethos*. Just as every culture and group has an ethos, so too does every organization. It is often not spelled out or put into writing, yet those who live within the system learn its "operating" principles, practices, assumptions and attitudes. It is the group personality and has great power to shape the lives of everyone in the system!

Ethos includes the intangible, invisible set of values, beliefs, and behaviors that shape the culture of an organization. It is the fundamental character and spirit of a group, based on the sentiments that inform beliefs and practices.

Ethos as a concept is seldom discussed or defined within a social system. It is just there! Members may find it hard to cognitively identify the philosophy and values making up their ethos, but they come to know them subjectively, on a feeling level. Ethos is rooted in the history of an organization, just as it is in a family or a culture. Early members form patterns of thinking and habits of behaving that are passed on through stories and other means. These become underscored by the behavior of leaders and reactions of members. "This is the way we do it here" is an expression of organizational ethos. Over time, the ethos may change, but it bears the indelible marks of the past.

Analyzing the ethos of a group or agency is enlightening. Doing so is an important beginning in a personnel care audit. Ethos is illustrative because, like nonverbal communication, it does not lie. An organization may say it cares well for its members, but how it actually does is reflected by what the members feel and how they respond. Leaders of an organization want to believe their policies are just, their communication is good, and that there is a high level of trust with their members. But whether it is actually true is reflected by the members' morale. If they feel in touch with their leaders, feel safe in disclosing openly to them, and feel they have a "say" in affairs, leaders are doing well. Members who feel they have influence in shaping the organization's policies, goals, and future feel best about their leaders. I encountered a shocking disconnect in an agency's stated care and the reality when a high-up leader said to me, "Of course, we never believe anything our members say...." Another shock was hearing a candidate tell me that in candidate school, the leader went to each room and looked at how well "students" had organized their drawers and suitcases! Such an invasion of privacy is outrageous!

The ethos of an agency or organization is largely maintained or changed by leaders. Therefore they have great power in shaping the experience of their members. In this regard it is helpful to consider the emotional intelligence (EQ) of any leader, as it can positively influence and shape the ethos.

Emotional intelligence refers to an accurate knowledge of self, an ability to monitor and manage oneself, and an accurate awareness of the impact one has on others. It includes the ability to manage that impact through sensitivity in emotion and communication. It includes understanding others accurately and supportively. Emotional intelligence is estimated to account for seventy percent of the success of a leader, far ahead of technical competence and leadership skills (see appendix in Goleman, Boyatzis and McKee, 2002).

Here are some specific elements of emotional intelligence that contribute to high morale:

Accessibility and availability of a leader is crucial. This does not mean a leader must answer every email or telephone message, every tweet and twitter, maintain an open door policy, or feel that he is on duty endlessly. Rather it means that the leader has established the habit of abundant, even lavish, communication. Depending on the context, a leader may himself answer every message personally or have a core of trustworthy staff to do this for him. It means showing warmth towards those he leads, and being with them often. It might include eating regularly in the lunch room, greeting people by name, hosting people in his or her home or finding other methods of hospitality. The goal is to be approachable and to build trust with those he or she leads. Essential to building trust is telling people the truth, both the good and bad news. It includes admitting faults and maintaining nondefensiveness. It is promoted by welcoming and soliciting feedback on his or her behavior, leadership style, and communication efforts.

Presence reflects care. A leader exhibits genuine care when he or she shows up at times of high emotion, either grief and sadness or events of celebration and joy. Going to the hospital when a staff member has a heart attack says "I care about you." By attending graduations or celebrations, a leader shows care. Being together in informal situations makes it easier for members to appreciate their leader as a person. Of course, there is no substitute for the leader knowing people's names!

Wise and timely affirmation is like water irrigating a parched desert in time of drought. People join humanitarian aid organizations because of a deep desire to help others, especially those in need. Given that the recipients of agency "caring" may never express their gratitude in words to those who serve them, it is even more important for leaders to say thank you. Having a leader say, "Good job!" can make a major difference in morale. It also builds trust when a worker knows his leader notices what he is contributing.

A mental health specialist was preparing for a trip to Asia and consulted with a globally experienced counselor as part of her preparation. The mental health worker also set up a luncheon appointment with a couple who had abundant international experience. During the lunch, the mental health worker mentioned the consultant she had contacted. The listening couple said, "She came to our country and met with us, and we were significantly strengthened." "What did she do, specifically?" asked the mental health worker. The couple thought and thought and then said, "She told us we were doing a good job, and we needed to hear that; it made all the difference." Such a few words, for such an impact!

Respect is a basic human need and giving it is part of emotional intelligence. It means noticing others and treating them as valuable simply because they are persons. It increases the recipient's self-esteem. Extending respect for the coping skills or productivity of the person or for his or her innovation and contributions does much to enhance motivation. Showing respect is easy when workers are coping well and performing well. It is much harder to extend respect when a worker is chronically arrogant, belligerent or passively aggressive toward supervision and leadership. Habits such as nit-picking and criticizing, whining and wheedling and subtly impeding the goals of a leader are maddening, but even then, workers deserve respect. Looking into the sources of their discontent can go a long way to helping them cope better.

Truly respecting a person means a leader will not allow someone to continue in dysfunction because respect also implies caring. Whether a person is violating the legal system or is behaving inappropriately, it has an impact on the reputation of the organization and is detrimental to the individual. It must be addressed. So too should inadequate performance be addressed. The leader or supervisor must find ways to identify the obstacle and address it. It is disrespectful to ignore a problem or pretend it does not exist. In perplexing situations, respect is communicated in how the problem is addressed and how the person is treated.

Respect is evident in policies related to discipline, grievances, the appeals process, confidentiality, and rehabilitation. Each policy must be scrutinized to see if respect is implicit in it. Fair policies enable all individuals to be treated with courage and respect, with their dignity honored.

Showing respect even in difficult situations with maddening people is a measure of a leader. Henry Cloud discusses three kinds of worker and offers suggestions for dealing with each one (2011). Wise workers, foolish workers, and evil workers are distinguished by their response to feedback. Each kind should be treated differently, but with respect.

Who Should Do the Audit?

When performing a personnel care audit, leaders must decide whether to call on the services of an external consultant or tap someone from within the staff. Typically, results will be viewed more objectively if an external consultant is engaged. On the other hand, if his or her recommendations seem unpalatable, it is easy for leaders to say, "He doesn't understand us! We are unique." We remember the tongue-in-cheek comment someone made to us, "You can't understand us until you've been bitten by our mosquitoes!"

Ten Steps for Doing the Audit[52]

If an organization is sincere about gathering truthful and full information, it is most helpful to obtain the services of an experienced outside consultant, preferably someone familiar with international aid, both faith-based and other humanitarian organizations. Taking this step exhibits a nondefensive stance, and a desire for full information. It ensures safety for the responders. It does mean that the recipients of the assessment, the leadership team, will have to weigh and evaluate the responses carefully—do they come from long-time members? Or new members? Do they reflect deeply held opinions, or spontaneous reactions based on current events? Is one arm of the organization more troubled than another?

Although there are values and drawbacks in either choice of internal consultants or external ones, it seems preferable to choose a researcher from outside the organization. This specialist could work in concert with a highly skilled leader within the organization, a person who knows the organization very well and can be trusted to respond with integrity.

---

[52] Note: This is a personnel care audit, not an evaluation of the financial soundness of the organization or an assessment of other factors of health. (See Volume II, Chapter 11, Organizational and Systems Issues.)

Step 1 . Create a profile of the organization. What kind of organization is this? The consultant needs history, contributions, locations, personnel information, leadership style, future goals and directions.

Step 2. Interview the leaders of at least the top three levels of management (senior management, mid-level management, and work supervisors).

Step 3. Become familiar with the legislation manual and personnel policy manual. Other helpful data will include the number of members who left the organization and the reason for and manner of their leaving, the growth rate of the organization, the ethnic diversity of the organization, the number of young people, women, and ethnically diverse people in management and leadership. The relationship of the organization's leadership to their board, the make-up of the board, and the model of governance followed by the board are also significant.

Step 4. Interview a random selection of staff workers from as many locations as practical and reasonable.

Step 5. Prepare a spreadsheet listing the values and goals of the organization (column one), the reactions and responses of leaders (column two), and the reactions and responses of the staff (column three). Evaluate for congruence or disparity.

Step 6. Evaluate the intentions of leaders and the reactions of staff workers against the personnel policies and procedures. Is there congruence?

Step 7. Identify areas where the organization is doing well and acknowledge these. Identify areas of discontent, weakness, or concern and offer recommendations to the leadership for change or sustained attention. These suggestions for change should be accompanied by a suggested time table, and some mechanism of accountability.

Step 8. Submit a written report to the person(s) authorizing the audit.

Step 9. Suggest revisiting the crucial and critical issues and proposed changes, by the same consultant, to be conducted in a year.

Step 10. Store collected data carefully. It should be lodged with both the leader or Human Resources person on the leadership team, as well as with the consultant. It should be treated as very confidential, though a number of actions will flow out of the findings.

Hopefully, the leaders' response to the personnel care audit is to ensure a robust member care program throughout the organization. If one does not yet exist, creating such a program is crucial. See Chapter 5 for a description of member care and the role of the Member Care Facilitator (MCF).

Summary

Any agency or organization that takes seriously the health and well-being of its members will take the extra care to perform a personnel care audit periodically. This is an excellent means by which to assess morale and to review the effectiveness and productivity of the members. As any group or agency changes over time, it is important to include this as part of the personnel or member care routine. Often an outside consultant can see the issues more clearly and solicit more honest feedback from members, especially if morale has diminished and there is any difficulty with workers trusting their leaders. Based on the personnel care audit and feedback from the consultant, leaders can make adjustments in the system to benefit the individuals as well as the team or organization. We recommend such an audit on each field of service, as well as for the organization as a whole. When top leaders in "headquarters" do not or have not lived in the field settings, this process is especially crucial, as they may actually be, or perceived to be, out of touch with the realities their members are facing.

Appendix One:
Essential Elements of a Member Care Program

Six essential elements of a good member care program include:

1. A vision. Leaders who have a vision for member care. Leaders are keepers of the ethos of an organization. They must be approachable, available, caring, and value and respect members.
2. A mandate. The role of Member Care Facilitator (MCF) must be board-approved and come with a philosophy statement and full support for this staff position. The MCF must have credibility. (Credibility usually comes only from successful field service, with a person who has "paid his dues"). He or she will be full-time, trained, and appointed. The role will include monitoring, listening, responding, and being proactive and creative. This person is to have the ear of top leaders and access to resources.
3. A champion. A key player who will place the MCF in a position to develop member care at the international headquarters and beyond.
4. A staff. MCFs placed geographically and allocated to international hubs where they are close to those members doing field work, while having good access to international resources.
5. An ethos of care. This must be expressed at all administrative levels by noticing, valuing, celebrating, confronting, challenging, and responding. It can be pervasive throughout all departments of the organization, both in the headquarters and abroad.
6. A budget. Making visits, gathering resources, phone calls—these things cost something. An organization that really cares for its people will both staff and fund the care functions.

Appendix Two:
A Model for Member Care

A helpful model for member care consists of concentric circles.[53] Beginning at the center, it includes the following six levels of providers or originators of caring.

1. Master Care at the center: nothing should replace God in a member's life; anything that can be done to strengthen members' relationship to God must be encouraged.
2. Self Care: resilience, hardiness, personal responsibility for self and family, for personal and spiritual growth, reading, thinking, listening, able to detect drift in self, and refocus.
3. Mutual care: friendship, hospitality, responsiveness to one another, mentoring, accountability relationships, serving as examples of life management one to another, etc.
4. Organizational care: policies, structures, caring leaders, awareness of issues, needs, and lifestyle of a member; helping to stimulate balanced living; knows members' tolerance for stress; insists on connection with other agents of care, such as the sending church.
5. Specialist care: counselors, educators, trainers, mediators, helpers of all kinds. The member care champion has a good network of helpers and care-givers.

Contact with and involvement of the sending church or other local entity which sponsors the individual member.

---

[53] This diagram and these ideas are attributed to Dr. Marjory Foyle, Dr. Kelly O'Donnell, and Dr. David Pollock (*Doing Member Care Well*).

Appendix Three:
Some Signs of Poor and Good Member Care

You know you're *not* practicing good member care when...
- Members display lack of satisfaction and low creativity.
- Members feel viewed as an expense rather than an asset.
- There is an atmosphere of fear and blame.
- Members feel disrespected and unvalued.
- Members feel distant from leadership and powerless.
- Members display low trust in leadership.
- There is high attrition.

You know you are practicing good member care when...
- Members are in touch with leaders and feel their input is valued.
- There is an atmosphere of safety; members feel free to try new things, freedom to express their opinions without fear of retaliation.
- Members are loyal toward the organization; they are good recruiters.
- Members feel they can use their gifts; they are given opportunities to grow.

Appendix Four:
"The Foundations of Member Care" and
"Implementing Member Care

Visual of Foundations of Member Care

Modeling and Mutliplying (Facilitating)

Heartstream Resources   Dodds

Knowledge and understanding with wise insight

Skills

FOUNDATIONS OF MEMBER CARE

Spiritual life qualities: discernment, spiritual gifts; personal maturity

Love, commitment, attitude, expressed empathy

Trust: honest, open, transparent; keeping confidences; ethical

			Knowledge and understanding with wise insight			Skills	
Family of origin	Moral & spiritual development	Hidden heart messages	Actualized "gifts & talents"	Counseling skills	Assertiveness	Listening and communication	Education self & others
Culture of origin	Physical development/ health	Actualized development/ health	Dimensions & stages of health development	Pastoral Skills	Analytical skills esp. Assessment	Mentoring skills	Conflict skills
Life stage	Generational differences			Resource skills	Hospitality skills Welcoming	Encouragement Skills	Debriefing skills
Host Culture	Personality types	Relational health		Stress management skills, assesment/intervention	Resource brokering	Emotional development	Affirmation skills
Significant past events	Basic human needs	Resource brokering				Organizational ethos	Mediation skills
	Impact of stress						
Leadership styles							

Visual of Implementation of Member Care

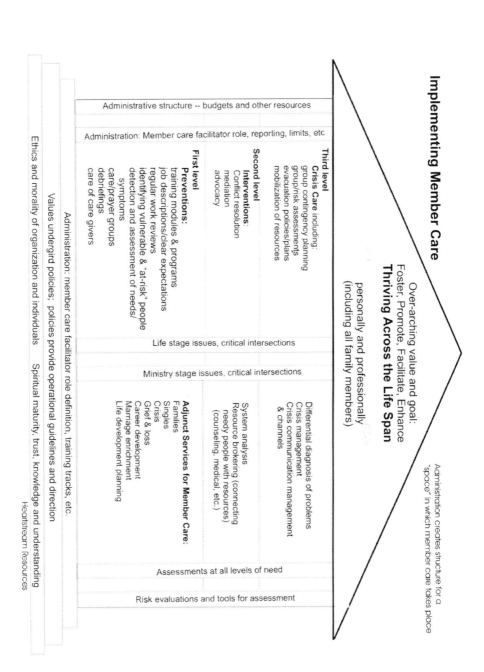

References and Recommending Reading

Arterburn, Stephen, and Felton, Jack. 2001. *Toxic faith: experiencing healing from painful spiritual abuse.* Colorado Springs: Shaw.

Bennis, Warren, and Goleman, Daniel. 2008. *Transparency: how leaders create a culture of candor.* San Francisco: Jossey Bass.

Cloud, Henry. 2011. *Necessary endings: the employees, businesses, and relationships that all of us have to give up in order to move forward.* NY: Harper Collins.

Goleman, Daniel. 1995 and 1996. *Emotional intelligence.* NY: Bantam Books

_____. 1998. *Working with emotional intelligence.* NY: Bantam Books.

Goleman, Daniel, Boyatzis, Richard and McKee, Annie. 2002 and 2004. *The new leaders.* London. Little Brown.

_____, _____, _____, _____: 2002 and 2004. *Prima leadership: realizing the power of emotional intelligence.* Boston: Harvard Business School Press.

_____. 2006. *Emotional intelligence: why it can matter more than IQ.* 10th anniversary Edition. Academic Internet Publ. Cram.

_____. 2006. *Social intelligence: the new science of human relationships.* NY: Bantam Books

_____. 2011. *Leadership: the power of emotional intelligence: selected writing.* Northampton: More than Sound.

Kohlberg, Lawrence. 1981. *The philosophy of moral development: moral stages and the idea of justice.* San Francisco: Harper and Rowe.

McAllister, Laurel. 2001. *Code of best practice in member care.* Vancouver, BC, Canada, Evangelical Fellowship of Canada.

Miller, Calvin. 1995. *The empowered leader: ten ways to servant leadership*. Nashville: Broadman and Holman Publ. pp. 135-153.

O'Donnell, Kelly, Ed. 2002. *Doing member care well.* Pasadena: CA. William Carey Library.

Chapter 10
Key Factors in Leaders and Leadership

The art and heart of agency care rests squarely on leaders! For caring attitudes and practices to permeate an organization, team, or agency, they must begin at the top with men and women who believe that those whom they lead are the most valuable resource without whom the organization's vision and purpose cannot be achieved. Leaders must validate their members as essential to the fulfillment of goals, and worthy of all that can be invested in them so that they may become most effective in their work roles and relationships. Given the huge challenges, chronic high stresses, and the obstacles inherent in fighting the evils of the world, we need a kind of leadership which believes in and invests in its people.

What kind of leaders and leadership philosophy can meet these objectives? We propose that the model of servant leadership, as defined and practiced by Robert Greenleaf, is the most effective. Servant leadership has been proven in myriad settings, including the humanitarian sector, in government,[54] and in business.[55]

---

[54] Dr. Larry Dodds was one of many leaders who practiced servant leadership in a local government setting, as he led the Public Health Department of Ventura County in Ventura, California, for ten years. With employees in the County system referring to his department of 240 employees as "the promised land," personnel often sought transfers into his department because of his approach to empowering and affirming the staff. When a top-down leader once criticized, "Dr. Dodds, I can't tell who is in charge here," Larry cheerfully responded, "Thank you! That is just the way it should be. Everyone knows his or her own job and does it well!"

[55] The Cornwall Coal Company in Tasmania, New Zealand, annual report with code of conduct. Available from Heartstream Resources.

We will examine the primary facets of servant leadership, the qualities and characteristics which are most important in leaders, and consider how leaders should be chosen and prepared. We will also explore leadership practices, especially those related to ethical treatment of members, identify some common errors to avoid, and discuss the challenges of leadership during periods of transition and change.

What is Servant Leadership?

Robert Greenleaf, who for decades served in American Telephone and Telegraph Company, is credited with coining the term "servant leadership." He practiced this kind of leadership and mentored many who became high-level leaders in the company. The Robert Greenleaf Center for Servant Leadership honors his enormous contribution, continuing to train leaders in this vital philosophy and model of leadership. See http://www.greenleaf.org/leadership/servant-leadership.

Robert Greenleaf described servant-leadership in this way.

> The servant-leader is servant first... It begins with the natural feeling that one wants to serve, to serve first. Then conscious choice brings one to aspire to lead. He or she is sharply different from the person who is leader first, perhaps because of the need to assuage an unusual power drive or to acquire material possessions. For such it will be a later choice to serve— after leadership is established. The leader-first and the servant-first are two extreme types. Between them there are shadings and blends that are part of the infinite variety of human nature.[56]

Greenleaf regarded that the best test of whether one is practicing servant leadership is whether those being led are growing as persons, becoming healthier and wiser, becoming more autonomous, and are more likely to themselves serve others.

---

[56] *Servant as Leader*, Robert Greenleaf, 1970.

Larry Spears of the Greenleaf Center has this to say about servant leadership:

> As we near the end of the twentieth century, we are beginning to see that traditional autocratic and hierarchical modes of leadership are slowly yielding to a newer model—one that attempts to simultaneously enhance the personal growth of workers and improve the quality and caring of our many institutions through a combination of teamwork and community, personal involvement in decision making, and ethical and caring behavior. This emerging approach to leadership and service is called *servant-leadership*.[57]

Many other fine leaders and authors have contributed to the literature and practice of servant leadership. Blanchard and Hodges identify a key value, "The duty of a servant leader is the ongoing investment of the leader's life into the lives of those who follow."[58] The servant leader notices his or her workers, and helps them—and that help may take many forms.

Leighton Ford's *Transforming Leadership* is an excellent study, as is Gayle Erwin's Jesus' *Style*. Ford echoes the key value of servant leadership, "Transforming leaders ...divest themselves of power and invest it in their followers."

Servant leadership stands in contrast to traditional top-down philosophies and styles of leadership, which typically view workers as commodities. For a discussion of this see Skye Jethani (2009). He describes how organizations attract good people, use them, use them up, get rid of them, and replace them. The difference is profound, considering that servant leadership views persons and teams as organisms, while traditional hierarchical leadership is mechanistic in its approach.

---

[57] From the Introduction to *Reflections on Leadership*, 1995, John Wiley Publ.
[58] Blanchard and Hodges, p. 83.

What Characterizes a Servant Leader?

A servant leader is identified through six characteristics described by the Robert Greenleaf Center and adapted to fit non-profit situations and leaders:

1.   The servant leader displays unlimited availability to others by accepting and empathizing—never rejecting. He or she responds to situations by listening first.

2. The servant leader knows him or herself well, and is an active learner immersed in the world. He or she believes growth begins "in here"—in a sense, lighting his or her own lamp. He or she is able to withdraw, be silent, re-orient, to recoup energy.

3. The servant leader holds liberating visions of a preferred future while understanding the ineffable nature of life. He or she is comfortable with the use of intuition and has dreams, foresight—can see a way and point to it.

4. The servant leader uses persuasion, working with one person at a time with gentle persuasion. He or she knows others can do what they must do for themselves which displays respect. He or she reinforces hope.

5. The servant leader builds community (teams), understanding that we build for all. This leader believes that work is as essential for workers as what they produce.

6. The servant leader uses power ethically, ensuring that no one is harmed by actions of a team. He or she accepts authority freely and knowingly, and uses it skillfully.

Note: In understanding the nature of servant leadership, it is helpful to describe the difference between "servant leadership" and "service" or "serving" in those usual definitions. (See Appendix One, by Gayle Erwin.)

Whom to Choose? Integrity is Key

Leadership literature in both for-profit and non-profit fields identifies integrity as one of the most essential qualities in a leader. Integrity and trustworthiness flow out of character and are key to leadership. The descriptions below are based in Judeo-Christian principles, which are shared by many other world religions and are prized in most cultures.

Character:
- Honesty and trustworthiness: The words and actions of people of integrity are congruent. Their lifestyle can stand up to scrutiny. They are worthy models, with highest integrity in moral and financial matter.
- Ability to build trust.
- Self-awareness and accurate self-assessment, demonstrated by a commitment to lifelong learning in all domains (academic, spiritual, emotional, interpersonal and professional).
- Personal vulnerability in regards to appropriate self-disclosure and appropriate risk taking.
- Taking responsibility rather than shifting blame.
- Flexibility which enables a leader to work harmoniously with multiple perspectives and in diverse contexts.
- Respecting authority and giving priority to accomplishing corporate vision and goals.
- Wielding power appropriately, remembering what Shakespeare said in his Sonnet # 94, "Who having the power to do harm, will do none."

Competence:
- Competency must be exhibited in many domains.
- Communication skills: The leader must be extremely competent in communication skills to connect with a widely diverse membership through many media. He or she should have very good listening skills, speak little, and use words that are positive, encouraging, and truthful.
- Finely honed interpersonal skills enable a leader to connect with people with sincerity and ease. The leader must be able to encourage, confront, teach, challenge, stimulate, weep with, rejoice with, and celebrate with people. He or she will be at ease

working with, leading, and promoting both genders. These skills must not be cosmetic or artificial; they must be anchored in a profound respect for people.

- Knowledge of personality types and styles: The leader must know her or his own personality type and style, as well as being able to recognize the unique personalities of those on the team. This knowledge enables a leader to accommodate other personalities and style preferences.

- Emotional intelligence: This crucial aspect of competency and self-awareness is discussed by Daniel Goleman in his many books on the subject. (See the bibliography for a listing of some of Goleman's books.)

- Cross-cultural and multicultural skills: These skills are essential in order to lead in today's diverse global environment. Humanitarian workers serve in many remote places in the world they come from and go everywhere. A competent leader in a diverse world must not be ethnocentric or nationalistic. Ideally, he or she will speak more than one language.

- A high tolerance for ambiguity is another crucial aspect of an ideal leader. Things seldom are as they seem to be; situations are often unpredictable, what worked yesterday will not work tomorrow, and change is everywhere. Being flexible and adaptable must come from a core of convictions and values that make him or her predictable, consistent, easy to trust.

- Hardiness: The leader is able to work hard and long. Leaders generally do work harder than most others because the responsibility rests on their shoulders. However, the leader must know how and when to take time off, to draw back, and how to recoup his or her energies.

- Accurate self-knowledge. This includes knowing what energizes him or her and what is draining and then arranging work accordingly.

- Skills in communication technology: These are vital in today's world, including both dissemination and storage of information. Being adept in technology will enable a leader to be more engaged in and to oversee all aspects of the organization.

- Organizational knowledge: A leader must know the history of the organization, its foundational principles, its guiding values and its core beliefs. He must be committed to the organizational goals.

- Appropriate understanding and use of power and what constitutes abuse of power. The Apostle Paul illustrates for us his own commitment to the best use of power, saying, "I want to use the authority the Lord has given me to build you up, not to tear you down."[59] In another letter he illustrates his loving care by saying, "I was like a nursemaid among you...."[60]

Additional skills, attitudes and qualities:

The following have been identified by Lester Hirst from the work of Greenleaf and Spears at the Greenleaf Center for Servant Leadership.[61] They are often called "soft skills" because they are hard to quantify and difficult to identify in oneself. The best way to determine if a potential leader has these skills is to elicit from past and present co-workers and previous supervisors how the person demonstrates these behaviors and attitudes:

- Acceptance of others
- Empathy—identifies with the concerns of others so as to better understand and lead
- Intuition
- Listening receptively—an act of will and commitment
- Awareness and perception—ability to see things as they really are highly developed powers of persuasion to lead the way ahead
- Ability to conceptualize—think beyond day-to-day concerns to place in context projects that are part of a larger vision
- Foresight—view the likely outcome of a given situation based on past lessons, realities of the present and consequences of the future
- Stewardship—best use and highest level of care of what has been placed in your trust
- A healing influence upon people and institutions—take opportunities to restore others to wholeness—to show caring
- Ability to build a sense of community in the workplace— promote opportunities for working together while respecting the dignity of individuals to provide service to the world

---

[59] II Corinthians 10:8, *New Testament.*
[60] I Thes. 2:7, J. B. Phillips paraphrase of the New Testament.
[61] Lester J. Hirst, Ph.D. Curriculum & Professional Development Manager for Compassion International.

- Commitment to growth of others—nurture personal, professional and spiritual growth of others, believing in the intrinsic value of individuals
- Willingness to change

How Do We Develop Servant Leaders?

We know from extensive experience and years of observation that the kind of leaders we have just described do not "just happen." They are developed over time through careful modeling, teaching, mentoring, and both professional and personal growth. I have been deeply involved in leadership development for the last twelve years (Gardner). In the early stages of this effort, I helped to develop a curriculum for the growth and development of young leaders. This curriculum has several elements:

Character development. Though it is currently fashionable to ignore one's weaknesses and build on one's strengths, some weaknesses become "deal breakers" for future leadership roles. A lack of integrity, arrogance, prideful disdain and lack of respect for people, and unwillingness to be a model and a coach are unacceptable in a leadership role. Unwillingness to receive feedback short circuits growth in the individual. Skills can be taught, but character qualities are harder to grasp and instill. Unless the individual sees and owns his or her own weaknesses and is willing to address them, his character is unlikely to change.

We suggest the Leadership Covenant (Appendix Two of this chapter) as a way to explore integrity and wholesome character. When a leader articulates his or her values, and is seen to live these out in private and public, it builds an atmosphere of trust and health. My own leader recently led a session in a leadership development event in which he outlined his twenty lifetime values. What a difference it makes to have a vulnerable and transparent leader express publicly the values that show he is a good and growing person!

Identification and formation of attitudes. Usually matters of skill, competence and performance occupy our minds first when we think of leadership development. But attitudes make or break a leader.

Organizational knowledge. The history of a given organization, including a time-line of the key events and context which have shaped it provides essential background knowledge for a leader. This is especially important in a multicultural context and differs with continent, country and culture.

Skills acquisition. Our curriculum emphasizes good communication skills, people management and care, interpersonal skills, strategic planning, networking, learning how to confront, how to do performance reviews with staff, how to engage with the public, how to gain ease with technology, and related functions of management and leadership. Knowledge is put into practice by developing skills. Knowledge without skills to support it is not as productive as it could be.

Feedback—inviting, receiving, and giving feedback. Participants in the leadership training programs prepare by completing a number of feedback instruments, such as the Strengths Finders test, a 360 review (four levels of feedback from supervisors, co-workers, peers, and others) and similar instruments. (See the bibliography for information on Strengths Finders.)[62]

Coaching. Each participant is assigned to a coach, an experienced person who will meet privately with the protégée. In addition, the two meet with a small group to work through the various instruments and to help the participant develop a personal and professional development plan. The plan is based on honing the individual's strengths and addressing the weaknesses. The coaching relationship is the key factor in the participant's growth.

The qualities of the coach are important! He or she should be able to give bad news in a good way, to point out the weaknesses as well as the strengths of the protégé, and to assist him or her in addressing weaknesses and honing strengths. The coach must have at his or mental

---

[62] https://www.gallup.com/cliftonstrengths/en/home.aspx

fingertips an array of resources for growth of the protégé. The coach may become the mentor to the protégé.

Knowledge of Personality Type. Our curriculum includes teaching potential leaders about personality type.

How Should Leaders be Chosen?

Besides the complexity of *whom* to choose, organizations must wrestle with the reality of HOW to choose leaders! The gap between the ideals of leadership and the practical reality is usually problematical and often large. What is most valued and desired is sometimes not achievable, as there is a limited pool of persons from which new leaders may be selected, especially in the humanitarian world which does not work on a normal salary-for-service system. It is helpful to review both the ideal and the practical, and to see that in actuality when a group looks for a new leader, they look for qualities from both lists. We want someone who exhibits impeccable character and trustworthiness, and who is competent and cross-culturally aware. We usually consider these factors in potential leaders:

Ideally	Practically
Character	Popularity
Competencies	Availability
Skills in many areas	Trustworthiness
Cross-cultural awareness	Field experience
Leadership style	Leadership style

Another practical matter is where one might find the potential leader. Some organizations will consider only someone from within their own ranks as opposed to looking elsewhere for a leader. Often, bringing in high level leaders from outside an organization makes a change in leadership more difficult because the person may not know the history, the values, or the uniqueness of the organization. If there is a need to change the ethos of the organization, any newly appointed leader must invest significant time getting to know the organization, have great powers of persuasion, high credibility, and the skill to bring about that change.

Other factors: In some organizations having **field experience** is considered to be an important factor, though not necessarily essential. **Popularity** is typically considered as well. To the degree that **personal charisma** a love for people and highly refined interpersonal skills contributes to popularity it is valuable. But if the person's popularity is because of being a hands-off leader who allows others to do "whatever," it is not wise to choose on that basis. Considering the **leadership style** of the person is important for best fit with a role and the context. Helpful questions include looking at the following: Is the person a visionary or a hands-on manager? Is he or she authoritarian, or does he or she manage power and authority appropriately? Does she or he seek consensus and consult others when making decisions? Does he or she hide behind his authority or remain open and vulnerable? We think about these things when the time comes to vote for who will lead us. And so we should.

Leadership Challenges in Times of Transition and Change

"Change is the only constant" is a saying attributed to Heraclitus, the Greek philosopher. Change is inevitable. Thus, managing change constitutes a major leadership challenge. This is acknowledged in more recent years by futurist Alvin Toffler, who says, "The illiterate of the 21st century will not be those who cannot read and write, but those who cannot learn, unlearn, and relearn." It seems this is a correct assessment. There are some things we must unlearn, relearn, and learn.

Hans Finzel says, "In today's organizations, change is not a response to a challenge, it is the challenge. Change is mandatory for any group that wants to make a mark today. Because if something works today, it is already half obsolete."[63]

Assessing transition readiness: William Bridges is a leading author and guru on the subject of transitions, an internationally recognized authority on managing change in the workplace. For more than two decades he has been helping clients with mergers, reorganizations,

---

[63] Finzel, Hans. 1994. *Ten Mistakes Leaders Make*, p 38.

leadership changes and cultural shifts. His ten books include *Transitions* and *Managing Transitions* (2003).

Bridges' definitions are illuminating. He says, "…change is a shift in the externals of any situation…" "By contrast, transition is the mental and emotional transformation that people must undergo to relinquish old arrangements and embrace new ones."[64] He reminds us that transitions include a beginning, a middle (neutral phase) and an end. Thus these two are fundamentally different. Poorly managed change and transition seem to be where many organizations meet disaster.

Bridges refers to "the human side of things," which includes understanding the impact of change and transition on people. He explains that *realizing* and *justifying change* is not sufficient to help people actually make the change. Having this awareness is essential to leaders.

Fifteen Kinds of Change and Transitions

The following are based on observed realities in humanitarian, religious, and altruistic organizations with international membership and worldwide areas of service:

1. New supervisor, old team
2. Change in policies handed down from the top (headquarters)
3. Budget cuts, "there is no money"
4. Conflict on the team
5. Loss of team members due to misconduct (much secrecy)
6. Loss of morale, people are losing heart
7. Loss of trust in the leadership; disunity among the team
8. Cultural differences causing conflicts and confusion
9. Differing expectations as to the role of a leader
10. Inexperienced leader who is not consistent or shows favoritism.
11. Change in organizational identity, e.g., a new name or a merger
12. Change of focus, e.g., changing from *doing* what we've always done to facilitating, mentoring, or consulting while others *do* it, often called "capacity building"

---

[64] Bridges, 1980.

13. Change in vision or style: "This is not the organization I joined, not the way it used to be."
14. The leader is unavailable; he or she is gone all the time.
15. The leader is unapproachable; though present he or she is feared or not trusted.

Characteristic emotions and behaviors typical during transitions: These include anger, criticalness, withdrawal, increase in gossip, lowered morale, decline in creativity, passive-aggressive behavior, taking of sides, defensiveness, and self-protectiveness. We will also see insecurity, self-centeredness ("What does this change mean to me?" "To my staff?") We may feel or hear, "Is anyone at the helm of this ship?"

Fear is another emotion common during times of transition, and it is contagious. Sometimes it is so strong that people resist the possibility of good news. Ambiguity is another inescapable element of change— when situations are unclear, vague, uncertain, and obscure. Transitions can be frightening especially for those who need predictability, routine, and security.

A leader who understands that negative emotions are normal responses to change can be supportive rather than condemning with his or her team. He or she can impart faith that things will work out, especially that God is present in times of difficulty. He or she will remember the Persian proverb which says, "A broken hand works, but not a broken heart."

Three Scenarios in One Case Study

Scenario 1: A young man is newly appointed by the International Office. He is Canadian, with a very shy wife and several small children. His leadership philosophy is authoritarian-- "I am the boss." This is evidenced in his approach to change. He cuts all budgets. He fires two people for holding opinions different from his. A team of ten decide together to subtly resist this leader. One of them quietly tells the leader the plan—and things get worse.

What did the leader do wrong?
What did the team do wrong?
How can this situation be 'fixed'? By whom?

Scenario 2: Another new leader is appointed, someone who is experienced, fluent in the local language, competent, and friendly. However *she* is a woman and also single. She inherits a demoralized, conflicted team due to budget cuts, cultural misunderstandings and loss of vision.

What should she do?
What would you do? Obviously, subtle gender issues are present that complicate her leadership. She can't change her gender.
Is there anything she *can* do?
What is the responsibility of the organization in this scenario?

Scenario 3: A local person, a good team member, is suddenly appointed as the field leader. He is popular with the members and staff but has no administrative or management experience.

How can he prepare for the leadership task? Who is responsible?
If *you* were asked to take on a major leadership role, how would you prepare?

An outstanding example of wisdom, discernment, longevity, and credibility in an organization is that of Billy Graham. What has enabled this group of highly visible persons to retain the integrity and credibility of their public group persona over a long period of time? My research reveals that they regularly and deliberately identified areas of temptation and vulnerability for highly visible people like themselves, and intentionally made commitments in four areas. My study of that group led me to write the Leadership Covenant which identifies nine areas of vulnerability for leaders. (See Appendix Two.)

Ten Ways to Practice Servant Leadership for Optimal* Health in An Organization
by Lois Dodds

1. **Create a climate of trust**. This involves warmth, acceptance, genuineness, respect, honesty, integrity, consistency and fairness.

2. **Model equality of persons**. Differentiate the hierarchy of roles and tasks from the value of each individual person and his or her contribution to the team.

3. **Match persons and job roles/tasks**. Based on temperament, motivations and job readiness/preparedness, persons should be placed in those roles which best allow for the expression of their gifts, motivations and experience. Persons not appropriately matched are more susceptible to burnout, as well as possibly being less effective and less motivated.

4. **Create challenge and opportunity** which foster the development of persons intellectually, spiritually, morally, and that enable acquiring new knowledge and skills.

5. **Invite participation**. Participatory leadership and decision-making enable a degree of involvement and "owning" of outcomes which contributes to the sense of worth of each person.

6. **Reward divergent thinking**. Allow for and encourage innovation, creativity and difference. In the long run these are the seeds for and source of organizational renewal and transformation.

7. **Be honest, open, and transparent**. Clearly communicate one's self (especially as leader), vision, purpose, goals, plans, etc. (Hidden

agendas on the part of leadership creates suspicion and mistrust.) Make expectations clear and give feedback regularly.

8. **Recognize, acknowledge, and reward** the contribution of each person, especially those who by temperament or task are likely to be overlooked.

9. **Provide support and resources** which enable persons to meet the expectations and goals established, both personal support (such as for family and educational needs) and organizational support, such as funding, space, etc.

10. **Affirm! Celebrate! Appreciate!** each person, each achievement, every effort.

* OPTIMAL implies the "best possible" growth and development of the individual which maximizes his or her potential. This is promoted through an enriching, nurturing, supportive and challenging environment. In comparison, "ADEQUATE," implies providing only what is needed.

Why Do Leaders Fail?

Hans Finzel, CEO and President of a large, reputable, nonprofit, global organization, identifies ten mistakes leaders make.[65]

These leadership mistakes are: top-down autocratic arrogance; giving paper priority over people; failing to affirm; allowing no room for mavericks; being dictators in decision-making; practicing "dirty delegation;" communication chaos; clues of corporate culture are missing; the hope for success without successors, and failure to focus on the future.

See Appendix Nine for a summary of Finzel's work.

---

[65] Finzel, Hans. 1994. *The top ten mistakes leaders make*. Colorado Springs, CO: David C. Cook.

Besides the kinds of errors which Finzel identifies, leaders can fail to relate to personnel or deal with issues in the most ethical ways. This is often manifested with a lack of commitment to care for people once they are chosen.

Ethical practice goes beyond the selection and training phases. Once an organization - selects its people, it should make a complete commitment to preparing and assisting those persons to be fully effective. This means ongoing care to enable them to contribute their best. Serious breakdowns in the caring process sometimes arise due to ethical mistakes.

Ethical Errors in Leadership.

1. **Making decisions about people's lives and work without consulting them**. This includes financial decisions, allocations, roles, relationships to children, decisions that affect children, and other highly personal matters. Ethical care includes people in all such decisions.

2. **Acting on third party information or allegations rather than on face-to-face interaction with the person**. Such third party information is always filtered by someone else's projections and interpretations, and labeled with their meanings. We know of several cases of people being "sent home" without even having a face to face interview about the perceived problem. Usually the allegations prove to be untrue, but great damage has already been done by robbing people of their ministries, their homes, their support network, and their honor. Ethical care involves due process, such as face-to-face interactions and fairness and justice.

3. **Giving away confidential information.** This is sometimes mistakenly justified on the belief that others have a "right to know." If there IS a need for others to know anything, the organization should work out **with the person** in writing exactly what is to be shared, and then stick to the script! Great hurt and damage is caused by inappropriate telling of secrets and confidential information. Ethical care safeguards confidence, personnel files, and other sensitive material.

Exchanging confidences between homeland and field is especially dangerous given today's ease of e-mail errors. Carefully managing records which contain any potentially damaging information is crucial. Access to files should be controlled, locked up and used only by those who have responsibility to guide the person's life and work. Extreme care is needed. We know of one situation in which an irresponsible personnel worker emailed everyone in the organization, "Mr. Nameless has resigned, but it has nothing to do with sexual matters."

This raises many relevant questions. What about storing records? How long do you keep them? Do you want to keep them? What about potential liability if you keep personnel records with some delicate information that might indicate a possible problem in the future? Do you destroy the documents to prevent "discovery" or keep them for possible future use? Are there legal issues or implications involved? Who is the custodian of those documents? When would they be destroyed, if ever? What do you do with written evaluations on new candidates? Do you keep them for follow up in case there are any difficulties? We have seen several people about whom we wondered how they ever got into a mission in the first place, because of things they reported to us, but there was no record of anyone noticing these things. Records do provide a valuable basis for research, so destroying them is not necessarily a good idea.

4. **Failing to keep confidences when sought out for advice and feedback**. Leaders who carelessly or deliberately pass on voluntarily shared information, misgivings, questions, or concerns do harm to the person and the organization. It is never appropriate to pass on information without asking permission of the person to do so. This is a fast way to destroy group morale! When something is important enough that it should be disclosed to someone else, the listener must ask the person to share it directly, not pass it on. Ethical care is listening, keeping confidences, and sharing with a third person only with permission.

5. **Failure to give regular performance reviews.** A person needs to know how he or she is doing, whether or not they are living up to expectations. Regular review provides a safe way to give appreciation, affirmation, and suggestions for growth and change. Ethical leadership coaches and teaches in order to support people's growth in ministry. Without feedback, people flounder, make mistakes, and may lose heart.

6. **Failure to give feedback for positive and appropriate behavior**. Criticizing failures or unmet expectations without positive feedback is hurtful. The first few years of any new assignment and allocation are highly stressful, and people need to be encouraged in what they are doing right and well. Thus, people especially need positive feedback during this phase.

7. **Failure to make expectations clear about the kind of work, the hours involved, the requirements, and so on.** Making expectations clear from the beginning and giving regular feedback helps in the adjustment process. Candidates should be told as much as is known about every facet of their work before going, especially the impact each will have on him or her and the family. Such "stress inoculation" is effective as a means of preventing a variety of problems. Knowing ahead of time one will not have electricity or running water, for instance, or that it usually takes a decade or two to instill major lifestyle changes averts the shock of learning such things on the spot after having established illusions of something better. Ethical care is pro-active care. It tries to avert, minimize and mitigate as much unnecessary stress as possible.

8. **Measuring people's "spirituality" with the wrong standards.** For instance, attributes such as lack of compliance or assertiveness are more likely indicators of personality type and conflict styles than of spiritual depth. Outspoken, articulate new members who point out redundancies and inaccuracies may be devalued; leaders may feel uncomfortable with such feedback. Young "prophets" usually don't get good reviews because by nature they observe and point out problems within systems. Ethical care by leaders means to be open to listen and slow to judge, and to acknowledge the insight and contributions of newer, younger and outspoken members.

9. **"Firing on furlough" and "hit and run" attacks.** To be fired in absentia, without having had any discussion of reasons, is devastating. This damages persons when they are not physically present to defend themselves or to seek resolution to a problem. We have seen this happen when people go home for a break, expecting to resume their field assignment, and then are told not to return. We have also seen an awkward "firing" take place as a leader drops someone off at the airport to go on home leave. These cowardly actions by leaders, who earlier

failed to engage in appropriate dialogue, does enormous damage. The sudden, unexpected action and lack of time for conversation is wounding and precludes closure. This recently happened to a couple based on allegations of wrong doing. These turned out to be lies by jealous national workers who later confessed. Even when corrected, the hurt and loss of trust so affects workers that it is very difficult to resume their former roles with those who have mistreated them. Ethical care provides regular, on-going feedback and confrontation when necessary.

10. **Forcing public confessions.** "Outing" someone or forcing a confession is harmful when a person is not ready to publicly address a problem behavior. This destroys trust and causes humiliation and shame. If a person agrees to confess wrong doing, and is supported by others in doing so appropriately, the outcome is faster healing for both the individual and the community. Ethical care means doing what is best for the troubled person, not making hasty attempts to satisfy the curiosity of or pressures from onlookers. The question also needs to be asked, "Is this something that **should** be confessed to a group? How many people have been affected by it?" If few have been, it may not need public confession. A wise leader will confront a wayward team member privately and discuss what actions to take.

11. **Misuse of power and "spiritual authority."** Because many humanitarian agencies are faith based, lines of power and authority may become blurred. It is crucial to differentiate organizational authority from what is considered to be spiritual oversight or mentoring. It is important to establish to whom one is accountable in both arenas. It is also important to establish who has the "final say" when a person must answer to various entities, such as sending groups, sponsors or donors, the field leaders, the home office, and a board of directors.

12. **Allowing persons to continue in service without intervention.** When someone has become exhausted, depleted, burned out, empty, or ineffective, appropriate intervention is essential. Loving, ethical care takes them out of the battle to provide time for restoration, without condemnation. Loving care provides resources for recovery, and for continued growth.

13. **Incongruity between recruitment and actual field life**. Incongruities seem especially glaring when the field experience and the

job role assignments bear little resemblance to what recruiters promised. For instance, recruiters cannot honestly say that anyone can work abroad in a humanitarian role. We know that is not true. Research bears out that those who are successful over the long haul have higher than average ego strength, resiliency, and coping skills.

Recommendations for Improving Ethical Practice

We want to see leaders provide ethical, moral and spiritual care with excellence. An ethical code of conduct regarding personnel and organization relationships is important to provide a standard for practice based on fairness and justice, as well as current legal mandates. One commonly in use is offered by People in Aid.[66] Another example of such a code comes from Missions Interlink of New Zealand.[67]

A second need is to establish a council of some kind, which will hear and adjudicate grievances of workers with their organizations. An impartial council with power to arbitrate would be a major step forward in protecting workers who are betrayed or violated in some way. Likely, just the existence of such a group and the public commitment of the organization to abide by its code would eliminate some abuse because leaders at all levels would be more alert to how people are treated.

So Then—What Shall We Say?

Though this chapter has focused on leadership and the qualities and competencies of leaders, ethical living is essential for everyone involved in the multicultural, humanitarian effort—both leaders and those whom they lead. We cannot help the world to change, or fight the evils we seek to right, without commitment from followers.

Graves and Addington tell us, "In searching so zealously for better leaders we tend to lose sight of the people these leaders will lead. Without his armies, after all, Napoleon was just a man with grandiose

---

[66] www.peopleinaid.org as of 2021, this website is no longer active
[67] Guidelines for good practice in member care. Available from Jenny Manson, Missions Interlink, www.pprofiles@maxnet.co.nz or www.info@missions.org.nz.

ambitions. Organizations stand or fall partly on the basis of how well their leaders lead, but partly also on the basis of how well their followers follow."[68]

Graves and Addington remind us of four necessary qualities of the followers who help to make leaders effective:
- Followers manage themselves well.
- They are committed to the organization and to a purpose, principle, or person outside themselves.
- They build their competence and focus their efforts for maximum impact.
- They are courageous, honest, and credible.

Summary

Considering the risk factors that many multicultural workers face, we suggest some specific leadership styles and organizational responses to help persons who are at risk. These behaviors in leaders and organizations are helpful:

Good leaders:
- Use their power to facilitate teams and build individuals.
- Attend to people, learn individual's needs, understand what is said and what cannot be stated.
- Are exceptional listeners.
- Exhibit and live trustworthiness and know how to build trust with all levels of workers, both local and distant.
- Are transparent and vulnerable.

What does leadership have to do with member care? Leadership is influence, and an effective member care worker has a great deal of influence. We must use it well. We must function as leaders, whether we have the mandate or the title or not. We must support well those who are leaders. Our member care responsibility must include our leaders, those with titles, positions and heavy responsibilities. We must bring

---

[68] Stephen R. Graves and Thomas G. Addington. 2002. Life@Work on *leadership: Enduring insights for men and women of faith,* p. 101. San Francisco: Jossey-Bass.

together a cohesive attitude that combines biblical truth – effective, responsible fulfilment of the Great Commission, and care of the team.

References and Recommended Reading

Annual Report Code of Conduct *of Cornwall Coal Company of Tasmania, New Zealand.* Available from Heartstream Resources.

Bennis, Warren, *et al.* 2008. *Transparency: how leaders create a culture of candor.* San Francisco: Jossey-Bass Publ. Also available in audio.

Blanchard, Kenneth, and Hodges, Phil. 2005. *Lead like Jesus: lessons from the greatest leader role model of all times.* Nashville: W. Publ. Group. p. 83.

Bradberry, Travis, and Greaves, Jean. 2009. *Emotional Intelligence 2.0.* San Diego, CA: TalentSmart.

Bratcher, Ed, *et al.* 1991. *Mastering Transitions.* Portland, OR: Multnomah Press.

Bridges, William and Bridges, Susan. 1980. *Transitions; making sense of life's changes.* Cambridge, MA: Perseus Books.

_____. 1991. *Managing transitions: making the most of change.* Reading, Mass: Addison Wesley Publ. Also 1997 in London: Nicolas Beasley Pub; also 2003 in Cambridge, Mass: De Capo Press

_____. 2001. *The way of transition: embracing life's most difficult moments.* Cambridge, Mass: Perseus Press.

Buckingham, Marcus, and Clifton, Donald. 2001. *Now, Discover Your Strengths:* New York: Free Press.

Clinton, J. Robert. 1988, 2012. The making of a leader, second edition. recognizing the lessons and stages of leadership development. Colorado Springs, CO. NavPress.

Covey, Stephen M. R. 2006. The Speed of trust. New York: Free Press.

Dodds, Lois A. 2010. Hot topic: Presentation on dual relationships. Mental Health and Missions Conference, Angola, Indiana. Nov. 18 to 21. Available Heartstream Resources.

_____. 2011.   A Christian Perspective on Dual or Multiple Relationships for Mental Health Professionals in a Community of Faith: A Body of Christ Perspective, with a Review of Eight Codes of Ethics. American Association of Christian Counselors World Congress. Nashville, Tennessee, Sept. 28 to Oct. 1. Available Heartstream Resources. Also on video from A.A.C.C.

Erwin, Gayle. 1983. *The Jesus style.* Palm Springs, CA: R. N. Haynes Publ.

Finkelstein, Sydney. 2003 and 2004. Why smart executives fail: and what you can learn from their mistakes. NY: Portfolio. Also in Chinese.

Finzel, Hans. 1994. *The ten top* mistakes an organization makes. Wheaton: Victor Books.

Ford, Leighton. 1993. Transforming Leadership. Downers Grove, IL: InterVarsity Press.

Gardner, Howard E. and Laskin, Emma. 1996. Leading minds: an anatomy of leadership. New York: Basic Books.

Gardner, John W. 1990. *On Leadership.* New York: The Free Press.

Goleman, Daniel. 1996. Emotional Intelligence. New York: Bantam Books.

_____. 2000. Working with emotional intelligence. New York: Bantam Books.

Goleman, Daniel, Boyatzis, Richard, and McKee, Annie. 2004. Primal Leadership: realizing the power of emotional intelligence. Boston, Mass: Harvard Business School Press.

_____. 2006. Emotional intelligence: 10th anniversary edition: why it can matter more than IQ. New York: Bantam Books.

_____. 2006. Social intelligence: the new science of human relationships. New York: Bantam Books.

_____. 2011. Leadership: the power of emotional intelligence. Northampton, MA: More Than Sound.

Graves, Stephen R., and Addington, Thomas G. 2002. *Life@Work on leadership: Enduring insights for men and women of faith.* p. 101. San Francisco: Jossey-Bass.

Greenleaf, Robert K. 1970. *Servant leadership.* New York: Paulist Press.

Hagberg, Janet. 1994. *Real power: Stages of personal power in organizations.* Salem, Wisc: Sheffield Pub. Co. Also 1984.

Hirst, Lester J. and Priscilla Hirst, *Leadership Development Learners Guide,* 2011.

Jethani, Skye. 2009. The Divine commodity: Discovering a faith beyond consumer Christianity. Grand Rapids, MI: Zondervan.

Kotter, John. 1996. Leading Change. Boston, Mass: Harvard Business School Press.

Schubert, Esther. 1993. Personality disorders and overseas missions: guidelines for the mental health professional. *Journal of Psychology and Theology.* Vol. 21, No. 1, pp. 18-25.

_____. 1996. The MMPI as a predictive tool for missionary candidates. *Journal of Psychology and Theology.* Vol. 24, No. 2, pp. 124-132.

Spears, Larry. 1995. *Reflections on leadership.* John Wiley & Sons.

Toffler, Alvin. 1971. *Future shock.* Boston: Little, Brown and Company.

Appendix One:
Service or Servanthood

Gayle D. Erwin, 1983

"Once, in a meeting with a neighbor pastor of an old established church, the conversation turned to what I had been writing about servanthood. He let out an "aha" as if a discovery had been made and said, "You are talking about service. We are old hands at that. We have been teaching service for years and our people are tired of that." At first I didn't know what to say until it dawned on me that there was a distinct difference between service and servanthood as I was hearing him.

"Service seemed to be something religious you could do that might not be a result of your own desires. "Service" could be a way of pigeon-holing spiritual life away from your everyday actions. "Service" could be a legalistic response to a desire for God's favor...a means of gaining points with God. "Service" could be what Paul spoke about in 1 Cor. 13 when he said, "though I give my body to be burned and have not love, it profits me nothing."

"This is not to infer that all service falls under the negative categories I have described. Indeed, thank God for all the energies put into His kingdom, but I must paint some contrasts.

"Service" can easily fall into the category of servitude in which one, though a volunteer, serves involuntarily, not out of choice but out of compulsion; whereas servanthood flows from choosing to lay down one's life and is not manipulated into its actions.

"Servanthood is a way of seeing people through the eyes of Jesus, not merely something else to do along the way. Servanthood involves another-centered attitude that does not put life into compartments. Servanthood without bothering to think of itself as service simply is service."

Reprinted from "Servant Quarters"

Appendix Two:
Leadership Covenant
By Dr. Larrie Gardner

1. Power: I will not use my position, title or authority to intimate others or to promote myself. I will use these to build others. II Co3. 13:10b

2. I will not pretend to know more or less than I do. I will ask for help when I need it and give credit. I will demonstrate an attitude of continual learning and growth.

3. Relationships: I will be faithful to my spouse in body, mind, emotions and thought. I will maintain friends though openness, reciprocity, mutual support and genuine encouragement.

4. Resources: I will be a good steward of time, money, and energy, remembering that, though all are limited, they should not be hoarded but directed toward the best pursuits.

5. Walk with God: I will love God supremely and enjoy Him fully, and rest in my relationship with Him. I will serve and worship the Lord of the Harvest, not substituting the Harvest for the Lord.

6. Thought life: My thought life is wholesome and could be published without embarrassment. I am honest in my view of myself and others. I will choose to fill my mind with positive goodness (Phil. 4: 7-8); my default will be one of good will and trust in God.

7. Fallibility: I am willing to admit mistakes and to ask for forgiveness when I offend.

8. Compassionate support: I want to shepherd people through change by being a "zone of safety" for them. I will be communicative and caring.

9. Generous humility: I will share what I have and know and think in order to strengthen others and reach our goal.

Leadership and people care come together. Good leadership is an aspect of member care. May we all carry out our leadership role with humility and sensitivity to the people entrusted to us. They are "the flock of God under our care" (I Peter 5:2).

Appendix Three:
Team Work Covenant
By Dr. Larrie Gardner, 2002

1. Acceptance: I will accept my supervisor as placed there by God and will support him or her by loyal speech, faithful workmanship, open communication, and sustained effort to help my group reach our larger goal. I will pray regularly for my supervisor and endeavor to make his task a joyful one (Heb. 13:17).

2. Contribution: I have expertise, experience, and insight and bring these as gifts to my supervisor and team. I will not be arrogant about my opinions or deceptive about my deficits in expertise and knowledge. I will continue to learn and grow in all areas of life.

3. Relationships: I will pursue peace (Rom. 12:18) with all because unity among believers is the most visible witness of godliness. I will be faithful to my task and a team player and friend to colleagues. I will honor my roles as spouse and parent as before God. Integrity, warmth, consistency, and communication will mark my relational style.

4. Resources: I will be generous with what I know and do and have. I will not compete when resources are scarce. While God has unlimited resources, I realize we do not. I will not hoard my time and energy but within reasonable boundaries, I will pursue corporate priorities.

5. Walk with God: I will work for God's approval (II Tim. 2:15) and behave like His child. I do not need to be policed because God's love constrains me to do good and to be good. I will love Him above all else and serve Him joyfully.

6. Thought life: Knowing I can't control fleeting thoughts, I will develop a wholesome and godly thought life by filling my mind with goodness and avoiding questionable movies, videos, books and other activities. I will not tolerate private sin. I will choose to think well of others and avoid judging motivations.

7. Conflict: Knowing conflict is inevitable, I will make every effort to resolve it quickly. I will disagree respectfully, when necessary, and pursue kind and gentle speech.

8. Receiving feedback: My supervisor must evaluate my performance, attitudes, etc. I will welcome feedback as necessary to continuing growth. I will not be defensive when corrected.

9. Integrity: I will not pretend, or attempt to deceive or impress others. I will own my mistakes rather than blaming someone else. I will be a responsible, honest, vulnerable, growing person, with God's help.

Appendix Four:
Trust Questionnaire Part 1
(to answer regarding oneself)

By Dr. Lester J. Hirst and Priscilla Hirst,
Leadership Development Learners Guide, 2011
Used by permission.

Directions:
For each statement, circle the number that best corresponds to your self-evaluation.

(1 = strongly agree; 2 = agree; 3 = don't know; 4 = disagree; 5 = strongly disagree.

1. I have a clear understanding of my values.   1 2 3 4 5

2. I behave consistently with my values.   1 2 3 4 5

3. I sincerely desire the best for others.   1 2 3 4 5

4. Others know I desire the best for them.   1 2 3 4 5

5. I possess the skills and abilities necessary to succeed.   1 2 3 4 5

6. I have a track record of producing results.   1 2 3 4 5

7. My track record gives others the confidence that I
   will produce results   1 2 3 4 5

8. I trust myself.   1 2 3 4 5

9. Others trust me.   1 2 3 4 5

Total Score_____

Appendix Five:
Trust Questionnaire Part 2
(for others to answer about you)

By Dr. Lester J. Hirst and Priscilla Hirst, *Leadership Development Learners Guide*, 2011 Used with permission.

Directions: Copy the following assessment and ask at least four people who know you well and with whom you work to answer.

.

Print your name in the blank spaces in each sentence. Request that the respondents do not put their name on the form (so that they will be more inclined to give an honest evaluation.) Explain that each person should fold the form in half (or put it in an envelope) before giving it back to you.

Directions: Circle the number that best corresponds to the statements using   the   scale   below:

1 = strongly agree; 2 = 2 agree; 3 = don't know; 4 = disagree; 5 = strongly disagree.

1. _____tells the truth, talks straight and doesn't leave false impressions.   1 2 3 4 5

2. _____generally cares for others.
       1 2 3 4 5

3. _____ treats people with respect, demonstrates concern for others and doesn't fake caring. 1 2 3 4 5

4. _____ has a track record of consistently delivering results and not making excuses. 1 2 3 4 5

5. _____ does not skirt the real issues with people. This person confronts reality and addresses difficult issues head-on. 1 2 3 4 5

6. _____ makes promises carefully and always keeps commitments no matter how small.   1 2 3 4 5

7. I trust _____. 1 2 3 4 5

8. Others trust _____.   1 2 3 4 5

9. _____ consistently interacts with others in a way that builds trust.   1 2 3 4 5

Total _____

Appendix Six:
Listening Quiz
(for yourself)

By Dr. Lester J. Hirst and Priscilla Hirst, *Leadership Development Learners Guide*, 2011 Used with permission.

Directions: Use the scale below to indicate your responses to the following questions. Put the number in the space before each statement.
1 = hardly ever; 2 = sometimes; 3 = often; 4 = nearly always; 5 = always

_____ When someone is talking to me, I think, "What does this have to do with me? Get to the point!"

_____ When someone is talking to me, I think about what I am going to say next.

_____ When someone is talking to me, I zero-in on things that matter to me because that is why we are talking.

_____ When someone is talking to me, I tend to go off on a personal tangent because the speaker reminded me of something.

_____ When someone is talking to me and my mind wanders, I tend to just nod my head and pretend that I understand what they're saying.

_____ When someone is talking to me, I relate everything the speaker says to my own experience.

_____ When someone is talking to me, I compare the speaker's speech patterns and content to that of other people.

_____ When someone is talking to me and I am not really interested in what they are saying, I say something to change the subject.

_____ When someone is talking to me and I find what they're saying to be trivial, I don't pay attention.

_____ When someone of the opposite sex is talking to me, I pay less attention than if the other person is someone of my same sex.

Total

Appendix Seven:
Thirteen Essential Leadership
Abilities and Attitudes
(self-rating)

By Dr. Lester J. Hirst and Priscilla Hirst, *Leadership Development Learners Guide*, 2011 Used by permission

Use this exercise to identify areas of strength and weakness and commit yourself to work on both areas, while focusing primarily on developing your strengths.

Rank the following abilities and attitudes and give yourself a rating of 1 – 4, with 1 = excellent; 2 = good; 3 = fair; 4 = needs improvement now.

_____Listening receptively – an act of will and commitment.

_____Acceptance of others .

_____Empathy - identifies with the concerns of others so as to better understand and lead.

_____Foresight and intuition.

_____Awareness and perception - ability to see things as they really are.

_____Highly-developed powers of persuasion - to go ahead and show the way.

_____Ability to conceptualize - think beyond day-to-day concerns to place in context projects that are part of a larger vision.

_____Foresight - view the likely outcome of a given situation based on past lessons, realities of the present and consequences of the future.

_____Stewardship - best use and highest level of care of what has been placed in your trust.

____A healing influence upon people and institutions - take opportunities to restore others to wholeness - to show caring.

____Ability to build a sense of community in the workplace - promote opportunities for working together while respecting the dignity of individuals to provide service to the world.

____Commitment to Growth of Others - nurture personal, professional and spiritual growth of others believing in the intrinsic value of individuals.

____Willingness to change.

___TOTAL

Appendix Eight:
Thirteen Essential Abilities and
Attitudes of Leadership

(you, scored by others)

By Dr. Lester J. Hirst and Priscilla Hirst, *Leadership Development Learners Guide*, 2011 Used by permission

Directions: Give this list of Thirteen Essential Leadership Abilities and Attitudes to four of your work colleagues, either those who work *for* you or those who are your peers and know you quite well. Ask them to rank the following list of ten abilities and attitudes and give you a rating of 1 – 4, with 1- excellent; 2 = good; 3 = fair; 4 = needs improvement.

_____Listening receptively – an act of will and commitment.

_____Acceptance of others.

_____Empathy - identifies with the concerns of others so as to better understand and lead.

_____Foresight and intuition.

_____Awareness and perception - ability to see things as they really are.

_____Highly-developed powers of persuasion - to go ahead and show the way.

_____Ability to conceptualize - think beyond day-to-day concerns to place in context projects that are part of a larger vision.

_____Foresight - view the likely outcome of a given situation based on past lessons, realities of the present and consequences of the future.

_____Stewardship - best use and highest level of care of what has been placed in your trust.

_____A healing influence upon people and institutions - take opportunities to restore others to wholeness - to show caring.

_____Ability to build a sense of community in the workplace - promote opportunities for working together while respecting the dignity of individuals to provide service to the world.

_____Commitment to Growth of Others - nurture personal, professional and spiritual growth of others believing in the intrinsic value of individuals.

_____Willingness to change.

Those who completed the form for you should not add their name to this evaluation.   Ask them to return the completed form to you in a plain envelope. Now compare the scores given to you by your colleagues with your own scores. Is there a discrepancy? Is this a blind spot for you, or is it simply that they do not know you very well. Does this discrepancy highlight an area of needed growth for you?

Appendix Nine:
Top Ten Mistake Leaders Make

By Hans Finzel
Compiled by Laura Mae Gardner

"I searched for a man among them who should...stand in the gap...but I found no one" (Ezekiel 22:30). Few prepare themselves or volunteer for leadership. Leaders have incredible power for good or ill in organizational life, and in people's lives. This book discusses what we can learn from mistakes, both how not to make them, and how to maintain a health-producing leadership style.

1. "The number one leadership sin is that of top-down autocratic arrogance" (p. 22).
Answer: **Servant Leadership** (Greenleaf). "A new moral principle is emerging which holds that the only authority deserving one's allegiance is that which is freely and knowingly granted by the led to the leader in response to, and in proportion to, the clearly evident servant stature of the leader."

2. Putting paperwork before Peoplework. The reason leaders do this is that "seen results take priority over unseen relationships; the material world predominates over the immaterial world, and we feel we are judged by what we do, not who we are" (p. 40).
Answer: **"...the most effective leaders spend most of their time being with people and solving people problems"** (p.43). "Jesus spent more time touching people and talking to them than in any other action" (p.45).

3. The absence of affirmation.
Answer: "One of my prime roles is to prepare God's people for works of service" (Eph. 4:12). I do that with a great deal of guidance and **encouragement**. We encourage by listening, (James 1:19), empathizing (Rom. 12:15), comforting (II Cor. 1:3-4), carrying burdens (Gal. 6:2), and encouraging (I Thes. 5:11)" (p. 61-63).

4. No room for mavericks.
Answer: "Have we made it impossible for bright rising stars and maverick go-getters to live within our organization? When we become

too preoccupied with policy, procedure, and the fine-tuning of conformity to organizational standards, we, in effect, squeeze out some of our most gifted people" (p. 66-67). (Caution: legitimate mavericks {creative free-thinkers} should be distinguished from troublemakers, malcontents and rebels) (p. 76). **Is there room for legitimate mavericks in our organization?** Legitimate mavericks are described on page 77.

5. Dictatorship in Decision-making. "I know all the answers."
Answer: **Facilitative leadership** is based on a commitment of respect for individual dignity and corporate creativity. This allows the person responsible for the job a certain amount of freedom to decide how it will be done. It involves others as much as possible in key decisions, and recognizes the wisdom and truth found in the membership. The ideal supervisor   is   described   on   page   90.

6. Dirty Delegation—over management or sloppy delegation with too many strings attached.
Answer: The four stages of delegation are: 1-assignment; 2-authority; 3-accountability, and 4-affirmation (p. 102). The most profound Scriptural example of delegation, is the Great Commission, which could also be called The Great Delegation (Matt. 28:19-20).

7. Communication Chaos. "The two words information and communication are often used interchangeably, but they signify quite different things. Information is giving out; communication is getting through" (p. 118). One worker complained about the lack of information in a rather vivid fashion: "I feel like a part of a mushroom farm—I'm left completely in the dark and fed more manure from time to time" (p. 117).
Answer: "The more people are informed, the more they feel a part of the whole organization and the less chance there is for misunderstanding" (p. 129). "The right to know is basic. Moreover, it is **better to err on the side of sharing too much information** than risk leaving someone in the dark. Information is power, but it is pointless power if hoarded" (Depree, 104-105).

8. Missing the Clues of Corporate Culture. "An organization's corporate culture is the way insiders behave based on the values and group traditions they hold" (p. 135). The difference between core values

(preferences) and beliefs (moral absolutes) are discussed, illustrating how conflicts arise within an organization due to the lack of understanding and clarity of member-held values and beliefs which are the guiding precepts of a given organization.

Answer: Some excellent examples of mission statements and guiding values of companies and churches are given on pages 144-5. **The core values and beliefs held by the leader and the clarity with which he communicates these** have much to do with cohesion and loyalty.

9. Success without Successors (hanging on too long; not developing people to take over; failing to mentor leaders.)

Answer: "**Mentoring** is a nonnegotiable function of successful leadership" (p 157). Four levels and kinds of mentoring are presented: upward mentoring downward mentoring, internal peer mentoring; external peer mentoring. (168-9). Finishing well was a final thought in this chapter.

10. Failure to Focus on the Future. "Vision is an effective leader's chief preoccupation" (p. 179).

Answer: The future is coming! "A leader is one who sees more than others see, who sees farther than others see, and who sees before others do" (Eims, p 183). One thing is constant: change. Not to change is a sure sign of imminent extinction. "There are two ways to **approach the future: as learners**, or as closed experts. The opposite of the learner is the know-it-all" (p. 188). Change is coming: explosion of technology, changes in the political landscape, new relationships between the First and Third Worlds, worldwide changes in social values, the role of women, and the changing balance of financial wealth in the world.

For humanitarian organizations: "The world outside is changing; the international community we want to touch is changing; our new workforce is different, with different expectations, and our donor base is changing dramatically. All across the US, churches are thinking differently about financial priorities. And the peoples in the nations we serve are thinking differently about our relationships to them." (p. 189)

CHAPTER 11
Medical Screening and Assessment
By Alice Chen, M.D., M.P.H.

Just as psychological screening and assessment is a vital aspect of selection for humanitarian, multicultural or cross-cultural service, physical health screening and assessment are also crucial. This is because the world of humanitarian work requires unusual stamina and strength, and persons without good physical resilience and hardiness may suffer unduly under the high load of stress. So, screening and assessment serves two purposes: to select and accept those who are healthy enough to endure the myriad stressors and to screen out those who may be harmed by exposure to the difficult lifestyles which typify most humanitarian roles and working environments. In some "in between" cases, a careful physical health evaluation may indicate a person can function adequately if medical services and resources are available in a given allocation.

The medical screening of the individual should be done thoroughly and carefully by a qualified and competent medical practitioner. At least ninety minutes should be allotted for a thorough personal assessment, including history-taking and physical examination. Spouses and children should be examined separately for the medical screening. Most established agencies have in-house forms they want the physician to use. It is very helpful if the physician has experience working abroad, as he or she can better understand what the candidate will face.

Studies have shown that people have more positive health outcomes when their healthcare providers have complete health history information (Smith, 2005). Thus, it is helpful to use one of the many questionnaires covering health history, fitness profile and immunization record. These forms may be given to the patient ahead of time so attention can be directed to areas of concern. In addition, the person coordinating the pre- field selection screening should be familiar with pertinent region-specific issues (Beattie, 2007).

The following factors should be considered in conducting a medical assessment of a candidate for international, cross-cultural service:

General Information for the Medical Screening

1. Issues related to age and seasons of life

a. **Role deprivation**: For the more experienced candidate who has enjoyed a productive career in the home country along with its associated esteem and prestige, "role deprivation" and the lack of structure in adjusting to life overseas can be especially stressful. Language study may also be particularly challenging for the older candidate. These are issues which should be raised and discussed with the candidate.

b. **Increased stress in humanitarian work**: Depending upon the candidate, the stresses of an international assignment may be overwhelming when compounded with the expected challenges of his or her particular stage of life. In addition, the convergence of the stresses with the natural changes of aging may cause already-distressing symptoms to worsen (Dodds, 2003).

For example, perimenopause (usually starting several years before menstrual periods cease altogether) often results in troublesome physical and emotional symptoms. Up to twenty-six percent of women in this stage of life have hypothyroidism which can cause weight gain, depression and low energy levels (Northrup, 2001). These symptoms, along with other issues such as sleep problems, menstrual irregularities and sexual dysfunction may all make the stresses of dealing cross-cultural living even more daunting.

c. **Young couples**: Clearly, different age groups have different health maintenance priorities and risk factors. Young couples applying for long- term service will likely want to start a family at some point, which calls for a knowledge of the obstetrical facilities at the destination site and/or other options for labor and delivery, as well as a discussion of their own tolerance of risk. Young mothers with pre-school children are at higher risk for depression, especially in cultures which do not allow women to be out in public or to have their own careers.

d. **Children with special needs**: Good screening of the family includes assessment of each child, especially to identify any learning or physical needs. They are another population deserving specific attention and careful matching with allocations where services are available. SHARE International is one resource that is very helpful to parents.[69]

e. **Second career persons**: With the growing number of "finishers" or second-career workers, agencies may need to be especially attentive to the age-related increase in chronic diseases, such as hypertension, diabetes, and coronary artery disease. The advanced ages of candidates require more careful consideration than in former times. A recent informal survey revealed that the average age of workers sent out by a Hong Kong agency was 47 years (D. Leung, personal communication, 2010). Age in itself is not a disqualifying factor but it has to be taken into consideration regarding placement, to ensure that facilities are available to support the management of chronic conditions that the older worker may have. Maturity, on the other hand, brings a host of benefits to the personnel force of humanitarian agencies, with increased wisdom and life experience.

2. Length of proposed assignment—long-term vs. short-term

a. **Long term**: The longer the duration of stay overseas, the higher the likelihood of events such as traumatic accidents (Hargarten, 2008). At the same time, with longer periods of time overseas and a deeper understanding of the language and culture, the successful long-term worker will usually have developed more effective cross-cultural skills which can decrease stress levels.

---

[69] SHARE organization is devoted to meeting the needs of children being educated in host countries because their parents work outside of the home culture. Shareeducation.org

b. **Short term**: The short term may be defined as a two-week stint for a specific task, or a one or two-year project. Those who go for a relatively short time have different expectations of their time overseas, which may affect attitudes and adjustment. Some persons stay in the "honeymoon" phase of adjustment for the entire time, thinking, "This is great!" Others may think, "I can put up with anything for two years." Such an attitude is helpful as a way of coping with the temporary discomforts of cross- cultural living.

3. **Projected time of travel and allocation**: Geographical features including climate and altitude need to be considered in assessing an individual for specific placements.

a. **Outbreaks of infectious diseases** which involve an animal vector often have seasonal variability. For example, Japanese encephalitis is a seasonal disease that usually occurs in the summer and fall in Asia (Fischer, et al., 2010). This may affect vaccination planning for those who will be departing at this time.

b. **Hot climates** such as in the Mediterranean, the tropics, South East Asia, may be very difficult for patients with conditions such as multiple sclerosis (MS). Hot and sunny climates may also be less suitable for those with medical problems with skin manifestations such as Systemic Lupus Erythematosus (SLE) or which require medications that cause skin reactions with exposure to sunlight.

c. **High altitude** locations would not be suitable for those with significant cardiovascular disease.

d. **Highly populated cities** located in basins such as Lanzhou, People's Republic of China or Taipei, Taiwan, may have severe pollution problems which are challenging for those with respiratory problems such as emphysema or asthma. Similarly, in Indonesia or Papua New Guinea, the smoke resulting from the periodic burning off of local forests can be problematic for workers with asthma. Lima,

Peru, is another locale fraught with conditions which perpetuate respiratory problems, due to the lack of rain which pollutes the city with dust, coupled with the ocean fogs and winds which keep the contaminants trapped in the air.

e. **Dark localities** pose other problems. Extreme north or south geographic regions may lead to Seasonal Affective Disorder (SAD). The farther north one lives, such as in Alaska or in Scandinavian countries, the higher the rate of this depression caused by lack of light. The same is true in the far south. Some of the problem can be minimized by the use of full-spectrum light, but persons already known to suffer from this disorder will be better off in other allocations. In one northern European country, a young wife found it extremely hard to care for her children, but when they moved to the Mediterranean coast, she returned to normal. Some studies show that supplementation with Vitamin D can help prevent and treat symptoms of SAD.

4. Living conditions and workplace situations in the host country should be considered. Screening for allocations needs to take into consideration several issues that will relate to the ease of living and working in the future place of work. These include:

a. **Degree of development and cultural difference** of the host country— developed vs. developing; urban vs. rural setting. The more different a country is from one's own home country, the more cultural perceptions may differ from one's own culture and the more stressful the transition usually is. Occasionally, however, persons experience culture shock because they expect a similar culture to have few differences. Friends assigned to England said they had more shock there, because of their expectations for greater similarity, than they did going to Papua New Guinea. They knew life would be really different there and thus had a mindset for having to adapt more.

b. **The practical problems of living**, including the degree of physical and mental effort required to meet the everyday challenges of living, can exact a heavy toll and vary according to assignment and location. For example, teaching in an urban international school is much different from serving as a relief worker in an isolated refugee camp. Even commuting to an urban school can add a measure of stress.

c. **Living arrangements** are highly variable, so it is good to learn ahead of time whether the individual will be living with a national host family or in a "compound-like" setting with other expatriates. The "compound" setting may offer more expatriate support but at the same time limit access to local resources and wisdom. Depending on the situation, the host family may be a significant source of valuable support or an additional stress to the individual, or both.

d. **Availability of amenities** (water, electricity, indoor plumbing), including Internet access (a valuable avenue of communication and social support as well as information) have considerable impact on the degree of stress that the candidate may expect to encounter. In this era of social networking, living in a country with highly censored Internet access which blocks social networks such as Facebook and Twitter may pose significant stress to those who are dependent on them for connecting with others. We might think of clean air and pleasant smells as amenities, in that doing without them is also difficult. Bad smells take their toll!

e. **Assignment** to solo work or to a team—What degree of infrastructure and physical and emotional support can be expected from on-site colleagues, medical or otherwise? These can make a difference in health outcomes.

f. **Assessment of stress and coping ability**—Prolonged living in a difficult cross-cultural setting is a major stressor in itself. The U.S. Foreign Service has estimated that sixty percent of all referrals for medical treatment have a stress-related basis (Gamble and Lovell, 2008). Stress can cause physical, cognitive, emotional, relational and behavioral changes. It can precipitate maladaptive coping mechanisms such as misuse of alcohol or prescription drugs, dependence on pornography, abuse of a family member, and other destructive attempts to deal with stress in ways which become problems in themselves. Extreme or chronic high stress can also unmask or worsen medical conditions such as gastroesophageal reflux, headache, irritable bowel syndrome and skin rashes (Callahan, 2008). In extreme cases, the person may experience a "tumble down" or cascade of ever-increasing medical problems. This happened to one woman we consulted with. Over a period of six years, she had surgery upon surgery, infection after infection, and ended up developing lupus, a severe auto-immune disorder. (See Volume 2, Chapter 7, on Stress and Coping, pages 137 to 166. Pages 150 and 151 illustrate the tumble-down effect of chronic high stress and its effects on the immune system. In our work worldwide, we have noticed that international workers seem to have many more assaults to the immune system, due to high stress coupled with environmental factors (Dodds).

5. Access to medical facilities:

a. **National medical facilities**—The resources listed in the "seeking health care abroad section" can inform the pre-field screening process, providing information about medical facilities as agencies consider the placement of workers who have underlying medical problems which need ongoing care, access to sophisticated investigations or emergency backup care (Riesland, 2008).

b. **Availability of on-site medical backup**—Does the team that the worker will be joining have medical staff on the same team or in the same locale that are available to provide medical attention?

c. **Availability of on-line medical resour**ces and translation services—these can be valuable sources of medical information and aid in comprehending local medical consultations.

6. Marital status and family dynamics

a. **The marriage relationship** and the family should be explored thoroughly through focused psychological screening. The medical assessment should also address this issue, as one's physical condition is intimately affected by one's relational and emotional health.

b. **The age of the children** at the time of departure should be considered. Older children, such as teens who are in high school, may find it more difficult to adjust to a new culture than younger children. Also, potential schooling options and opportunities for social interactions need to be considered for the children. Though this is not specially a medical question, raising the issue can help parents think ahead.

b. **Special needs of children**: It is advisable to assess the needs of the family's children such as for speech pathology, special education, physiotherapy and support for learning disabilities, chronic physical disabilities, etc. Some agencies have access to specialists who are able to go to the field to conduct assessment and therapy, but this is exceptional. It is strongly advised to proactively explore potentially sensitive issues such as social adaptation, attention deficit disorder with/without hyperactivity (ADHD), etc. despite the resistance one might encounter, in order to determine level of support required.

c. **International adoptions**: Increasingly, international workers are adopting children from their host countries. It would be important to be aware of such intentions and to assess the resources available to support the couple in pursuing this decision, especially in dealing with potential issues such as cognitive and physical developmental delays, attachment issues, and behavioral problems (Chicoine & Tessier, 2008).

Medical History

A careful medical history should be taken, covering the following areas:

1. Current medical problems:

It is important to identify long-term problems which could have impact on the individual's well-being and service.

a. Be alert to conditions/**medication**s requiring regular specialist or laboratory follow-up or special or limited/controlled medications.

b. **Seizure disorders**: Patients with active seizure disorders such as epilepsy may react to anti-malarial medications such as mefloquine (P. Fischer, personal communication, February 22, 2011); regular monitoring of drug levels is also recommended.

c. **Congestive heart disea**se (CHF), if not controlled and clinically monitored, can cause significant disability and death.

d. **Atrial fibrillatio**n or history of cardiac valve replacement often require anticoagulant treatment and regular INR testing.

e. **Reactive airway disease** (asthma) is a potentially life-threatening condition which is often aggravated by environmental allergies and air pollution. Patients in the field need to assess the local risks and availability of inhalers and medications.

f. **Celiac disease** and other malabsorption conditions may limit the variety of local foods which can be tolerated. Example: gluten is found ubiquitously in Asia, including in soy sauce and other frequently-used seasonings, in addition to wheat products. Because south Asia relies more heavily on rice products than wheat as a staple, this area may be a better fit for those with gluten intolerance. As processed foods and condiments vary from region to region, ingredients in the same products may vary, so the product may be tolerated in one region but not in another. In addition, unfamiliar foods may prove to be offenders; knowing local resources could be very helpful. For example, a common vegetable called "jiucai" or garlic chives frequently eaten in north China cuisine has an especially high fructose content (S. Rowe, personal communication, April 20, 2011). Though the quantity of this seasoning used is usually quite small, it can wreak havoc on those with fructose intolerance.

g. **Ulcerative colitis** and other forms of inflammatory bowel disease.

h. **Obesity:** There is growing interest in using BMI (body mass index), a measure of obesity which is calculated by dividing the body weight in kilograms by the height in meters squared, as a measure of health and wellness in the pre-field assessment (R. Pruitt, personal communication, April 8, 2011). Obesity is a global epidemic that poses high risk for cardiovascular and cerebrovascular disease, diabetes and a host of other medical conditions. In addition, the obese worker will find the physical challenges of overseas life, including walking, carrying loads for distances on foot, climbing stairs in the absence of elevators, etc., difficult to negotiate. Overweight is defined as having a BMI of 26-30 (25-28 in Asians) and obesity, BMI of greater than 31 (greater than 29 for Asians). Weight loss may constitute a condition for approval for obese candidates, however, typically most people regain weight when lost to meet special purpose, so we do not recommend conditional acceptance. Before departure, overweight candidates should be advised regarding weight loss and continue weight control while on the field.

i. **Asplenia** -- Patients who have their spleens removed, or non-functioning due to a disease such as sickle cell, should also be identified. These individuals run a greater risk of severe infections, especially meningitis, malaria and influenza, so placement in areas with the potential for Falciparum malaria infection should be avoided if possible. These individuals must be fully immunized including against pneumococcus (Prevnar 13® and Pneumovax 23® vaccines), meningitis (Menveo® and Bexsero® vaccines), Haemophilus (Hib vaccine) and seasonal influenza (influenza vaccine). They should also have a course of antibiotics on hand, e.g., amoxicillin-clavilanate or Levaquin in case of possible bacterial infection and seek immediate medical care if fever develops.

j. **Hearing loss** may severely impair language learning and would require learning special learning strategies (J. Long, personal communication, February 1, 2011).

k. **Chronic fatigue**: This common condition is often worsened by travel and stress. It is best to wait until symptoms are largely resolved before any extensive or demanding travel (Lankester, 2011); awareness of one's own activity limitations and need for rest is essential.

l. **Fatigue** is a symptom of hypothyroidism, anemia, heart disease, depression and other conditions for which thorough pre-field investigation may be a condition for approval.

2. Current medications

a. **Availability in host country**—Special attention should be paid to medications which may not be available in the host country; in such situations, one needs to assess the ease with which such medications could be safely and legally imported into the country. Examples include interferon for MS, controlled medications for ADHD, etc.

b. **Potential drug interactions**—Workers taking medications purchased in the host country may also develop adverse drug interactions between their own medications and medications purchased in the host country. This type of reaction occurs typically between a newer prescription medication and a drug in the host country that is not available in the worker's home country. An example is the interaction between halofantrine, a drug used to treat severe malaria, and amiodarone, a type of medication used to treat cardiac arrhythmias. This interaction of these two drugs can cause serious heart arrhythmias

(Callahan, 2008). To minimize these complications, the health care provider should consider replacing newer-generation medications that the patient is using with older medications which have fewer drug interactions and a better-known drug profile. Patients should also be well-informed about the side-effects and potential drug interactions of their prescription medications.

3. Allergies – to medication and foods:

a. **Medication allergies**: patients who are allergic to anti-malaria medications (artemisin, quinines, etc.) should not be placed in malaria-endemic regions of Asia and Africa.

b. **Airborne allergies**: Finding out about environmental hazards, such as dust and other air pollution is very important, as patients will have little or no control over these.

c. **Chronic allergic sinusitis and asthma**—Persons who suffer from these may expect to experience frequent recurrences while located in areas which are heavily polluted or where anti-smoking laws are not strictly enforced.

d. **Food allergies**: If severe and resistant to management, food allergies may preclude effective long-term service. For example, peanuts are ubiquitous in many parts of the world, including the Middle East and Asia, so severe peanut allergy causing anaphylaxis may be a excluding condition (N. Ohanian, personal communication, December 31, 2010).

e. **Severe allergic reactions**—The allergic individual should be advised to carry antihistamines such as chlorpheniramine (Chlor-Tripolon®) or diphenhydramine (Benadryl®) at all times. If there is a history of previous anaphylaxis or breathing difficulties, the individual should carry adrenaline (EpiPen®) at all times. Seek medical advice after any severe reaction even when taking antihistamines or self-injecting with adrenaline is effective (Lankester, 2011).

4. Family history:

a. A strong family history of illness and/or death from heart disease or stroke warrants further investigation and education regarding lipid levels, weight control, diet, exercise, etc. and requires regular monitoring on the field.

b. Extra vigilance in screening may be necessary for those with a positive family history of conditions which may impact service, especially if some signs of the condition are already apparent, such as in certain forms of muscular dystrophy, breast cancer, colonic polyps (affected individuals an increased risk for colorectal cancer), malignant melanoma, aneurysms and others.

c. Genetic markers for increased cancer risk are becoming more available and can help the screening process. Some of the more common examples are BRCA 1 & 2 for breast cancer, and MLHL, MSH2, MSH6, PMS2, *and* EPCAM for Lynch Syndrome.

5. Risk factors for chronic conditions:

Hypertension, high cholesterol and diabetes mellitus are all risk factors for coronary heart disease and stroke; otherwise suitable candidates should be advised how to monitor and manage these conditions while on assignment. Regular check-ups should then be mandatory.

6. Sexual history:

Though it may be awkward to broach this topic, especially with those who are applying for service in religious agencies, it is important to identify problems in this area. A previous history of sexually-transmitted diseases (STDs), use of pornography, a history of extramarital sexual involvement, whether heterosexual or homosexual, and a history of sexual abuse or rape are all "red flags" pointing to potential problems. In addition, the stress of cross-cultural adaptation, loneliness and anonymity compounded with the increased availability of sexual outlets such as commercial sex workers in some areas of the world create an irresistible trap for the vulnerable individual. Depending on the sexual history, testing for AIDS/HIV and STDs may be needed.

7. Psychological issues:

Although a thorough psychological assessment is essential (See Chapter One), the medical practitioner also should be attentive to a past history of psychological problems, including a history of depression or anxiety or personality disorders which may be manifested in physical complaints or behaviors. These may be indicated on medical history records while there may not be any psychological records.

8. Immunization history:

See the Appendix on vaccinations. Increasingly, organizations are encountering candidates who refuse immunizations for both themselves and their children. As a result, there has been a resurgence in recent years in the incidence of vaccine-preventable diseases such as measles and pertussis with significant negative sequelae (L. Lorenz, personal communication, June 7, 2013). The weight of medical evidence strongly supports full immunization of both adults and children with vaccination against routine childhood diseases. From an organizational point of view, it is worth noting that a candidate who refuses to obtain vaccinations may also be non-compliant in future with other medical treatment, including obtaining specific vaccinations required by different host countries.

The Physical Examination

The screening must include a full physical examination including the following:

- Weight
- Height
- Body-mass index (BMI = body weight in kilograms/height in meters squared)
- Waist measurement[70]
- Heart
- Respiratory rate
- Basic eye examination
- Dental check-up

---

[70] There is growing evidence that the waist circumference, especially in Asians, is a better measure of central adiposity and high risk of heart disease and stroke than BMI. Normal waist circumference for Asian females is less than 80 cm. (31.5 inches), and for Asian men 90 cm. (35.5 inches) as per the International Diabetes Federation. Other ethnic groups have different cut-off points.

Laboratory tests, including:

- Complete metabolic panel, including renal function and liver function tests
- CBC
- Lipid panel
- Blood group and type
- TSH – for women > 40 years old
- PSA – for men > 50 years old[71]
- Pap smear for sexually active women (previously and currently)
- Mammogram – for women > 40 years old[72]
- Chest X-ray
- ECG
- Mantoux test (PPD) – This skin test for TB requires reading the result by a trained person 48-72 hours later. Long-term travelers, disaster assistance personnel, medical providers, and expatriates who are likely to have longer periods of contact with the local population are often at higher risk of tuberculosis, especially in Africa, Central America, Southeast Asia, and the Indian subcontinent. This increased risk underscores the need for tuberculin skin testing prior to and, ideally, 3 months after travel (Callahan, 2008). If there is a question about the meaning of a positive Mantoux reading because of childhood BCG vaccination, the medical consultant can order an interferon-gamma release assay test (IGRA) to check for latent TB infection.

When the results of investigations have returned, it is important for the medical practitioner to review them with the individual, and to explain the significance of new findings as well as how to manage known conditions. The importance of self-care should be emphasized and the key role of the individual him/herself in health maintenance. Results should be forwarded to the agency for screening and placement purposes. We recommend that a selection committee include a

---

[71] The use of PSA for screening for prostatic cancer is controversial and should be discussed with the physician.

[72] There is some debate about the recommended starting age for mammographic screening for breast cancer. Some authorities such as US National Cancer Institute (NCI) recommend starting to screen at age 40 while others recommend starting age 50. This issue should be discussed with the clinician.

physician or a member who fully understand implications of recommendations from the screening physician.

On-line Tools for Medical Screening

1. Problem-Knowledge Coupler software (PKC):

The PKC is a commercially available on-line service which provides over one hundred "couplers" or electronic questionnaires which the individual self-administers. regarding the individual's current conditions and symptoms, medications, allergies, exposures, etc. through a series of questions which the individual answers on-line. The program then "couples" the responses with a database of medical information and offers guidance that is tailored to the individual's needs in the answers given. The individual is then advised to review the report with a medical practitioner provider who is able to address the issues brought out by the report and to complete the assessment with a physical exam and lab investigations. Over one hundred of these "couplers" or software modules are available; for pre-field screening, the "General Health Screening" and "Mental Health" couplers are commonly used; the "Wellness and Health Review" coupler is used for returning workers. This tool is used by a number of NGOs and humanitarian organizations.

2. RealAge: A similar on-line coupler tool, RealAge, which is now managed by the same group as PKC, is available free of charge.[73] It takes about twenty minutes to do, and asks a battery of questions about your history, diet, exercise and emotional health, and then give personalized health advice according to your answers. Though not specifically geared for screening for international service, it is an accessible source of generally sound medical advice to potential workers.

Medical Assessment after Re-entry and Home Assignment

We recommend what a number of agencies require. They ask their personnel to undergo a complete physical examination and/or

---

[73] Sharecare.com/static/realage, click Log in to Find out your Real Age

psychological assessment upon return to the home country and at regular intervals in order to clarify issues that need addressing and strengthening, manage newly-arisen medical problems, determine that workers are still fit to continue their work and to provide debriefing about their term of service (Hay, 2007).

Summary

Evaluation for physical health is a crucial aspect of screening, assessment and selection of candidates. The process must include a thorough health history, assessment of current conditions, evaluation of medications, and the hands-on physical examination. In addition, the more the examiner knows about the likely allocation, in terms of climate, environmental factors, and availability of medical services, the better judgment can be rendered. It is best if the examination is done by a physician knowledgeable about the risks and stresses of overseas living. Results should be passed on to the selection committee of the agency, and evaluated along with all the other assessments made of the individual   and   his   or   her   family.

References and Recommended Reading
See Chapter 12 for these.

CHAPTER 12
Medical Advice for International Workers
By Alice Chen, M.D., M.P.H.

Before embarking on an overseas assignment, you may be overwhelmed by all the preparations that you will need to make. Near the top of the list of questions will likely be "What do I do if I or a family member gets sick overseas?" or "How do we keep healthy while we're travelling or living abroad?"

Studies show that expatriates do develop medical conditions while traveling and working overseas. The most common ailments encountered are: diarrhea, respiratory illness, injury, skin problems, and conditions causing fever. In one study surveying nearly 27,000 U.S. government civil servants and family members, the most common reasons for out-patient visits were, in order of frequency: upper respiratory infections, diarrhea, non-traumatic musculoskeletal complaints, mental health problems, dermatology, injuries and fever. Trauma and heart disease are the most common causes of hospitalization, followed by infectious diseases such as malaria, dengue fever and gastrointestinal infections, determined largely in some cases by location, with Africa carrying the highest risk of infection, mostly due to malaria (Riesland, 2008).

This chapter provides general advice on how to minimize your health risk and how to deal with commonly encountered medical problems. An exhaustive discussion, however, is beyond the scope of this chapter; the intent is to provide a general checklist as you prepare, with a strong emphasis on self-care and prevention. Please note that medical information is constantly changing and needing updating; this chapter seeks to offer basic advice about common problems and provide some resources. If you have any questions and certainly if you experience any symptoms, you should seek your health care provider.

Selecting an organization which shares the responsibility for maintaining your good health is also important. Gamble and Lovell list the following as important factors to look for in a sending organization (Gamble & Lovell-Hawker, 2008):

- Commitment to a "Code of Good Practice" ("People in Aid," 2003)[74] which places a priority on care for workers.
- Financial policies which ensure adequate on-field living and work funds as well as language learning and pension. Inquire as to how finances are obtained – is support-raising necessary or is a salary guaranteed?
- Provision of pre-field training and orientation
- Adequate medical and psychosocial support – does the organization have an ethos that promotes health and emotional care for the worker?
- Policies regarding vacation, schooling for children (including provision for special needs), evacuation/repatriation, medical insurance, etc.
- Provision for debriefing and resettlement on completion of the assignment as well as follow up of ongoing problems related to the assignment.
- Effective communication channels which are easily accessed, especially in the event of emergencies.

---

[74] The People in Aid "Code of Good Practice" is a widely respected set of standards that aims at improving the quality of the human resources management of humanitarian aid and development agencies. It provides a comprehensive framework that can be applied to organizations of varying size and mission (www.peopleinaid.org).

At the same time, if you are a potential international worker, you should inform yourself about common health concerns that might be encountered when traveling and living abroad. Such issues that are covered in this section include:

1) Food and water safety and traveler's diarrhea
2) Injury prevention
   a) Traffic accidents
   b) Water-related injuries
   c) Other water-related hazards
3) Sun protection
4) Malaria and other vector-transmitted diseases

Additional resources are provided in the bibliography.

1. Food and Water Safety and Prevention of traveller's diarrhea (TD):

CASE[75]
An active American 2-year-old boy playing in the courtyard of his home in rural India during the rainy season scooped up and swallowed a mouthful of run-off water from a puddle. Within twenty-four hours, he developed a high fever, bloody diarrhea, irritability and abdominal discomfort. On the second day, his fever, which was unresponsive to fever-reducing medication, peaked at 41C and he had a generalized seizure. He was seen at a provincial level hospital for assessment where stool culture eventually confirmed the growth of the bacterium Shigella, one of the few causes of diarrhea that require antibiotics. He did not suffer any lasting effects from the seizure but continued to have bloody diarrhea, weight loss and abdominal pain. Over the course of his six-week illness, he received four courses of antibiotics but continued to have symptoms. Eventually, his diarrhea did resolve, and on the following day, his 7- month-old sister developed bloody diarrhea. The family continued to deal with this infection when the young boy was re-infected by his sister. The family's gastrointestinal problems finally resolved spontaneously three months after the original infection.

[75] All the cases in this chapter are based on actual, and in some cases, composites of several people, but names and details have been altered to protect identities.

Acute diarrheal disease or traveler's diarrhea (TD), also known as "Delhi belly," "Montezuma's revenge," "Hong Kong Dog," the "Aztec Two- Step," the "Trotskies" and other colorful names, constitutes a significant proportion of the medical ailments encountered by international workers and travelers. Every year, over 80 million individuals from developed nations travel to less developed areas of the world and it has been estimated that over half of these international travelers will suffer diarrhea over the course of their visit abroad (Ericsson, 2008). The causes of TD include bacterial, viral, protozoal and parasitic organisms, but the most common source is bacterial, enterotoxigenic E. coli (ETEC). Symptoms result not from the bacterial infection itself, but rather from a toxin released by E. coli after it has entered the gastrointestinal system. This infection is transmitted through water or food that has been contaminated at its source such as with the use of night soil (human excrement to fertilize crops), during food preparation because of poor personal hygiene on the part of the food preparer, or inadequate food handling and storage practices.

TD usually presents as acute diarrhea and vomiting, resolving completely in several days, though about one in ten cases may last up to 2 weeks. In general, TD is a mild, self-limited illness but anyone who has experienced it can attest to how distressing and incapacitating it can be despite its short duration. Dehydration is also a concern in children and with severe cases in adults, so being vigilant and informed about this common problem is important. A very good source on this topic is the CDC "Yellow Book" which provides valuable health information for travelers.

What can I do to prevent TD?

Traditional wisdom holds that TD is easily prevented if common-sense guidelines are followed, but experience has borne out that even while following preventative guidelines, many travelers and international workers still become ill. However, this does not eliminate the need to be careful in choosing what to eat and drink when one is living in a new setting. Below are general recommendations offered by Connor (2012), Ericsson (2008) and Acheson (2011) regarding safe food and water consumption while traveling or living in a developing country.

Safe food and water recommendations:

- Wash and scrub raw fruits and vegetables thoroughly before eating or storing them. Use dishwashing detergent or a cleanser designed for washing fruits and vegetables and rinse several times. Rinse with filtered water if they are to be eaten raw.
- Refrigerator temperature should be maintained at 40oF (4.4oC) or lower, the freezer at 0oF (-17.8oC) or lower.
- Refrigerate foods promptly. Do not leave cooked foods at room temperature for more than two hours (one hour if the room temperature is above 90oF/32oC). For large amounts of leftovers, divide them into smaller batches for storage in the refrigerator or freezer so that each batch will be cooled to a safer temperature more quickly.
- Precooked, perishable, or ready-to-eat food that needs to be refrigerated should be served as soon as possible. Cook hotdogs, sausages and other precooked meats and fish to kill bacteria that may have contaminated them in the processing plants.
- Rinse all meat, poultry and fish with water before cooking or storing. Store them apart from other food; wrap them well and contain any juices that may run out of the meat.
- Don't cut meat and fish on the same cutting board that you use for other foods; use one for meats and fish and another one for produce. Use different knives to cut different foods to prevent cross-contamination.
- Wash your hands, knives, and cutting boards thoroughly with hot water and dishwashing detergent each time you handle uncooked food such as produce and raw meat, fish, seafood or poultry.
- When cooking raw food from animal sources, make sure the internal temperature reaches the following levels: ground beef 160oF (71oC); chicken 170oF (77oC); turkey 180oF (82oC); pork 160oF (71oC). Use a thermometer for monitoring the temperature when roasting meat; with frying, stir-frying or boiling, make sure the meat is cooked through and no longer shows any sign of blood.
- Seafood should be cooked thoroughly. Raw fish (such as sushi) presents a risk for a variety of parasites, on top of the risk of infection by organisms carried by food handlers. Freezing kills only some, not all, harmful microorganisms. Prawns or shrimp should first have the intestinal tract removed from the ridge along the back

half of the shrimp, a process also called deveining, before being prepared for consumption. Filter feeders such as clams and mussels are best avoided due to the risk of hepatitis A and other diseases.

- Be sure to cook chicken eggs thoroughly so that the yolk is no longer runny.
- As freezing does not necessarily kill bacteria, wash meats and poultry thoroughly after thawing, handling them the same as you would handle fresh meats.
- Wash your hands after handling food or using the toilet.

The following chart (adapted from Ericsson, 2008) ranks various drinks and foods in terms of risk of contracting TD. In general, consuming contaminated food is a more significant source of TD than water.

Recommendations regarding food and drink:

Type	Safe for consumption	Likely safe: use with discretion	Unsafe for consumption: avoid
Beverages	Sealed/bottled carbonated soft drinks,[76] rinse and dry the exterior of the container before drinking the contents	Sealed, bottled fresh citric juices	Unpasteurized milk
	Sealed/bottled carbonated water	Sealed bottled water	Water from the faucet; do not use tap water for brushing teeth
	Bottled water (boil for 3 minutes to kill	Commercial or machine-made ice	Unpasteurized milk Chipped ice

[76] Rare cases of TD resulting from bottled carbonated beverages have been reported, but the appearance of fizzing on breaking the seal usually indicates that carbonation was complete and that the drink is safe.

	bacteria, viruses and parasites); if you want to store and cool the boiled water, make sure you use clean containers		(freezing does not kill organisms)
	Purified water: five drops of tincture of iodine or two drops of 5% sodium hypochlorite (bleach) per quart or liter of water will kill most bacteria within 30 minutes (but may leave an unpleasant taste)		
	Filtered water[77]		
Food	Hot foods which are grilled thoroughly or boiled (with cooking temperatures reaching to 160°F or 70°C)	Dry Items	Salads

[77] Multi-Pure (http://www.multipureco.com/) and Tealbrook (http://www.tealbrook.com/Home.html) are both reliable, commercially available water filters.

	Processed and packaged foods	Highly-concentrated processed foods, such as jam and syrup	Sauces and 'salsas' (especially if they have been displayed at room temperature for a period of time)
	Cooked vegetables and peeled fruits	Washed vegetables and fruits	Unpeeled fruits
			Raw or poorly cooked meats
			Uncooked seafood
			Unpasteurized dairy products
			Cold desserts
Setting	Recommended restaurants	Local homes, or ready-to-eat food purchased from supermarkets	Road-side vendors

How is TD treated?

In general, TD is a condition that resolves on its own so antibiotics are not necessary. Keeping up adequate fluids, avoiding solid food and resting for several days usually are adequate. It is advisable to be cautious in your use of anti-diarrheal medication such as diphenoxylate (Lomotil®) or loperamide (Imodium®). The use of antibiotics may benefit the following individuals (Wanke, 2010):

1. Those who have the following symptoms:

    a) More than four loose stools/day
    b) Fever
    c) Blood, pus or mucus in the stool

2. Those who may have less serious symptoms, but whose work responsibilities or travel plans are seriously curtailed by them:

Self-medication with antibiotics (see chart below) is usually adequate, but medical attention may be needed for those who have:

a) A high fever
b) Abdominal pain
c) Large amounts of bloody stools
d) Vomiting
e) No effect with preventative antibiotics
f) Symptoms lasting 10 to 14 days.

The following chart (adapted from Ericsson, 2008) lists currently recommended medications for the prevention and treatment of TD. Note that preventive therapy is taken daily for the duration of being at-risk for TD; duration of antibiotic treatment of established TD is three days (except for azithromycin which is most effective as a one-time dose of 1 gram).

Self-medication:

Medication	Daily oral dose for prevention (and treatment)	Usage and adverse effects
Bismuth subsalicylate (Pepto-Bismol®)	30 ml. or two tablets chewed, four times/day, with meals (for both treatment and prevention)	Black tongue (rinse and brush mouth and tongue after each dose) and stools. May cause ringing of the ears and salicylate overdose. Avoid using with coumadin or non-steroidal anti-inflammatory medications like aspirin or naproxen.
Quinolones		Avoid use in children under the age of 14 or in pregnant women. **Not recommended in SE Asia because of antibiotic resistance of *Campylobacter jejuni.***
Ofloxacin	300 mg once/day for prevention (for treatment X three days)	GI upset, rash, dizziness, insomnia, and anxiety

Medication	Daily oral dose for prevention (and treatment)	Usage and adverse effects
Norfloxacin	400 mg once/day for prevention (for treatment X three days)	
Ciprofloxacin	500 mg once/day for prevention (for treatment, twice/day X three days)	May increase caffeine levels and cause jitteriness in individuals who take caffeine-containing beverages
Levofloxacin	500 mg once/day for prevention (for treatment X 3 days)	
Rifaximin	200 mg once or twice/day for prevention (for treatment three times/day X 3 days)	Adverse effects no different from placebo
Azithromycin	1-gram, one-time dose for treatment (not for prevention)	Drug of choice in SE Asia because of widespread quinolone resistance by *Campylobacter jejuni*

What medications are used to prevent TD?

The mainstay of prevention of TD is still food and beverage precautions as discussed earlier. However, chemoprophylaxis, the prevention of TD with the use of medications before the onset of symptoms, has also proven to be effective. The regular use of bismuth subsalicylate (eg. Pepto-Bismol®) offers 40-65% protection (Ericsson, 2008) while antibiotics when used against organisms that are sensitive to them offer 80-90% protection. However, the use of antibiotics for the prevention of a self-limited condition is a somewhat controversial issue, as widespread use of antibiotics leads to antibiotic resistance, a growing problem globally. Those individuals who are at high risk for TD as well as those who are travelling on important business may opt for the use of chemoprophylaxis after discussion with their health care provider.

Noted to be at high risk for TD are the following individuals:

- Those who have suppressed immune systems, such as cancer patients
- Those with low gastric acidity
- Those who anticipate not being able to avoid eating food under unsanitary conditions
- Those who have not travelled to tropical areas in the preceding six months
- Those of higher socioeconomic status

Is there a vaccine that prevents TD?

Dukoral® (available in Canada) an oral cholera vaccine has been found to be also effective against ETEC, enterotoxigenic E. coli, the most common organism causing TD. It is approved in both the US and Canada for the prevention of TD, but opinions vary as to the effectiveness of this vaccine. Two studies indicated that Dukoral reduced the incidence of diarrhea caused by ETEC by 67% in a trial in Bangladesh and 52% among travelers to Morocco, but another study estimates that in view of the global rate of ETEC infection and the effectiveness of the vaccine, the vaccine may only prevent less than 7% of cases of TD (Wanke, 2011). Research is currently underway in the development of a vaccine available as a skin patch which may show promise for the prevention of moderate to severe TD. In summary, the Infectious Diseases Society of America in 2006 recommended that the use of the vaccine should take into consideration its cost, adverse effects, effectiveness and the cost of treatment in the event of developing TD.

This is another issue you may want to discuss with your health care provider who will help you decide whether you should receive this vaccine, based on your destination, duration of time overseas, health condition, etc.

2. Injury Prevention

CASE1:
A 40-year-old British NGO CEO working in Russia was a passenger in a jeep driven by a prominent local businessman whom he had just met. For "face" issues, the local businessman had insisted on driving, though he was an inexperienced driver. He was speeding on a mountain pass when the vehicle swerved on the gravel road, flipped and then rolled several times. The driver and the expatriate, both in the front seat, were wearing seatbelts. The expatriate was lurched violently by the impact and when the car stopped rolling, he found himself suspended by the seatbelt. He experienced numbness and severe pain of his right shoulder and all extremities after impact, feeling as though he had "broken both legs and both arms." After extricating himself from the vehicle with the help of local villagers, he noted that he continued to have numbness and paralysis of his right arm in addition to neck and shoulder pain. He tried to "work it off" by walking and shaking his arm, with some effect. The vehicle surprisingly was still drivable, so he and the driver continued their trip. The driver, rattled at being responsible for the injury of a foreigner, attempted to calm his nerves with alcohol at a meal-stop, despite the protests of the expatriate.

Over the course of the nine-hour return trip, the expatriate developed increasing neck and shoulder pain and numbness and paralysis of his right arm. When, they returned home, medical colleagues from his agency assessed him and immediately transported him by taxi to the local university hospital for medical attention. Cervical spine X-rays showed fractures at the C5-C6 level with a rupture of the intervertebral disc causing compression of the spinal cord. He was immediately immobilized on a bench in the hospital waiting-room by his medical colleagues to stabilize his neck. Hospital admission was advised, but in view of the hospital's relatively primitive conditions, the patient and his colleagues opted for observation and care at his home. He was transported home on a wooden door which served as a backboard, and spent the next two weeks attached to a jury-rigged traction system set up in the living room of his apartment. He was cared for by his family and colleagues, as well as a local orthopedic surgeon who made house-calls. After two weeks of improvised traction, during which the patient suffered considerable anxiety, the agency made plans to repatriate the patient for further treatment. A Philadelphia cervical collar was obtained locally with some difficulty and he flew home with his family on a commercial aircraft on business class, which allowed him to maintain a semi-reclining position.

Subsequent assessment and treatment in the UK resulted in being his being fitted with a modified halo brace for three months. He returned to work overseas after a four-month medical leave and within a year's time, he had recovered over 90% of his physical function. However, for over a year following the accident, he suffered symptoms of post-traumatic stress syndrome, including flashbacks and anxiety attacks.

CASE2:
An Australian teacher of English, working with a mission organization in a European country, was driving out of a parking lot in a car when a young man on a bicycle pulled out quickly in front of him. The driver braked quickly but could not avoid hitting the cyclist who was thrown from his bicycle and landed head-first on the road. The driver was not injured, but the cyclist was taken to hospital, arriving in a coma, from which he never recovered. In hospital, imaging studied showed that he had sustained a severe cerebral bleed. Despite having surgery, his condition did not improve.

The driver of the car visited the young man in hospital regularly, where he continued in a vegetative state. In addition to experiencing great personal remorse, he was also subjected to ongoing overt and implied accusations and demands for compensation from the family of the cyclist. Legal proceedings were taken against the driver which dragged on for several years, adding to the heavy emotional toll on him and his family. Finally, when a large anonymous monetary gift designated as compensation to the cyclist's family was received, the tension between the two parties was eased. The cyclist remains in hospital in a vegetative state; the driver and his family have since transferred to another country of service.

Statistics show that injuries top the list for the number of travel-related deaths worldwide, with up to 25 times more deaths resulting from trauma than from infectious diseases (Hargarten, 2008). Worldwide, road traffic injuries top the list of traumatic causes of injury and death while drownings take second place. Less common causes of injury and death in international settings include violent acts, natural disasters (tsunamis, earthquakes, etc.), airplane crashes, extreme environmental exposures, and bites and stings (Hargarten, 2008). According to the World Health Organization, about 5 million people died as a result of an injury in 2000 – a rate of 83.7/100 000. This is a significant burden to not only health care facilities, but also to the individuals and families involved; as this case vividly shows, dealing with trauma is a grueling experience for all involved.

a) Traffic accidents

Seventy percent of collisions involving international travelers or dwellers occur in developing countries. The victims of motor vehicle accidents in developing countries are not predominantly the occupants of cars, but rather pedestrians, motorcyclists, bicyclists, and other non-motorized vehicle occupants. Most road traffic deaths occur amongst pedestrians, with about half of these deaths being in children (Hargarten, 2008). The most common cause of death by injury for international travelers is traffic accidents, involving motor vehicles, pedestrians, and other non-motorized transportation, such as bicycles and rickshaws. Bicycle helmets reduce the risk of head and brain injury for riders of all ages by 75%. Bike helmets have also been shown to reduce the number of facial injuries among riders by 65%.

Studies in Australia have shown that the main reasons foreign visitors are involved in crashes are the following: disorientation, fatigue, not driving on the correct side of the road, head-on crashes and overturning vehicles. In contrast, speeding and alcohol-related incidents were the most common reasons for crashes involving local residents (Hargarten, 2008).

In summary, road crash accidents are very common. Death to the pedestrian is more frequent than to drivers or passengers. Children are particularly vulnerable. Non-motorized transportation also carries a high risk of injury and death. In view of these alarming facts, it is essential to take steps to prevent traffic-related injuries, such as the use of bicycle helmets and other measures. It is wise to keep in mind that for the most part, trauma is a preventable disease! Below are included some specific recommendations (Hargarten, 2008; Steffes & Steffes, 2002) for reducing the risk of death and injury from road accidents:

Traffic safety recommendations:

1) As much as possible, choose to sit in the backseat of any vehicle.
2) Wear a seatbelt regardless of where you are sitting in the vehicle. Small children should be seated in a car seat, as per the guidelines issued by your home country.[78]
   a) Children who have outgrown their booster seat should use the vehicle seatbelt and they should always use lap-and-shoulder seatbelts for optimal protection.
   b) Children younger than 13 years should be seated in the back seat of vehicles with seatbelts for optimal protection.
3) In most countries (and particularly in developing countries), avoid driving as much as possible and hire reliable drivers familiar with the driving culture and roads. Avoid using drivers who may be under the influence of drugs or alcohol.
4) If you cannot avoid driving:
   a) Avoid driving at night and especially all-night driving.
   b) Avoid driving when you are fatigued or jet-lagged or under the influence of alcohol.
   c) Familiarize yourself with local road signs, roads, driving customs and laws. Check with authorities or your embassy in the country of your destination for requirements regarding licensure, road permits, auto insurance, local road rules, driving culture and road conditions.
   d) Carry a cell phone for emergencies when you are driving. Avoid talking on the cell phone or texting while driving.

---

[78] Regulations governing seatbelt and car seat use vary from country to country. Such regulations may not exist in the developing country where you may be serving. Familiarize yourself with the regulations in your home country, and purchase only car seats which bear a mark that certifies that the seat has been made by an authorized manufacturer and meets prescribed safety standards, such as the Canadian "National Safety Mark" (Transport Canada, 2013).

e) Consult a map before you set out. Use a Global Positioning System (GPS), as available. These are now available on cell phones and are a standard feature in many vehicles. Alternatively, if you have access to the Internet, use an on-line web-mapping service such as Google maps (www.maps.google.com) or MapQuest (www.mapquest.com) to plan your route; these maps can be downloaded to your mobile device or printed out.

f) Familiarize yourself as to how to respond to an emergency in the event of a crash. Some embassies recommend that you do not exit your car to exchange licenses in the event of an accident. If no policeman is readily available, drive directly to either the embassy or the police station. Staying with your car can be dangerous, and in some developing countries, accidents are deliberately staged as a form of extortion.

g) If you are driving in a country that drives on the opposite side of the road from that with which you are familiar, be extremely careful. As skilled a driver as you may be, in an emergency, your automatic reflexes may not be your friend.

5) If you plan to rent a vehicle (with or without a driver):

a) Check if the vehicle is equipped with seatbelts for all seats, air bags, and the LATCH (lower anchors and tethers for children) System if you have small children.

b) Select commonly available cars when renting (with or without a driver), and ask that any obvious rental car markings be removed.

c) Obtain a map, directions, list of local traffic signs and traffic laws, and a full introduction to the rental vehicle from staff of the rental agency prior to departure. Do a safety inspection of the tires, brakes, lights, airbags, and seatbelts.

6) Avoid riding on or driving a moped or motorbike. If you do use these vehicles, all passengers, whether adults or children, should wear

helmets. You may need to bring appropriately fitting helmets, especially for children, from home.

7) All bicyclists and bicycle passengers, especially children, should wear properly-fitting bicycle helmets. If necessary, take these with you to your destination.

8) Keep the doors of the vehicle locked and windows shut at all times. Be vigilant regarding potential car-jacking scenarios.

CASE3:

A 15-year-old American boy and his father attended an organized father-son camping weekend at a training camp in an African country. At the end of the weekend, as the men were breaking camp, several of the teenagers decided to try out the on-site military-style training facilities. After crossing the river on a cable bridge, the boys decided to not cross back to the camp the same way, but rather to swim across. The mountain stream, swollen by three weeks of heavy spring flooding, had a much higher water level than usual and rocky outcroppings at the site where the boys chose to swim across both contributed to a strong undertow. The boy set out with the others, but tired quickly and was washed away by the powerful current. After an intensive search, his body was recovered a week later many kilometers downstream. Both the boy's father and the dorm father who was in charge of the camp suffered for years from guilt and depression because of what they perceived as their responsibility in this accident.

Drowning is a serious but largely preventable cause of death. About 450,000 people drown worldwide each year (Hargarten, 2008) and it is a leading cause of death due to injury among tourists. Near-drowning, or submersion in water not leading to death, is also a significant cause of injury. Annually, about 15% of injury deaths of US citizens traveling abroad are caused by drowning. A study of children from the UK traveling abroad over an eight year period showed that 74% of deaths were due to drowning in a swimming pool. For even strong and experienced swimmers, swimming in a strange setting environment can be fraught with danger. Unfortunately, as with many injuries sustained abroad, drowning often occurs when travelers are engaging in unfamiliar activities in unfamiliar settings. Taking preventive measures is   essential.

Following are recommendations for swimmers in unfamiliar settings adapted from Hargarten (2008); another excellent source of information is the CDC website (n.d.).

Water safety and drowning prevention recommendations for travelers:

1) Adult non-swimmers and children should use personal flotation devices (PFDs) when they are in and around water (lakes, ocean,

   swimming pools, etc.). Bring these along from home if they are not available at the destination.
   a) Use proper-sized and coastguard-approved PFDs. Check the label for safe and correct fitting.
   b) Use PFDs for:
      i) Water-skiing or other towed activities
      ii) On personal watercraft
      iii) While white-water boating, sail boarding and on moving vessels of < 26'/7.9 meters
      iv) Children under 13 years of age should use them at all times when they are around water, even if they know how to swim.
   c) Make sure you know where the PFDs are when you board a yacht or cruise ship.
   d) Avoid inflatable swimming aids as they are not a substitute for approved PFDs and can give both adults and children a false sense of security.
2) Before leaving home, learn how to do cardio-pulmonary resuscitation (CPR) as CPR is essential for resuscitating someone who has had a near-drowning. Maintain your CPR certification with re-examination every two years.
3) If you have children, choose accommodations where there is four-sided, four-foot (1.2 m.) climb-proof isolation fencing around the pools and/or where there is a barrier between your living space and any body of water in which your child may drown. Ideally, the fence should have self-closing and self-latching gates.
   a) Children aged 4 or older should learn how to swim. Educate children regarding behavior around bodies of water: avoid

running on slippery pool decks; avoid diving into shallow water; always swim with a companion.

b) Adults who take on the supervision of children around water should be:
   i)   Experienced
   ii) Fully focused on supervising those under his/her care, providing "touch supervision," i.e. remaining within an arm's length away from the child.
   iii) Know how to perform CPR (cardiopulmonary resuscitation)
   iv) Know how to initiate an emergency response plan, including where to seek help
   v)   Free from the influence of alcohol.

c) Even children who are considered excellent swimmers need supervision in and around water.
d) While watching children near water, avoid distracting activities like reading, using a mobile device (browsing, listening to music, talking or texting), or playing games.
e) Keep rescue equipment (a shepherd's hook, a long pole with a hook on the end, and life preserver) and cell phone at hand at the pool-side. Rescue equipment should be made of fiberglass or other materials that do not conduct electricity.

4) Avoid alcohol if you are planning to be around or in water or on a boat as alcohol suppresses the gag reflex, as well as affecting your ability to think clearly.
5) Use designated swimming areas, preferably equipped with trained and certified lifeguards thereby improving survival in the event of a near-drowning.
6) Learn about animal-related risks and other environmental risks in and near the water where you are located (e.g. crocodiles, hippopotami, submerged rocks, thick water weeds). Pay attention and heed signs posting surf and weather conditions, as well as coliform counts or other environmental risks that may be present in natural bodies of water.
7) Travelers planning on diving and/or participating in more physically demanding water-related activities than normal should be assessed for physical, mental and medical fitness prior to departure. Reassessment should be done at regular intervals and following an

illness or injury. Guidelines regarding flying after diving should be adhered to rigorously to prevent barotrauma (i.e., 'the bends').

c) Other Water-related Hazards:

Schistosomiasis

Another potential hazard presented by swimming in natural bodies of water in certain areas of the world is parasites. One particular infection is called schistosomiasis. Schistosomiasis (sometimes called "bilharziasis") is caused by an infestation of a parasitic blood fluke called schistosomes which has a complex lifecycle involving both a definitive host (humans) and an intermediate host (snails). In areas where this organism is endemic (different species are found in specific regions of the world), avoid swimming, bathing, or wading in natural bodies of water. Contact of short duration such as through swimming or rafting and even from being sprayed by infected water is a potential source of infection in some regions of the world (Leder & Weller, 2010).

A larval form of the organism, called cerceriae, not seen by the naked eye, develops in the snail and is released into the water. On exposure to human skin, the cerceriae tunnel directly through the skin in a few hours and may cause a syndrome known as "swimmer's itch" usually within one day of exposure.

If contact with possibly infested water occurs, towel-dry the exposed skin rapidly and briskly to reduce the risk of infection. In addition, rubbing the skin with alcohol may also help. Swimming in chlorinated or salt water is safe.

What are the symptoms of schistosomiasis?

At the time of contact, tingling and itching at the site of entry may develop immediately, followed by an intensely itchy, raised rash 12 to 24 hours later, which can last more than a week, though some individuals do not have any symptoms on infection. Previous contact to schistosomiasis results in a more rapid immune response to subsequent infection and more severe symptoms (Leder and Weller, 2010). With high parasitic load and prolonged duration, the infection can then progress to serious disease of the gastrointestinal tract, liver, urinary and neurological systems, requiring medical treatment.

If, after leaving a schistosomiasis-endemic area, you become acutely ill with a fever, or develop ongoing vague gastrointestinal or genitourinary symptoms, along with fatigue or general unwellness, be sure to inform your doctor that you have been in an area endemic for schistosomiasis, as the adult form of the parasite may remain in the body for long periods of time. Blood serological tests can be done to determine whether you have been infected.

Leptospirosis

Water-related activities, including exposure to flood waters, can also result in infection with other parasites and bacteria; one such example is leptospirosis (Leder & Weller, 2010). As a general rule, it is advisable never to swim or have body contact with fresh or brackish water whilst overseas as many diseases can be contracted from such water.

3. Sun protection

Sun protection should be a major consideration for those working in areas of intense sun exposure. The following are guidelines from the American Academy of Pediatrics (AAP) released in February 2011 (Balk, 2011). Whether exposed in the course of everyday living or through intentional sun-tanning, ultraviolet radiation (UVR) is a major contributing cause of the three major forms of skin cancer: basal cell carcinoma, squamous cell carcinoma and malignant melanoma of the skin. UVR is the main environmental cause of the first two types which are the most common forms of skin cancer. In addition, the incidence of melanoma, the third category of sun-related skin cancer, is increasing, continuing the upward trend of the last 30 years. Recently, melanoma has been increasingly diagnosed in young white women and in white adults older than 65 years. Melanoma represents less than 5% of all skin cancers but causes the most skin cancer deaths. If diagnosed early by consultation with a dermatologist and skin biopsy, prognosis is excellent but once it has metastasized, there is no successful treatment for this potentially fatal condition. Clearly, prevention and early diagnosis are very important.

Who are at risk for skin cancer?

- People with light skin and eyes and who freckle easily
- People who sunburn easily
- People with a family history of melanoma
- People who had high levels of sun exposure in childhood
- People who have a large number of moles

What are other effects of UVR?

Other effects of UVR exposure include premature aging of the skin and, with long-term sun exposure, eye changes including cataract formation.

Adverse reactions can also occur when with sun exposure is combined with medication use. Common medications that can cause such reactions include: nonsteroidal anti-inflammatory medications (ibuprofen, aspirin, etc.), tetracyclines, tretinoin, phenothiazines, psoralens, sulfonamides, thiazides and para-amino benzoic acid (PABA) esters which are found in some sunscreens. In addition, some sunscreens, fragrances, sulfonamides, and phenothiazines are associated with allergies that are compounded by sun exposure.

Sun protective strategies, recommended by leading authorities include the following:

1) Avoid sunburn; avoid sun-tanning and tanning beds.
2) Time activities to avoid being outside at times of peak intensity UVR (midday between 10 AM and 4 PM), as much as possible. This is especially important if you are located near the equator.
3) Wear protective clothing and hats.
   a) Clothing is an excellent barrier against UVR. Unlike sunscreen, the clothing provides constant protection throughout the day unless it becomes wet. The more surface area of the body the clothing covers, the more protection it offers. For adequate coverage, wear clothing that covers to the neck, elbows, and knees. Wool and synthetic materials, heavily or tightly-woven fabrics and dark colors as well as chemically treated fabrics are superior with regards to sun protection. Hats with brims are most protective.

4) Stay in the shade.
5) Be aware, though, that you can still sunburn in the shade, as the UVR is scattered and reflected. If you have fair skin, you can burn in less than an hour sitting under a tree. Clouds decrease UVR intensity, but not to the degree that they decrease the intensity of heat. As a result, on a cloudy day, you may feel as though you are being protected while in reality, you are still being exposed to significant levels of UVR.
6) Be especially careful about protecting against sun exposure when you are near water, snow, sand, concrete and glass or if you are in a high-altitude location.

7) Use sunscreen liberally.
   a) SPF (Sun Protective Factor) is a ranking system used to indicate the degree of protection from sunburn provided by using a sunscreen; the higher the SPF, the greater the protection. For example, a person who ordinarily would develop sunburn in 10 minutes would be protected for about 300 minutes (10 X 30) with an SPF-30 sunscreen. The recommended amount is 2 mg/cm^2 which is approximately 1 oz (30 ml, or one capful) of sunscreen at one sitting for coverage of all the sun-exposed areas of an average adult wearing a bathing suit.
   b) Use sunscreen with an SPF of at least 15, spread liberally on the skin 15 to 30 minutes before going outside to allow for adequate absorption into the skin and to decrease the chance of the sunscreen being washed off. The sunscreen should then be reapplied every two hours and after swimming, sweating, or drying off with a towel.
   c) High SPF sunscreens do provide greater protection, and are recommended for those who have had skin cancer, but, in general, using sunscreen properly and reapplying it regularly are more important than using a sunscreen with a higher SPF.
   d) Avoid using sunscreens that contain oxybenzone, which may have weak estrogenic effects when absorbed through the skin.
   e) Two inorganic physical sunscreens approved by the US Food and Drug Administration which create a physical barrier to the penetration of UVB and UVA into the skin are zinc oxide and titanium dioxide.

    f)   Sunscreen is advised for children over age 6 months, along with the use of sun protective strategies such as UVR avoidance and clothing. Infants younger than 6 months of age should be kept out of direct sunlight and dressed in protective clothing and hats. When sun avoidance is impossible, sunscreen may be applied to infants, but only to exposed areas. Special attention should be taken to avoid sun exposure of pre-term infants as they may at a higher risk of absorbing sunscreen components.

8) Wear sunglasses.
    a)   Sunglasses protect against sun glare and harmful radiation. Visual health organizations recommend the use of sunglasses that absorb upwards of 97% of the full UVR spectrum.

    b)   Sunglasses should be used while working, driving, participating in sports, taking a walk, running errands, or doing anything in the sun.

9) People taking medications or using topical agents that are known to cause toxic or allergic reactions should limit sun exposure and avoid all unnecessary UVA exposure. Fully protective clothing and sunscreen with a high SPF that also blocks UVA wavelengths are recommended.

10) Parents are advised to discuss sun protection with their children beginning at 9 or 10 years of age to encourage their taking responsibility for ensuring sun protection.

What about tanning salons?

In most of the developing world, light-colored skin is more highly-esteemed than the Western ideal of the "healthy suntan" so sun-safe practices are often more the norm in these countries than the exception. However, a word about tanning salons and sun lamps is warranted. These artificial sources of UVR should be avoided as evidence shows an increased rate of skin cancer in those who frequent tanning salons. Large, powerful tanning units used by tanning salons may generate 10 to 15 times the intensity of UVA radiation than the midday sun (Balk, 2011).

In addition, it is often wrongly thought that obtaining a "pre-vacation tan," at a tanning salon or elsewhere, provides protection against sunburn while one travels to sunnier climes. This faulty practice actually leads to increased radiation exposure, as people tend to use fewer sun protection precautions while on vacation, thinking that their suntan will protect them. Such a pre-vacation tan results in virtually no protection against sunburn or against sun-induced DNA damage and skin aging.

What about sun exposure and vitamin D?

The medical community is divided regarding recommendations regarding sun exposure, because of the strong association between sun exposure with skin cancer, as well as vitamin D status. Vitamin D production by the skin requires sunlight exposure, and adequate vitamin D is needed for bone and muscle health as well as for other physiological functions. Although vitamin D is available through the diet, supplements, and non- intentional sun exposure, many people have low vitamin D concentrations; up to one-third of teenagers and young adults in the US have Vitamin D deficiency (25(OH)D less than 50nmol/L). In order to maintain an adequate level of vitamin D while promoting sun protection, adequate dietary and supplemental vitamin D is necessary for all age groups, but especially for children, pregnant women, breastfeeding mothers and post- menopausal women. Guidelines regarding vitamin D supplementation for breastfed and formula-fed infants and other children should be followed. In addition, it is recommended that all individuals under age 70, whether adult or child, receive at least 600 IU of vitamin D daily; adults over age 70 should receive 800 IU (Institute of Medicine, 2011).

"Sensible sun exposure" (exposure of arms and legs for 5–30 minutes, depending on the time of day, season, latitude and skin pigmentation, between 10 AM and 3 PM twice weekly) has also been recommended to maintain vitamin D concentrations (Balk, 2011).

4. Malaria and other vector-transmitted diseases:

CASE 1:
A Canadian couple serving on the Kenyan highlands was requested by their agency, with one week's notice, to temporarily move to another part of the country to meet a pressing need. The family traveled with their 6-year-old son to this area of lower elevation, leaving their two older children in boarding school at their home base. With the urgency of the request and the fact that malaria was not a problem in the highlands, the family neglected to take chemoprophylaxis (preventive treatment) for malaria. They stayed in a house where they noticed the screens on the windows had a number of holes, but because it was a borrowed residence, they did not feel at liberty to make repairs.

Two and a half weeks later, their son developed a high fever accompanied by vomiting, inconsolable crying and drowsiness. Despite their leaving the next day for medical attention, the child fell into a coma and died.

CASE 2:
A 9-year-old girl is brought in to see the doctor because the family is planning to move to Ghana, West Africa, to work with a medical development project. The child had had several seizures in the first three years of her life, for which she was treated with phenobarbital, an anti-seizure medication. She has now been off this medication for three years and has remained seizure-free. She currently has no evidence of any other health problems. Her mother, a nurse, has heard that anti-malarial medications can cause seizures, so she does not want her daughter to take chemoprophylaxis for malaria. The doctor explains to the mother that mefloquine, a commonly-used anti-malarial medication, can cause increased seizure frequency in patients with an active seizure disorder. This child, however, has a very low risk of running into trouble using mefloquine and the benefits of chemoprophylaxis far outweigh the possible side-effects of the medication, especially with the high prevalence of malaria in West Africa.

---

a) **Malaria** is an infectious disease, caused by a protozoan organism, spread largely by the female mosquito of the Anopheles genus. It is present in a significant proportion of the world and brings a high rate of illness and death, yearly causing 350–500 million infections worldwide and approximately 1 million deaths (Arguin & Mali, 2012). The WHO estimates that 10,000–30,000 travelers contract the disease annually. West Africa and Oceania have the highest risk of infection for travelers, while other parts of Africa, South Asia, and South America have moderate   risk   for   infection.   Regions   with   lower estimated risk are Central America and other parts of Asia. However, there is marked variation between countries and even between seasons in the same area. Less frequently, malarial transmission can also occur through blood transfusion, organ transplantation, the use of contaminated needles, or through the placenta from mother to fetus.

Prevention by taking medication (chemoprophylaxis) is very important in minimizing the risk of being infected by malaria. Reports of compliance to prophylaxis recommendations among travelers vary from as high as 82% to as low as 16%. Studies of long-stay travelers and/or expatriates have shown that the risk of malarial infection increases with the length of time spent in endemic areas. One study noted that the most striking feature of expatriates who developed malaria was their failure to use chemoprophylaxis consistently. In one study of 36 patients who were infected with malaria, 84% reported no or inconsistent chemoprophylaxis use (Riesland, 2008).

What type of medication should I take against malaria as I travel?

As you prepare to head overseas to serve, you and your travel medicine consultant should discuss what type of precautions against malaria you should take. This would depend upon your destination, your specific itinerary, what type of accommodation you will be living in, the specific season and style of travel, and the pattern of drug resistance against anti-malarial drugs in the geographical area of your service. The travel medicine consultant will also need to know about any pre-existing conditions you may have, medications and whether you are pregnant. Be prepared to provide this information when you see the consultant. For some individuals, taking precautions against mosquitoes may be adequate, while others will need to take medication regularly before and during their time abroad, as well as after their return. Also, note that no chemoprophylaxis provides 100% protection, so mosquito control and being attentive to clinical symptoms of malaria are also very important.

The website for the Centers for Disease Control (www.CDC.gov) provides excellent information on this topic, as well as helpful tools to determine what level of protection you need. If you are going to an area endemic for malaria, you would be well-advised to look at this website for further information to supplement your discussion with your travel medicine consultant. Along with other information, it includes a very useful chart delineating what medications are effective for prevention, arranged geographically (CDC, June 6, 2013).

What preventive measures should I take against malaria?

The following discussion is derived from the CDC website as well as other sources (Arguin & Mali, 2012).

Malaria prevention consists of a combination of mosquito avoidance measures and chemoprophylaxis.

Mosquito avoidance measures:

The best way to avoid insect bites is to physically reduce exposure to mosquitoes in your environment, apply DEET (see below) to your skin and wash your clothing with permethrin (according to instructions) prior to departure.

a) The *Anopheles* mosquito, the insect responsible for malaria transmission, is most active between dusk and dawn, its primary feeding time. Avoid being out and about at this time. (Note that mosquitoes carrying the virus causing dengue fever are most active during the day.)
b) Cut your contact with mosquitoes by staying in areas that are screened-off – check the screens for holes and for a tight fit in their frames. Keep screens and doors closed, and open windows at night only if they have screens. At night, look for mosquitoes around ceilings, curtains,   and   closets   and   kill   them.
c) Spray your living space with permethrin-based insecticide in the

evening; spray your bedroom an hour before you retire.
d) The mosquitoes carrying malaria do not fly well in turbulent air. If
your room has a fan, use it, directing the air flow over your bed.
e) As the climate permits, wear long sleeves and long pants made of a
tightly-woven material. White or light-colored clothing is preferred, as
mosquitoes avoid such clothing due to lack of camouflage.
f) Don't wear strong scents such as after-shave, cologne, perfume, or
perfumed skin lotion, to avoid attracting mosquitoes. g) Eliminate
breeding sites for mosquitoes by getting rid of sources of standing water,
such as the bases of potted plants and plants with water-holding leaf
structures (e.g. bromeliads). Cover open drains with netting.

The most effective broad-spectrum insect repellent is DEET (*N,N*-
diethyl- metatoluamide), an ingredient found in many commercially
available insect repellents. It is effective against mosquitoes, biting flies,
chiggers, fleas and ticks over a long period of time. DEET preparations
come in many concentrations but adults should use a repellent that
contains at least 15% DEET for adequate protection, although some
authorities recommend concentrations of up to 50% DEET.
Formulations with higher DEET concentrations are effective for a
longer duration but may have increased toxicity. The following chart is
from Gradin & Day's work on comparing various insect repellents
(2002).

Active Ingredient and Concentration	Commercial Name	Duration (minutes)
24% DEET	OFF! Deep Woods™	302
20% DEET	Sawyer Controlled Release™	234
5% DEET	Off! Skintastic for Kids™	88
IR3535, 7.5%	Skin-So-Soft Bug Guard Plus™	23
Citronella, 0.1%	Skin-So Soft Bug Guard™	14

Please note that citronella formulations and Skin-So-Soft lasted less
than 20 minutes so are inadequate for protecting against mosquitoes.

• DEET is safe for both adults and children older than 2 months of
age but neurologic effects have been reported with very heavy use

of DEET in children. It can also cause rash and allergic reactions, and can damage some plastics as well as clothing made of spandex and rayon (Breisch, 2011).

- Picaridin, available in the US as Sawyer Insect RepellentTM (20%), Cutter Advanced SportTM (15%) and Cutter AdvancedTM (7%) is a safe repellent which has similar effectiveness to DEET when used for short periods; however, DEET remains effective for a longer period of time. It is also odorless, non-sticky and non-greasy and does not irritate skin, stain fabrics or degrade plastics. (Breisch, 2011).
- Permethrin is a related, safe and biodegradable insecticide that repels mosquitoes, ticks, flies, and other insects effectively. It is applied only to fabric, binding tightly to it without harming or staining it and withstands multiple launderings, lasting two-three weeks. Like picaridin, it will not soften or melt plastic or synthetic material.

Because of the potential toxicity of using repellents over a long period of time, the following recommendations have been made by the US Environmental Protection Agency (EPA), to increase effectiveness and decrease side-effects (1996).

- Apply a thin layer of repellent to the skin to just cover, but not saturate, the skin.
- Apply repellents to exposed skin and clothing during high- mosquito periods, but not under clothing.
- Apply the repellent to your face by rubbing a small amount into your palms and then onto your face. Wash your palms after applying to prevent contact with your eyes, mouth and genitals.
- Never use repellents over cuts, wounds, rashes or broken skin.
- Don't apply repellent to the hands of small children, to avoid being rubbed into the eyes.
- The repellant does not need to be applied frequently. However, protection is decreased by swimming, washing, sweating, exercise and exposure to rain.
- When using sunscreen, apply sunscreen first and then repellent.
- Repellent should be washed off with soap and water at the end of a day before going to bed.

Effective protection against mosquitoes is vital to protecting against malaria infection. Regular and wise use of repellents for both adults and children is an important and effective strategy to this end.

Chemoprophylaxis for malaria:

The importance of taking chemoprophylaxis as recommended for the specific area that you will be travelling through or living in cannot be overemphasized. In nearly all deaths, patients were using either no chemoprophylaxis or an unsuitable regimen, had a delay or errors in the diagnosis of malaria by physicians and laboratories, or received incorrect initial treatment (Schlagenhauf-Lawlor and Kain, 2008). Malaria is a serious but preventable infection that can be averted with careful and mindful attention. However, no one anti-malarial drug is 100% effective in preventing malaria and must be combined with the use of protective measures as mentioned above.

Recommended chemoprophylaxis regimens involve taking medication for an extended period of time: before departure, during the actual time spent in the malaria-endemic area, and for a period of time after leaving the malaria endemic area. A thorough discussion of the specific medications is beyond the scope of this chapter as recommendations for drugs to prevent malaria differ by country of travel. This information can be found in the country-specific tables of the CDC "Yellow Book." Recommended drugs and their comparable efficacy in various countries are listed in alphabetical order of the country names. Some areas, however, are known to have high levels of transmission, for example, West Africa, where exposure for even short periods of time can result in transmission, so chemoprophylaxis for those traveling and working in this area is strongly recommended (Arguin & Mali, 2012).

It is wise to discuss this issue with your health care provider (or travel medicine consultant) well in advance (at least four to six weeks) of your departure. By starting the drug before travel, anti-malarial medication is able to build up to an effective level in the blood before you are potentially exposed to malaria parasites. Be careful to follow the instructions that your travel medicine consultant gives you. Malaria kills!

Special points regarding chemoprophylaxis:

The following discussion is taken from Arguin & Mali (2012).
a) Children travelling to malaria-endemic areas also need chemoprophylaxis at doses appropriate for their weight.
b) Malaria is a particularly dangerous for pregnant women as it can cause serious complications such as prematurity, abortion, and stillbirth. Pregnant women should avoid travel to malaria-endemic areas until after delivery. If travel is unavoidable, chemoprophylaxis is essential.
c) As anti-malarial drugs, particularly chloroquine, can be fatal if taken in large doses, medication should be stored in childproof containers out of the reach of infants and children.
d) Chemoprophylaxis can be started earlier if there are particular concerns about tolerating one of the medications. For example, mefloquine can be started three to four weeks in advance to allow potential adverse events to occur before travel. If unacceptable side effects do develop, there would be adequate time to change the medication before departure.
e) Although medications used for anti-malarial chemoprophylaxis are generally well-tolerated, side effects can occur. While minor side effects usually do not require stopping the drug, those who have serious side effects should see a health-care provider to determine if symptoms are related to the medicine and make an appropriate medication changes as needed.

f) Do not delay seeking medical attention if you suspect that you or one of your family members, team mates or companions has malaria.
g) Be careful if you are taking bismuth subsalicylate (Pepto- Bismol®) for the prevention of traveler's diarrhea at the same time as doxycycline for malarial prophylaxis. Bismuth subsalicylate can affect decrease the effectiveness of doxycyline by reducing its bioavailability.

What are the symptoms of malaria?

Prevention of malaria is essential to the international worker. However, 100% prevention of malaria is not achievable, so you should be aware of the symptoms of malaria and seek attention immediately if you or a family member develop any of these symptoms. The following section draws heavily from Steffes and Steffes (2002) and Magill (2008).

Malaria is characterized by fever (as high as 41°C/105°F) and influenza-like symptoms, including chills, sweating, which usually occurs over a 4–6 hour period. The patient may also experience headache, dizziness, muscle and bony aches, gastrointestinal symptoms (including nausea, vomiting,   diarrhea,   cramps),   dry   cough and malaise. After several days, the patient may develop an enlarged spleen and liver. Because of the cyclic nature of the infection, these symptoms may occur at intervals, every two to three days. The patient may feel generally well, though fatigued, between the episodes. Malaria may be associated with anemia and jaundice and with severe disease, most commonly caused by a strain called P. falciparum, the patient may develop seizures, mental confusion, renal failure, acute respiratory disease syndrome (ARDS), coma, and death.

Malaria symptoms can develop as few as 7 days (but usually 14 days) after initial exposure in a malaria-endemic area and as late as several months or more after departure. Many cases do not surface until the patient has returned home from the malaria-endemic area.

After you leave the affected area, if you experience any severe viral-like symptoms in the following year, you should have a high index of suspicion that you have malaria and seek medical attention immediately. Symptoms might include:

- unexplained fever that lasts more than 24 hours
- a prolonged severe headache
- severe muscle and joint pains
- persistent diarrhea or vomiting that does not respond to treatment.

Seek immediate treatment and if your doctor seems to make light of the problem, seek medical attention at a university center or a travel medicine clinic. Any delay in receiving treatment could be fatal.

b. Other vector-transmitted diseases

Dengue fever and Chikungunya are other vector-transmitted diseases which can also be controlled by mosquito control (Leder & Weller, 2010).

Dengue fever is an infectious disease endemic in tropical Asia, Central and South America, and the Caribbean, that is also transmitted by mosquito, in this case, the Aedes aegypti mosquito. Though it can affect anyone in a dengue-endemic area, it primarily affects long-term residents in endemic areas vs. travelers (Rothman, 2010). As this infection has no known treatment, nor is a vaccine available (though current efforts at developing a vaccine are promising), mosquito control is particularly important. Insecticide spraying, as a measure to counter dengue outbreaks, is not extremely effective against A. aegypti mosquitoes, which is often found within houses. The same mosquito control measures mentioned for malaria prevention also hold for dengue fever control, with the exception that bed netting is not very effective against dengue infection as the mosquitoes are most active during the daytime. Note that previous infection with dengue fever does not provide immunity against dengue in the future, as there are four main subtypes of dengue, and infection with one subtype does not offer cross-immunity.

Walking barefoot or in loose-fitting footwear on beaches, on soil, or in water that may be contaminated with human or canine feces may lead to contact with hookworm or Strongyloides larvae. Infestation of the larvae can cause cutaneous larva migrans, hookworm, or strongyloidiasis. Cutaneous larva migrans is the leading cause of skin infections in international travelers (Wilson, 2010). These infections, as well as bites by ticks, sand-flies, chiggers and other insects can also be avoided by the same preventative measures mentioned above re: mosquito control in addition to the following:

- Wear shoes instead of sandals. Appropriate footwear can help prevent infection from parasites, fungi and other injuries (snakebites, cuts, puncture wounds)
- After being out-of-doors, do a thorough body check at the end of the day to look for embedded insects
- When you pick up a piece of clothing or linen or a towel, shake it out first.
- When walking at night, use a flashlight.

5. Conclusion
International living is full of adventures, medical and otherwise. Having a basic understanding of common problems encountered, coupled with a vigilant, proactive attitude, is vital in maintaining health as one navigates the shoals of cross-cultural living.

CASE:
In May 2003, at the height of the SARS crisis in China, a German nurse posted in one of the SARS hotspots developed a low-grade fever. It was just days before she was to return to her home country for home leave, and adhering to national regulations, she presented for a checkup to the local hospital mandated with assessing foreign SARS cases. She had been assured by a Chinese medical friend that this was merely a formality. The hospital, however, kicked into high gear, and much to her surprise and consternation, the nurse found herself admitted to the SARS ward, sharing an isolation ward with 23 confirmed SARS cases. Though her temperature remained low-grade and she did not develop any symptoms of SARS, and in fact, her lab tests suggested that she had a *Mycoplasma* infection which would explain her fever, the hospital quarantined her for monitoring for 5 days, fearful of being responsible for introducing the first SARS case to Germany. The nurse's hospitalization created great concern within her agency, prompting phone calls with the home office, discussing

the need for medical evacuation, and with her family and constituency as the patient herself had no way of contacting them from hospital.

Anxiety escalated when a local TV station broadcast a short video clip of the patient in the hospital SARS ward, as part of a "What were you doing on May 1, Labor Day?" public relations stint. Within minutes of this showing, the executive director of her agency received the first of dozens of phone calls from colleagues and neighbors who'd all had contact with this outgoing foreigner in the preceding days. In an already charged atmosphere of near-hysteria about this deadly and poorly-understood virus, this development only heightened the general level of suspicion and fear. The agency monitored the patient's progress closely, negotiating with the hospital for early discharge to avoid her being actually infected by the confirmed cases of SARS with whom she was hospitalized. In addition, the agency played a public health role, consulting and advising quarantine for known contacts, in keeping with national regulations. This was complicated by the fact that this occurred in the late spring when many of the known foreign contacts already had made plans to return to their home countries.

The patient was discharged from hospital after five days, when her fever had subsided and she had not developed full-blown symptoms of SARS. She voluntarily underwent another week of quarantine in her home before returning to Germany. By June, 2003, the WHO proclaimed the SARS outbreak contained; China, in total, reported 235 deaths as a result of the SARS outbreak.

1. What are the main groups of people involved in this scenario who need attention? What issues are to be considered by the agency?
2. If you were the head of the agency to which this worker belonged, what concrete steps would you take in managing this situation?
3. What lessons were learned? How could this case affect future emergency and contingency planning?

Appendix One:
Vaccinations

Vaccinations

Vaccinations are an essential part of preparing both yourself and your family for international service as many diseases you will encounter at your destination, as in your home country, are now preventable by vaccines. In recent years, there has been a resurgence of childhood diseases such as measles[79], mumps and pertussis (whooping cough) because of a growing number of individuals who did not receive routine vaccinations for fear that vaccines, like the MMR (measles, mumps and rubella vaccine), are linked to problems such as autism (K. McClean, personal communication, January 30, 2011). Please note that A.J.

---

[79] Before measles immunization, nearly all children got measles by age 15, resulting in 48,000 being hospitalized, 7,000 having seizures and 1000 suffering permanent brain damage or deafness. After measles immunization, these numbers dropped significantly such that by the year 2000, measles originating in the US had dropped virtually to zero, with rare cases being imported cases. However, in 2011, 222 cases of measles were reported in the US. and from 2012 to 2013, outbreaks in the United Kingdom resulted in more than 2750 cases, occurring primarily in unimmunized children, aged 5-14 years (Auwaerter, 2013).

Wakefield, the UK investigator who was responsible for the 1998 report that set off these fears was convicted of fraud in 2010 and that he and the report, which contained falsified content, have both been thoroughly discredited.

Besides routine vaccinations, families preparing to serve overseas will also be required by the host country to obtain additional vaccinations. It is in your best interests to obtain the vaccinations that your travel medicine consultant recommends.

What factors determine whether I need a vaccination?

As a general principle, whether you need a certain vaccine depends on the following factors (Freedman, Virk & Jong, 2008):

- the risk of contracting a disease which could be prevented by a vaccine
- the severity of the disease if you were to be infected
- the risk of the vaccine itself

The decision to receive a certain vaccination also depends on personal factors specific to the individual. Be prepared to tell your travel medicine consultant the following information:

- Your anticipated activities in the destination area
- Living conditions and accommodations
- Length of time you will be spending in the destination area
- The degree of intimate contact with national residents (including sexual relations)
- The season of the year that you will be travelling
- Your age
- Any known allergies
- Your general condition of health
- Any medications you are taking on an ongoing basis
- Whether you are pregnant, are possibly pregnant or are likely to become pregnant on location
- Past history of immunizations

Practical guidelines:

a. Visit a travel clinic four to six weeks before your time of departure in order to finish your complete immunization series.

b. No vaccine provides 100% protection against a disease, so take preventative measures regarding food and water safety, general hygiene and avoidance of insect bites, even if you have been vaccinated.

c. All commonly given vaccines can be given on the same day, without affecting their protective effect or increasing the risk of adverse reactions. This is especially important if you are preparing for or already involved in international work, as you may be exposed to several infectious diseases within a very short period of time. It is recommended that all advised vaccines be given according to the schedule for your age. If not administered on the same day, an inactivated vaccine may be given at any time before or after a different inactivated vaccine or a live-virus vaccine (Kroger & Atkinson, 2012).

d. If more than one live vaccine (measles, mumps and rubella [MMR]; varicella; zoster; yellow fever; or live attenuated influenza vaccine) is to be given, they should either be given on the same day, or at least a month apart from each other, in order to maximize protection from each vaccine.

e. Seek medical advice from your agency, local medical authorities or experienced workers about the safety and reliability of locally-produced vaccines in your location. Disruptions in the cold chain (not maintaining the vaccines at 35°F/2°C to 45°F/8°C during transport and storage), use of expired vaccines and counterfeit vaccines (Xu, 2010 as cited in ProMED, 2010)[80] can all affect the effectiveness of the vaccination. You may also want to take along your own syringes if the

---

[80] This was a significant concern in China in 2009-2010 over the sale of counterfeit and contaminated rabies vaccines. In September 2010, the news reported the sale of counterfeit rabies vaccine which caused the death of a child and threatened the lives of more than a thousand others.
http://english.cri.cn/6909/2010/09/26/1821s596358.htm from a ProMED-mail post (www.promedmail.org)

hygienic practices at the medical facility where you are receiving vaccinations   are   questionable.

f. If you forget to return for a follow-up dose of vaccine or booster at the time specified by your doctor or are delayed for any reason, you can get the dose whenever you go in next to see the doctor. It is unnecessary to start the vaccinations series over again, or to add any extra doses except for oral typhoid. For maximal protection, you need to complete the full oral typhoid immunization schedule at least one week before travel. If you miss an oral typhoid vaccine, you should consult with your travel medicine specialist (Lexi-Comp, 2011). Some vaccines require regular   boosters   in   order   for   ongoing   protection.

g. Individuals with decreased immune function (altered immunocompetence) should not be given live vaccines until their immune function has recovered, as the immune response will not be able to mount an adequate protective response to the vaccine. This includes patients with leukemia, cancer, HIV infection, undergoing cancer chemotherapy, prolonged therapy with high dose steroids or having conditions such as asplenia (lack of spleen) and chronic renal disease. It is recommended that patients with mild immune suppression receive the MMR   and   varicella   vaccines   (Manning,   et   al.,   2008).

h. Pregnant women require particular attention re: vaccinations. If you are pregnant, you should discuss specific recommendations pertaining to pregnant women with your travel medicine consultant. As these recommendations are modified regularly in the light of new data, specific recommendations are not included in this chapter. One set of current recommendations for pregnant women can be found on the CDC website.

    i.   Pregnant women should not receive live attenuated viruses including HPV, BCG (TB), MMR, oral typhoid, yellow fever and varicella vaccines. They should also not receive the Human Papillomavirus (HPV) vaccine (Sutton, 2012).

    ii.   Women in the second and third trimesters of pregnancy are at increased risk for hospitalization from influenza. Because vaccinating against influenza before the season begins is critical, and because predicting exactly when the season will begin is impossible, routine influenza vaccination is recommended for all women who are or will be pregnant (in any trimester) during influenza season, which in the United States is usually early October through late March (Manning et al., 2011). However, pregnant women should not receive the live attenuated influenza vaccine.

i. Routine vaccines can be given if the adult or child has symptoms of a minor ailment, even with a fever. However, if you have a moderate to severe illness such as a severe cold or flu or other infection, with or without fever, it is best to postpone the vaccination. Giving it at this time may affect the immune response and also cover up any adverse symptoms you may have towards the vaccine. If you have a history of a serious large localized or systemic allergic reaction to a previous dose of a vaccine or its components, using the same vaccine formulation again may not be advisable. In some cases, other brands or formulations of the vaccine may be available.

j. Arrange to have your last shots in a series at least ten days before your departure date in order to let any fever and pain subside and to make sure you are not having any adverse reactions (Steffes & Steffes, 2002).

Specific Vaccinations:

Regarding travelling to distant destinations, Freedman, Virk, Jong (2008) divides specific vaccinations into three categories: required, recommended and routine vaccinations.

Required vaccinations:

1. Yellow fever vaccination is required for all travelers to certain endemic countries that have established this requirement under the International Health Regulations; these countries are located mainly in equatorial Africa and parts of South and Central America. Travelers to these endemic regions will need proof of immunization when they enter other countries, which are not endemic for (infected with) yellow fever (Freedman, Virk & Jong, 2008).

2. In order to obtain a Hajj or Umrah visa to Saudi Arabia, one needs a proof of vaccination against meningococcal meningitis (Rendi-Wagner & Kollaritsch, 2008).

Recommended travel vaccinations:

Depending on the factors mentioned above, these may include hepatitis A, hepatitis B, typhoid, influenza, rabies, Japanese encephalitis, tick-borne encephalitis and cholera (in some countries, the cholera vaccine is approved for the prevention of travelers' diarrhea caused by enterotoxigenic E. coli).

Routine vaccines:

Vaccinations which may need updating prior to a trip include tetanus/diphtheria/pertussis, measles/mumps/rubella, polio, pneumococcal, varicella, zoster, HPV (Freedman, Virk & Jong, 2008). If you have not completed the primary series or received required boosters for any of these childhood diseases, you should definitely do so before travelling overseas. The most current schedules for vaccinations for children, adolescents and adults can be found on the CDC Vaccines and Immunization website at www.cdc.gov/vaccines.

Special notes on specific vaccines:

1. Measles, mumps and pertussis:
As mentioned earlier, infectious disease experts have observed that there has recently been a resurgence of measles and mumps, probably because of waning immunity in individuals who were immunized in childhood rather than getting natural diseases and the lack of boosting from regular outbreaks (K. McClean, personal communication, January 30, 2011). You may be at high risk with lowered immunity if you are just starting to serve in an area with high risk for exposure and have not received boosters for these diseases since childhood. These childhood diseases are often more severe when acquired as an adult. You should have at least two MMRs if you are going to a high-risk area, possibly including one MMR given in adulthood. Ensure that your children are also adequately vaccinated.

Similarly, you should receive TdaP, which includes the pertussis vaccine in addition to tetanus and diphtheria vaccines, versus Td vaccine, as cases of pertussis have also been noted (Ibid.).

2.Rabies:

Rabies deserves particular attention as it is 100% preventable yet fatal when contracted. It has regularly been attributed with the highest number of infection-related deaths in areas of the world such as China in recent years (CDC, 2013).[81] More than 55 000 people, mostly in Africa and Asia, die from rabies yearly (CDC, 2013). Travelers and international workers on these continents and in Latin America run the greatest risk of infection. The rabies virus is transmitted through the bite of rabid mammals which serve as vectors, such as dogs, cats, raccoons, skunks, bats, and foxes. In the US, more than 90% of cases reported to the CDC occur in wildlife, but global figures show that exposure to rabid dogs is the cause of over 90% of human rabies infections and of over 99% of human deaths from rabies (CDC, 2013a).

It is estimated that the risk of children being bitten is four times greater than that of adults (Gamble & Lovell-Hawker, 2008). In addition, children tend to be bitten higher on the body or face (DeMaria & Techasathit, 2011). These bites are more severe, yet they are often are minimized and neglected as parents may not recognize their seriousness.

Vaccination for rabies is highly effective when given properly and in time, granting close to 100% protection. Vaccination includes two series: the pre-exposure series (for protection before being bitten) and the post-exposure series (for protection after being bitten).

The pre-exposure series can be given according to various schedules; the US Advisory Committee on Immunization Practices (ACIP) recommends vaccination at 0, 7 and 21 or 28 days, with the injections

---

[81] In November, 2010, Guangdong, China, reported 33 deaths due to rabies, second only to AIDS (80 deaths) and tuberculosis (14 deaths). These three top causes of mortality due to infection accounted for 95.49 percent of fatalities. In contrast, 1-3 people die every year in the US from rabies, usually due to exposures to indigenous rabid bats, skunks, or raccoons, or to exposure to rabid dogs while travelling overseas. China reports about 2000 deaths due to rabies per year (CDC, June 6, 2013b).

given intramuscularly or intradermally (Manning et al., 2008). Recent studies show that the lower-dose intradermal mode (which requires one-tenth the dose of the intramuscular dose, and is thus significantly less expensive) is more effective than originally thought, with evidence of immunological protection three years after the injection. This may be an option available overseas, e.g. in Thailand, but is not offered currently in the US (DeMaria & Techasathit, 2011).

In the event that an individual is bitten, he/she will require post-exposure vaccination (PEP), whether or not he/she has received pre-exposure vaccination (i.e. a series of shots before being bitten). If the individual received pre-exposure vaccination, two PEP vaccinations are required, one on day 0 (as soon as possible after the bite) and another on day 3 (Manning, et al. 2008). If the individual did not receive pre-exposure vaccination, he/she requires a four-dose PEP regimen, the first dose given on day 0, followed by doses administered on days 3, 7, and 14 after the first vaccination. This PEP regimen, recommended by the ACIP (Rupprecht, 2010), advises giving only four post-exposure immunizations as opposed to five, as previously recommended. For maximal immune response, McClean recommends this regimen only with the use of purified chick embryo cell vaccine (PCEC, commercially available as RabAvert™, Novartis) or human diploid cell vaccine (HDCV, available as Imovax™, Sanofi Pasteur) vaccines, not with other vaccines (personal communication, January 30, 2011). Also, depending on the characteristics of the actual bite (location, degree of contamination, etc.), the individual may need to receive rabies immunoglobulin. These are decisions that your health care provider will need to make.

If you know that you will be living and working in a region with a high proportion of animals carrying the rabies virus, you should seriously consider getting pre-exposure rabies vaccination. In addition, the following individuals should strongly consider vaccination:

i.   Families with children
ii.   Families with pets
iii. Personnel with limited access to care or transportation to where prompt post-exposure treatment can be received.

iv.   Personnel in countries where access to Human or Purified Equine Rabies Immune Globulin and/or modern tissue culture vaccines is limited

v.   Personnel who visit or travel into remote or rural regions or explore caves for work or recreation

vi.   Veterinarians or personnel who will be working with animals

Avoidance of animal bites:

Avoiding animal bites is a key factor in minimizing the risk of rabies. Do educate both yourself and your children on how to avoid animal attacks, and in the unfortunate event of such an attack, how to handle yourselves. Callahan (2008) offers the following guidelines:

1. In general, stay away from unfamiliar animals and animals exhibiting unusual behavior, even if the owner tells you that it is safe and won't bite. Especially avoid animals which are in a cage, pen or crate.

2. Avoid opportunities to pet or be photographed with a wild animal, an attraction offered by some commercial animal farms. Although they claim that the animals are safe, guests have been attacked and as they are usually required to sign a

   waiver, all financial costs for the result of attack are the responsibility of the guest alone.

3. Avoid visiting animal parks or zoos which do not provide adequate protective facilities (sturdy vehicles, trained staff, adequate barriers, etc.).

4. Knowing whether the animal is attacking for reasons of self-defense or predation is helpful in determining one's response to an attack (Callahan, 2008). A number of unprovoked attacks have occurred when the predator mistakes the victim, or a part of the victim, for prey.

   a. An animal that is sick or injured, or is trying to protect itself or its young is best avoided with non-threatening behavior (backing away quietly, moving slowly, playing dead). If knocked over, roll into a ball and lie still.

   b. If the attacking animal, such as solitary polar bears, tigers and lions, sees the traveler as prey and advances without provocation, one should make oneself as difficult, large and unattractive a potential meal as possible.

i. Yelling, making oneself appear larger by opening your jacket, standing tall, placing one's bags overhead can be helpful.
ii. As small children are specifically targeted by hyenas and big cats, lift them up and carry them on the shoulders or back.
iii. When being attacked, do not turn away and run, as this may trigger a chase reflex and you may expose yourself to attack.

5. When walking in an area which may be populated by stray dogs, carry a sturdy stick. In the event that a dog attempts to attack you, keep the stick between you and the animal, as it will regard the stick as an extension of you and will attack the stick rather than a part of you. However, do not attempt to strike the animal with the stick as its reflexes are faster than yours.
6. Do not attempt to separate pets from animals that have attacked them.
7. Train your children to immediately report any bite to an adult. Wash the wound with soap and water, scrubbing it out vigorously to remove any trace of saliva. Contact health authorities immediately.

Influenza: Seasonal Influenza and Avian Flu:

With the H1N1 pandemic and avian flu threats of 2009, 2010 and 2012-13, most authorities advise a yearly influenza shot at the beginning of the flu season (October-March). This is not only to protect against seasonal flu, but also to prevent the chance of human-human transmission in the event of pandemic avian influenza (seasonal influenza is spread from person to person, while avian flu is not). If someone who is infected with both influenza viruses and these combine to produce a recombined form of the virus, it could spread more easily from one human to another, something that the avian flu rare does on its own. All individuals six months old and over are recommended to receive the influenza vaccine. It is strongly advised those at high risk of flu complications be vaccinated, including pregnant women, children younger than 5 years old but especially younger than 2 years old, older adults 65 years and older, and people with chronic conditions like asthma, diabetes, and heart disease (CDC, March 15, 2013).

Why do Guidelines Regarding Immunization Vary So Much?

While preparing for overseas service, the prospective cross-cultural worker may wonder why so many guidelines exist which, in some cases, seem to conflict with each other. Different countries vary in their recommendations, and even different organizations within the same country will have varying guidelines. According to Magill and Shlim (2010), guidelines or recommendations, such as for vaccinations, preventative medications (e.g. malaria prophylaxis) or therapy (e.g. self- treatment for diarrhea) are established by many sources including the following:

- The governmental, regulatory body of each country which approves which drugs are to be available in that country
- International organizations such as the WHO, which often provides guidelines for smaller countries which do not have their own regulatory body.
- National governmental agencies such as the Centers for Disease Control and Prevention (CDC) in the US.
- Professional organizations such as the Advisory Committee on Immunization Practices (ACIP) and the American Academy of Pediatrics (AAP) in the US, which form their recommendations based on medical literature and expert opinion.
- Many unmonitored opinions on the Internet.

These different sources all have their own priorities in establishing recommendations such as the availability of products in their respective countries, the mandate of the specific government agency, cultural differences regarding the perception of the risk presented by a disease, different interpretations of the scientific evidence for a medication or intervention or just plain differences of opinion amongst experts (Magill & Shlim, 2010).

How then Should You Make Wise Decisions for Yourself and Your Family?

Be sure to seek a good travel clinic in your home country. You should choose a travel medicine consultant who is up-to-date, informed about current standards of care and vaccine practices for your country, and able to communicate clearly the risks and benefits of the interventions you are concerned about. Make sure you see your travel medicine consultant at least four to six weeks before departure; he/she will likely offer recommendations besides those regarding immunizations, especially if you are planning on living overseas long-term. Be sure to ask your travel medicine consultant to recommend other reliable resources that can be accessed while you are overseas to help you keep informed. At your international destination, your local healthcare provider ideally will have access to information from national public health agencies on standard vaccine practices in that country.

The following are helpful links:

- Children are usually immunized against common childhood diseases within the first 24 months of life. These vaccinations are often referred to as the "routine" immunizations of childhood. Routine immunization schedules for children recommended by various countries can be found on the WHO website: http://apps.who.int/immunization_monitoring/globalsummary/schedules
- The CDC offers guidelines and information for international travelers which is available at www.cdc.gov/travel as well as recommended immunization schedules at http://www.cdc.gov/vaccines/schedules/easy-to-read/index.html
- Other countries have similar guidelines, accessible as below: Canada: http://www.phac-aspc.gc.ca/im/index-eng.php Australia: http://immunise.health.gov.au

As numerous diseases encountered in the developing world can now be prevented by vaccines, an essential part of preparing for international work is to take timely and active steps to be informed and appropriately vaccinated before heading for the field.

Appendix Two:
Travel Medical and First-aid Kits

The majority of travelers experience some kind of health problem upon travelling to a developing country. The longer your stay, the greater your risk of illness or injury, with the risk rising by 3–4% with each day of travel (Weiss & Franco-Paredes, 2008). Diarrhea and respiratory tract symptoms are the most common problems encountered with traveling to developing countries. Nearly 25% of travelers experience symptoms related to the respiratory tract during their trip, while approximately 8% of travelers experience skin problems, and about 5% of travelers experience trauma from accidents or injuries. Most injuries are minor, requiring only self-treatment with what can be found in a basic first aid kit. In view of these facts, be prepared! Carrying a travel medical kit that is well thought-out and comprehensive is a key part of that preparation.

Before you leave, take time to browse in your local pharmacy and buy the items that you usually use when you are feeling unwell. These will be the basis of your travel medical kit. As you assemble your medical kit, consider your destination (what are common local diseases?), duration of time to be spent abroad, accessibility to medical care at your destination, your general health and that of your family, including pre-existing and/or chronic conditions, and your own level of medical knowledge and ease in giving self-care.

What should be included in a general medical kit?

Weiss and Franco-Paredes (2008) and Whatley and Marshall (2012) suggest the following contents:

1.All prescription medications:
a. If you have any pre-existing medical conditions, make sure you carry enough medication for the duration of your trip and an extra supply in case of a delayed return. Any supplies or medications that are needed for the management of flare-ups of existing medical conditions should be carried as well (e.g. Ventolin nebules for acute asthma attacks, etc.). Make sure you consult with your health-care provider before departure about other precautions and preparations.

b. Include copies of all prescriptions and extra medications in case of loss or extended period of travel, as well as a note from the prescribing physician (on formal letterhead), if you are using controlled substances and/or injectable medications. In addition, some medications are not allowed in certain countries so if you are on any medications that may fall under these restrictions, particularly with controlled substances such as narcotics, contact the embassy or consulate of the destination country.
c. Keep medications in their original container (preferred) in a small pill case or bottles labeled with name, strength, expiration date, and instructions.

2. Medication related to the region you will be traveling or located in, e.g. malaria chemoprophylaxis medications as needed (see section on malaria) or high-altitude medication.
3. Antibiotics for self-treatment
    a. Azithromycin 250mg capsules: for bacterial throat infections, ear infections, bronchitis, pneumonia, sinusitis, traveler's diarrhea (especially in SE Asia), skin infections, urethritis, pelvic infections
    b. Amoxicillin clavulanate 500mg tablets, cefuroxime or cephalexin 500mg tablets for: bite wounds, skin infections, pneumonia, urinary tract infections, ear infections, bronchitis, tonsillitis and sinusitis
    c. Ciprofloxacin 500mg tablets (or other fluoroquinolone) for: diarrhea including traveler's diarrhea (but not in SE Asia), urinary tract infections, pelvic infections, bone infections
    d. Metronidazole 250mg tablets for: infections with Giardia or amoebae, intra-abdominal infections including peritonitis and appendicitis, dental infections
4. Allergy medications
    a. Antihistamines such as diphenhydramine for: allergic reactions, as a sleep aid, and relief of cough and cold symptoms
    b. Injectable epinephrine (Epi-pen®) for those with a history of anaphylaxis with bee stings, food allergies (such as peanut allergy), etc.
    c. Non-sedating antihistamines such as loratadine or cetirizine are helpful during the day for rhinitis, allergic conjunctivitis, etc.

5. Anti-motion sickness medications such as dimenhydrinate
6. Non-prescription items such as antidiarrheal medications (loperamide, bismuth salicylate), laxatives (as bowel habits may be affected by jet lag, travel, dietary changes, and dehydration)
7. Anti-inflammatory medication or analgesics such as acetaminophen, ibuprofen, naproxen or other related medications for pain relief and fever control (pediatric formulations for children)
8. Cough suppressant (lozenges or syrup) and/or expectorant such as dextromethorphan or guafenisin
9. Decongestant such as pseudephedrine 25 mg.
10. Antacids and/or H2 blockers; (e.g., cimetidine, ranitidine) or proton-pump inhibitors (omeprazole, etc.)
11. A mild sedative (e.g. zolpidem), other sleep aid, or anti-anxiety medication
    a. Travel-related items such as a digital thermometer, antibacterial wipes or towelettes/alcohol-based hand gel (containing at least 60% alcohol), sunscreen (SPF of at least 15), DEET-containing insect repellents, antifungal powder, lotion or cream (e.g. clotrimazole, mycostatin), 1% hydrocortisone cream for contact dermatitis, poison ivy/oak or insect bites, itch relief cream or solution (e.g. calamine lotion), saline eye drops (artificial tears), lip balm (with sunscreen), tea tree oil (melaleuca oil) for skin infections/blemishes, water purification tablets, oral rehydration salts and latex condoms.
12. 12. N95 respirator (facemask): one-time use only; helps block droplets, splashes, sprays or splatter that may contain germs (viruses and bacteria) from reaching your mouth and nose
13. 13. Neti pot or equivalent: for sinus irrigation with normal saline (mix 1 liter or water, 1 tbsp. of salt, 1 tsp. of baking soda and adjust as needed). Dry, dusty and/or polluted locations can precipitate sinus problems. (Often a local product such as a teapot, soya sauce dispenser or plastic squeeze bottle will work well too) 14.For women: a course of antifungal vaginitis treatment such as fluconazole 150mg single-dose tablets or intravaginal suppositories (e.g. clotrimazole, miconazole) 15. A spare set of eyeglasses or contact lenses and a small eyeglass repair kit with screwdriver, magnifying lens, and extra hinge screws; sunglasses with protection against at least 97% of UV radiation (bring eyeglass prescriptions, if not older than 1 year) 16. Tweezers and scissors to remove splinters, stingers, cactus

thorns   or   ticks

17. For pregnant women: consider including a blood pressure cuff to monitor blood pressure, urine dip sticks to check for protein in the urine (proteinuria) when regular prenatal visits are not possible, chewable antacids for heartburn, hydrocortisone cream for hemorrhoids, prenatal vitamins and constipation medications (Sutton,   2012).

18. Dental supplies: mouth mirror, dental floss, oil of cloves (a dental   anesthetic)

19. Surgical supplies (for lacerations, cuts, injuries, etc.):

    a. Povidone iodine solution USP 10% (Betadine®) to disinfect water and when diluted ten-fold with water, to clean out wounds. This may also help to kill the rabies virus in wounds inflicted by animals.

    b. Tincture of benzoin: an adhesive in liquid form that increases the stickiness of wound closure strips, moleskin, or tape

    c. One-quarter by four-inch wound closure strips (such as Steri- StripsTM) which, when used with benzoin, can be used to close shallow, non-gaping lacerations. They are stronger, longer, stickier, and more porous than adhesive bandages.

    d. Polysporin® or double-antibiotic ointment. Avoid triple-antibiotic ointment because of allergic reactions to neosporin

    e. First-aid cleansing pads with lidocaine, a topical anesthetic: for use while scrubbing dirt and embedded objects out of abrasions

    f. Antiseptic towelettes with benzalkonium chloride

    g. Surgical scrub brush: for cleaning embedded objects and dirt from abrasions

    h. Aloe vera gel: A topical gel for treating and soothing burns, frostbite, and poison oak/ivy dermatitis

    i. Petroleum jelly: for preventing dressings from sticking to the wound and as a lubricant or moisturizer.

    j. Scalpel with No. 11 blade: for incising and draining abscesses

    k. Gloves: avoid latex if you are allergic
    l. Four by four inch sterile dressings
    m. Non-stick sterile gauze pads or dressings
    n. Gauze roller bandages for dressing limbs and digits (Kling®) and elastic bandages for sprains (Ace® bandages)
    o. A variety of different sizes of adhesive bandages
    p. Rolls of different widths of adhesive tape
    q. Safety pins
    r. Stockinette bandage: A net style bandage for holding dressings in place over joints and over the head
    s. Moleskin or gel pads: adhesive material for application on pressure points to prevent blisters and to protect them when they occur

What else should I be aware of?

- If your destination is a developing country and you are not certain what medical facilities will be available, you may want to take along needles, syringes, and intravenous catheters for immunizations and other injections, as these supplies are sometimes re-used under non-sterile conditions and are a key source of blood-borne viral infections such as HIV and hepatitis B and C. In sub-Saharan Africa, in particular, gloves should always be used whenever you may come in contact with body fluids (blood, saliva, urine, semen and vaginal discharge) because of the high risk of HIV infection (M. Elmer, personal communication, January 13, 2011).
- Commercial "suture/syringe kits" are also available which you can take along and use when you need local medical attention; see Travel Medicine, Inc., Tel: 800 872 8633, www.travmed.com (Weiss & Franco-Paredes, 2008).
- Carry your travel medical kit in your carry-on luggage for easy accessibility. Use plastic bottles (vs. glass) for liquids, and adjust amounts according to the duration of your stay. Note that in keeping with current security regulations, tweezers, nail clippers, scissors and fluids in a container larger than 100 ml cannot be carried in your carry-on bags and must be placed in your checked baggage.

- Use a waterproof bag or plastic container with a tight seal to contain the medical kit, and pack the individual components and medications in reusable plastic bags (such as Ziploc® bags).
- Some meds need to be stored separately to protect them from extreme temperatures. For example, capsules and suppositories will melt at temperatures above 37°C, and many liquid medicines (such as insulin) should be protected from freezing.
- Preparing a medical kit also provides the opportunity for you to consult your family physician or travel health consultant to discuss your specific risk of travel and for you to take steps to protect your health while you are working abroad.
- Contact card (Whatley & Marshall, 2012): It is important for you to be able to find and record important contact information. This information often needs to be accessed quickly and having a contact card with the following items will help save time in these urgent   situations:

The address, phone numbers and email addresses of the following:

- Family member or close contact in your home country Place of residence at the destination
- Health-care provider at home
- Health insurance, travel insurance and evacuation insurance information
- Hospitals or clinics at the destination, including emergency facilities
- Embassy or consulate in the destination country or countries

A list of your medications (including doses and frequency of dosing), allergies, significant medical history

For more details, see Appendix 3: Health Insurance, Evacuation Insurance   and   Accessing   Health   Care   Abroad.

Commercial medical kits are also available. Below is a list of websites supplying a wide variety of medical kits, some to meet specific needs such as managing diabetes, dealing with dental emergencies, and handling aquatic environments. If you purchase one of these ready-made kits, make sure you review it for completeness; you may need to add it for your own particular needs.

- American Red Cross: www.redcrossstore.org
- Adventure Medical Kits: www.adventuremedicalkits.com
- Chinook Medical Gear: www.chinookmed.com
- Travel Medicine, Inc.: www.travmed.com
- Wilderness Medicine Outfitters: www.wildernessmedicine.com

Counterfeit and Substandard Medications

An increasingly prevalent problem is that of counterfeit and substandard medications, that is, medications which are not manufactured by an authorized source but sold as if it were. This problem is especially prominent in the developing world with estimates of over 50% of all drugs being sold in Asia, Africa and Latin America being counterfeit or subpar (Green, 2010). An example of this disturbing increase is the high proportion of antimalarial drugs purchased in pharmacies and shops in SE Asia which are counterfeit (Weiss & Franco-Paredes, 2008). This may result in ineffective treatment, the development of adverse effects or toxic effects from contaminants.

How can I avoid the problem of counterfeit medications?

1. As much as possible avoid buying medications abroad.
2. Take along adequate amounts of the medications you need to use for chronic conditions or for possible anticipated problems such as traveler's diarrhea or GI conditions, and for chemoprophylaxis for infections such as malaria.
3. Before departure, buy all the medications you will need for your trip; bring along extras in case of travel delays, and make sure you have easy access to them in your carry-on bags.

4. Carry a list of your medications, with the common generic and brand names, doses, side effects, drug interactions, precautions.

5. Arrange to have all your recommended vaccinations before you leave home; counterfeit and outdated vaccinations are also a problem. If you need vaccinations while abroad and if the quality of local vaccines and their storage and transport are questionable, you may wish to import vaccines. However, this is generally not advised because of the difficulty of maintaining the cold chain in transit, and also because of legal issues in crossing borders with biological products. It is best to consult a reliable medical practitioner in your area for the best solution to this problem.

What if I have to buy medications abroad?

1. Buy medications from a reputable pharmacy. Seek the advice of local residents or expatriates as to the best place to buy medications. Avoid buying from street vendors, or open markets. Ask for a receipt.

2. Do not buy medications which are substantially less expensive than the standard price.

3. Be familiar with the medications you use. Keep samples of your medications to compare with ones that are available for purchase.

Check the packaging and information insert. Though these can be very cleverly duplicated, watch out for misspelled words, ink color, quality of printing and packaging, etc.

Appendix Three:
Health Insurance, Evacuation Insurance and Accessing Health Care Abroad

CASE:

A retired Canadian engineering professor was invited to work with graduate students at a Chinese university for six months. He and his wife had enjoyed an initial few months of engaged involvement at the university when he developed a flu-like illness. When he started coughing and experiencing shortness of breath, he was seen at the university clinic where the doctor diagnosed pneumonia and gave him oral antibiotics. When he did not improve on the antibiotics, he was sent for a chest X-ray which showed significant changes from a previous film and he was admitted to a university-affiliated hospital. As the H1N1 flu was endemic at the time (November 2009), he was hospitalized and underwent a very extensive battery of investigations, including blood tests, numerous ECGs, and several ultrasound scans and CT scans. The doctors could not confirm the cause of his lung problem but treated him for pneumonia with antibiotics and anti-viral medications, and drained fluid from his lungs several times. Despite treatment, he continued to deteriorate, much to the dismay of his family at home. His hosts at the university were also very concerned, and assigned graduate students to tend to him in hospital around the clock.

A Chinese friend helped the patient negotiate the cultural nuances of the situation, working behind the scenes to collect details about his medical condition that were not accessible to the patient or his family. This data was then relayed to the patient's physician-son at home in Canada. Finally, when his condition had somewhat stabilized after twelve days in hospital, the patient was given medical clearance to return to Canada. However, he was informed that his hospital records would not be available until three days after his discharge (and after his scheduled flight) and it took further "pulling of connections" to obtain them. He finally left China, accompanied by his wife, by commercial flight. At home in Canada, he was immediately placed under the care of a pulmonologist and cardiologist at a major university hospital. There, specialists confirmed the diagnosis of pneumonia made by the doctors at the Chinese hospital.

The total payment for hospitalization was 13 000 RMB (USD 2 000) for twelve days of hospitalization, which the patient had to pay in cash before receiving any medical care. After his return home, he was completely reimbursed for all medical expenses by his provincial health insurance plan and the extended health insurance policy he had purchased before departure. The patient reported that without the advocacy of the Chinese friend who spoke the local dialect, he would not have been able to receive the care that he did.

While living overseas, international workers can and do develop serious medical conditions. When these illnesses strike, you may find yourself unable to effectively communicate about your medical condition or to understand the treatment being offered nor how to pay for such treatment. At a time when you are already feeling unwell, vulnerable, anxious, and likely in considerable pain, this can be an extremely stressful time.

Preparation is of utmost importance; taking adequate measures before departure can help minimize the stress that these unwelcome events cause. You should have a plan in place in case you or a family member falls ill and have prepared resources for that possibility. This section will deal with measures that you can take beforehand to minimize anxiety and stress, addressing the issues of health insurance, medical evacuation and finding and paying for medical treatment while overseas.

Health insurance is essential if one is to work overseas for any length of time. The CDC website on travel insurance is an excellent resource (Johnson & Sommers, 2012). Medical expenses for even relatively minor ailments may become prohibitive and if ongoing treatment is needed, these expenses can necessitate one's premature return home. In addition, obtaining treatment in local hospitals often requires payment up front, before any medical attention is given, clearly a dangerous situation in an emergency situation.

Who should have health insurance?

The Australian national website's wry comment about travel insurance is: "If you can't afford travel insurance, you can't afford to travel." If you answer "yes" to the following questions listed in the CDC website (Johnson & Sommers, 2012), you should, in particular, consider obtaining   health   insurance:

a. Do you plan to remain outside of their home country for an extended period of time?
b. Do you have any pre-existing conditions? If you have a medical condition, you should make sure that the complications of your condition will be covered by the insurance policy.
c. Do you engage in high–risk activities which run a greater chance of injury? This applies to many cross-cultural workers who work and travel in isolated, primitive or rural areas where there is an increased risk of infectious diseases such as rabies and malaria and where road conditions are more treacherous and fewer medical facilities are available.

How do I know if I need to buy insurance?

In preparing for overseas service, the first step is to carefully review your existing health insurance policies. Some health insurance carriers in the home country may cover emergencies that occur while traveling. Examine your current insurance coverage and analyze your anticipated medical needs while abroad.

What should I look for in an insurance policy?

When considering an insurance policy, make sure you receive satisfactory answers to the following questions provided by the CDC Yellow Book:

a. Does the insurance company arrange and guarantee payment of medical bills directly to medical facilities abroad?
b. Is there a need for pre-authorization for treatment, hospital admission, or other services? This is often the case for health management organizations (HMOs). (Riesland, 2008)
c. Is a second opinion required before obtaining emergency treatment?
d. Is there 24-hour physician-assisted support? This is especially important for evacuation insurance coverage.
e. Is emergency medical evacuation covered, including transportation to one's home country vs. to the nearest site of available medical help?

f. If medical evacuation is advised, are the costs of hospitalization covered (Riesland, 2008)?

g. What are the restrictions for the treatment of flare-ups of pre-existing medical conditions?

h. What is the company's policy for "out-of-network" services? Most insurance companies have a designated network of health care providers that provide medical services for the insured. However, in the event of an emergency, you must seek the closest available help, which may not necessarily be within your company's network, which will be the case if you are working out of the country (Larson, 2009).

i. If needed, what coverage is there for the complications of pregnancy? Is there coverage for unexpected childbirth away

from home? Is there coverage for medical evacuation specifically for any obstetrical problem (Mackell, 2008)?

j. Are there restrictions for high-risk activities such as extreme sports (skydiving, scuba diving, bungee-jumping, mountain climbing, etc.)?

k. Is there coverage for injuries sustained as a result of being under the influence of alcohol or drugs?

l. What are the restrictions of the policy regarding psychiatric emergencies or injuries related to terrorist attacks or acts of war?

m. Is care obtained at specific medical facilities at your location ineligible for coverage? At least one insurance company insuring development workers in Asia does not reimburse expenses incurred in a particular international health facility because of that facility's high rates, as there are other local, good-quality and considerably more affordable alternatives.

Make sure that you clarify all questions and details about the policy directly with the insurance company before purchasing and departing, and obtain written confirmation of the policy.

If your existing insurance coverage is not adequate for your needs abroad, you may need to consider purchasing supplemental insurance.

Where can I buy supplemental insurance?

Travel insurance can be purchased through most insurance and credit card companies and through travel agencies, as well as from travel insurance firms. Some companies may have more experience and resources in certain destination area than others.

The following are resources for purchasing travel insurance and medical evacuation insurance:

1. U.S. Department of State: Medical Information for Americans Abroad: http://travel.state.gov/travel
2. International SOS: www.internationalsos.com/en
3. MEDEX: www.medexassist.com
4. International Association for Medical Assistance to Travelers: www.iamat.org

Some credit cards offer travel insurance as a benefit of the care. If you plan to use this insurance exclusively, make sure you qualify for the insurance and obtain, in writing, the exact details of the insurance coverage (Australian government website, n.d.).

Additional notes about health insurance:

a. Note that insurance must be purchased in the home country before departure (Suh, 2008).
b. Carry the details of your insurance policies with you, including policy numbers. In addition, leave contact information for the insurance carrier with family or friends at home.
c. Most policies do not cover the cost of cancellation resulting from official advisories against travel to particular destinations or modified travel advice (Australian government website, n.d.).
d. For American workers: Medicare and Medicaid, in general, will not cover medical expenses incurred outside the United States.
e. Those without insurance coverage will not easily be admitted to most private overseas hospitals and will likely need to rely on the local public healthcare system (Riesland, 2008).

What if I have a pre-existing medical condition?

Those with underlying medical conditions should take the following precautions when traveling:

a. Before leaving, appoint a health care proxy, advanced directive (living will) or medical power of attorney to make medical decisions on your behalf in the event that you are unable to do so on your own. Specify your desires clearly in each of these proxies. For an example of an advanced directive, see Five Wishes by Aging with Dignity (www.agingwithdignity.org).

b. If you have complicated or ongoing medical problems, store your records with an Internet vendor in "a cloud," (Conroy, 2007) or on a USB drive that you can carry with you so you can access it easily from any destination. For more services, register with a medical assistance company such as Medicalert (www.medicalert.org) which stores your medical conditions, allergies and advance directives, and provides your emergency medical information and identification to health care providers through a live 24/7 emergency response service (Riesland, 2008).

c. Carry a letter from your physician with the details of your medical conditions, allergies, specific instructions and all current medications (including their generic names), preferably in the local language(s) of the areas you plan to visit.

Evacuation Insurance:

Case 2:
A woman from New Zealand visited a South American city where she had previously worked for several years as an independent English teacher, not associated with an agency. In the intervening years, she had worked sporadically at home, while dealing with the fallout of a failed marriage. On this visit, she sought out old friends and students as well as investigated opportunities for resuming English teaching. Over the course of her visit, she was noted to be increasingly irrational and impulsive and not sleeping or eating regularly. When she began to aggressively pursue an intimate relationship with one of her previous students, who was happily married and not interested in her advances, it was evident that she was

delusional, possibly suffering from acute mania. An expatriate doctor who worked in the city prescribed antipsychotic medication and initiated steps to repatriate her. These arrangements were complicated, however, by her unwillingness to leave, difficulties in contacting her family and financial issues, as she did not have a sending agency to coordinate the repatriation process. Eventually, funds were secured, and when her condition had stabilized somewhat, she was accompanied back to her home country by another visitor to the area.

In a setting where local medical facilities and staff are inadequate to meet an individual's needs, evacuation may be required. As the above case illustrates in a negative way, evacuation insurance for those working overseas is strongly recommended. According to a 2004 study of 36 evacuations from a population of 50,000 travelers, 11 had traumatic injuries, eight had cardiovascular diseases (including heart attack and stroke), five had acute abdominal problems, four had mental health problems and three had lung problems (US Department of State, 2005, as cited in Riesland, 2008). In other series, obstetrical emergencies were noted to be a common cause for evacuation. Sand, et al. (2010) found that of 504 patients who were evacuated by air to Europe, the top five diagnoses for adults were hip fracture (fracture of the femoral neck) (14.7%), stroke (14.6%), heart attack (8.3%), head trauma (7.5%), and multiple trauma (3.4%). For children, the top three diagnoses were meningitis (20.9%), head trauma (16.7%), and fracture of the lower leg (8.4%).

As medical evacuation can be extremely expensive, costing anywhere from a few thousand dollars to over $100,000 USD for an air ambulance, and requires payment in advance if there is no evacuation insurance, many international organizations now require evacuation insurance.

When investigating evacuation insurance, one should check for the following:

    a.   Does the insurance include coverage for repatriation, and not just transfer to a center where better treatment may be obtained?

   b. Certain companies may have more expertise and contacts in certain geographical areas; clarify which company is best-situated and well-resourced for your location.

If medical evacuation is needed, but the worker is unable to arrange it, some private charitable organizations and commercial airlines offer compassionate rates (Riesland, 2008). Embassies may also help with accessing resources. Such charitable organizations include:

The Air Care Alliance (http://www.aircareall.org)
Angel Flight (http://www.angelflight.com)
Doctors Without Borders (http://www.doctorswithoutborders.org)
Make a Wish Foundation (http://worldwish.org)
Medical Wings (http://www.medicalwings.com)
Operation Smile (http://www.operationsmile.org)
Send Hope Organization (http://www.send-hope.org).

Accessing Health Care Abroad

What do I do if I get sick overseas?

Healthcare standards vary greatly throughout the world, and may differ significantly from those in the country of residence. Dealing with any illness, which in itself can be a very distressing experience, is made even more difficult by less-than-ideal medical facilities and care, an unfamiliar setting, language barriers and the individual's own stress reaction (Suh, 2008).

What should I keep in mind when I seek health care in the local system?

As mentioned earlier, if you do not have travel insurance, you will most likely have difficulty gaining access to local private hospitals and will need to use to the national public medical system in the destination country. Here are some general comments and suggestions about these facilities:

1. **Local hospitals**: The national hospitals in many countries are efficient, up-to-date and well-run. However, in many developing countries, the facilities and services will be inferior to what one is accustomed to in one's home country (Riesland, 2008). The quality of private clinics, including in-house hotel doctors, can be hard to assess. However, if you are faced with a serious medical condition,

   you may not have much choice but to access such resources. The key issue is often deciding between using local resources and opting for a timely transfer, assuming that you have evacuation insurance.

2. **Specialist hospitals**: Many medical facilities abroad, from clinics to hospitals, are dedicated to one specialty, for example, anorectal problems, dermatological problems, sexually-transmissible diseases, obstetrics or men's problems. You may receive adequate care in that particular specialty at one of these facilities, but if problems outside this specialty develop, you may receive inferior comprehensive care.

3. **Local wisdom and resources**: As much as possible, try to find a local contact who can advise you when you face health dilemmas such as deciding which hospital is best for your condition. Local staff working for your agency may be such a resource. A medical person working within the system is ideal, as access to medical care often depends on connections which can expedite the process. This is especially important in emergencies. As a long-term international worker, make friends with neighbors and colleagues who can introduce you to helpful contacts in your time of need. In the absence of such connections, at minimum, enlist the help of someone who is conversant in the local language.

4. **Resources from other expatriates**: Seek advice from other expatriates living in the same area. They can often recommend accessible and acceptable physicians, medical facilities and services.

5. **Be aware of the commercialization of medical care**: The medical systems in some countries are highly commercialized with doctors' salaries relying heavily on commissions or kickbacks, usually a percentage of the monetary value of the prescriptions written or the investigations ordered. Unfortunately, the treatments and tests these doctors prescribe are often not necessary so it is best to obtain a second and even a third opinion. A sympathetic local medical

consultant or a trusted medical practitioner accessible by phone or Internet can be extremely helpful as you decide what investigations or treatments are necessary.

6. **High-level consultants**: In some local national hospitals, outpatient clinics offer varying levels of care, which is reflected in the registration fee. The lowest fee is charged by the most junior staff physicians, the highest by the professor or consultant level physician, indicating not only their degree of experience and training, but also, at times, objectivity and lack of self-interest. A registration fee of up to 10-20 times the amount of the lowest fee may signal that this consultant receives only this fee as payment for his/her services, thus assuring a more objective assessment; his/her payment would not rely on kickbacks from writing prescriptions or ordering tests. If you encounter such a situation, you may be better off paying the higher registration fee for a potentially less biased assessment.

7. **"Face" issues**: In many countries, such as in Asia, cultural dynamics may influence the quality of care that you receive. Younger doctors may be expected to carry out the orders of more senior physicians and not to challenge these judgments if they have differing opinions, which may impact negatively on the care you receive (Riesland, 2008). Similarly, an outside, foreign medical opinion may not be well- received by the local doctor, who may regard such suggestions as a threat or a criticism. When dealing with complicated or critical medical conditions, being aware of this cultural dynamic may tip the balance you decide whether to seek care in a national medical facility or to transfer to an international hospital.

8. **Foreigners' clinics**: These are increasingly available and can offer an adequate medical option for foreign travelers or long-term international workers. These clinics often provide amenities to which Westerners are accustomed (private examining rooms, individual hospital rooms with ensuite bathroom, etc.) and may have English- speaking doctors. Higher level services and facilities like these also carry higher rates. Many former communist countries have established "VIP" hospitals initially established for the care of political leaders, but which now receive foreign patients. These facilities may have better equipment and amenities than local public hospitals, but may still fall below the standards expected by many Westerners (Riesland, 2008).

9. **International medical assistance companies**: These companies also run clinics in many locations around the world, providing an environment that is familiar to travelers and expatriates and offering amenities and medications that are not widely available locally (Riesland, 2008). The employees of these clinics are often well-informed about the quality of local facilities and consultants and sometimes follow the care of subscribing patients who are admitted to local hospitals. In addition, these clinics are usually affiliated with

   medical evacuation companies which maintain networks of contacts and databases about regional medical facilities, a valuable resource in the event of medical evacuation.

10. **Embassy clinics**: Though often not accessible to travelers, embassies and consulates can offer valuable information about local health facilities and risks. For example, the American Citizen Services branch of embassy consular sections maintains and makes available upon request updated lists of local medical facilities and clinics which are considered reliable, though they do not usually indicate which facilities or consultants are preferred.

11. **Medical mission facilities**: Another resource is missionary clinics or hospitals, where available. Serving expatriates and travelers generally is not the focus of these clinics, but they can be an invaluable source of medical help, especially in remote areas.

12. **English language proficiency of medical and nursing staff**: Some doctors may speak English, especially in foreigners' clinics, but nurses generally have lower English levels. In addition, in the national hospitals of developing countries, nurses often do not do practical hands-on patient care (baths, use of bedpan, changing of position, transfers, even the administration of medications, etc.) and meals are not provided, leaving the family member to supply these services. As a result, a hospital stay requires a personal care assistant and/or someone to deliver meals to the hospital.

13. **Medical equipment**: The medical investigation equipment found in local hospitals is often state-of-the-art, and the tests are affordable, compared to most host countries, but a key determinant of quality is the qualifications and experience of the person reading the results. Most results can be scanned or photographed with a digital camera and easily forwarded electronically. In addition, MRI, CT and other radiological imaging results can often be saved electronically by the

operator and given to the patient on CD, making consulting with an experienced specialist about the results either on-site or electronically very convenient. Keep copies of all lab and imaging investigations for future reference.

14. **Alternative medicine**: Alternative medical options may exist in your area, such as traditional Chinese medicine (TCM) including moxibustion, cupping, acupuncture, therapeutic massage, qigong, coining or traditional healers in Africa. Some of these modalities may be helpful, but only in limited cases, and usually are not appropriate for dealing with emergency situations. Other modalities

may be downright harmful. For example, TCM can be helpful for "re- equilibrating" the patient with chronic conditions and therapeutic massage and acupuncture can provide symptomatic relief for those with neuromuscular problems. On the other hand, relying on traditional modalities may delay timely diagnosis and treatment. In addition, the sale of traditional medications generally is not regulated, so their effectiveness and side-effects are not always known. It is best to seek the advice of a local cultural mentor or medical professional about the credibility and effectiveness of alternative medicine modalities before you go this route.

How should I prepare if we plan to have a baby overseas?

The following are specific suggestions for women who are pregnant, or plan to become pregnant:

a. When seeking a hospital for delivery, ask for a tour of the labor and delivery suite and inquire about the neonatal resuscitation facilities – do they have incubators, 24/7 NICU nursing care, monitoring equipment and oxygen?

b. How long is the average hospital stay following a delivery? Is there a rooming-in policy, allowing mom and babe to share a room?

c. What is the C-section rate? Caesarean section rates are rising around the world. In the US, the caesarean section rate was 32% in March 2010; in China, the C-section rate approaches 50%; Ecuador and Paraguay report rates of 40 and 42 percent rates respectively (Menacker & Hamilton, 2010). Having the pregnant woman suffer pain during childbirth is considered unacceptable in some areas of the world, such as the Mediterranean (Turkey), whereas in other areas, very little analgesia is given for natural delivery or even after C-section (one American woman who delivered in China received only one injection of pethidine after a C-section and no further painkillers).

d. Check into the availability of an anesthesiologist. Is epidural anesthesia (or other form of pain control) available during labor? In the event of a C-section, what type of anesthesia is used (general, local, spinal, epidural, etc.)? In the West, general anesthesia is usually used for C-sections; if an epidural was used during labor, it can be topped up to provide enough anesthesia for a C-section as needed.

e. Ask about private rooms; often hospitals will provide "deluxe" services and amenities for those who can afford them, i.e. private hotel-style hospital rooms with adjoining bathrooms and meals (vs. the family having to provide them).

f. If you have had complications related to pregnancy, labor and delivery or a pre-existing condition (uncontrolled diabetes or hypertension, habitual miscarriage, premature labor, history of C-section or other instrumental assistance for obstructed labor, bleeding problem, heart problem, etc.) you should discuss with your obstetrician where best to deliver your baby (Sutton, 2012).

g. Home births are not advisable in a foreign setting, especially where you are unfamiliar with the means of access to and availability of local emergency obstetrical facilities.

h. Be clear about what services and amenities are available, so that you can make an informed decision about where to deliver. Even if you do not have a lot of options, knowing what to expect will help you to manage your expectations and decrease the surprise element in an already-stressful setting.

i. For those international workers who work closely with the national people, and where obstetrical facilities are adequate though not as luxurious as one may wish, one may opt to give birth in the host country for the purpose of deepening relationships. Choosing to submit to the same conditions as one's national peers, especially when one has the choice to seek better care elsewhere, is a powerful form of identification with those who do not have that choice. Also, by delivering a child locally, the expatriate mother can forge strong bonds with local friends and neighbors as they help to meet practical needs when she is in a position of weakness and vulnerability. One of the unexpected by-products of one expatriate woman's emergency C-section of a premature child in a Chinese hospital was the strong bonding that resulted between her and her friends, Chinese and expatriate, who cared tirelessly for her and her family. This may not be a viable option for some women, but is a factor worth considering when making the decision of where to deliver.

Where can I find out about medical services and options abroad?

Commercial services:
The following commercial travel medical advisory services provide health services to travelers and expatriates. These companies have access to information about medical facilities in many destinations. Note that some of the listed physicians and/or clinics listed, such as embassy-associated clinics or those linked with multinational corporations, are not available to every subscriber (Suh, 2008). These organizations collect and offer to subscribers databases of local medical facilities and providers throughout the world and can be a significant resource in seeking the best medical care, be it through a local facility or consultant or by medical evacuation.

    a. The International Association for Medical Assistance to Travelers (IAMAT) (www.iamat.org). Membership is free; donations are accepted. This website also offers extensive travel medicine resources, including how to deal with mental health issues such as dealing anxiety, depression, stress, etc. while traveling http://www.iamat.org/editorials.cfm

    b. MASTA, (www.masta-travel-health.com) – registered office in the UK.

    c. The Travel Doctor TMVC, (www.traveldoctor.com.au)– Australian-owned and operated.

    d. Shoreland's Travax® (www.shoreland.com).

    e. International SOS travel insurance (www.internationalsos.com).

    f. The International Society of Travel Medicine website (www.istm.org) provides a 'Travel Clinic Directory' of members from more than 80 countries with contact information

g. Credit card companies and health insurance plans may also be a source of overseas healthcare information. Tour groups usually make provisions for travel health events but policies and expertise vary. Be aware of what is actually covered.

Government resources:

Many governments also offer helpful travel advice on websites for their citizens. Riesland (2008) lists the following government travel websites.

For British citizens	www.fco.gov.uk and click 'Passports, Travel and Living Abroad'
For American citizens[82]	www.travel.state.gov/ and choose topics under 'International Travel'
For Canadian citizens	www.voyage.gc.ca/ and choose topics under 'Travelling Abroad'
For Australian citizens	www.smartraveller.gov.au/ and click 'Travel Information"
For New Zealand citizens	www.safetravel.govt.nz/
For South African citizens	www.safrica.info/ and click 'South Africans Abroad'
For Irish citizens	www.dfa.ie/home/index.aspx?id=35 and click 'Travel Advice'

Falling ill or being injured while traveling or working overseas can be a stressful and dangerous predicament. In order to minimize risks, it is wise to be prepared for the possibility of a medical event and/or emergency. Obtaining adequate health insurance, including evacuation insurance, and being informed all help to minimize anxiety and improve outcomes in the event of a medical crisis.

---

[82] For American citizens who become seriously ill or injured abroad, a U.S. consular officer can help access medical services, inform family or friends and, possibly, transfer of funds from the United States. Payment of all medical expenses is the responsibility of the traveler, however.

Appendix Four:
Emergency Action Plans

One organization working in Asia uses the following contingency plans for emergency and disaster management. Also provided is information on how to build a "safe-room." These sample plans are provided as examples for you in the development of your own organization's contingency planning. Feel free to use these plans, while taking care to modify them in keeping with the specifics of your situation.

Appendix Four includes the following sections:

1. Emergency Action Plan
2. Security and Safety Guidelines
3. Personal Information File – to be filled out by workers upon arrival on the field.
4. Crisis Management Policy
5. Emergency Personal and Family Information Sheet and Instructions
6. Earthquake Contingency Plan
7. Avian Pandemic Influenza Contingency Plan
8. Developing a "Safe Haven" in Your Home

1. Emergency Action Plan

Current evaluation of security situation

An emergency constitutes a worsening of security issues for workers in Asia. When facing an emergency situation and making decisions about possible evacuation, consider the following questions:

1. Are you rendered ineffective or inoperative?
2. Are national workers agreed that you're staying is a problem for the work?
3. Does your presence create a security threat to your neighbors?
4. Has a decision been made by the joint or seconding agency for evacuation?
   Is your embassy bringing pressure to bear on you to leave and is transport being provided?

5. Is normal transport available?
6. Is there proven physical danger?
7. Is there an opportunity for re-deployment either until the emergency is over, or for future service?
8. Is the safety of the family of concern?
9. Is there a feeling that repatriation is advisable?

One of these factors alone may not be sufficient reason to evacuate but several factors may constitute sufficient reason. It is also understood that any person with inability to function under perceived danger, families with young children, or anyone who has received a specific threat may be evacuated without reference to the Security Levels listed below.

The following codes for Security Levels, and guidelines, will be used when notifying workers and head office of the Security Level in the host country.

GREEN: Normal Caution
Life is running normally with no greater than usual personal risk.

1. Follow the usual Security & Safety Guidelines (Appendix A) for living and working.
2. Review the EAP from time to time with family members and co-workers.
3. Ensure your passport and residency/visa papers are accessible and in date, with photocopies of such.
4. Ensure you have access to cash in the event of an emergency – enough to cover air tickets if necessary. If possible, have a credit card with you. Remember, in an emergency availability of funds will be limited.
5. Ensure that the **Personal Information form** (Appendix B) and the **EMERGENCY PERSONAL AND FAMILY INFORMATION SHEET** – (Appendix C) have been completed and updated annually. Each family and individual worker needs to complete these forms within one week of arrival on the field (the worker keeps one copy for reference and one is sent to the field leader).

6. Ensure you are registered with your embassy.
7. Keep a list of contact information (e.g. field leader, embassy, emergency services).

YELLOW: Preparation
Increased level of personal risk due to significantly heightened local or regional tension involving:

Terrorist events increasing in frequency, an increasing dislike of or threats and violence to foreigners/Christians, an increase in military presence, increase in crime, travel requiring extra precaution, communication lines being damaged, medical or food and water supplies becoming limited, a colleague experiencing significant stress which requires local help.

1. Be prepared for possible delay in placement of new workers in the area.
2. Be ready for a possible movement to Security Level Red or higher.
3. Be prepared for restrictions in your movements and possible exit by a pre-determined route.
4. Keep informed by talking with local people, listening to the news and advice given by the embassies.
5. Contact the field leader who will consider advice or requests from the local authorities, non-agency workers in the area, agency workers, and the home office; and make decisions based on these.
6. Postpone any travel away from home. If travel is necessary contact your team leader and make sure you are contactable while away.
7. Arrange to back up your computer and delete sensitive information.
8. The field leader will keep in touch with the home and local offices as far as possible.

RED: Partial Exit

High level of personal risk due to: increasingly widespread disturbances, acts of terrorism that threaten the collapse of central or regional government, the imminent outbreak of hostilities between the host country and another power, serious threat to the life of foreigners/Christians, religion-based violence, local medical, food and water supplies being very limited, breakdown of law and order, communication lines being cut, a colleague being under significant stress for a long period, a colleague only having minimal local support.

1. All non-essential field workers will be advised to leave. Those who stay should not move away from the normal location unless approved by the field leader.
2. Workers who stay should make preparations to leave, if needed, within one hour.
3. Workers who leave will do so by pre-arranged routes. They should notify their field leader of their leaving and attempt to inform as soon as possible after their arrival at their destination.
4. Hand over work to a local colleague.
5. Attempts should be made to keep in regular contact with the field leader and home office.
6. Those staying in the area will keep in daily contact with each other.
7. If leaving, and there is time, personal belongings should be packed and stored in a suitable place.
8. Workers should keep a low public profile.

BLACK: Mandatory Exit

Unacceptably high level of personal risk due to: war between the host country and another power, the outbreak of civil war, the outbreak of a regional war that results in significant unrest, a natural disaster or epidemic, complete breakdown of law and order, a personal threat, local medical, food and water supplies having run out, all outside communication being cut with no hope of repair in the near future, a colleague being overwhelmed by stress, a colleague not having support locally, a colleague not having access to funds, a colleague being subject to assault/robbery.

1. All workers are required to leave immediately, though by this stage it may be impossible to do so.
2. The leaving strategy, communications, etc should be as Security Level Red above.
3. If unable to leave, workers should assess the situation, have their emergency bag with them, and move to the safest place, being sure to communicate whenever possible with the field leader, and other remaining field workers.
4. If staying in their home, workers should make this as safe as possible, preserving water and other supplies.
5. Exceptions may be granted for workers to stay in country during a mandatory exit. These exceptions will be made only with the permission of both the partner's team leader, field leader, and regional director and will be given on the basis of special circumstances. In this instance the worker will take personal liability for him/herself.

2. Security and Safety Guidelines

While trusting in God do the following things:

1. Limit travel to essential trips.
   a. While driving, keep car doors locked and watch for anyone following you.
   b. Avoid travelling alone.
   c. Vary timings and routes of daily travel as much as possible.
2. Choose a "security partner" and keep him/her informed of your movement away from home / office.
   a. In particular, short term members should note this.
   b. Read and follow Warden advisory notices.
   c. Avoid scheduled meetings with casual contacts away from office or home.
3. Maintain low public profile regarding dress, vehicles, language, shopping, lifestyle, etc.
4. Watch for suspicious people and circumstances (and especially possible surveillance).
   a. Report concerns to your team leader.

5. We require that each unit carries a cell phone while travelling. (A personal GPS which can be triggered to alert a remote party in an emergency is an affordable option as well.)
6. Avoid locations frequented by, and large gatherings of, foreigners such as fancy hotels, markets, restaurants, etc.
7. Determine a "safe-room" in your home.

The Warden for the US embassy sends out warden notices as he receives them from the embassy. All American workers are registered with the US embassy. Other nationalities should register with their embassies.

3. Personal Information File Crisis Management

Crisis Management

THIS FORM MUST BE FILLED OUT WITHIN 7 DAYS OF ARRIVAL ON THE FIELD

Name(s) _____

Date _____

Passport information page and visa page should be attached to this form

Please list children living with you and attach passport copies.
_____
_____
_____

If children reside in a boarding school for part of the year, please list times when boarding is generally in session and school contact information.
_____
_____
_____

Please list children living in another country and their contact information (email and postal addresses, telephone numbers)

_____

_____

_____

_____

Person(s) to be notified if you are unable to be contacted (due to crisis restrictions, hostage situation, severe injury or death)

Name_____

Relationship_____

Telephone number _____

Address _____

Email address _____

Identity/Financial information: If you would rather not list this information, please list a contact in your home country who could provide the information or close accounts.

Contact person _____

Relationship_____

Telephone number _____

Postal Address _____

Email address _____

Social Security Number(s) _____

Credit Cards: numbers, names and customer service address and phone numbers

_____

_____

_____

Bank Accounts: Bank name, address and phone
number_____

_____

_____

Type of account/ account number

_____

_____

_____

Health insurance Company

_____

Name(s) as registered

_____

Account number(s)

_____

Proof of life questions: please list three bits of trivia about yourself (and spouse) that only you would know (for a hostage situation)

_____

_____

_____

_____

Untimely death on the field: Please indicate whether you wish to be buried in-country, or have your body sent back to your home country. Please note that expenses related to sending a body overseas will be borne by the family.

_____

_____

_____

Please include with this sheet a DNA sample, for example—a lock of hair or fingernail clipping from each member of the family who resides in this country. Place each DNA sample in an envelope and write the person's name on it.

Given to home office in year _____.

_____

Please make a photocopy of this form for your files and send the original BY HAND to the Field Chairman

4. Crisis Management Policy

Evacuation:

1. The Executive Council and the Crisis Management Team (CMT), in consultation with the home office, will make decisions regarding evacuation of field workers. All workers will abide by any decision to evacuate.
2. Costs of evacuation will normally be paid by the individual's work funds. If work funds are not available, costs will be borne by the field.

Hostage Situation:

1. The remaining spouse or children will be immediately relocated to a safe location, most likely out of the country.
2. All communication with supporters or friends must be approved by the CMT handling the crisis.
3. Negotiations will be supervised by the CMT only, on behalf of the worker and his/her family.

I (we) agree to the policies as stated above

Name (please print) _____

Signature_____

Spouse name _____

Signature _____

EMERGENCY PERSONAL AND
FAMILY INFORMATION SHEET
(Instructions)

This form is for emergency use only by the agency in the event you or a family member is at risk.

The agency is conscious of the fact that many of you live and work in areas of the world where your personal safety is at some measure of risk. Like other agencies, we have procedures and policies for contingency and crisis situations so we can respond appropriately in an emergency.

Preparations for such emergencies require that we have up-to-date information. Even though some information requested on this form is redundant with material already in one or more of your files here at the home office, it is in this format for emergency purposes only. Should we ever need outside professional or government assistance in managing a crisis, this information will be vital.

Please be assured this information will be kept in strict confidence and will only be accessed by a Crisis Team should there be an emergency involving you.

Remember to include an up-to-date photo of yourself and your family members.

We do hope this information is never needed. Thank you for taking the time to help us in this way.

Please return to your field leader.

Strictly Confidential
Emergency Personal and Family Information

Name of employee: _____

SS#: _____

Date: _____

	Employee	Accompanying Family Members					
Name							
Date Of Birth							
Height							
Weight							
EYE Color							
HAIR COLOR							
Distinguishing Marks If Any							
Passport Number							
* Country							
* Issue Date							
* Expiry Date							
* Issuing Authority							
Names Of Special, Regular Medication							
* Dosage							

EMERGENCY CONTACT:
NAME: _____
ADDRESS: _____
PHONE: _____

6. Earthquake Contingency Plan

Mitigating steps to:
- a.   Reduce the probability
- i.   We cannot control the probability of earthquakes happening, but can reduce the consequences by reasonable preparation before such an event occurs.
- ii.   THE REALITY - EARTHQUAKES
- 1.   If a major earthquake struck in your area you may be without direct assistance for up to 72 hours.
- 2.   Are you prepared to be self-sufficient?
- a.   *Is your family?*
- b.   *Is your organization?*
- 3.   Don't plan to rely on others for assistance – resources will be taxed
- b.   Reduce the consequences
- i.   INDIVIDUAL & FAMILY Preparedness
- 1.   What to KNOW & DO BEFORE & DURING an earthquake (OSHA website 2009)
- a.   Pick "safe places". A safe place could be under a sturdy table or desk or against an interior wall away from windows, mirrors, bookcases, tall furniture, hanging objects, or fireplaces that could fall on you. The shorter the distance to move to safety, the less likely you will be injured. Injury statistics show that people moving as little as 10 feet during an earthquake's shaking are most likely to be injured.
- b.   Practice drop, cover, and hold-on in each safe place. Drop under a sturdy desk or table and hold on to one leg of the table or desk. Protect your eyes by keeping your head down. Practice these actions so that they become an automatic response.

c.   Wait in your safe place until the shaking stops, then check to see if you are hurt. You will be better able to help others if you take care of yourself first, then check the people around you. Move carefully and watch out for things that have fallen or broken, creating hazards. Be ready for aftershocks.

d.   Be on the lookout for fires. Fire is the most common earthquake-related hazard, due to broken gas lines, damaged electrical lines or appliances, and previously contained fires or sparks being released.

e.   If you must leave a building after the shaking stops, use the stairs, not an elevator.

f.   If you're outside in an earthquake, stay outside. Move away from buildings, trees, streetlights, and power lines. Crouch down and cover your head. Many injuries occur within 10 feet of the entrance to buildings. Bricks, roofing, and other materials can fall from buildings, injuring persons nearby. Trees, streetlights, and power lines may also fall, causing damage or injury.

g.   Get training. Take a first aid class from your local Red Cross chapter. Get training on how to use a fire extinguisher. Keep your training current. Training will help you to keep calm and know what to do when an earthquake occurs.

2.   What to DO - BEFORE an earthquake

a.   *Conduct drills and physically place yourself & your children in safe locations*

b.   *Have a list of emergency phone numbers including an out-of-state relative / friend*

c.   *Decide where your family will reunite if separated*

d.   *Important medications – do you have extra?*

3. What to DECIDE - BEFORE an earthquake

e.   *What about the kids?*

  i.   Know the policies of the school your children attend.

 ii.   Make plans to have someone pick them up if you are unable to do so.

f.   *What about pets?*

  i.   Your safety should take priority

 ii.   Store extra food and water for them

 ii.   HOME Preparedness

 1.   What to KNOW - BEFORE an earthquake

a.   *Learn how to shut off gas, water, and electricity*

2. What to DO - BEFORE an earthquake
a. Put latches on cabinet doors to keep them closed during shaking
b. Keep flammable or hazardous liquids in cabinets or secured on lower shelves in closed containers
c. Secure water heater and appliances that could move enough to rupture utility lines
d. Keep breakable and heavy objects on lower shelves
e. Secure hanging plants and heavy picture frames or mirrors, especially those hanging over beds
f. Maintain emergency food, water, and other supplies
  i. Medicine
 ii. First aid kit
iii. Clothing
 iv. Fire suppression equipment
g. Conduct a survey with evacuation in mind
  i. Look for potential post-earthquake hazards INSIDE
  1. Designate evacuation routes that avoid as many hazard areas as possible
  2. Decide on alternate routes
 ii. Look for potential post-earthquake hazards OUTSIDE
  1. Power lines down
  2. Routes past concrete block walls (brick walls don't crumble as easily)
  3. Areas where debris could fall from overhead

iii. VILLAGE Preparedness
  1.   What to KNOW – BEFORE an earthquake
  a. All mud and rock village houses are potential death traps in an earthquake. If you live in northern Pakistan, entering such houses exposes you to extreme risk in an EQ

  2. What to DO – BEFORE & DURING an earthquake
  a. Avoid, when culturally appropriate, entering mud or rock homes in villages. Ask, when possible, to sit out in the fresh air as your preference.
  b. If you are in such a house during an earthquake, your best option is to move outside as quickly as possible.

iv.   WORK & OFFICE Preparedness
1.   What to KNOW - BEFORE an earthquake
a.   *Basic health profile of employees including blood type, prescription medications, allergies*
b.   *Home location and contact information for employees' families*

2.   What to DO - BEFORE an earthquake
a.   *Emergency plan? (aka: contingency plan)*
i.   Crisis management team within the organization
b.   *Full assessment as you did at home*
i.   Gas and water shutoffs, safe areas in the building
ii.   Conduct a survey with evacuation in mind
1.   Look for potential post-earthquake hazards INSIDE
a.   Designate evacuation routes that avoid as many hazard areas as possible
b.   Decide on alternate routes
2.   Look for potential post-earthquake hazards OUTSIDE
a.   Power lines down
b.   Routes past concrete block walls (brick walls don't crumble as easily)
c.   Areas where debris could fall from overhead
c.   *Plan potential escape routes?*
d.   *Search and rescue*
i.   Meeting point to determine who is accounted for

Resolution Steps:
c.   Indicators for recognition and acknowledgment of the crisis
i.   Physical damage to buildings
ii.   Power & other utility disruption during tremors
iii.   Physical harm due to tremors

d.   Containment of the crisis
i.   Initial investigation
1.   Is it safe to stay in your home or office?
a.   *Gas lines and electrical service intact?*
b.   *Potential hazardous materials issues?*
c.   *Structural integrity of the building?*
2.   If at work, decide whether to shelter at the facility, nearby or return home?
a.   *Consider distance, roadway conditions*

3. Survey with evacuation in mind
a. Designate open areas outside that are without overhead hazards and removed from potential danger spots
b. Everyone should be informed about evacuation plans
ii. What else could go wrong and what are the chances it will?
iii. Identify possible secondary crises
1. Prepare for aftershocks
2. Move to a better location, if the present one does not look safe.

iv. Secure valuables as much as possible against potential looting.
v. Evacuation should never be automatic!
1. There may be more danger outside than inside
2. There may be no safe areas outside
3. There may be no clear routes to get outside
4. Before a decision to evacuate is made someone must determine if:
a. There is a safe route out of the building
b. There is a safe place to assemble or move to
e. Isolation
i. Activate contingency plans and Crisis Management Team (CMT)
1. The CMT is the same as specified for other crises on the field
ii. Communicate to the organization
1. Each family and institution should report to a CMT member within two hours, if possible
2. If normal avenues are destroyed, use satellite phones
3. Use messengers if able to travel between locations

f. Assessment
i. Gather information about each individual, family and institution
ii. Ask who, what, when, where, why, how?

g. Action Plan
i. Decide appropriate location and accommodations for the CMT
ii. Set up communications and reporting for the CMT
iii. Reassess primary and secondary crises (ongoing, modify as needed)
iv. Identify pivotal (most pressing) crisis of the moment (may be secondary)
v. Issues to plan for
1. Infrastructure Damage
a. Buildings damaged

    b. Water supply

    c. Electricity

    d. Gas lines

    e. Communications

    2. Optional Actions

    a. Helping victims

    b. Safe staging areas

   vi. Action plan

    1. When personnel are cared for we will look for opportunities to reach out to the community in repairs, disaster relief, medical assistance, trauma counseling, etc.

  vii. The agency-run hospital will shift priorities in order to care for earthquake victims. The field will offer its services as people and funds are available.

 viii. Identify intended results

   ix. Determine media style (open/closed/reserved)

    h. Implementation of the plan

    i. Specific assignments

   ii. Report completion

  iii. Beware of independent actions

    i. Evaluation and modification of the plan

    i. Measure actions against intended results

   ii. Continually reassess primary and secondary crises

  iii. Always recognize the pivotal crisis

   iv. Modify the plan as necessary

    v. Notify all members of changes to the plan

    j. Closure

    i. Recall all resources

   ii. Identify "consequences"

  iii. Plan follow-up actions

    1. Thank you's

    2. Counseling

    3. Training

7. Pandemic Contingency Planning

1. Pandemic General Principles
    a. Definition of a pandemic: A global outbreak of illness, usually caused by a virus, which is most often an influenza virus.
    b. Phases of a pandemic[83]
        i.   **Phase 1** – (the inter-pandemic period) no viruses circulating among animals have been reported to cause infections in humans.
        ii. **Phase 2** - an animal…virus circulating among domesticated or wild animals is known to have caused infection in humans and is therefore considered a potential pandemic threat.
        iii. **Phase 3** – (the pandemic alert period begins) an animal or human-animal…virus has caused sporadic cases or small clusters of disease in people but has not resulted in human-to-human transmission sufficient to sustain community-level outbreaks.
        iv. **Phase 4** - characterized by verified human-to-human transmission of an animal or human-animal…virus able to cause community-level outbreaks.
        v.   **Phase 5** - characterized by human-to-human spread of the virus into at least two countries in one WHO region.
        vi. **Phase 6** – (the pandemic period) characterized by community level outbreaks in at least one other country in a different WHO region in addition to the criteria defined in **Phase 5**.

2. Pandemic phase-specific recommendations:[84]
    a. Phases 1 and 2 (Inter-Pandemic Period)
        i. Individuals and families should:

---

[83] Adapted from https://www.ncbi.nlm.nih.gov/books/NBK143061/
[84] These are offered to help mitigate risk where possible, but with the understanding that serving in remote locations for the sake of the Gospel is never risk-free.

1. Be up to date on immunizations! Make sure this includes an annual influenza vaccine.
2. Be as healthy as possible: physically, mentally, emotionally, spiritually.
3. Avoid live animal markets and contact with wild and domestic animals, birds, poultry, rodents, and their bodily secretions.
4. Practice frequent thorough hand washing (20 seconds with soap and water). Carry and use alcohol-based hand sanitizer having at least a 60% alcohol content, or sanitizing wipes before eating and after using the toilet.
5. Foods should be thoroughly cooked before eating, particularly meats, poultry and eggs.
6. "Bleach it, boil it, peel it or forget it" -- a pretty good rule of thumb for locally purchased fruits and vegetables.
7. Avoid traveling to countries or regions known to have infectious disease outbreaks.

ii. Local mission communities should:

1. Manage information--Appoint someone to serve as a pandemic "point person," whose responsibilities may include:
   a. Keeping current on potential pandemic threats through reference to the WHO website and other news services
   b. Passing on relevant information to colleagues in timely fashion
   c. Serving as a consultant when questions arise
   d. Serving as liaison with the home office
2. Plan for contingencies
   a. Each mission community should engage in pre-crisis planning (see below), which includes, at a minimum, the development of clear criteria for evacuation of personnel and decision-making authority during crises.
   b. Each area leader should have the ability to keep in contact via email or phone with each team member.
   c. Each family unit should have their documents and important papers, including passports,

medical information, wills and emergency contact persons in a designated place in their home which they have communicated to their ministry area leader. This information should include what to do with their children in case of their death and their burial arrangements.

d. In case of symptoms of illness, each family unit should decide on a general treatment protocol, i.e., which hospital or doctor to contact, etc. This protocol must be communicated to their area leader in case they are unable to assist themselves.

e. Consider pre-designating and training a field Crisis Management Team (CMT).

iii. Mission organizations should:

1. Develop organization-wide contingency plans including clear pathways of decision-making authority (such as an organizational CMT) in advance of situations such as political unrest, infectious disease outbreaks, kidnapping/hostage taking, death of missionaries. Organizations such as Crisis Consulting International https://cricon.org/ may be of benefit.

2. Require and assist each field/mission community to develop field-specific contingency plans.

b. Phases 3 through 5 (Pandemic Alert Period)

i. For individuals and families

1. Decide whether evacuation is appropriate (reference personal and field contingency plan). Considerations include:

a. Presence of pre-existing heart or lung disease in yourself or family members, increasing your risk of a poor outcome should you contract the illness.

b. Prevalence of the illness in your local area vs. the prevalence in an area or country to which you might be evacuated.

c. Availability and quality of local medical care:

          i. Facilities offering respiratory support (ventilators) if the illness severely impacts the respiratory system.

          ii. Anti-viral medications or other medications

    d. Likelihood and timing of border closure or travel restrictions eliminating the possibility of later evacuation.

2. Avoid contact with contagious people (Phase 4):

    a. Stay home as much as possible. Some families in highly urban settings may want to arrange to live outside of the city, perhaps with other colleagues.

    b. Wear masks that fit snugly and cover nose and mouth whenever you leave home. N95 masks are most effective. If not available or not tolerable, KN95 masks, surgical masks or cloth masks are also effective, (listed in descending order of effectiveness). Check CDC or WHO websites for tips on mask choice and proper wearing.

    c. Avoid crowds and public transportation.

3. Wash hands and clothes thoroughly.

4. Disinfect your home environment to the extent possible.

5. Begin preparations for at least a 2 to 4-week period of quarantine (i.e. not leaving your dwelling), which should include:

    a. Food supply

          i. Buy and store any foodstuffs that you would use normally and that do not require refrigeration.

          ii. This may include simple canned meats, fruits and vegetables, peanut butter, boxed or powdered milk.

    b. Extra disinfectant hand soap, bleach/other disinfectant for use in the house and any sickrooms.

    c. Extra daily household supplies

    d. Bottled water

    e. Flashlights with extra batteries

        f.   Extra bottled gas if you use it for cooking
        g.   Prescription medications
        h.   Masks
        i.   Basic medical supplies/medications: thermometer, ORS packets, Paracetamol (acetaminophen)

ii.   Local mission communities should:

1. Manage information—the pandemic "point person," should continue to execute his/her duties including:
   a. Frequent referring to WHO and CDC websites, updates from local health authorities and other news services
   b. Communicating regularly with the US embassy
   c. Passing on relevant information to colleagues at least weekly
   d. Serving as a consultant when questions arise
   e. Serving as liaison with the home office
2. Activate the previously designated CMT.

iii.   Mission organizations should:

1. Regularly communicate with field leadership and any crisis management organizations that have been engaged.
2. Regularly communicate with the field CMT and other field leadership.
3. When possible, honor and support field decisions regarding individual or field evacuation.

c.   Phase 6 (Pandemic Period) -- Continue the above recommended activities

Self Quarantine

i)   Each family needs to be prepared to stay in their home for at least one month.

(1) Prepare enough food for 2 - 4 weeks of reverse quarantine. Simple canned meats and vegetables, peanut butter, boxed milk that won't spoil or milk powder. Buy and store any food stuffs that you would use normally and that don't require refrigeration.

      (2) Buy extra disinfectant hand soap as there will be much hand-washing, bleach or other disinfectant for use in the house and sickroom. Buy extra daily household supplies so you don't have to go out to the market very often.

      (3) Store some bottled water.

      (4) Buy flashlights with extra batteries

      (5) May want to store an extra bottle of gas if you use bottled gas for cooking

      (6) Make sure you have a good supply of your own personal prescription medications if you take any.

      (7) Purchase masks for your family.

      (8) Purchase some basic supplies/medications: thermometer, ORS packets, Paracetamol

b. Some families in highly urban settings may want to arrange to live outside of the city, perhaps with other colleagues.

c. All necessary provisions of food, clothing, and shelter must be on hand to avoid   having to leave your dwelling.

d. Each area leader should keep in contact via email or phone with each team member.

e. In case of symptoms of illness, each family unit must decide on their treatment protocol; which hospital or doctor to contact, etc. This must be communicated to their area leader in case they are unable to assist themselves.

f. Each family unit should have their documents and important papers, including passports, medical information, wills and emergency contact persons in a designated place in their home which they have communicated to their ministry area leader. This information should include what to do with their children in case of their death and their burial arrangements; although in a pandemic, transportation of bodies will be restricted.

b) The Sick Family Member in Quarantine

1. If hospitalization is an option:
   a) Take the family member to the hospital.
   b) Keep cell phone & charger to maintain contact
   c) Only one parent should stay if the patient is a minor, so the other is not exposed to as much risk.

2. If hospitalization is not an option:
> a) Isolate the patient with closed door
> b) All who enter wear face masks
> c) Wear protective clothing
> d) Protect wounds or cuts
> e) Disinfect patient's room—all surfaces
> f) If sick one showers, etc, disinfect afterwards

For more information on avian flu, check out the following websites: http://www.who.int/mediacentre/factsheets/avian_influenza/en/index.html CDC http://www.cdc.gov/flu/avianflu/

8. Developing a Safe-Haven in Your Home

A. Purpose of a safe-haven in your home:

1. To hold off home-invaders while help is called.
2. A shelter during war (if there is insufficient advance warning to move to a safer location or area).
3. A shelter following an earthquake (if still intact).

B. Identify a suitable room:

1. Center of the building if possible.
2. No outside walls, or else walls very close to other buildings.
3. No windows, or else small windows, or close to another building.
4. Strong, solid door (not hollow-core).
5. Attached bathroom is a bonus.

C. Improvements to increase security:

1. Add tower bolts to top and bottom of door.
2. Always keep the door key in the lock on the inside.
3. If window is large, some panels to hang on the grillwork to absorb shattered glass from nearby explosions.
4. Modify window grillwork to provide an emergency exit, if possible.

D. What to keep in the room:

1. Fire extinguisher (Dry powder type).
2. Phone (even if the room is only used for storage, keep a phone present along with a list of emergency, agency, co-workers' and home country numbers).
3. One week's supply of drinking water (bottles or large containers - keep fresh).
4. One week's supply of tinned food (with extra can-opener).
5. Emergency lantern or flashlight (with spare batteries, kept fresh).
6. Reading material, including a Bible.
7. Cushions or pillows for temporary comfort.
8. Mobile phone and charger (take in with you if cellular signal is strong enough there).

9. Bucket with a lid (temporary toilet, if no attached bath - can be used to store the following items until needed)
   a. First-aid kit
   b. Transistor radio (with spare batteries, kept fresh)
   c. Candles and matches
   d. Extra amount of regular prescription medications (use and replace to keep fresh)
   e. Wooden wedges to jam under door and along sides (makes it extra hard to get through the door - kick or push sideways to remove)

Acknowledgements for Chapter 12

In preparing to write this chapter, I received much encouragement and helpful input from others committed to the care of international workers. Listed in alphabetical order, these individuals include: John and Angela Condie, Pam Davis, Lois Dodds, Steve Edlin, Curt Elliott, Muriel Elmer, Phil Fischer, Ken Gamble, Laura Mae Gardner, Ted Lankester, David Leung, Judy Long, Lynn Lorenz, Karen McClean, Nairy Ohanian, Jan Potz-Hartford, Michael Pocock, Roni Pruitt, Suzanne Rowe and Stan Haegert. In addition, I would like to acknowledge Paul Douglas, Michelle O'Hara and Suzanne Rowe for their help in proofreading.

References and Recommended Reading

Acheson, D. W. K. (2011). Food poisoning (food-borne illness). In S. B. Calderwood (Ed.). *UpTodate*. Available from http://www.uptodate.com

Aging with Dignity. (2010). Five wishes. Retrieved from http://www.agingwithdignity.org/five-wishes.php

Arguin, P. M. & Mali, S. 2012. Malaria. *CDC Yellow Book*, chapter 2, Pre-travel Consultation. http://wwwnc.cdc.gov/travel/yellowbook/2012/chapter-3-infectious-diseases-related-to-travel/malaria

Australian government, Dept. of Foreign Affairs &Trade

Retrieved http://www.smartraveller.gov.au/tips/insurance.html

Auwaerter, P. G. May 30, 2013. Measles vaccine at 50 years: still not over the finish line. Medscape News Pediatrics. Retrieved from http://www.medscape.com/viewarticle/804814?nlid=31605_45 5&src=wnl_edit_medp_peds&uac=90644MX&spon=9

Balk, S. J. and the Council on Environmental Health and Section on Dermatology Pediatrics (February 28, 2011). Ultraviolet radiation: a hazard to children and adolescents. DOI: 10.1542/peds. 2010-3502.

Breisch, N. L. 2010. Prevention of arthropod and insect bites: repellents and other measures. In D. B. Golden & A. M. Feldweg (Eds.). *UpToDate*. Available at www.UpToDate.com.

Callahan, M. & Hamer, D. H. 2008. Remote destinations. In J. S. Keystone, P. E. Kozarsky, D. O. Freedman, H. D. Nothdurft & B. A. Connor (Eds.). *Travel Medicine* (Chapter 32). Available from http://www.expertconsultbook.com

Callahan, M. 2008. Bites, stings and envenoming injuries. In J. S. Keystone, P. E. Kozarsky, D. O. Freedman, H. D. Nothdurft & B. A. Connor (Eds.). *Travel Medicine* (Chapter 47). Available from http://www.expertconsultbook.com/

Centers for Disease Control and Prevention (CDC). June 7, 2013. Immunization schedules. Retrieved from http://www.cdc.gov/vaccines/schedules/index.html

CDC. June 5, 2013. Malaria information and prophylaxis, by country. Retrieved from http://www.cdc.gov/malaria/travelers/country_table/c.html

CDC. June 6, 2013. How can you prevent rabies in people? Retrieved from http://www.cdc.gov/rabies/prevention/people.html

CDC. June 6, 2013a. Rabies around the world. Retrieved from http://www.cdc.gov/rabies/location/world/index.html

CDC. June 6, 2013b. Rabies information for specific groups. Retrieved from http://www.cdc.gov/rabies/specific_groups/index.html

CDC. June 7, 2013. Protecting the ones you love: drowning. Retrieved from http://www.cdc.gov/safechild/Drowning/index.html

CDC. March 15, 2013. What you should know for the 2012-2013 influenza season. Retrieved from http://www.cdc.gov/flu/pastseasons/1213season.htm

CDC National Center for Zoonotic, Vector-borne and Enteric Disease. July 22, 2010. Travelers' diarrhea. Retrieved from http://www.cdc.gov/nczved/divisions/dfbmd/diseases/travelers_diarrhea/

Chicoine, J-F & Tessier, D. 2008. International adoption. In J. S. Keystone, P. E. Kozarsky, D. O. Freedman, H. D. Nothdurft & B. A. Connor (Eds.). *Travel Medicine* (Chapter 28). Available from http://www.expertconsultbook.com

Connor, B. A. 2012. Travelers' diarrhea. In *CDC Yellow Book* (chapter 2). Retrieved from http://wwwnc.cdc.gov/travel/yellowbook/2012/chapter-2-the-pre-travel-consultation/travelers-diarrhea

Conroy, S. February 11, 2009. Storing data "in a cloud". *CBS News.* Retrieved from http://www.cbsnews.com/stories/2007/08/15/scitech/pcanswer/main3169392.shtml

DeMaria, A. & Techasathit, W. 2011. When to use rabies vaccination. In M. S. Hirsch, McGovern, B. H. (Eds.). UpToDate. Available from www.UpToDate.com

Dodds, Lois, and Dodds, Lawrence. 1997. Selection, training, member care and professional ethics: choosing the right people and caring for them with integrity. IFMA/EFMA Personnel Conference. Orlando, Florida. Dec. 4-6. Available in booklet at www.heartstreamresources.org.

Durbin, D. R. & Committee on Injury, Violence and Poison Prevention. March 21, 2011. Child passenger safety. DOI: 10.1542/peds.2011-0215.

Ericsson, C. D. 2008. Prevention of traveler's diarrhea. In J. S. Keystone, P. E. Kozarsky, D. O. Freedman, H. D. Nothdurft & B. A. Connor (Eds.). *Travel Medicine* (Chapter 17). Available from http://www.expertconsultbook.com.

Fischer, P. February 23, 2011. Malaria: what's new for kids? [PowerPoint slides]. CMDA-CMDE Symposium, Chiang Mai, Thailand.

Fradin, M. S. & Day, J. F. July 4, 2002. Comparative efficacy of insect repellents against mosquito bites. *New England Journal of Medicine,* 347, 13-18.

Freedman, D. O., Virk, A. & Jong, E. C. 2008. Immunization of healthy adults. In J. S. Keystone, P. E. Kozarsky, D. O. Freedman, H. D. Nothdurft & B. A. Connor (Eds.). *Travel Medicine* (Chapter 10). Available from http://www.expertconsultbook.com

Gamble, K. (n.d.). Checklist for expatriate preparation. Unpublished document.

Gamble, K. and Lovell-Hawker, D. 2008. Expatriates. In J. S. Keystone, P. E. Kozarsky, D. O. Freedman, H. D. Nothdurft & B. A. Connor (Eds.). *Travel Medicine* (Chapter 30). Available from http://www.expertconsultbook.com/

Green, M. D. (2010). Perspectives: counterfeit drugs. In *CDC Yellow Book* (Chapter 2). Retrieved from wwwnc.cdc.gov/travel/yellowbook/2010/chapter-2/counterfeit-drugs.htm

Hargarten, S. & Cortés, L. M. 2008. Injury and Injury Prevention. In J. S. Keystone, P. E. Kozarsky, D. O. Freedman, H. D. Nothdurft & B. A. Connor (Eds.). *Travel Medicine* (Chapter 49). Available from http://www.expertconsultbook.com/

Hay. 2007. Personal communication.

Institute of Medicine. 2010. DRIs for calcium and vitamin D, report at a glance, released 11/30/2010. Retrieved from http://iom.edu/Reports/2010/Dietary-Reference-Intakes-for-Calcium-and-Vitamin-D/DRI-Values.aspx

Johnson, K. J. & Sommers, T. E. 2012. Travel insurance and evacuation insurance. In *CDC Yellow Book* (chapter 2). Retrieved from http://wwwnc.cdc.gov/travel/yellowbook/2012/chapter-2-the-pre-travel-consultation/travel-health-insurance-and-evacuation-insurance

Kroger, A. & Atkinson, W. 2012, General Recommendations for
     Vaccination and Immunoprophylaxis. In *CDC Yellow Book*
     (chapter 2). Retrieved from
     http://wwwnc.cdc.gov/travel/yellowbook/2012/chapter-2-the-
     pre-travel-consultation/general-recommendations-for-
     vaccination-and-immunoprophylaxis

Lankester, Ted. 2011. Pre-travel preparation of aid workers and
     volunteers [PowerPoint slides]. CMDA-CMDE Symposium,
     February 17, 2011.

Larson, N. January 21, 2009. When should I obtain out-of-network
     health care? *About.com.* Retrieved from
     http://healthinsurance.about.com/lw/Health-
     Medicine/Conditions-and-diseases/ When-Should-I-Obtain-
     Out-of-Network-Health-Care.htm.

Lexi-Comp., Inc. Copyright 1978-2011. Typhoid vaccine: drug
     information. Available from www.UpToDate.com.

Leder, K. & Weller, P. F. 2010. Travel advice. In D. J. Sexton and E.
     L. Baron (Eds.). *UpToDate.* Available at
     http:www.UpToDate.com.

Leung, D. 2010. Personal communication.

Lorenz, L. 2013. Personal communication.

Mackell, S. M. & Anderson, S. A. 2008. The pregnant and breast-
     feeding traveler. In J. S. Keystone, P. E. Kozarsky, D. O.
     Freedman, H. D. Nothdurft & B. A. Connor (Eds.). *Travel
     Medicine* (Chapter 20). Available from
     http://www.expertconsultbook.com

Magill, A. J. 2008. Malaria: epidemiology and risk to the traveler. In J.
     S. Keystone, P. E. Kozarsky, D. O. Freedman, H. D. Nothdurft
     & B. A. Connor (Eds.). *Travel Medicine* (Chapter 12).
     Available from http://www.expertconsultbook.com

Magill, A. J., Shlim, D. R. 2010. Perspectives: why guidelines differ. In *CDC Yellow Book* (chapter 1). Retrieved from http://wwwnc.cdc.gov/travel/yellowbook/2012/chapter-1-introduction/perspectives-why-guidelines-differ

Manning, S. E., Rupprecht C. E., Fishbein D., Hanlon C. A., Lumlertdacha, B., Guerra, M., Hull, H. F. May 23, 2008. Human rabies prevention --United States, 2008.

Recommendations of the Advisory Committee on Immunization Practices. *Morbidity and Mortality Weekly Report (MMWR), 57(RR03); 1-26, 28.* Retrieved on April 26, 2011 from http://cdc.gov/mmwr/preview/mmwrhtml/rr5703a1.htm

McCarthy, A. E. 2008. Travelers with pre-existing disease. In J. S. Keystone, P. E. Kozarsky, D. O. Freedman, H. D. Nothdurft & B. A. Connor (Eds.). *Travel Medicine* (Chapter 24). Available from http://www.expertconsultbook.com.

McClean, K. January 30, 2011. Personal communication.

Menacker, F. & Hamilton, B. E. March, 2010. Recent trends in Cesarean delivery in the United States. National Center for Health Statistics (NCHS) Data Brief (35). Retrieved from http://www.cdc.gov/nchs/data/databriefs/db35.pdf

Ohanian, Nairy. 2010. Personal communication.

People in Aid. 2003. Code of Good Practice. Retrieved from http://peopleinaid.org/pool/files/code/code-en.pdf

ProMED. September 26, 2010. Rabies – China: (Guangxi) counterfeit human vaccine. Received February 12, 2011 by email.

Pruitt, Roni. 2011. Personal communication.

Rendi-Wagner, P., Kollaritsch, H. 2008. Principles of immunization. In J. S. Keystone, P. E. Kozarsky, D. O. Freedman, H. D. Nothdurft & B. A. Connor (Eds.). *Travel Medicine* (Chapter 9). Available from http://www.expertconsultbook.com.

Riesland, N. 2008. Healthcare abroad. In J. S. Keystone, P. E. Kozarsky, D. O. Freedman, H. D. Nothdurft & B. A. Connor (Eds.). *Travel Medicine* (Chapter 50). Available from http://www.expertconsultbook.com

Rothman, A. L. 2010. Prevention and treatment of dengue virus infection. In M. S. Hirsch and B. H. McGovern (Eds.). *UpToDate.* Available at UpToDate.com

Rowe, S. 2011. Personal communication.

Rupprecht, C. E., Briggs, D., Brown, C. M., Franka, R., Katz, S. L., Kerr, H. D., . . . Cieslak, P. R. March 19, 2010. Use of a reduced (4-dose) vaccine schedule for post exposure prophylaxis to prevent human rabies, Recommendations of the Advisory Committee. Morbidity and Mortality Weekly Report (MMWR), 59(RR-2). Retrieved from http://cdc.gov/mmwr/preview/mmwrhtml/rr5902a1.htm

Sand, M., Bollenbach, M., Sand, D., Lotz, H., Thrandorf, C. Cirkel, C., . . . Bechara, F. G.MD. 2010. Epidemiology of aero medical evacuation: an analysis of 504 cases. *Journal of Travel Medicine*, 17(6), 405–409. DOI: 10.1111/j.1708-8305.2010.00454.x

Sanders, J. W., Riddle, M. S., Brewster, S. J. & Taylor, D. N. (2008). Epidemiology of traveler's diarrhea. In J. S. Keystone, P. E. Kozarsky, D. O. Freedman, H. D. Nothdurft & B. A. Connor (Eds.). *Travel Medicine* (Chapter 16). Available from http://www.expertconsultbook.com

Schlagenhauf-Lawlor, P. & Kain, K. C. 2008. Malaria chemoprophylaxis. In J. S. Keystone, P. E. Kozarsky, D. O. Freedman, H. D. Nothdurft & B. A. Connor (Eds.). *Travel Medicine* (Chapter 13). Available from http://www.expertconsultbook.com

Steffes, B. & Steffes, M. (2002). *Handbook for Short-term Medical Missionaries.* Harrisburg, PA: ABWE Publishing.

Stephenson, I. 2013. Treatment and prevention of avian flu. In M. S. Hirsch and A. R. Thorner (Eds.). *UpToDate.* Available at UpToDate.com

Suh, K. N. 2008. Elderly. In J. S. Keystone, P. E. Kozarsky, D. O. Freedman, H. D. Nothdurft & B. A. Connor (Eds.). *Travel Medicine* (Chapter 22). Available from http://www.expertconsultbook.com.

Sutton, M. 2012. Traveling while pregnant. In CDC Yellow Book (chapter 8). Retrieved from http://wwwnc.cdc.gov/travel/yellowbook/2012/chapter-8-advising-travelers-with-specific-needs/pregnant-travelers
Transport Canada. June 6, 2013. Child Safety. Retrieved from http://www.tc.gc.ca/eng/roadsafety/safedrivers-childsafety-car-time-stages-1083.htm

US Department of State. 2005. Medical Office.

US Environmental Protection Agency (EPA), Office of Pesticide Programs. 1996. Using insect repellents safely. Retrieved from www.epa.gov/pesticides/insect/safe.htm.

Wanke, C. A. 2011. Traveler's diarrhea. In S. B. Calderwood and E. L. Baron (Eds.). *UpToDate.* Available at UpToDate.com

Weiss, E. A. & Franco-Paredes, C. 2008. Travel health and medical kits. J. S. Keystone, P. E. Kozarsky, D. O. Freedman, H. D. Nothdurft & B. A. Connor (Eds.). *Travel Medicine* (Chapter 8). Available from http://www.expertconsultbook.com/

Weiss, E. L. & Batchelor, T. 2008. Expedition medicine. In J. S. Keystone, P. E. Kozarsky, D. O. Freedman, H. D. Nothdurft & B. A. Connor (Eds.). *Travel Medicine* (Chapter 31). Available from http://www.expertconsultbook.com

Whatley, A. D. & Marshall, C. M. 2012. Travel health kits. In *CDC Yellow Book* (chapter 2). Retrieved from http://wwwnc.cdc.gov/travel/yellowbook/2012/chapter-2-the-pre-travel-consultation/travel-health-kits

Wilson, M. E. 2010. Skin lesions in the returning traveler. In K. Leder and   E. L. Baron (Eds.). *UpToDate.* Available at UpToDate.com

Wolfe Acosta, R. & Wolfe M. S. 2008. Structure and organization of the pre-travel consultation and general advice for travelers. In J. S. Keystone, P. E. Kozarsky, D. O. Freedman, H. D. Nothdurft & B. A. Connor (Eds.). *Travel Medicine* (Chapter 5). Available from http://www.expertconsultbook.com

Xu, L. (Ed.). September 26, 2010. Eight arrested over fake rabies vaccinations. *Xinhua.* Retrieved from http://english.cri.cn/6909/2010/09/26/1821s596358.htm